Using

QuickBooks Accountant

FOR ACCOUNTING

2015

Glenn Owen

Allan Hancock College

CENGAGE
Learning·

Australia · Brazil · Mexico · Singapore · United Kingdom · United States

Using QuickBooks Accountant® 2015 For Accounting

Glenn Owen

Vice President, General Manager: Balraj Kalsi

Product Director: Mike Schenk

Senior Product Manager: Matt Filimonov

Content Developer: Ted Knight, J.L. Hahn Consulting Group

Senior Product Assistant: Adele Scholtz

Senior Marketing Manager: Robin LeFevre

Senior Marketing Coordinator: Eileen Corcoran

Art and Cover Direction, Production Management, and Composition: Cenveo Publisher Services

Media Developer: Lysa Kosins

IP Analyst: Christina Ciaramella

IP Project Manager: Betsy Hathaway

Manufacturing Planner: Doug Wilke

Cover Designer: Alisha Webber, Cenveo Publisher Services

Cover Image: ©iStock.com/Christopher Futcher

Library of Congress Control Number: 2015939189

ISBN: 978-1-305-08477-3
Student Edition ISBN: 978-1-305-08478-0
Student Edition with CD ISBN: 978-1-305-08477-3

Cengage Learning
20 Channel Center Street
Boston, MA 02210
USA

Cengage Learning is a leading provider of customized learning solutions with office locations around the globe, including Singapore, the United Kingdom, Australia, Mexico, Brazil, and Japan. Locate your local office at: **www.cengage.com/global**

Cengage Learning products are represented in Canada by Nelson Education, Ltd.

For your course and learning solutions, visit **www.cengage.com/school**

Visit our company website at **www.cengage.com**

Printed in the United States of America
Print Number: 01   Print Year: 2016

Brief Contents

Contents

What if you could integrate a popular computerized accounting program into your classroom without using complicated and confusing manuals? What if your students could use this program and reinforce basic accounting concepts in an online and interactive case setting? What if you could accomplish both without spending a fortune and a vast amount of time preparing examples, cases, and illustrations? In fact, *Using QuickBooks Accountant® 2015 for Accounting* by Owen is a textbook that fulfills and expands upon all three of these "what ifs."

Why Is This Textbook Needed?

The first course in accounting has evolved significantly over the last several years. Educators are responding to the demand of accounting and nonaccounting faculty who rely on this course to lay a foundation for other courses. Moreover, the accounting profession relies on this course to attract the "best and the brightest" to become accounting majors. The evolution of this course has also put pressure on instructors to integrate computers into the classroom and, in so doing, develop students' skills in intelligently using and interpreting accounting information.

Faculty often want to incorporate computerized accounting into the first course but are reluctant to invest the time and effort necessary to accomplish this laudable goal. Existing materials are often "preparer" driven in that they focus on the creation of financial reports only. Students are often discouraged in their use of computers in the first accounting course because of the confusing and complicated accounting software manuals that concentrate on accounting mechanics.

This text responds to all of these needs. It provides a self-paced, step-by-step environment in which students use *QuickBooks® Pro 2015* or *QuickBooks® Accountant 2015* to create financial statements and other financial reports, to reinforce the concepts they learn in their first course, and to see how computer software can be used to make business decisions.

QuickBooks Pro vs. QuickBooks Accountant

This text includes a student version of *QuickBooks® Accountant 2014*. However, it can be toggled between various editions: General Business, Contractor, Manufacturing & Wholesale, Nonprofits, Professional Services, Retail, and Pro. The text itself will focus on the Accountant version.

New Features in This Edition of the Textbook?

New to this edition is Assignment 4, found in Chapters 6 through 12, called Drone City. This is a sole proprietor providing drone consulting and sales.

What Are the Goals of This Textbook?

This textbook takes a user perspective by illustrating how accounting information is both used and created. QuickBooks Accountant is extremely user friendly and provides point-and-click simplicity with excellent and sophisticated accounting reporting and analysis tools. The textbook uses a proven and successful pedagogy to demonstrate the software's features and elicit student interaction.

The text's first and foremost goal is to help students learn or review fundamental accounting concepts and principles through the use of QuickBooks Accountant and the analysis of business events. The content complements the first course in accounting and thus should be used in conjunction with a core text on accounting.

A second goal is to enable students to view financial statements from a user perspective. After an initial tour of QuickBooks Accountant, students learn how to use QuickBooks Accountant to understand and interpret financial statements.

A third goal of the text is to provide students a means to investigate the underlying source documents that generate most financial accounting information, such as purchase orders, sales invoices, and so on. Students will experience this process by entering a few business events for later inclusion in financial reports.

A fourth goal is to provide students a means of exploring some managerial aspects of accounting by performing financial analysis and comparisons. Budgets are created and compared to actual operating results, and receivables and payables are aged for the purpose of analyzing cash management and cash flow projections.

A fifth goal of this text is to reduce the administrative burdens of accounting faculty by providing a self-paced environment, data sets, cases, and a correlation table describing how this book might be used with a variety of popular accounting texts.

What Are the Key Features of This Textbook?

This text is designed to work with *QuickBooks® Accountant 2015*. It can be used with other versions of QuickBooks, but the screen shots and instructions are based entirely on *QuickBooks® Accountant 2015*.

The text is divided into two parts. Part 1 is designed to help you navigate through QuickBooks Accountant. It provides a foundation for Part 2, which will show you how to create new QuickBooks Accountant files and to record a variety of operating, investing, and financing transactions. Part 2 consists of seven chapters, each with its own set of questions, assignments, and case problems. All chapters in Part 1 revolve around Larry's Landscaping & Garden Supply. Larry's specializes in landscaping new and existing homes and is well known in town for its high-quality work and timely completion of projects. You've answered an ad for a part-time administrative assistant and are about to learn more about what QuickBooks Accountant can do for a business. Chapter 1 gives you a quick interactive tour of QuickBooks Accountant, in which you will restore data files and become familiar with QuickBooks Accountant's essential features. Chapters 2, 3, 4, and 5 introduce you to creating and preparing the balance sheet, the income statement, the statement of cash flows, and supporting reports.

Part 2 is designed to teach you how to use QuickBooks Accountant and the accounting methods and concepts you've learned in your introductory accounting course. This part is divided into seven chapters, each with its own set of questions, assignments, and case problems. You will follow the adventures of Donna and Karen at Wild Water Sports, who have hired you to help them set up their business in QuickBooks Accountant, capture various business transactions, make adjusting entries, set up and use budgets, and generate key business reports. You will utilize QuickBooks Accountant's EasyStep Interview to establish accounts, customers, vendors, items, and employees and then record business transactions using key source documents like sales receipts, invoices, bills, deposit forms, and checks. You will learn how to create journal entries in QuickBooks Accountant to accrue revenues and expenses, adjust deferred assets and liabilities, and record depreciation of long-lived assets. Finally, you will learn how QuickBooks Accountant's budgeting and reporting process can help Wild Water Sports plan and control their business activities.

A tested, proven, step-by-step methodology keeps students on track. Students enter data, analyze information, and make decisions all within the context of the case. The text constantly guides students, letting them know where they are in the course of completing their accounting tasks.

Numerous screen shots include callouts that direct students' attention to what they should look at on the screen. On almost every page in the book, you will find examples of how steps, screen shots, and callouts work together.

Trouble? paragraphs anticipate the mistakes that students are likely to make—or problems they might encounter—and then help them recover and continue with the chapter. This feature facilitates independent learning and frees you to focus on accounting concepts rather than on computer skills.

With very few exceptions, QuickBooks Accountant does not require the user to record journal entries to record business events. An appendix on traditional accounting records gives you the flexibility to teach journal entries at your discretion. It provides the information necessary for students to make journal entries to record the events described in Chapters 6 through 12.

Questions begin the end-of-chapter material. They are intended to test students' recall of what they learned in the chapter.

Matching exercises follow the questions. Each matching exercise lists key concepts/terms used or introduced in each chapter, terms that the student must match with the appropriate definition. This helps reinforce the student's grasp of the accounting and QuickBooks Accountant concepts.

Assignments follow the matching exercises. In the first five chapters, the assignments involve continuing the students' exploration of QuickBooks Accountant by viewing Larry's information. Three additional cases are used to extend their practice and exploration of QuickBooks Accountant files. The first is Sierra Marina, a sole proprietorship renting boats in the Sierra Mountains. The second is Kelly Jennings, an advertising agency doing business as a corporation. The third is Jason Galas Attorney at Law PC, a law firm doing business as a professional corporation.

In Chapters 6–11, exercises follow the matching exercises. Each exercise revolves around Boston Catering where students are asked to add customers, vendors, items, employees, and operating, investing, and financing activities. Each exercise stands alone and does not require completion of the previous exercise.

In Chapter 12, the end-of-chapter material includes questions, matching exercises, and three assignments. These are designed to help students apply the knowledge gained in the chapter on managing a firm's fixed assets including creating a new client, creating a fixed asset item list, depreciating fixed assets, and recording a journal entry in QuickBooks Accountant.

In Chapters 6–11, four assignments follow the exercises. Each assignment in Chapters 7–11 includes a beginning backup data file, which is used to get the student started. This includes an extension of the Wild Water Sports continuing business problem used in the chapter, followed by the Central Coast Cellular, Santa Barbara Sailing, and Drone City assignments. Three additional cases follow these assignments. None of these cases include a beginning data file; students continue the case from the previous chapter. These include the Forever Young, Ocean View Flowers, and Aloha Properties cases.

Five comprehensive problems appear at the end of Chapters 7 and 11. These problems provide an opportunity for students to demonstrate their comprehensive understanding of QuickBooks Accountant procedures and accounting knowledge.

The Student version of the text web site includes all beginning data files for each chapter and for each assignment. Students should navigate their browser to http://www.cengage.com. Click Higher Education, then type Glenn Owen in the Search for Books or Materials text box, and then click Find. Locate and then click the QuickBooks 2015 text from the listing provided. Click the text **Students: Access Free Companion Content**. Click **Access**. Book resources should be listed including student data files.

The Instructor's Manual includes solutions to all questions, matching exercises, assignments, cases, and comprehensive problems. Completed QuickBooks Accountant backup files are provided for the assignments, cases, and comprehensive problems to enable instructors to see what the student completed data file should look like after each chapter. The instructor's section of the text web site includes student data files and instructor completed data files. Instructors should navigate their browser to http://www.cengage.com. Click Higher Education, then type Glenn Owen in the Search for Books or Materials text box, and then click Find. Locate and then click the QuickBooks 2015 text from the listing provided. Click the text **Instructor Companion Site**. Book resources should be listed including both student and instructor data files. Instructor completed backup files, solution manual, rubrics, etc., are locked and require registration and login available at this site.

Dates

QuickBooks Accountant, like all accounting programs, is extremely date sensitive. This follows from the accounting periodicity concept, which requires accounting information to be organized by accounting periods such as months, quarters, or years. It is most important that, when using this text, you enter the proper dates to record business transactions or view business reports. For example, if you are using this book in 2016 (and thus your computer has a system date of 10/1/16, for example) then you will need to adjust the date references. In the Employee Center, for instance, the concept of "The Calendar Year" means 2016. However, if you are using this book in 2017 (and thus your computer has a system date of 2/1/17, for example) then the reference to "The Calendar Year" refers to 2017. The Larry's Landscape & Garden Supply file used in Chapters 1–5 is a sample file created by Intuit which automatically sets the system date to 12/15/2014. Thus you won't have to worry about differences in report dates.

The end-of-chapter assignments, cases, and comprehensive problems often have dates that differ from the date you might be entering business transactions. For example, the Central Coast Cellular assignment is dated 2014. When entering dates for transactions, QuickBooks Accountant automatically warns you of transactions being recorded more than 30 days into the future or more than 90 days in the past as shown by the following windows:

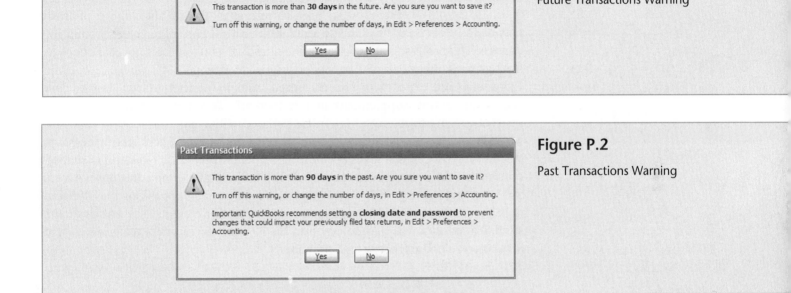

Figure P.1

Future Transactions Warning

Figure P.2

Past Transactions Warning

Click the **Yes** button when this occurs and then go to the Edit menu, click **Preferences**, click **Accounting**, and then click the **Company Preferences** tab. Uncheck the two check boxes located in the Date Warnings section as shown below.

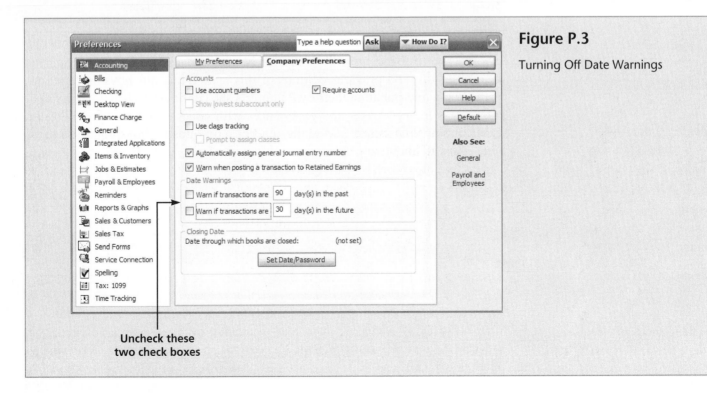

Figure P.3

Turning Off Date Warnings

About the Author

Glenn Owen is a tenured member of Allan Hancock College's Accounting and Business faculty, where he has lectured on accounting and information systems since 1995. In addition, he is a retired lecturer at the University of California at Santa Barbara, where he taught accounting and information systems courses from 1980 to 2011. He has also been a lecturer at the Orfala College of Business at Cal Poly San Luis Obispo teaching financial and managerial accounting courses. His professional experience includes five years at Deloitte & Touche as well as vice president of finance positions at Westpac Resources, Inc., and Expertelligence, Inc. He has authored many Internet-related books and accounting course supplements and is currently developing online accounting instruction modules for his Internet-based financial accounting courses. Mr. Owen previously released a 2013 edition of his Excel and Access in Accounting text, which gives accounting students specific, self-paced instruction on the use of spreadsheets (Excel 2013) and database applications (Access 2013) in accounting. His innovative teaching style emphasizes the decision maker's perspective and encourages students to think creatively. His graduate studies in educational psychology and his 39 years of business experience yield a balanced blend of theory and practice.

Dedication

I would like to thank my wife Kelly for her support and assistance during the creation of this and previous editions of this text. While our boys are now out of the house and pursuing their own interests she continues to listen to my often crazy ideas for new cases and experiences with college students, providing an excellent sounding board and reality check. You and the boys continue to be what life is all about.

Note to the Student and Instructor

QuickBooks Version and Payroll Tax Tables

The text and related data files created for this book were constructed using *QuickBooks® Accountant 2015* release R4P. To check your release number, open *QuickBooks® Accountant 2015* and type **Ctrl 1**. If your release is less than number R5, use the QuickBooks Update Service under the Online menu to update your version. This is a free service to version 2015 users and requires an Internet connection. The files accompanying this text can be used in any *QuickBooks® Accountant 2015* release R5 or higher. If you are using a higher release number, QuickBooks Accountant will automatically offer to update your file when you try and restore from the Data Files CD. Click **Yes** in the corresponding Update Company window.

In this version of QuickBooks Accountant, Intuit continues its use of a basic payroll service. This is a requirement in order to use the QuickBooks Accountant payroll features that automatically calculate taxes due to federal or state agencies. QuickBooks Accountant initially comes with the current tax tables; however, these tables soon become outdated, and the payroll feature is disabled unless the user subscribes to the payroll service.

Some previous versions of this text applied whatever tax tables were in effect at the time of publication. Users who had different tax tables often noted differences in solutions as a result. This new requirement solves that problem. The author decided to use the manual payroll tax feature, which requires that students manually enter the tax deductions. This alleviates the discrepancies between the solutions manual and the students' data entry and removes the burden of having to purchase the tax table service for each copy of QuickBooks Accountant installed in a lab environment. Instructions on how to set up payroll for manual calculation of payroll taxes are provided in the text. For more information, see your QuickBooks Accountant documentation.

All reports have a default feature that identifies the basis in which the report was created (e.g., accrual or cash) and the date and time the report was printed. The date and time shown on your report will, of course, be different from that shown in this text.

Getting Started with QuickBooks Accountant

part 1

In this Part, you will:
- Take an interactive tour of QuickBooks Accountant
- Create a balance sheet and modify its presentation
- Create an income statement and modify its presentation
- Create a statement of cash flows and modify its presentation
- Create supporting reports and modify their presentation

Part 1 is designed to help you navigate through QuickBooks Accountant. It provides a foundation for Part 2, which shows you how to create a new QuickBooks Accountant file and record a variety of operating, investing, and financing transactions.

This part is divided into five chapters—each with its own set of questions, assignments, and case problems. Chapter 1 gives you a quick interactive tour of QuickBooks Accountant, in which you will become familiar with the essential features of QuickBooks Accountant. Chapters 2, 3, 4, and 5 introduce you to creating and preparing the balance sheet, the income statement, the statement of cash flows, and supporting reports.

An Interactive Tour of QuickBooks Accountant

Student Learning Outcomes

Upon completion of this chapter, the student will be able to:

- Discuss QuickBooks Accountant's basic features
- Restore, open, back up, and close a QuickBooks Accountant file
- Identify the components and menus available in the QuickBooks Accountant window
- Use QuickBooks Accountant Help resources
- Examine a few forms and reports available in QuickBooks Accountant

Case: Larry's Landscaping & Garden Supply

You've been working in a part-time job at a restaurant, and today you decide that you've served your last hamburger. You want a new part-time job—one that's more directly related to your future career in business. As you skim the want ads, you see an ad for an administrative assistant at Larry's Landscaping & Garden Supply. The ad says that job candidates must have earned or be earning a business degree, have some computer skills, and be willing to learn on the job. This looks promising. And then you see the line "Send a résumé to Scott Montalvo." You know Scott! He was in one of your marketing classes two years ago; he graduated last year with a degree in business. You decide to send your résumé to Scott right away.

A few days later you're delighted to hear Scott's voice on the phone. He remembers you well. He explains that he wants to hire someone to help him with clerical and other administrative tasks. He asks if you could start right away. When you say yes, he offers you the job on the spot! You start next Monday.

When you arrive Monday morning, Scott explains that the first thing he needs you to learn is how to use a software package called QuickBooks Accountant. You quickly remind Scott that you're not an accounting major. Scott laughs as he assures you that you'll have no problem with QuickBooks Accountant because it is so user oriented. He chose QuickBooks Accountant exactly for that reason and has been using it for about three months. Scott wants accurate, useful, and timely financial information to help him make sound business decisions—and he's not an accountant, either.

Scott explains that the company has been using QuickBooks Accountant since its inception. He has become so busy at the company that he needs someone else in the office who can enter transactions, generate reports for the managers, and so on. So he says that today he will give you a tour of QuickBooks Accountant and teach you some of the basic features and functions of this package. You tell him that you're familiar with Windows and you're ready to start.

(*Note:* The file used in Chapters 1 through 5 is a service-based practice file created by Intuit. This file is used because it automatically sets the system date and no changes are made to the data.)

Using This Text Effectively

Before you begin the tour of QuickBooks Accountant, note that this textbook assumes that you are familiar with the basics of Windows: how to control windows, how to choose menu commands, how to complete dialog boxes, and how to select directories, drives, and files. If you do not understand these concepts, please consult your instructor. Also note that this book is designed to be used with your instructor's and/or another textbook's discussion of essential accounting concepts.

The best way to work through this textbook is to read the text carefully and complete the numbered steps, which appear on a shaded background, as you work at your computer. Read each step carefully and completely before you try it.

As you work, compare your screen with the figures in the chapter to verify your results. You can use QuickBooks Accountant with any Windows operating system. The screen shots used in this book were captured in a Windows 7 environment. So, if you are using an earlier or later version of Windows, you may see some minor differences between your screens and the screens in this book. Any significant differences that result from using QuickBooks Accountant within different operating systems will be explained.

Don't worry about making mistakes—that's part of the learning process. The *Trouble?* paragraphs identify common problems and explain how to correct them or get back on track. Follow those suggestions *only* if you are having the specific problem described.

After completing a chapter, you may do the questions, assignments, and case problems found at the end of each chapter. They are carefully structured so that you will review what you have learned and then apply your knowledge to new situations.

Demonstrations

Demonstrations are available throughout this text and are referenced by a Video Demonstration Icon in the margin. These demonstrations are stand-alone full-action videos with audio showing step-by-step illustrations of business processes explained in this text.

Video Demonstration

All of these are available via the text's companion web site located at http://www.cengagebrain.com. Navigate your browser to http://www.cengagebrain.com. Type Glenn Owen in the Search for Books or Materials text box, and then click Find. Locate and then click the QuickBooks 2015 text from the listing provided. Click the **Free Materials** tab and then click **Access Now**. Book resources should be listed including Student Data Files and Video Demonstrations.

When you navigate your browser to the student companion site for the text, you should see two Book Resources: Student Data Files and Video Demonstrations.

Student Data Files are addressed in the next section of this text. Video Demonstrations need to be downloaded from the companion site to your computer by clicking the Video Demonstrations text. Usually these files are downloaded to a folder on your computer called Downloads. In some cases you may be asked where you want these files downloaded.

The file you download is a very large compressed zip file. When you double-click the file downloaded you'll see a list of files. All of these need to be extracted (decompressed) first before you can view them. Click **Extract to a folder** and then create a folder on your computer or flash drive that you want to contain all of your demonstration files. Remember where you extracted these files so you can find them later.

QuickBooks Accountant Application Installation CD

To complete the chapters and exercises in this book, you must have access to the QuickBooks Accountant application. Your instructor might make the application available in a lab environment or you may already own the software. Alternatively, the CD located in the inside back cover of this text, labeled "Intuit Quickbooks Accountant 2015," contains all the files you need to run QuickBooks Accountant on your computer. Insert the CD in your computer and the setup installation program should begin automatically. Follow the instructions provided to install the QuickBooks Accountant application onto your computer. If it does not start automatically, use Windows Explorer to open the CD and double-click the setup application.

In this edition of the textbook, Intuit provides a student trial version of QuickBooks: Premier Accountant 2015. If you use the Premier Accountant 2015 version of the software, the figures in this book will match what you see on your computer screen. You may also use QuickBooks Pro 2015. In this case, some of the figures in the text may not match what you see on-screen. However, the differences are minor. The backup and restoration process is the same for both QuickBooks Pro 2015 or QuickBooks: Premier Accountant 2015 and student data files can be restored in either version. The only exception is that the newly added Chapter 12 contains material that is only available in the Accountant version.

Data Files

To complete the chapters and exercises in this book, you must have access to data files. Download the data files from the text's companion site at http://www.cengagebrain.com. Navigate your browser to http://www.cengagebrain.com. Type Glenn Owen in the Search for Books or Materials text box, and then click Find. Locate and then click the QuickBooks 2015 text from the listing provided. Click the **Free Materials** tab and then click **Access Now**. Book resources should be listed including student data files.

The file you download is a very large compressed zip file. When you double-click the file downloaded you'll see a list of files. All of these need to be extracted (decompressed) first before you can restore them to QuickBooks. Click **Extract to a folder** and then create a folder on your computer or flash drive that you want to contain all of your student data files. Remember where you extracted these files so you can find them later.

You will then need to restore the backup files to their original format. (As a reminder, there are no differences in the restoration of backup files in QuickBooks Pro and QuickBooks: Premier Accountant versions and student data files can be restored in either version.) The files are named to correspond to chapters and sessions in this book.

Working from your computer's hard drive is the most efficient way to use the QuickBooks Accountant program. However, if you are in a lab environment and want to take your file with you when you leave, you'll need to copy that file to a removable disk (ideally a portable USB drive). More on this later.

What Is QuickBooks Accountant?

Scott is excited about using QuickBooks Accountant because it is the best-selling small business accounting software on the market today. He explains that QuickBooks Accountant is an automated accounting information system that describes an entity's financial position and operating results and that helps managers make more effective business decisions. He also likes the QuickBooks Accountant reports and graphs, which quickly and easily organize and summarize all the data he enters.

Scott says he especially likes QuickBooks Accountant because it can handle all of the company's needs to invoice customers and maintain receivables and can also be used to pay bills and maintain payables. It can track inventory and create purchase orders using on-screen forms—all without calculating, posting, or closing. Scott can correct any previously recorded transaction, and an "audit trail" automatically keeps a record of any changes he makes.

Scott explains further that QuickBooks Accountant has four basic features that, when combined, help manage the financial activity of a company. The four features—lists, forms, registers, and reports and graphs—work together to create an accounting information system. Let's take a closer look at each of these four features. Don't start the QuickBooks Accountant program yet. Just read through the following to better understand QuickBooks Accountant's features.

Video Demonstration

DEMO 1A - Overview and introduction

Lists

Lists are groups of names—such as customers, vendors, employees, inventory items, and accounts—and information about those names. Lists are created and edited from a list window or while completing a form, such as an invoice, bill, or time sheet. Figure 1.1 shows a list of customer names with jobs for each of these customers, balances owed for each job, and any explanatory notes.

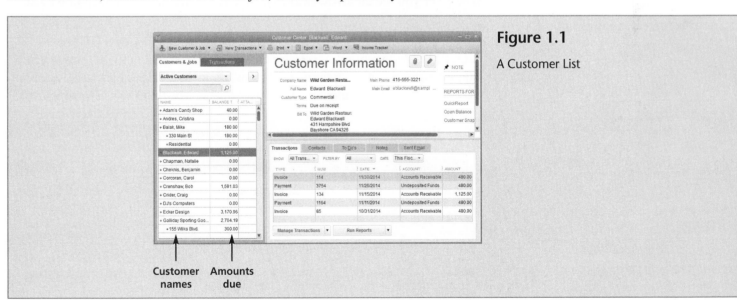

Figure 1.1

A Customer List

Customer names   Amounts due

Forms

Forms are QuickBooks Accountant's electronic representations of the paper documents used to record business activities, such as customer invoices, a vendor's bill for goods purchased, or a check written to a vendor. The customer invoice form in Figure 1.2 contains many **fields**, or areas on the form that you can fill in.

If you fill in a field, such as the Customer: Job field, QuickBooks Accountant often automatically fills in several other fields with relevant information to speed up data entry. In Figure 1.2, for example, the Bill To, Terms, and Invoice # fields are filled in as soon as the Customer: Job field is entered.

Figure 1.2

An Invoice Form

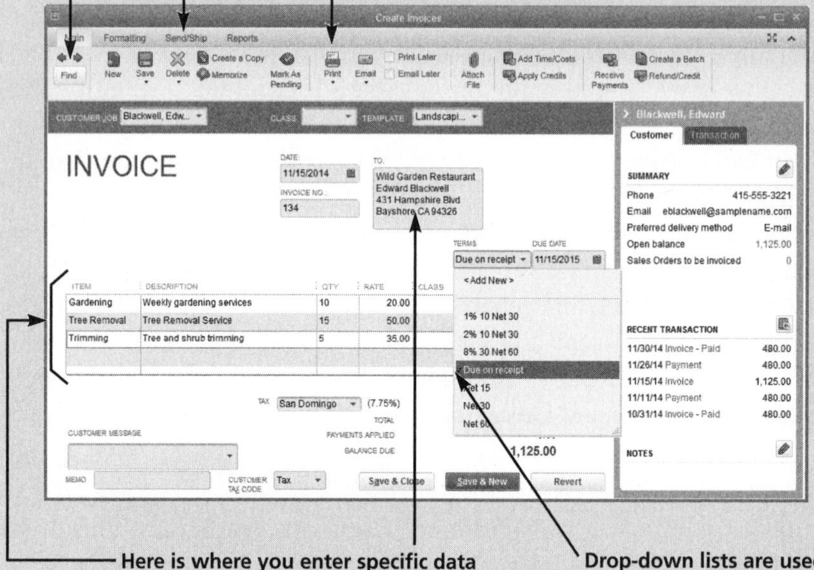

Your screen may show the words Print, Send, Ship, and Find if your Create Invoices window is expanded. QuickBooks Accountant automatically removes words to save space when the window size is reduced.

Here is where you enter specific data for each invoice

Drop-down lists are used to enter preformatted data

Also, filling in a field is made easier through the use of drop-down lists. Whenever you see an arrow next to or in a field, that field is a drop-down list.

Registers

A QuickBooks Accountant **register** contains all financial activity for a specified balance sheet account. Examples of registers include checking (cash), accounts receivable, inventory, and accounts payable. The checking register in Figure 1.3

Figure 1.3

A Section of the Checking Register

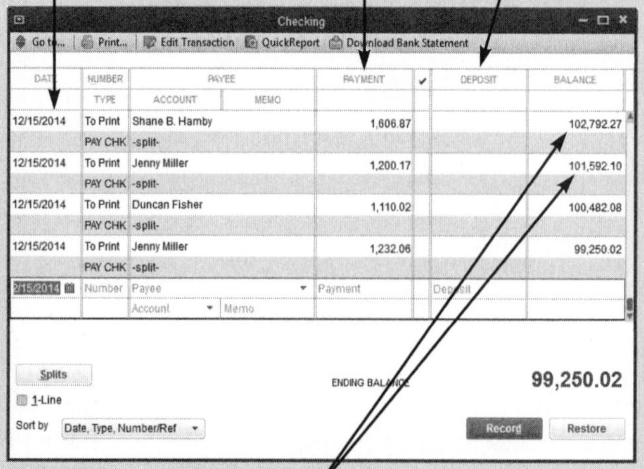

Note the four-digit year

Cash payments

Cash receipts

Balances are calculated after each transaction

shows some cash payments and cash receipts; it also provides cash balances after each transaction.

The financial effects of business transactions may be entered directly into the register or into the forms that automatically record the effects of these transactions in the relevant register. For example, if an owner's cash contribution is recorded on a Deposit form, the increases in both the checking account and relevant owner's equity account are simultaneously recorded in the Checking register and Contributed Capital register.

Reports and Graphs

QuickBooks Accountant **reports** and **graphs** present the financial position and the operating results of a company in a way that makes business decision making easier. The Profit and Loss report in Figure 1.4 shows the revenues and expenses for a specific period of time. Note that QuickBooks Accountant uses the title "Profit & Loss," but the generally accepted accounting title for this report is "Income Statement." Titles for this and other reports are all changeable using QuickBooks Accountant's Header/Footer tab. You can modify

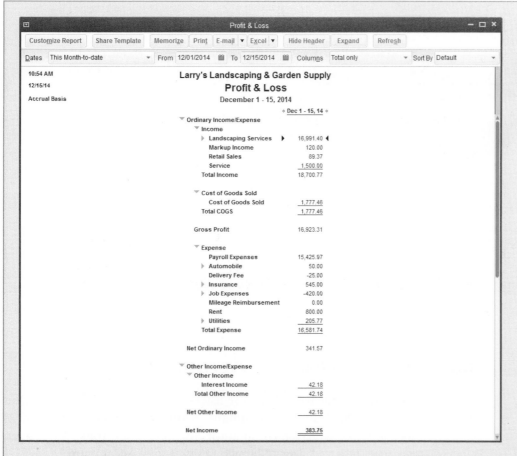

Figure 1.4

A Profit and Loss Report (Income Statement)

reports in many other ways, such as by comparing monthly periods, comparing this year with prior years, or examining year-to-date activity.

QuickBooks Accountant can also graph data to illustrate a company's financial position and operating results. For example, the bar chart in Figure 1.5 illustrates sales by month, and the pie chart illustrates sales by construction category.

Figure 1.5

A Sales Graph

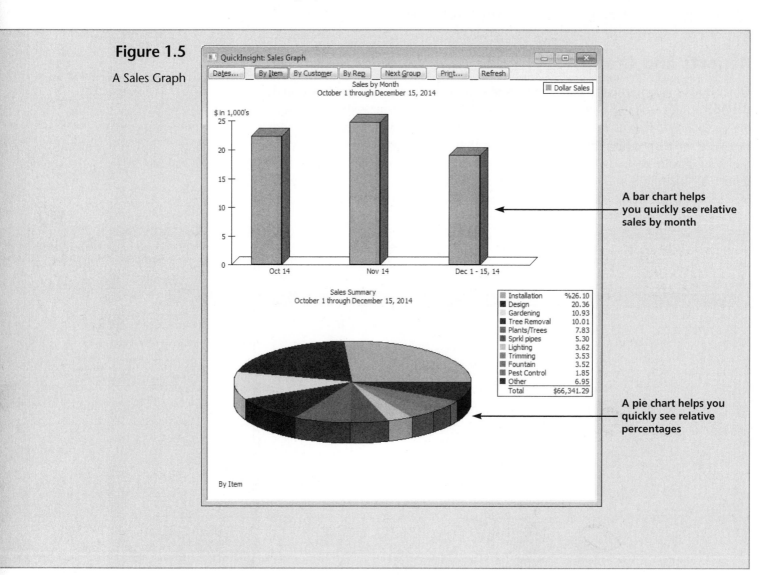

Launching QuickBooks Accountant

Now that you know about lists, forms, registers, and reports and graphs, you are ready to launch QuickBooks Accountant. Scott invites you to join him in his office and use his large-screen monitor to start your tour. You open Windows, and Scott tells you how to launch QuickBooks Accountant.

To launch QuickBooks Accountant in Windows:

1 Click the **Start** button.

2 Select the **Programs** menu and look down the list for QuickBooks Accountant.

3 Once you've located the QuickBooks Accountant program, click the QuickBooks Accountant icon or name.
Trouble? If, when QuickBooks Accountant was last used, the file being worked on was closed, you will see a No Company Open window. If, however, a QuickBooks Accountant file is open, click **File**, and then click **Close Company**. Be sure to close any open files before you proceed to the next set of steps.

Now that you have launched QuickBooks Accountant, you can begin to learn how to use it.

Restoring and Opening a QuickBooks Accountant File

Scott hands you a disk and asks you to restore the Larry's Landscaping & Garden Supply QuickBooks Accountant file. (*Note*: This file is one of the files you already downloaded and extracted from Cengage.)

Video Demonstration

DEMO 1C - Restoring and backing up a file

To restore a backup file to its original format:

1 Download the data files from the textbook's web site as previously described.

2 Launch QuickBooks Accountant if you closed it above. (*Note:* if a QuickBooks Setup window appears, close it.)

3 Click **File** and then click **Open or Restore Company** or, if a QuickBooks Setup window appears, click the **Other Options** tab and then click **Open Existing File**.

4 Choose the **Restore a backup copy** option button and then click **Next**.

5 Choose the **Local backup** option button and then click **Next**.

6 Locate the Larry's Landscaping & Garden Supply (Backup) file wherever you downloaded the file from the textbook's web site. Select it and then click **Open**.

7 Click **Next** in the Restore Backup: To Location window, which appears next.

8 Navigate the Save Company File as window to the location where you want the file to be restored on your computer's hard drive. Be sure to note its location for future use. In the example shown in Figure 1.6, we chose to save the restored file in a folder called "Restored QuickBooks Accountant files."

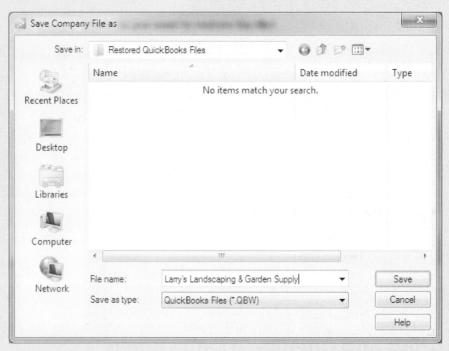

Figure 1.6

Restoring a Backup File

9 Type **Larry's Landscaping & Garden Supply** as the file name and then click **Save**. (*Note:* you may be asked if you want to update your company file. This happens when QuickBooks is automatically updated to a new release. If this happens, click **Yes** to continue.)

10 Click **OK** in both of the QuickBooks Accountant Information windows, indicating that the file has been successfully restored.

11 Click the **Begin Using QuickBooks Accountant** button if presented.

Later, you can continue this process for all the backup files on your Data Files CD as you need them. As mentioned before, you may be working in a lab environment where the files you work on today may be erased tomorrow. To preserve your work, you should back up your files to removable data storage (e.g., a USB drive). See Appendix 3 for more information on file management as well as backing up and restoring files.

The QuickBooks Accountant Window

Scott explains that QuickBooks Accountant operates like most other Windows programs, so most of the QuickBooks Accountant window controls should be familiar to you. He reaches for the mouse and quickly clicks a few times until his screen looks like Figure 1.7. The main components of the QuickBooks Accountant window are shown in this figure. Let's take a look at these components so that you can become familiar with their location and use.

The **title bar** at the top of the window tells you that you are in the QuickBooks Accountant program and identifies the company file currently open. The **menu bar** contains the **command menus**, which open windows within QuickBooks Accountant. The File, Edit, View, and Help menus are similar to other Windows programs in that they allow you to perform such common tasks as open, save, copy, paste, find, and get help.

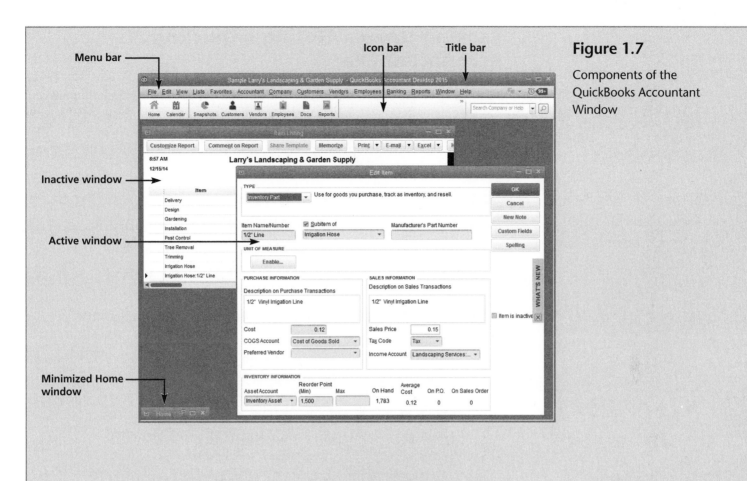

Figure 1.7

Components of the QuickBooks Accountant Window

The Lists menu gives you access to all lists, including the chart of accounts, customers, vendors, employees, and inventory items. The Company, Customers, Vendors, Employees, and Banking menus provide easy access to QuickBooks Accountant Centers as well as common tasks unique to that menu. For instance, in the Customers menu you can create invoices, enter cash sales, create credit memos, receive payments, and so forth. The Reports menu will give you quick access to common reports and graphs for easy creation. The Window menu allows you to choose the format for window displays, such as cascade or tile vertically. Finally, the Help menu will give you immediate access to an index of help topics.

The **icon bar** gives you one-click access to the QuickBooks Accountant Centers and Home page. From time to time, you may want to hide the icon bar so you can have more horizontal space for the customizable icon bar.

The icon bar includes icons representing tasks you do every day, such as entering and paying bills, creating invoices, and receiving payments. If you use QuickBooks Accountant's payroll system, you might consider adding icons for your payroll forms. Icons can be added, removed, or reordered to fit your needs. Use the View menu to hide or display the icon bar and make any changes.

The **active window** is the window in which you can enter or edit data, and it is identified by a solid window title bar. Only one window can be active at a time. Other windows may be open, but they are inactive. If the active window is closed, or if a window behind it is selected, it becomes **inactive**, and the newly selected window becomes active.

Backing Up and Closing a QuickBooks Accountant File

Now that you have seen the components of the QuickBooks Accountant screen, Scott wants to show you how to *back up* and close a file so that you will always be able to save your work and exit QuickBooks Accountant.

"Maintaining backups is important just in case your original file is somehow damaged or lost," Scott explains.

To create a backup file for later use and then close the file:

1 In Windows Explorer, create a folder on your USB or other external drive called "My QuickBooks Backups."

2 In QuickBooks Accountant, click **File** and then click **Back Up Company**.

3 Choose the **Create Local Backup** option button and then click **Next**.

4 Identify the location where you want to *back up* your file for later use. (In this example, the backup location is K:\My QuickBooks Accountant Backups\, where K is the drive letter assigned by the Windows operating system for the USB drive. [Your drive letter may be different. If you back up to your hard drive you may receive a warning message about backing up to your hard drive. If so, click **Use this Location**]. The My QuickBooks Accountant Backups is the folder created in Step 1.) Uncheck the **Add the date and time of the backup to the file name** check box and then uncheck the **Remind me to back up when I close my company file** check box. Then click **OK**.

5 When the Create Backup window appears, choose the Save it now option and then click **Next**.

6 Your screen should look like Figure 1.8. Click **Save**.

Figure 1.8

Backing Up a Data File

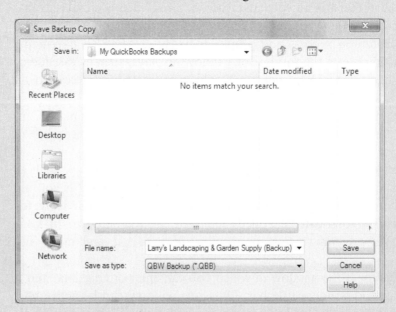

7 Click **OK** in the QuickBooks Accountant Information window, which indicates your backup was successful. Keep this QuickBooks Accountant file open.

Then Scott tells you something very unusual. He says that, unlike other Windows programs, QuickBooks Accountant *does not have a Save command.* In other words, in QuickBooks Accountant you cannot save a file whenever you want. You stare at Scott in disbelief and ask how that can be possible. Scott explains that *QuickBooks Accountant automatically saves all of the data you input and the changes you make as soon as you make them and click OK.* Scott admits that, when he first used QuickBooks Accountant, he was uneasy about exiting the program until he could find a way to save his work. But he discovered that there are no Save or Save As commands on the QuickBooks Accountant File menu as there are on most other Windows programs. He reassures you that, as unsettling as this is, you'll get used to it once you become more familiar with QuickBooks Accountant. See Appendix 3 for more information on file management as well as backing up and restoring files.

QuickBooks Accountant's Menus and Shortcut List

Scott explains that to enter sales receipts, create invoices, pay bills, receive payments, and so on, you use QuickBooks Accountant menu commands. Some of these functions are also available from buttons on the QuickBooks Accountant icon bar.

Some QuickBooks Accountant menus are dynamic; in other words, the options on the menu change depending upon the form, list, register, or report with which you are working. For instance, when you enter sales receipts information, the File and Edit menus change to include menu commands to print the sales receipts or to edit, delete, memorize, or void the sales receipts, as shown in Figure 1.9.

Because all these are new to you, Scott suggests that you first become familiar with how managers use QuickBooks Accountant to make business decisions.

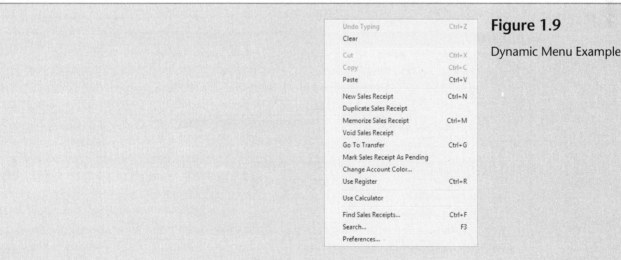

Figure 1.9

Dynamic Menu Example

Using QuickBooks Accountant to Make Business Decisions

Once transactions are entered into the QuickBooks Accountant accounting information system, they can be accessed, revised, organized, and reported in many ways to aid business decision making. This capability is what makes a computerized accounting information system so valuable to managers.

While you're sitting with Scott, he receives a phone call from Laurie McConnell. Laurie needs some information on whether any accounts are past due. You know from your accounting course that Laurie is really asking for information about **accounts receivable**, or amounts due from customers from previously recorded sales. Laurie wants to know how much is due from customers and how current those receivables are; specifically, which customers owe the company and when their payments are due. Scott tells Laurie he'll look into this immediately and call her right back.

Be aware that dates are critical to retrieving relevant information in QuickBooks Accountant. In most cases when you ask for a report, QuickBooks Accountant will give you that report as of the system date (today's date, whatever that might be). For example, if you are working on this assignment on January 5, 2016, and you request a report on receivables, QuickBooks Accountant will give you a report of receivables as of January 5, 2016. If you want a report as of March 31, 2014, you will need to change the date on the report and then refresh the report to see that information. Note that the Larry's Landscape file is a special "Sample Company" file and it will always present a current system date of 12/15/2014 regardless of what day you are working on the file. This will not be true when you are working with all other QuickBooks Accountant files.

To identify the customers who owe the company money and the total amount of receivables due from these customers:

1 Click **Reports**, click **Customers & Receivables**, and then click **A/R Aging Summary**. Now click the **Collapse** button at the top of the report. The report in Figure 1.10 will appear.

Figure 1.10

Accounts Receivable Aging Summary

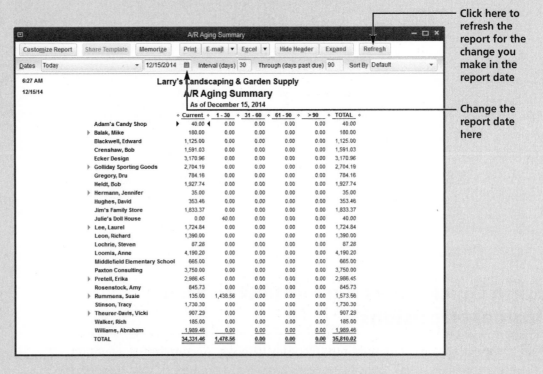

Trouble? The report you see might be slightly different from the one shown in Figure 1.10. Some column widths have been altered. Use the scroll bars to view this report both vertically and horizontally.

2   Note that customers owe the company a total of $35,810.02.

3   Scott wants to see a graphic illustration of this information. From the Menu bar, click **Reports**, click **Customers & Receivables**, and then click **Accounts Receivable Graph**. The graph in Figure 1.11 will appear.

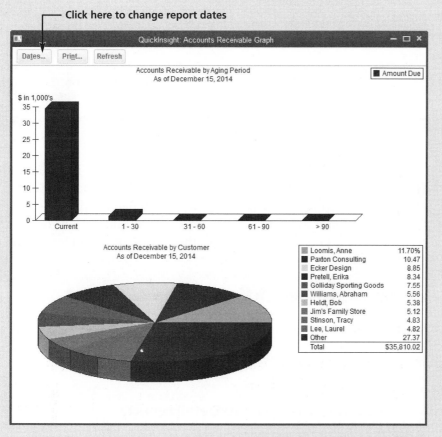

Figure 1.11

Accounts Receivable by Aging Period and Customer

Scott calls Laurie back and tells her that $35,810.02 is due from customers. He explains that Susie Rummens ($1,438.56) and Julie's Doll House ($40.00) are past due. Laurie would like to know specifically what invoices were sent to Susie Rummens, when payments were made, and in what amounts. Scott knows he can easily get this information by accessing the Customer Balance Detail report for Susie Rummens.

To access the Customer Balance Detail for Suzie Rummens:

1   From the Menu bar, click **Reports**, click **Customers & Receivables**, and then click **Customer Balance Detail**.

2   Scroll down the report to Susie Rummens detailed information shown in Figure 1.12. This report describes the two invoices that billed her for services rendered.

Figure 1.12

Customer
Balance Detail

You would click here
to print this report

| | Customer Balance Detail | | | | — □ ✕ |

| Customize Report | Share Template | Memorize | Print | E-mail ▼ | Excel ▼ | Hide Header | Refresh |

Dates All ▼ From [ ] To [ ] Sort By Default ▼

6:31 AM
12/15/14

Larry's Landscaping & Garden Supply
Customer Balance Detail
All Transactions

◇ Type ◇	Date ◇	Num ◇	Account ◇	Class ◇	Amount ◇	Balance ◇
Rummens, Susie						
2877 S Rosebush						
Invoice	12/12/2014	128	Accounts Receiva...	Landsca...	1,438.56	1,438.56
Total 2877 S Rosebush					1,438.56	1,438.56
721 Fern Lane						
Invoice	12/11/2014	126	Accounts Receiva...		135.00	135.00
Total 721 Fern Lane					135.00	135.00
Total Rummens, Susie					1,573.56	1,573.56

◄— Use this scroll bar
to view the rest
of this report

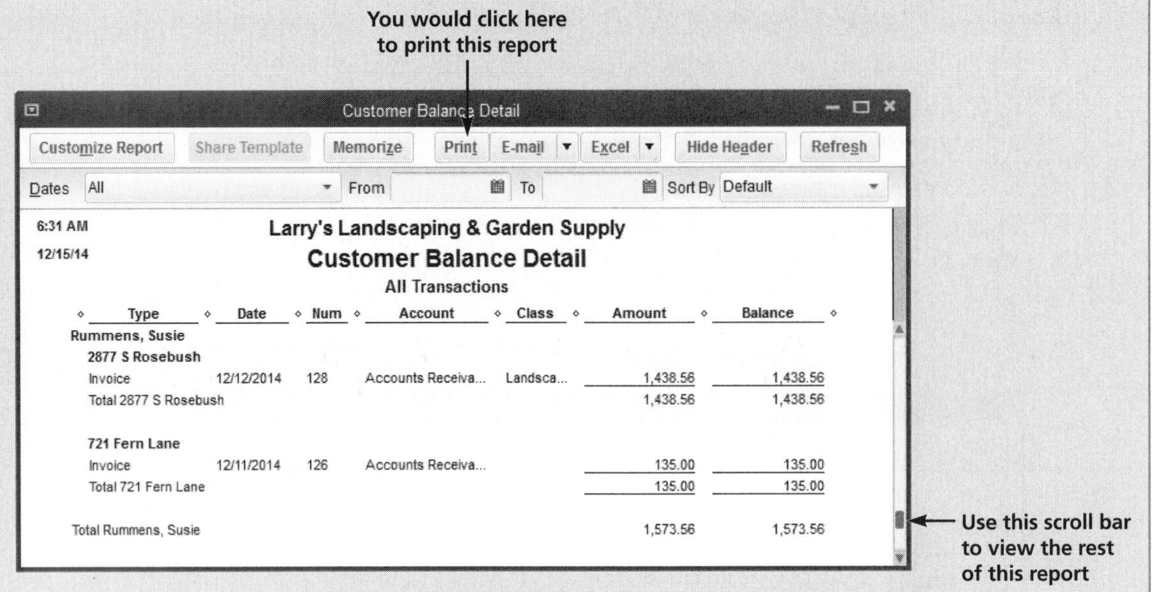

Scott calls Laurie back and tells her that the past due invoice is number 128. He has quickly and easily accessed financial information from the company's QuickBooks Accountant data file, and Laurie thanks him. She is grateful for his quick response so she can make her decision. She asks if, before the end of the day, he would print out a copy of this information and leave it on her desk. Scott is happy to oblige.

Printing in QuickBooks Accountant

Scott suddenly remembers a meeting he must attend. But before exiting Quick-Books Accountant, you remind him that he promised to print a Customer Balance Detail report for Laurie.

To print a Customer Balance Detail report:

1 If you have closed the Customer Balance Detail report, click **Reports**, click **Customers & Receivables**, and then click **Customer Balance Detail**.

2 Click the **Print** button located on the button bar. See Figure 1.12.

3 Click **Print** in the Print Reports dialog box. The report prints out. *Trouble?* You might have to set up a printer before printing. If necessary, click **Cancel** in the Print Report dialog box. Then select **Printer Setup** from the File menu. QuickBooks Accountant allows you to set up different printers for different functions. Click the **Settings** tab and select the printer you would like to use from the printer name drop-down list.

4 You've opened several windows and not closed them. Click **Window** in the menu bar, and then click **Close All** to close all open windows and return to the QuickBooks Accountant opening window.

Since you may have modified the settings for one or more reports, a Memorized Reports window may appear. Since we don't plan to use this report again, click **No**.

Scott asks you to drop off this report at Laurie's desk sometime after lunch.

Using QuickBooks Accountant Help

Scott suggests you explore QuickBooks Accountant's Help features while he is at his meeting. He tells you that QuickBooks Accountant Help has the standard features and functions of Windows Help and also has other help features specific to QuickBooks Accountant. These other features are listed in the main Help menu shown in Figure 1.13.

As with other Windows programs, you can access Help by clicking on the Help menu or pressing **F1**. In QuickBooks Accountant, pressing F1 opens a Have a Question window. QuickBooks Accountant Help is context sensitive—that is, different help screens appear depending on where you are in the program. You can get help for a specific topic by choosing the Help Index menu item.

You decide to follow up on Scott's suggestion to look at a help feature he finds very useful, the Help Index. You are specifically interested in how QuickBooks Accountant uses accounts.

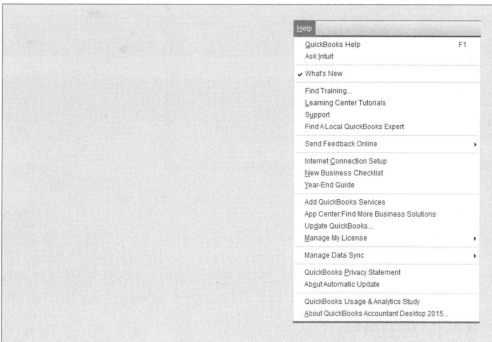

Figure 1.13

The Help Menu

To use the Help Index:

1 Click **Help** from the menu bar. Then click **QuickBooks Help** on the menu.

2 Type the phrase **add a new account** in the text box and then click the magnifying glass icon and then click the **Show more answers** text until you see the text Add accounts and subaccounts.

3 Click the text **Add accounts and subaccounts**. Your screen should look like Figure 1.14 showing both the Have a Question? and Help Article windows.

Figure 1.14

The Help
Window

Type here —

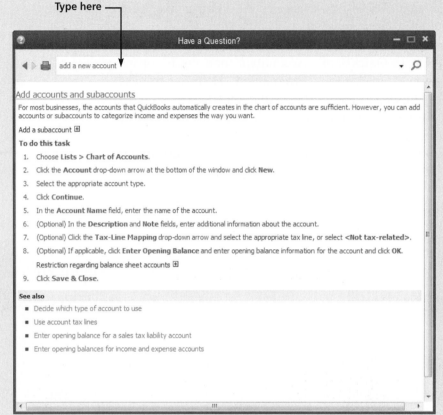

4 Click the **Printer** icon, and then click **Print** to print this screen.

5 Close both windows.

You will have an opportunity to use most of these options in this and later chapters.

Date Formats

You mention to Scott that the default four-digit year format in QuickBooks Accountant (12/15/2014) seems a bit excessive, and perhaps they should return to the more standard date format (12/15/14). Scott agrees and decides to show you the steps necessary to change the date preferences.

To change date preferences:

1 In the Larry's Landscaping & Garden Supply file currently open, click **Edit**, and then click **Preferences**.

2 Click the **General** icon on the left of the Preferences window, and then click the **Company Preferences** tab.

3 Uncheck the Always show years as 4 digits (1999) check box.

4 Click **OK** to save the changes, and close the Preferences window.

5 To restore the home page, click **Home** in the Navigation bar.

Scott confirms that all dates in QuickBooks Accountant registers, report windows, and so forth will now be in the standard format of a two-digit year (12/15/14).

The QuickBooks Accountant Home Page

Scott reminds you that another feature he previously mentioned was the Quick-Books Accountant home page, shown again in Figure 1.15. The QuickBooks Accountant home page provides a big picture of how your essential business tasks fit together. Tasks are organized into logical groups (Customers, Vendors, Employees, Company, and Banking) with workflow arrows to help you learn how tasks relate to each other and to help you decide what to do next.

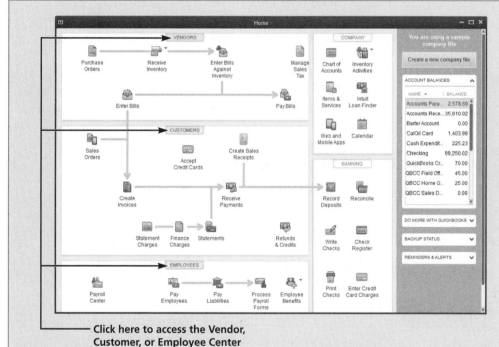

Figure 1.15

The QuickBooks Accountant Home Page

Video Demonstration

DEMO 1B - Using navigation centers

The workflow arrows indicate a logical progression of business tasks in QuickBooks Accountant. However, these arrows do not restrict you from doing tasks in a different order or in an order that works better for your business needs.

The Customers portion of the home page includes two main activities: invoicing and receiving payments. Note, however, that invoices may receive input from the vendor section (when we're billing customers for parts purchased from a vendor) as well as the employee section (when we're billing customers for employee time).

The Vendors portion of the home page includes four main activities: creating purchase orders, receiving items, establishing a liability, and paying that liability. QuickBooks Accountant provides you the means of managing all of these tasks with the click of an icon.

The Employees portion of the home page includes two main activities: recording employee time and paying employees and tax authorities. The work flow here does require sequential input, in that employee time must be entered *before* employees and tax authorities can be paid.

The Banking and Company portions of the home page are generic to the whole company and aren't necessarily business processes requiring workflow steps. The Company section allows you to update your chart of accounts, items, services, and physical quantities of items on hand. The Banking section allows you to record deposits, write checks, and reconcile your bank accounts.

The home page also provides you access to lists of customers, vendors, and employees via the Customer, Vendor, and Employee Centers, respectively. In these Centers, QuickBooks Accountant provides easy access to managing customers, vendors, and employees and allows entering transactions for each. For example, in the Employee Center you can view an employee's recent paychecks, edit that employee's information, enter a new employee, enter time worked, and write a new paycheck.

Scott reminds you that the home page is one of many ways to access the core features of any accounting information system like QuickBooks Accountant. There are menus, icons, centers, and workflow diagrams, all of which eventually take you to the same place to edit, enter, or process business events. He also notes that there are several sections on the right of the home page that may be closed or minimized. He suggests you open and close the Getting Started and Account Balances sections, which might have been minimized when you first viewed the home page but that are open in Figure 1.15.

After you have learned the basics about QuickBooks Accountant in this course, you might decide to use QuickBooks Accountant Centers and workflow diagrams more often. But for now, follow the steps as they are written in this text.

To view and explore the home page:

1 Click **Home** from the icon bar.

2 Click the **Enter Bills** icon in the Vendors section to view the Enter Bills window shown in Figure 1.16, where later you'll enter bills received from vendors.

Figure 1.16

Entering Bills

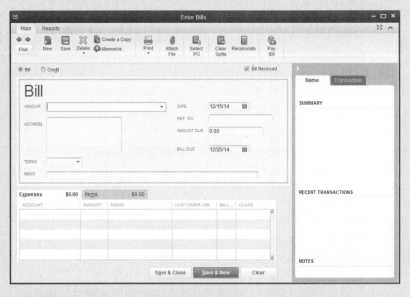

3 Close the Enter Bills window.

4 Click the **Receive Payments** icon in the Customers section to view the Receive Payments window shown in Figure 1.17, where later you'll enter amounts received from customers. Click **No Thanks** if a Get More From QuickBooks Accountant window appears.

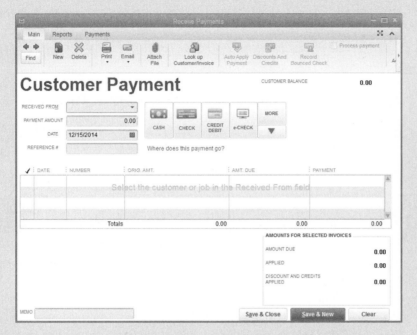

Figure 1.17

Receive Payments

5 Close the Receive Payments window.

6 Click **Employees** to view the Employee Center and then make sure the Date text box reads. This Calendar Year as shown in Figure 1.18.

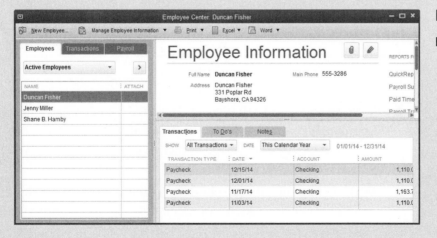

Figure 1.18

Employee Center

7 Close this window.

QuickBooks Learning Center Tutorials

QuickBooks Learning Center Tutorials are designed to help you get started. They provide an overview of important concepts and instructions for key tasks.

After Scott returned from his meeting, he asks if you've tried the tutorials. He's found them to be an effective way of learning about key business tasks in QuickBooks Accountant. Note: You must have a working Internet connection to view these tutorials.

To experience QuickBooks Learning Center Tutorials:

1   Click **Help** from the File menu, and then click **Learning Center Tutorials**. Your window should look like Figure 1.19.

Figure 1.19

QuickBooks Learning Center

2   Click **Adding your bank accounts** from the list of tutorials in this section. Approximately 8 seconds into the tutorial, click the **Pause** button located in the lower left-hand corner of the window. Once you have paused the tutorial, your window should look like Figure 1.20.

3   After viewing the tutorial, close the Tutorial window. Click other sections of QuickBooks Accountant and view other tutorials as you would like.

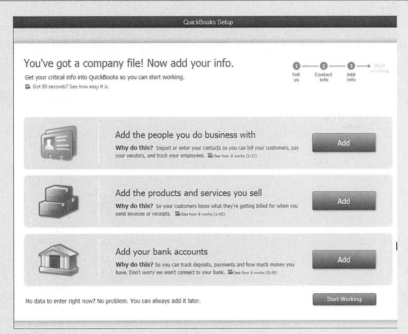

Figure 1.20

Tutorial on Adding Your Bank Accounts

4 When done, close the QuickBooks Accountant Learning Center window.

Exiting QuickBooks Accountant

You thank Scott for taking the time to introduce you to QuickBooks Accountant as he rushes off to yet another meeting. You know you can probably exit QuickBooks Accountant on your own, using standard Windows commands. You choose to use the Exit command on the File menu.

To exit QuickBooks Accountant:

1 Click **File** on the QuickBooks Accountant menu bar to display the File menu.

2 Click **Exit**. Once again, a dialog box might display the message "Intuit highly recommends backing up your data to avoid any accidental data loss. Would you like to *back up* now?"

3 Click **No** to exit QuickBooks Accountant and return to Windows. Good accounting practice encourages backing up data files, but backup is not necessary now with these sample files.

End Note

Scott has shown you some of the features of QuickBooks Accountant, how to navigate these features, and how business decisions can be aided by the reporting and analysis of accounting information afforded by QuickBooks Accountant. You are impressed by the speed at which information is made available and are anxious to learn more.

Chapter 1 Questions

1 Describe, in your own words, the various uses of QuickBooks Accountant.

2 List the four basic features of QuickBooks Accountant.

3 Describe how lists are used in QuickBooks Accountant.

4 Describe how forms are used in QuickBooks Accountant.

5 Name three forms used in QuickBooks Accountant.

6 Describe how registers are used in QuickBooks Accountant.

7 Describe how reports and graphs are used in QuickBooks Accountant.

8 Describe the function of the centers in QuickBooks Accountant.

9 Describe how to print a report in QuickBooks Accountant.

10 Describe two of the Help features available in QuickBooks Accountant.

Chapter 1 Matching

Select the letter of the item below that best matches the definitions that follow.
Use the text or QuickBooks Accountant Help to complete this assignment.

a. Data Files CD   _____ A repository for all financial activity for a specific balance sheet account.

b. Lists   _____ A means of presenting the financial position and the operating results of a company in a way that makes business decision making easier.

c. Forms   _____ The process of creating a copy of a QuickBooks Accountant file for safe-keeping or transporting to a different computer.

d. Registers   _____ Contains backups of all the practice files needed for chapter work and completion of assignments.

e. Reports and graphs   _____ Groups of names such as customers, vendors, employees, items, and accounts.

f. Restoring a backup   _____ A big-picture approach of how your essential business tasks fit together organized by logical groups such as customers, vendors, and employees.

g. Icon bar   _____ Electronic representations of paper documents used to record business activities such as customer invoices, vendor bills, and checks.

h. Home page   _____ The process of rebuilding a backup file to a full QuickBooks Accountant file ready for additional input.

i. Backing up a file   _____ One click access to QuickBooks Accountant Centers and Home page.

Chapter 1 Assignments

1 *Working with Files*

Open the Larry's Landscaping & Garden Supply file you used in the chapter to practice opening, closing, and printing. Create a Customer Balance Summary report as of 12/16/2014 from the Customers & Receivables menu item on the Reports menu. Click the Collapse button to condense the report and then print the resulting report.

sole proprietorship

merchandising

2   *Practice Using the QuickBooks Accountant Help Menu*

Use the QuickBooks Accountant Help menu to learn more about Quick-Books Accountant's features.

a.   Search on printing reports and print this topic.

b.   Search on add a customer. Print this topic.

c.   Search on calculating payroll taxes manually. Print this topic.

d.   Click **Chart of Accounts** from the Company menu. Press **F1** (which will open QuickBooks Accountant's Help window) and then print the topic.

3   *Using the QuickBooks Accountant Learning Center Tutorials*

From the Help menu, select **Learning Center Tutorials**. Click **Inventory**, and then watch the tutorial on using reports to manage inventory. Explain what information is provided on the Inventory Valuation Summary report.

4   *Accessing Inventory Data*

Scott Montalvo wants to know the amount and nature of inventory on hand as of December 15, 2014. Open the Larry's Landscaping & Garden Supply file you used in the chapter. Open an Inventory Valuation Summary report. Write your responses to questions below and print the Inventory Valuation Summary report.

a.   What is the item description of inventory item Pump?

b.   How many of this item were on hand on that date?

c.   What was the average cost of this item on that date?

d.   Print the Inventory Valuation Summary report in landscape orientation.

5   *Accessing Sales Data*

Scott has questions about the company's sales for the month of December. Open the Larry's Landscaping & Garden Supply file you used in the chapter. Open the Sales by Customer Detail report. Write your responses to the following questions.

a.   What amount was DJ's Computers billed this period?

b.   What was Jim's Family Store billed this period?

c.   What was the total amount billed during this period?

Preparing a Balance Sheet Using QuickBooks Accountant

Student Learning Outcomes

Upon completion of this chapter, the student will be able to:

- Create a comparative balance sheet and a summary balance sheet
- Investigate detail supporting balance sheet items
- Use the Balance Sheet Report button bar
- Create a balance sheet as of a specific date other than the system date
- Print a balance sheet

Case: Larry's Landscaping & Garden Supply

It's your second day at your new job, and you arrive early. Scott is already hard at work at the computer. He tells you he is preparing for Larry's quarter year-end on December 31, 2014. Since this is the first time he will prepare financial statements using QuickBooks Accountant, he's a little nervous.

You recall from your accounting course that a balance sheet reports the assets, liabilities, and owners' equity of a company at a specific point in time. As part of your continued training on QuickBooks Accountant, Scott asks you to watch what he does while he prepares the balance sheet. He explains that his immediate goals are to familiarize himself with how to prepare a balance sheet using QuickBooks Accountant and to examine some of the valuable features that QuickBooks Accountant provides for helping managers analyze and interpret financial information.

Creating a Balance Sheet

You know from your business courses that the information on a balance sheet can be presented in many ways. Scott tells you that QuickBooks Accountant provides four preset ways to present a balance sheet; QuickBooks Accountant also allows him to customize the way he presents the information. He decides to examine one of the preset balance sheets first. He chooses what QuickBooks Accountant calls the Standard Balance Sheet report.

Scott is amazed at how rapidly QuickBooks Accountant creates this balance sheet compared to how long it has taken him to create one manually in the past. As you both look over this balance sheet, Scott comments that—because he generated this information so quickly and with so little effort—he might now be able to add information to balance sheets that he didn't have time to include before. For example, he has always wanted to include comparative information on balance sheets to help him make better business decisions.

Video Demonstration

DEMO 2A - Creating a balance sheet

To create a Standard Balance Sheet report:

1 Open Larry's Landscaping & Garden Supply QuickBooks Accountant file you used in Chapter 1.

2 Click **Reports** from the icon bar. Click **Company & Financial** on the left (if it is not already selected). Click the **Standard** tab at the top of the Report Center window. In the upper right hand corner of the Report Center window, click the **List View** icon (place your mouse over the three icons shown noting that the List View is the middle icon). Scroll down the window, and then double-click **Balance Sheet Standard** under the heading **Balance Sheet & Net Worth**. Click the **Customize Report** button on the button bar, click the **Header/Footer** tab, uncheck the **Date Prepared, Time Prepared**, and **Report Basis** check boxes, and then click **OK**. A partial view of QuickBooks Accountant's Standard Balance Sheet appears. See Figure 2.1.

Figure 2.1

Top Portion of Larry's Standard Balance Sheet

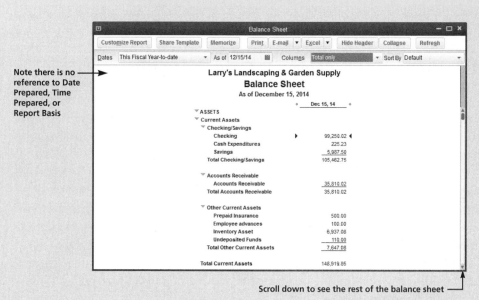

Note there is no reference to Date Prepared, Time Prepared, or Report Basis

Scroll down to see the rest of the balance sheet

3 Scroll down the Balance Sheet. Notice that this report shows the balance in each account, with subtotals for assets, liabilities, and owners' equity. Unlike standard accounting practice, QuickBooks Accountant displays net income for the year to date as part of owners' equity. In particular, take note of the current assets, fixed assets, current liabilities, long-term liabilities, and equity.

4 Do not close this window.
Trouble? On many of these reports, when you change the size of a column and then close the window, a "Memorized Report" window pops up asking if you want to memorize these new settings ("Would you like to memorize this report?"). I suggest that at this point you just click **No**.

Creating a Comparative Balance Sheet

By using the help function of QuickBooks Accountant, Scott discovers how easy it is to create a comparative balance sheet. He learns that he can modify the existing standard balance sheet by creating one that compares each month of the quarter just ended. When Scott sees how easy it is to create a comparative balance sheet, he decides to create one comparing the balance sheets of October, November, and December.

To create a comparative balance sheet report:

1 Change the Columns text box from Total Only to **Month**. Your window should look like Figure 2.2.

Check here to change
columns to months

Figure 2.2

QuickBooks Accountant's
Comparison Balance Sheet Report

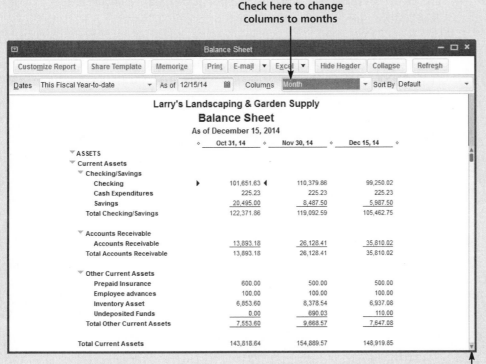

Scroll down to see more of this balance sheet ⸻

2 Scroll down and across this balance sheet. Note that this report is similar to the Standard report except that the columns compare the amounts by month for a three-month period as compared to just one date. *Trouble?* The balance sheet on your screen might not look the same as Figure 2.1 because the column widths are different. To change the column widths on any QuickBooks Accountant report, click and hold the mouse over the small diamond-shaped symbols to the right or left of any column. Drag to the right or left to increase or decrease each column's width. A dialog box might appear asking if you want to make all columns the same width. You may answer yes or no.

3 Close this window.

Creating a Summary Balance Sheet

Scott wonders if QuickBooks Accountant has a preset report that summarizes balance sheet information—in other words, one that provides no detail, only totals. In annual reports, such a summary is useful to external financial statement users, who usually do not have much interest in detailed balance sheet information. Scott again consults Help and learns that QuickBooks Accountant has a Summary Balance Sheet preset report.

To create a Summary Balance Sheet report:

1 From the Report Center, click **Company & Financial**, if it is not already selected, and then double-click **Balance Sheet Summary**. (*Note:* This is not clicking the Reports menu item; it's clicking **Company & Financial** from the Report Center.) Remove the Date Prepared, Time Prepared, and Report Basis as you did in the previous balance sheet. Your window should look like Figure 2.3.

2 Scroll down the summary balance sheet if necessary. Note that it is a brief version of the Standard Balance Sheet; it shows amounts for each account type, such as Other Current Assets, but not for individual accounts within each account type.

Figure 2.3

QuickBooks Accountant's
Summary Balance Sheet Report

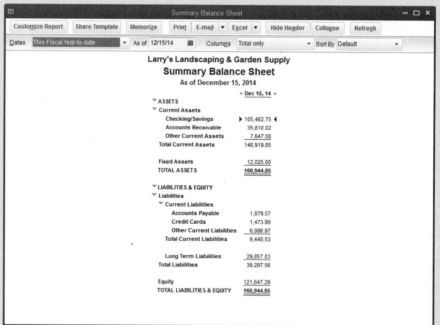

Investigating the Balance Sheet Using QuickZoom

Now that Scott knows he can generate the type of reports he wants, he decides to investigate QuickZoom—a feature he has heard QuickBooks Accountant provides for most reports. He tells you that QuickZoom shows you what transaction or transactions underlie any amount found in a report. You know that this is a helpful feature because managers must often explain report balances quickly; thus, knowledge of the underlying detailed transactions is essential.

Scott decides to practice using QuickZoom by analyzing the transactions that make up the Accounts Receivable balance.

To use QuickZoom:

1 Place the cursor over the Accounts Receivable balance of **$35,810.02**. A cursor shaped like a magnifying glass and containing a "Z" appears. This cursor indicates that a QuickZoom report is available for this amount. See Figure 2.4.

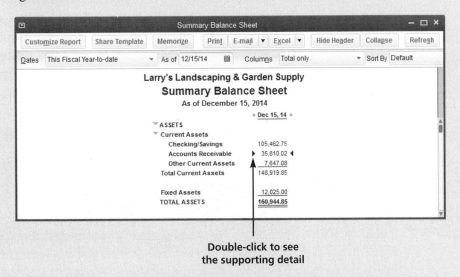

Figure 2.4

Using QuickZoom

Double-click to see the supporting detail

2 Double-click the amount **35,810.02**. The Transactions by Account report appears.

3 Remove the Date Prepared, Time Prepared, and Report Basis items as you did previously. The resulting Transactions by Account report now appears with all changes to Accounts Receivable occurring from October 1, 2014, through December 15, 2014, as shown in Figure 2.5.

Transactions are listed for 10/1/2014 to 12/15/14

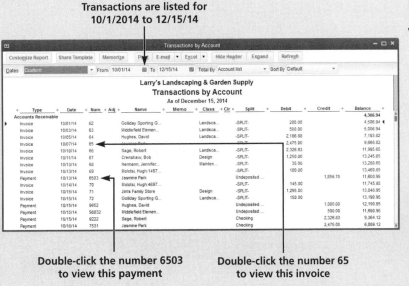

Figure 2.5

Viewing Transactions by Account

Double-click the number 6503 to view this payment

Double-click the number 65 to view this invoice

4 Double-click invoice **65** in the Num column to examine one of the actual invoices that increased accounts receivable. See Figure 2.6.

Figure 2.6

Examining Invoice Number 65

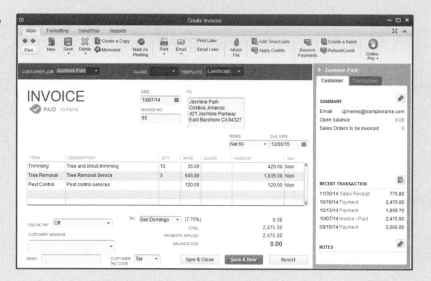

5 Close the Create Invoices window. The Transactions by Account report, which was hidden while you examined invoice 65, reappears. *Trouble?* If the transactions report does not reappear, activate the Transactions by Account report by clicking **Transactions by Account** on the Window menu; or, if you closed the window, repeat Steps 1 through 4 as necessary.

6 Double-click anywhere on the row containing the payment reference 6503. A Receive Payments window appears (see Figure 2.7). Note that this payment was a payment on account and was applied to invoice 49.

7 Close the Receive Payments window.

8 Close the Transactions by Account window.

Figure 2.7

Customer Payment Received

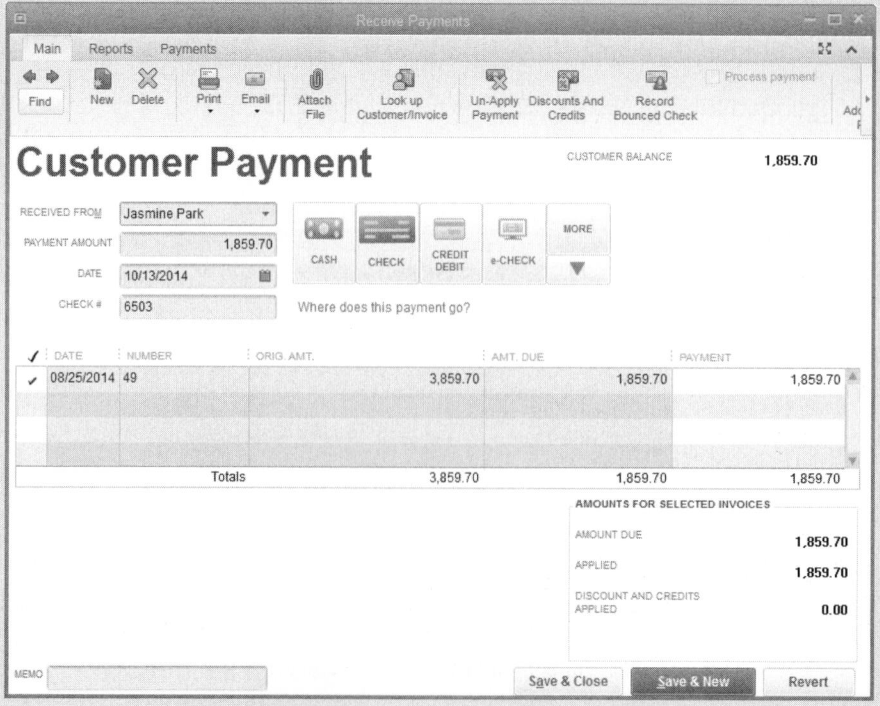

Scott is pleased with the QuickZoom feature of QuickBooks Accountant because it allows him to quickly and easily investigate any of the balances reported.

Modifying Balance Sheet Reports

The balance sheet report, like all other reports created in QuickBooks Accountant, can be modified using the report button bar located on the menu bar. Scott decides that since this summary balance sheet is for internal use, he wants to change the heading, include the previous month's balances, report the numbers in thousands, and make a few other appropriate cosmetic changes.

To modify the Summary Balance Sheet report:

1   Click the **Customize Report** button on the report button bar. (*Note:* The summary balance sheet should still be open. If not, re-create it.)

2   Click the **Display** tab if it is not already active; then leave the From date as **10/1/2014** and then change the To date to **11/30/2014**, change Display columns by setting to **Month**, and check the **% of Column** check box, as shown in Figure 2.8.

3   Click the **Fonts & Numbers** tab as shown in Figure 2.8.

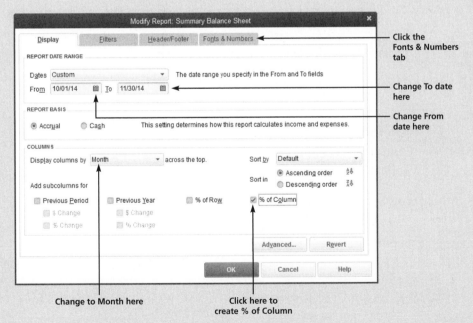

Figure 2.8

The Modify Report Dialog Box Display Tab

4   Click the **Divided By 1000** and **Without Cents** check boxes under the Show All Numbers section of the Modify Report dialog box. See Figure 2.9.

Figure 2.9

The Modify Report Dialog Box
Fonts & Numbers Tab

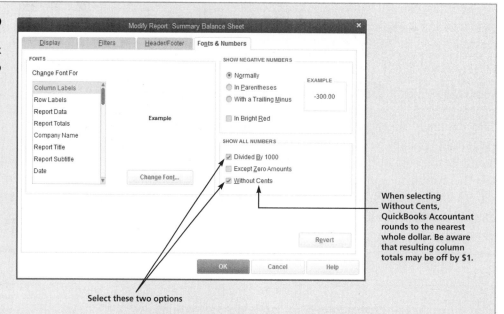

Select these two options

When selecting
Without Cents,
QuickBooks Accountant
rounds to the nearest
whole dollar. Be aware
that resulting column
totals may be off by $1.

5 Click the **Header/Footer** tab.

6 Click inside the Report Title edit box. Change the name of the report
from Summary Balance Sheet to Comparative Summary Balance Sheet
by adding the word **Comparative** as shown in Figure 2.10. (*Note:* To
properly identify this report as yours, you may want to type your name
in the Extra Footer Line of the Header/Footer tab.)

Figure 2.10

The Header/Footer Tab

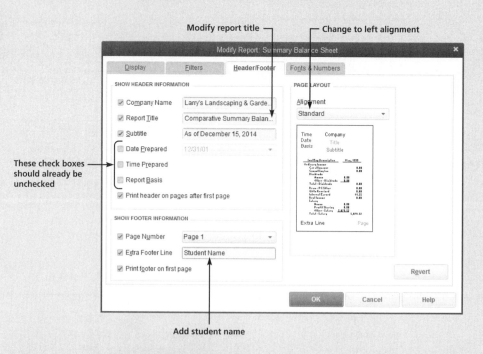

Modify report title

Change to left alignment

These check boxes
should already be
unchecked

Add student name

7 Change the alignment by clicking the **Down Arrow** in the Page Layout
section and clicking **Left**. This changes the alignment of the title text to
a left alignment.

8 Click **OK** to close the Modify Report window. The resulting report is shown in Figure 2.11. Do not close this report.

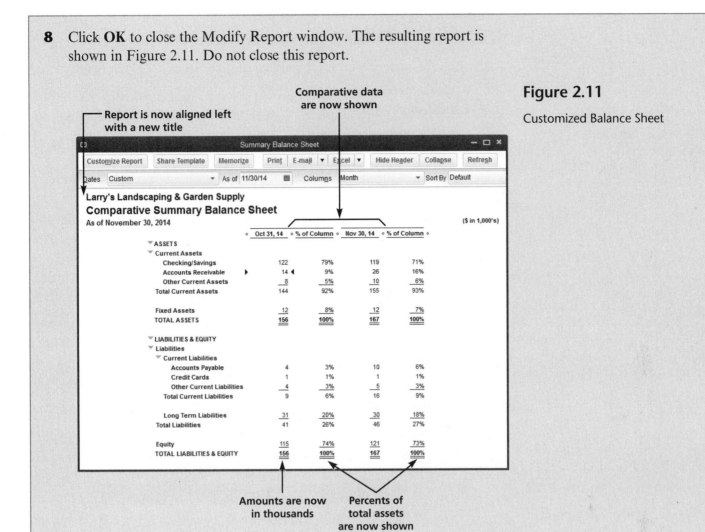

Figure 2.11

Customized Balance Sheet

Scott knows that this modified balance sheet will help him analyze the financial information more easily and quickly. You will have an opportunity to explore other report modification features available in QuickBooks Accountant in the chapter assignments.

Memorizing a Report in QuickBooks Accountant

Scott, knowing that he wants you to be an efficient QuickBooks Accountant user, suggests that you learn how to memorize the report just created so it can be produced again. He explains that, while standard reports are always available, unique reports like the one you just created should be memorized. Later they can be accessed, dates changed if necessary, and then re-created.

"How will I know where they are when I need them?" you ask.

Scott explains that he will create a memorized report group for you using your name. That way, when you need them again, they will be easy to find.

To memorize the comparative balance sheet just prepared:

1 Activate the Report Center window. If you closed it, open it again.

2 Click the **Memorized** tab at the top of the Report Center and then click **Edit Memorized List**.

3 Click the **Memorized Report** button at the bottom of the Memorized Report List window, and then click **New Group**.

4 Type your name as the new group, and then click **OK**. (For illustration purposes, the list will show "Student Name" as your name.)

5 Go to the Summary Balance Sheet still open in QuickBooks Accountant by clicking its name from the Open Windows List.
Trouble? If the Open Windows List is not present, click the **View** menu and then click **Open Windows List**.

6 Click the **Memorize . . .** button at the top of the report.

7 Check the **Saved in Memorized Report Group** check box, and select your name from the drop-down list.

8 Click **OK** to memorize the report accepting the default report title provided.

9 Click **Memorized Report List** from the Open Windows list to view the Memorized Report List window, which should look similar to that shown in Figure 2.12. Then close the Memorized Report List.

Figure 2.12

Memorized Report List

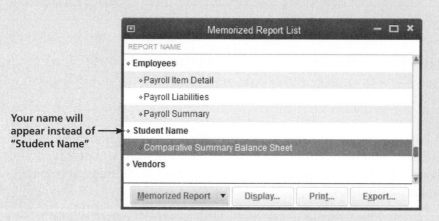

Your name will appear instead of "Student Name"

Printing the Balance Sheet

Scott receives a phone call from Frances Wu, an accountant with the company's CPA firm of Stoddard & Wong. Frances says she needs a printed copy of the company's comparative summary balance sheet as of 11/30/2014 to analyze the need for an allowance for uncollectible accounts. Scott knows that printing the balance sheet he just created will provide her with the information she needs. He also knows that printing a balance sheet is just like printing any other report in QuickBooks Accountant.

To print the Comparative Summary Balance Sheet report:

1 Click **Print** on the report button bar.

2 Click **Preview** in the Print Reports dialog box to preview the report.

3 Click the **Zoom In** button to see what the report will look like when printed. (Alternatively, you could have clicked anywhere on the screen to zoom in on the report.) See Figure 2.13.

Figure 2.13

Preview the Balance Sheet

Larry's Landscaping & Garden Supply
Comparative Summary Balance Sheet
As of November 30, 2014

	Oct 31, 14	% of Column	Nov 30, 14	% of Column
ASSETS				
Current Assets				
Checking/Savings	122	79%	119	71%
Accounts Receivable	14	9%	26	16%
Other Current Assets	8	5%	10	6%
Total Current Assets	144	92%	155	93%
Fixed Assets	12	8%	12	7%
TOTAL ASSETS	156	100%	167	100%
LIABILITIES & EQUITY				
Liabilities				
Current Liabilities				
Accounts Payable	4	3%	10	6%
Credit Cards	1	1%	1	1%
Other Current Liabilities	4	3%	5	3%
Total Current Liabilities	9	6%	16	9%
Long Term Liabilities	31	20%	30	18%
Total Liabilities	41	26%	46	27%
Equity	115	74%	121	73%
TOTAL LIABILITIES & EQUITY	156	100%	167	100%

4 Click the **Print** button if you would like to print the report.

5 Close all windows and, if you are not proceeding to Chapter 3, exit QuickBooks Accountant. If a Memorized Report window appears, click in the check box next to Do not display this message in the future, and then click **No**.

Scott feels much more confident about using QuickBooks Accountant. You are quickly becoming more comfortable with QuickBooks Accountant as well.

In the next chapter, you will expand your QuickBooks Accountant knowledge to include the creation, modification, and printing of another useful financial statement—the income statement.

Chapter 2 Questions

1 List the preset ways in which QuickBooks Accountant can present a balance sheet.

2 What time period alternatives does QuickBooks Accountant provide for a balance sheet?

3 List the steps you would take to create a balance sheet for a date other than the current system date.

4 Describe the steps to generate a balance sheet in QuickBooks Accountant.

5 Describe the steps to resize the columns of a comparative balance sheet.

6 Describe the different types of transactions you might find in a Transactions by Account report on accounts receivable.

7 Describe how QuickZoom gives you more information about a balance sheet.

8 How might a manager use QuickZoom to analyze a business's financial position as reported in a balance sheet?

9 List five ways you can customize a QuickBooks Accountant report.

10 Suppose you wanted to include a column in a balance sheet that described what percentage each asset, liability, and owners' equity account was of the total assets amount. How would you do this in QuickBooks Accountant?

Chapter 2 Matching

Select the letter of the item below that best matches the definitions that follow. Use the text or QuickBooks Accountant Help to complete this assignment.

a. Balance Sheet Standard report

b. To date

c. Summary Balance Sheet report

d. QuickZoom

e. Transactions by Account report

f. % of Column

g. Memorizing a report

h. Divided by 1000

_____ When selected in the Modify Report window, this check box requires QuickBooks Accountant to add a column representing the percentage of each item compared to total assets.

_____ When selected in the Modify Report window, this check box requires QuickBooks Accountant to round amounts to the nearest whole dollar.

_____ The start of the reporting period.

_____ A financial statement reporting in detail the assets, liabilities, and equities of a business as of a certain date.

_____ A process by which modified reports are saved for later use.

_____ When selected in the Modify Report window, this check box requires QuickBooks Accountant to report amounts in thousands.

_____ The end of the reporting period.

_____ A QuickBooks Accountant feature that allows you to view the transaction details of underlying amounts in a report.

i. Without Cents   _____   A report generated when using QuickZoom.

j. From date   _____   A financial statement reporting in summary form the assets, liabilities, and equities of a business as of a certain date.

Chapter 2 Assignments

1   *Creating a Balance Sheet for Larry's Landscaping & Garden Supply*

Scott asks you to help him prepare a balance sheet. Use the Larry's Landscaping & Garden Supply file you used in the chapter. (Be sure to type your name in the Extra Footer Line of this report.)

sole proprietorship

merchandising

a. He asks you to prepare and print a summary balance sheet as of October 31, 2014. He wants the amounts represented in thousands without cents and with no date prepared, time prepared, or report basis shown. Print, then memorize this report with Name: Summary Balance Sheet October 2014, and save it in your report group.

b. Scott also asks you to prepare and print a standard balance sheet as of October 31, 2014. He wants amounts to be displayed in thousands, without cents, and with the page layout left-aligned but with no date prepared, time prepared, or report basis shown. Click the Collapse button to reduce the size of the report so it fits on one page. Print, then memorize this report with Name: Standard Balance Sheet October 2014, and save it in your report group.

2   *Investigating the Balance Sheet Using QuickZoom*

Scott asks you to help him investigate the Accounts Receivable balance as of October 31, 2014. Use the Larry's Landscaping & Garden Supply file you used in this chapter. Create a summary balance sheet as of October 31, 2014, and then investigate the Accounts Receivable balance.

a. Print the resulting Transactions by Account report.

b. Examine and print a copy of invoice 76.

3   *Customizing a Balance Sheet*

Use the Larry's Landscaping & Garden Supply file you used in this chapter. Modify the balance sheet you created in Assignment 1a (remember, you memorized it, so it is easy to recall) to include October and November amounts with a % of column. Change the report title and format the page as shown in Figure 2.14. (**Hint:** Use the Modify Report button.) Print the report with your name in the Extra Footer Line in portrait orientation.

Figure 2.14

Comparative Balance Sheet

Larry's Landscaping & Garden Supply Comparative Balance Sheet As of November 30, 2014 ($ in 1,000's)	Oct 31, 14	% of Column	Nov 30, 14	% of Column
ASSETS				
Current Assets				
Checking/Savings	122	79%	119	71%
Accounts Receivable	14	9%	26	16%
Other Current Assets	8	5%	10	6%
Total Current Assets	144	92%	155	93%
Fixed Assets	12	8%	12	7%
TOTAL ASSETS	156	100%	167	100%
LIABILITIES & EQUITY				
Liabilities				
Current Liabilities				
Accounts Payable	4	3%	10	6%
Credit Cards	1	1%	1	1%
Other Current Liabilities	4	3%	5	3%
Total Current Liabilities	9	6%	16	9%
Long Term Liabilities	31	20%	30	18%
Total Liabilities	41	26%	46	27%
Equity	115	74%	121	73%
TOTAL LIABILITIES & EQUITY	156	100%	167	100%

Chapter 2 Cases

Chapter 2 Case Problem 1

SIERRA MARINA

Meagan Casey is the sole proprietor and owner of Sierra Marina, located at the north end of Shaver Lake in the California Sierra Mountains. She has been in business for a few years and decided on July 1, 2014, to automate her accounting using QuickBooks Accountant. Meagan has already entered the June 30, 2014, ending balances from her previous accounting system as well as all transactions for July and August 2014, and she has asked you to help her prepare some basic financial reports related to the company's assets, liabilities, and equities.

Requirements:

Prepare, memorize, and print the following reports using Meagan's Sierra Marina QuickBooks Accountant file. (Remember, you'll have to restore this file from the Data Files CD. Be sure to include your name in the Extra Footer Line of each report where possible.)

1 A standard balance sheet as of July 31, 2014.

2 A summary balance sheet as of July 31, 2014.

3 A comparative summary balance sheet for June and July 2014 without cents, with a % of column, and in a left alignment. Be sure to change the report title to include the word "comparative."

4 A report of those transactions recorded in July 2014 that affected accounts receivable. (*Hint:* From your summary balance sheet created in Step 2, double-click **Accounts Receivable** and make sure the From date is 7/1/14 and the To date is 7/31/14.)

Chapter 2 Case Problem 2

JENNINGS & ASSOCIATES

corporation

service

Kelly Jennings has just started working full time in her new business, an advertising agency named Jennings & Associates and located in San Martin, California. Like many eager entrepreneurs, she started her business while working full time for another firm. At first, her billings were quite small. But as her client base and her billings grew, she decided to leave her job and set out on her own. Two of her colleagues and friends—Cheryl Boudreau and Diane Murphy—see Kelly's eagerness and dedication, and they decide the time is right for them, too. Cheryl and Diane ask Kelly if they can join her sole proprietorship as employees, and so together they leave the traditional corporate agency environment.

Kelly knows that one of the first tasks she must accomplish is setting up an accounting system for Jennings & Associates. Also, she has just received a request from her banker to submit a balance sheet as documentation for a business loan. As a close friend you recommend she use QuickBooks Accountant, and you volunteer to help her get started.

Kelly tells you that in 2014 she borrowed $5,000 to start the business. Now she is applying for a loan to help expand the business. She also reminds you that, although she did conduct some business in 2014, her first full-time month was January 2015.

Requirements:

Prepare, memorize and print the following reports using Kelly Jennings.qbw (include your name in the Extra Footer Line of each report where possible). Remember, you'll need to restore this file from your Data Files CD.

1   A standard balance sheet as of December 31, 2014.

2   A standard balance sheet as of January 31, 2015.

3   A Transactions List by Date report for the month of January 2015 in landscape orientation. (*Hint:* This report is listed in the Report menu section labeled Accountant & Taxes.)

4   A summary balance sheet as of January 31, 2015, formatted in thousands and without cents and without the date prepared, time prepared, or report basis included.

5   A report of those transactions recorded in January 2015 that affected accounts payable. (*Hint:* Create a summary balance sheet and double-click accounts payable.)

Chapter 2 Case Problem 3

JASON GALAS, ATTORNEY AT LAW PC

corporation

service

Jason Galas has a well-deserved reputation as a leader in innovative and cutting edge corporate tax planning with over 20 years of experience. His firm's diverse practice extends beyond ordinary tax issues. Jason decided to automate his accounting using Peachtree. His bookkeeper has already entered the December 31, 2011, ending balances from the previous manual accounting system as well as all transactions for January and February 2012, and they have asked you to help them prepare some basic financial reports related to the company's assets, liabilities, and equities.

Requirements:

Prepare and print the following reports or answer questions using the Jason Galas, Attorney at Law PC file. (Remember, you'll need to restore this file from your Data Files CD.)

1   A standard balance sheet as of 1/31/12 formatted without cents and without the date prepared, time prepared, or report basis fields included. Memorize as Balance Sheet 1 in a group with your name.

2   A standard balance sheet as of 2/29/12 formatted without cents and without the date prepared, time prepared, or report basis fields and with a % of column. Memorize as Balance Sheet 2 in a group with your name.

3   A transactions list by date report for the month of January 2012 in landscape orientation without a date or time prepared stamp. Memorize as Jan Transactions in a group with your name.

4   A transactions list by date report for the month of February 2012 in landscape orientation without a date or time prepared stamp. Memorize as Feb Transactions in a group with your name.

5   A report of those transactions recorded in January 2012 that affected accounts payable in landscape orientation without a report basis or date or time prepared stamp. Memorize as Jan AP Transactions in a group with your name.

6   Drill down from the accounts payable balance owed at 1/31/12. Locate a bill dated 1/26/12 from Randol Leasing. What is this bill for? What is the amount due?

7   A report of those transactions recorded in January 2012 that affected accounts receivable in landscape orientation without a report basis or date or time prepared stamp. Memorize as Jan AR Transactions in a group with your name.

8   Drill down from the accounts receivable balance due at 1/31/12. Locate invoice 563. Who is the client? What was billed to this client?

9   Drill down from the accounts receivable balance due at 1/31/12. Locate a cash receipt on 1/27/12. Who is the client making the payment? What is this payment for?

Preparing an Income Statement Using QuickBooks Accountant

3

Case: Larry's Landscaping & Garden Supply

Now that Scott has created a balance sheet, he is ready to create an income statement for the period October 1, 2014, through November 30, 2014. You recall from your accounting course that the income statement reports revenues and expenses for a specific period.

Again, as part of your training with QuickBooks Accountant, Scott asks you to watch how he prepares the income statement. He expects to use many of the same functions and features to prepare an income statement that he used to prepare the balance sheet.

Creating an Income Statement

As with the balance sheet and other reports available in QuickBooks Accountant, the income statement can be presented in preset ways and can also be customized. Scott decides to examine one of the preset income statement formats first—the format called Standard.

Before doing so, he mentions that QuickBooks Accountant does not use the traditional name for this report. Instead of calling it the income statement, QuickBooks Accountant refers to it as the "Profit & Loss" report. Scott prefers "income statement" because it is really the most accurate name for this report. Although the report title on the menu cannot be changed, Scott will show you how you can change the title on the report.

Video Demonstration

DEMO 3A - Creating an income statement

To create a standard income statement:

1 Open the Larry's Landscaping & Garden Supply QuickBooks Accountant file you used in Chapter 2.

2 Open the Report Center, click the **Standard** tab, and then click **Company & Financial**, and then double-click **Profit & Loss Standard**. Change the From date to **10/1/14** and the To date to **10/31/14**. Then click **Refresh**.

3 Click **Customize Report**, click the **Header/Footer** tab, and then uncheck the **Date Prepared, Time Prepared**, and **Report Basis** check boxes and then click **OK**.

4 Click the **Collapse** button to view Figure 3.1 and then scroll down the income statement. This report summarizes revenues and expenses for this month-to-date. Notice that QuickBooks Accountant does not use the standard accounting term "revenue" but instead uses the term "income." Subtotals are included for revenues and expenses. Observe also the period specified for this particular report is October 1–31, 2014, the span of this report period.

Figure 3.1

Income Statement for the Month
of October 2014

Called "Income Statement"
in traditional accounting

Note that now the
From and To dates are
formatted to two digits

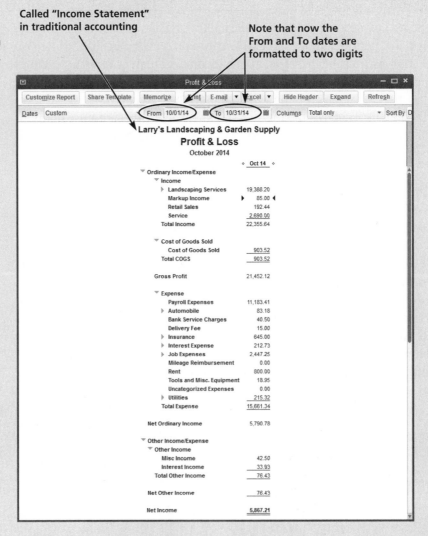

Scott changes his mind and wants a year-to-date statement for his preliminary income statement.

Modifying an Income Statement

Scott decides to revise the previously created income statement to make it a year-to-date statement for the period January 1, 2014, through December 15, 2014. He also wants to show you how to change the report title from "Profit & Loss" to the more accurate "Income Statement." For this title change you will modify the header, a task you learned how to perform previously with the balance sheet.

To revise the period of time and the report title:

1 Change the From date on the previously created income statement to **1/1/14** and the To date to **12/31/14**. Click **Refresh**. The revised report appears as in Figure 3.2.

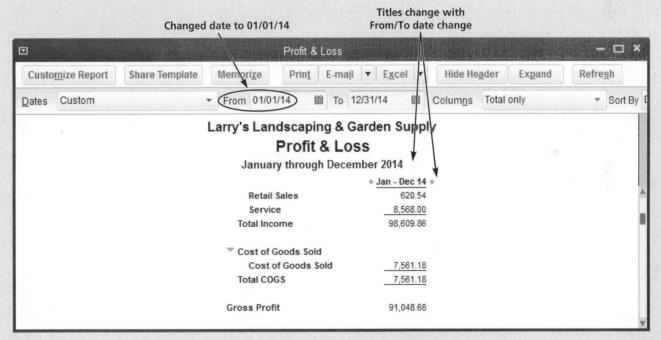

Figure 3.2 Revised Income Statement for the Period January 1 to December 31, 2014

2 To change the report title, click **Customize Report**, and then click **Header/Footer**. The Header/Footer tab appears (see Figure 3.3).

3 Move the cursor to the Report Title edit box and delete Profit and Loss. Type **Income Statement** and then click **OK**. (*Note:* To properly identify this report as yours, you may want to type your name in the Extra Footer Line of the Header/Footer tab.)

4 Click the **Memorize** button.

Figure 3.3

Header/Footer Tab

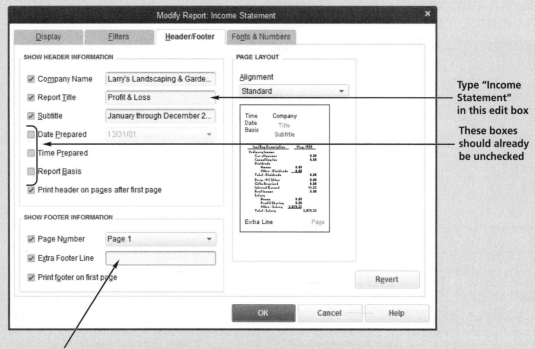

Type "Income Statement" in this edit box

These boxes should already be unchecked

You may want to type your name here to identify this as your report

Figure 3.4

Revised Income Statement with Corrected Title

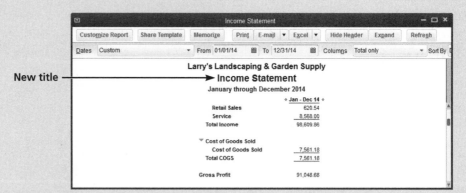

New title

5   Save this report, as shown in Figure 3.4, as Income Statement in the Memorized Report Group you created in the last chapter and then click **OK** and then close the Income Statement report window.

Once again, Scott comments on how remarkably fast this process is compared to creating income statements manually. As with the balance sheet, he decides to create a comparison report—this time with the income statement.

Creating a Comparative Income Statement

QuickBooks Accountant has several features that allow you to create comparative reports as you did with the balance sheet. Scott suggests that you help him create a comparative income statement illustrating the performance of Larry's Landscaping in October and November. You guess that the process will be similar to how you prepared the comparative balance sheet. Scott also suggests changing the name and look of the statement as you've done previously.

To create a comparative income statement for October and November:

1 From the Report Center, click **Company & Financial**, and then double-click **Profit & Loss Standard** located under the title Profit & Loss (income statement).

2 Set the From date to **11/1/14** and the To date to **11/30/14**, click **Collapse**, and then click **Refresh**.

3 Click the **Customize Report** button, and then check the **Previous Period, $ Change**, and **% Change** check boxes located under the caption Add subcolumns for (see Figure 3.5).

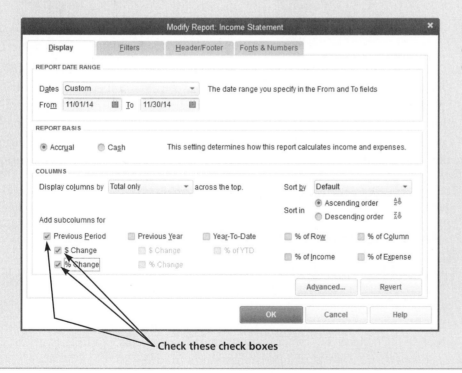

Figure 3.5

Creating a Previous Period for a Comparative Income Statement

Check these check boxes

4 Click the **Header/Footer** tab, and then uncheck the **Date Prepared, Time Prepared**, and **Report Basis** check boxes.

5 Change the name of the statement from Profit & Loss to **Comparative Income Statements**, align the statement **Right**, put your name in the Footer, and then click **OK** to see the revised report. See Figure 3.6.

Figure 3.6

Comparative Income Statements
for October and November 2014

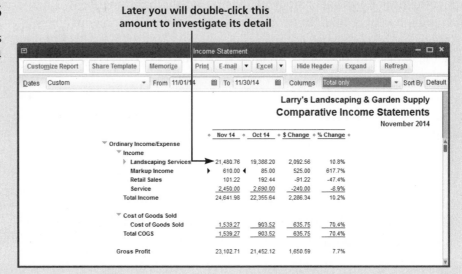

6 Do not close this report, as it will be used in the next section.

Scott had been concerned about the company's performance in November and can now see how things differed between November and October. He is pleased to discover that total income increased 10.2% and that gross profit increased 7.7% from the previous month. He scrolled down the income statement to discover that job expenses had decreased in November, but automobile and tools and misc. equipment expenses had increased. Overall, the company's net income increased from the previous month by 45.6%. He decides to further investigate the increase in tool and misc. equipment expenses.

Using QuickZoom with the Income Statement

To investigate the increase in tools and misc. equipment expenses, Scott uses the QuickZoom feature of QuickBooks Accountant to examine the underlying source of various business events. He knows that he can "drill down" behind the income statement to view Transaction Detail By Account reports and further to an invoice. He explains that the invoice in this example is referred to as a *source document* and will prove helpful in his analysis.

To use QuickZoom with an income statement:

1 Scroll down the statement until the Tools and Misc. Equipment line appears, then place the QuickZoom cursor over the November Tools and Misc. Equipment amount of $716.05 and then double-click that amount to reveal a Transaction Detail By Account report (see Figure 3.7).

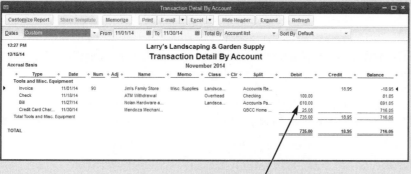

Figure 3.7

Transaction Detail By Account Report

Double-click here to view detail

2 Double-click the **$610.00** as shown in Figure 3.7 to reveal the bill from Nolan Hardware and Supplies as shown in Figure 3.8.

3 Close the Enter Bills and Transaction Detail by Account windows and then memorize your newly created Comparative Income Statements report into your previously created Report Group. Close the Comparative Income Statement report window.

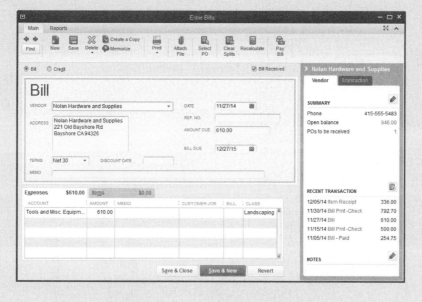

Figure 3.8

Bill from Nolan Hardware and Supplies

You have now seen that the QuickZoom feature of QuickBooks Accountant is available with the income statement as well as with the balance sheet and that it provides background detail relating to revenues and expenses.

Modifying the Income Statement Report

The Income Statement report, like all other reports created in QuickBooks Accountant, can be modified using the report button bar. Scott knows from experience that when he works with income statements in the future he will definitely need to add columns, change report dates, use different number formats, modify headings, and so on. He therefore decides to explore additional ways of modifying an income statement. He decides first to create a third-quarter income statement and to add a percentage of net income column.

To add percentage of net income columns and to change the dates on an Income Statement report:

1 From the Report Center, click **Company & Financial**, and then double-click **Profit & Loss Standard** from the list of Profit & Loss Reports.

2 Click the **Customize Report** button on the report button bar, and then select the **Display** tab if it is not already selected.

3 Click the **% of Income** check box in the Columns section to report monthly amounts as a percent of total income—actually a percent of total revenue.

4 Click the **From** edit box, and change the date to **7/1/14**.

5 Click the **To** edit box, and change the date to **9/30/14** (see Figure 3.9). These two changes customize the report so it reports on the months of July through September only. (Alternatively, you can select the calendar icons and click the arrows to specific dates.)

Figure 3.9

The Modify Report Window

Change these dates

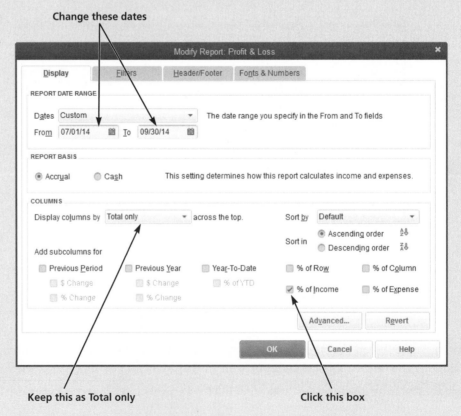

Keep this as Total only   Click this box

6 Select the **Header/Footer** tab, and uncheck the **Date Prepared, Time Prepared**, and **Report Basis** check boxes.

7 Click **OK** to accept these changes and then click the **Collapse** button. The revised report appears as Figure 3.10. Do not close this report window.

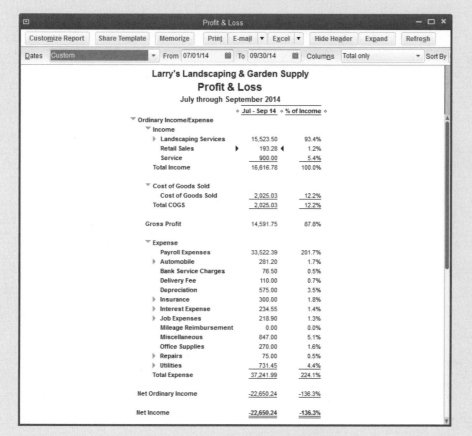

Figure 3.10

Quarterly Income Statement with a % of Income Column

Scott decides that he wants to report the numbers without cents and to expand income and expense detail.

To report the amounts without cents:

1 Click **Customize Report** on the report button bar, and then click the **Fonts & Numbers** tab.

2 Click the **Without Cents** check box under the Show All Numbers section of the Format Report window. A check mark appears in the box.

3   Click **OK** to accept these changes.

4   Click the **Expand** button on the report button bar to view a portion of the revised quarterly Income Statement (see Figure 3.11).

Figure 3.11

Income Statement with Numbers Reported without Cents

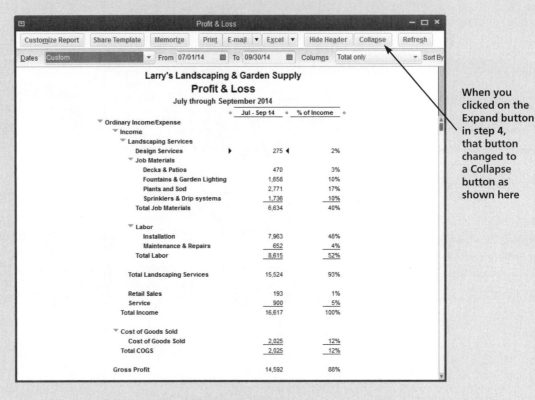

When you clicked on the Expand button in step 4, that button changed to a Collapse button as shown here

As Scott looks over this latest version of the income statement, he sees that he must correct the report title again. Also, he decides the title would look better if it appeared in the center of the report and if it included each separate month.

To modify the title and its layout:

1   Click **Customize Report** on the report button bar, and then click the **Header/Footer** tab.

2   Click inside the **Report Title** edit box, and change the name of the report from Profit & Loss to **Income Statement** as you have done before.

3   Change the title alignment by clicking the **Down Arrow** in the Page Layout section and changing the selection from Standard to **Centered**.

4   Before you accept these changes, look at the Subtitle edit box. Notice that QuickBooks Accountant had changed the subtitle of this report.

QuickBooks Accountant does this automatically for you whenever you change the dates in the To and From edit boxes. (*Note:* Once again, you may want to type your name in the Extra Footer Line.)

5   Click **OK** to accept the changes. Change the Columns text box from Total Only to **Month**. The modified income statement appears as shown in Figure 3.12.

Figure 3.12

Modified Income Statement

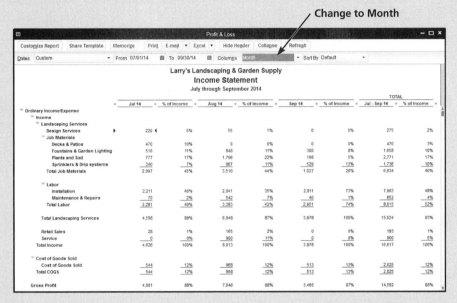

6   Do not close this report window. Memorize this report with a title of 3rd Qtr. Income Statement.

QuickBooks Accountant provides many other ways to modify a report—grouping and subtotaling data, sorting transactions, and specifying which columns appear in a report, to name just a few. Scott encourages you to explore these additional options when you generate reports in the future.

Printing the Income Statement

Scott would like to print this modified report so that he can show some Larry's Landscaping and Garden Supply managers an example of the type of reports he can generate for them. He'd like this example to fit on one piece of 8½″ × 11″ paper—both to save paper and to make analysis of the report easier. He decides to use QuickBooks Accountant's preview option to see if the report will fit onto a single page.

To preview the modified income statement:

1   Click **Print** on the report button bar.

2   Click **Preview** in the Print Reports window. A miniature reproduction of the report appears. See Figure 3.13. (Do not resize the columns.) The heading "Page 1 of 4" may appear at the top of the window. This indicates how many pages the report contains and which page you are previewing.

Trouble? Your screen may indicate Page 1 of 1 depending on your computer and printer settings. If so, skip to step 4, but continue reading so that you are familiar with the options that can help fit a long report on one page. In addition, if you did not memorize this report as instructed to previously, the name of your report may be incorrect.

Figure 3.13

The Print Preview Window

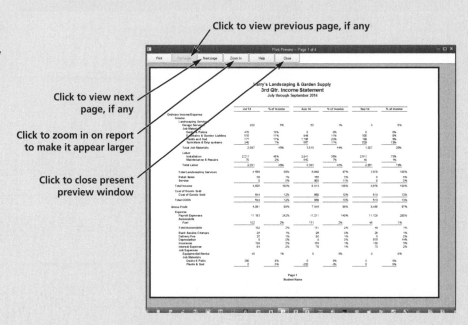

Click to view previous page, if any

Click to view next page, if any

Click to zoom in on report to make it appear larger

Click to close present preview window

3   Notice the Next page and Prev page buttons below the window heading. The Prev page button is grayed out, which indicates that there is no previous page. But the Next page button is not grayed out. Click **Next page** to preview Page 2 of the report.

4   After previewing the statement, click the **Close** button on the button bar, and then click **Cancel** in the Print Reports window. The report reappears.

Scott has seen that the report is not much more than one page; he might make it fit onto one page by reducing the size of the type font.

To reduce the font size of the type in a report:

1   Click **Customize Report** on the report button bar, and then click the **Fonts & Numbers** tab. See Figure 3.14.

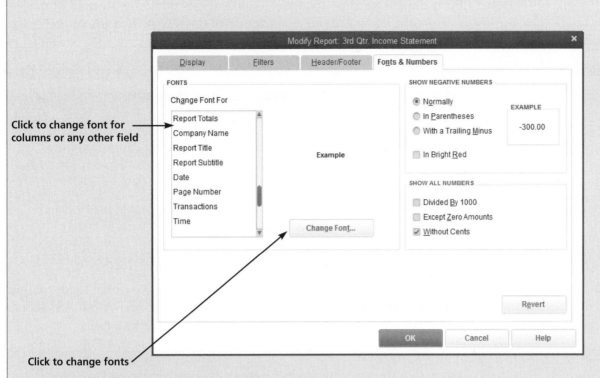

Figure 3.14

The Modify
Report Window

Click to change font for
columns or any other field

Click to change fonts

2   Click the **Change Font** button located in the bottom center of the window. The Column Labels window appears.

3   Choose **Arial** as the font, **Narrow Bold** as the font style, and **8** as the size as shown in Figure 3.15.

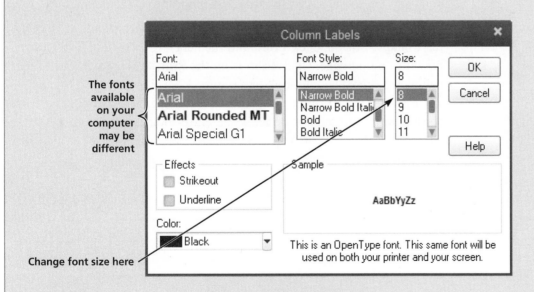

Figure 3.15

The Column Labels Window

The fonts
available
on your
computer
may be
different

Change font size here

4   Click **OK** to accept this new size. A Changing Font window will appear asking if you want to make the change to all related fonts. Click **Yes**. Then click **OK** again. The revised report appears—now in a different font.

Scott hopes that this change will make the example report now fit on one page. To see if it worked, he again previews the report. If it fits on one page, he'll print it.

To preview the modified income statement again:

1 Click **Print** on the report button bar.

2 Click **Preview.** The Print Preview window appears. Notice that the heading for this window may still include the words "Page 1 of 4." The change of font size has reduced the report size but not enough that it will fit on one page.

3 Click **Close**, and then click **Cancel** in the Print Reports window.

Suddenly, Scott realizes there might be another way to fit the report on one page. He decides to change the orientation of the page from portrait, the default vertical orientation, to landscape, which is a horizontal orientation.

To change a document from portrait to landscape orientation:

1 Click **Print** on the report button bar to view the Print Reports window.

2 Click the **Landscape** button in the Orientation box.

3 Click **Fit report to 1 page(s) wide** (see Figure 3.16).

4 Click **Preview** once again. The report still does not fit on one page. Thus your only option is to collapse the report and forgo the detail.

5 Click **Close** and then click **Cancel** in the Print Reports window, click the **Collapse** button, click **Print**, and then click the **Preview**. The report now fits on one page. Click **Print** from the Print Preview window. Your completed report should look like Figure 3.17.
Trouble? If your printer still prints this document on two pages, consult with your lab personnel. Different printers may generate different output.

6 Close all windows, and exit QuickBooks Accountant as you have done before.

Figure 3.16

The Print Reports Window

Your information may be different

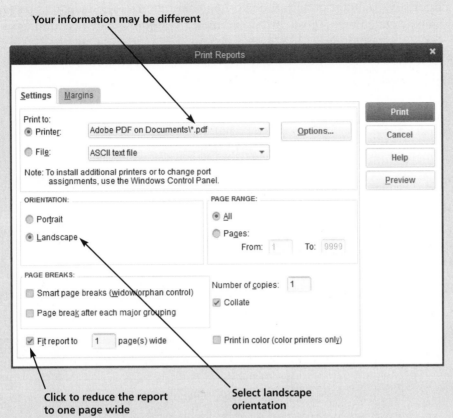

Click to reduce the report to one page wide

Select landscape orientation

Figure 3.17

Modified Income Statement on One Page

Larry's Landscaping & Garden Supply
3rd Qtr. Income Statement
July through September 2014

	Jul 14	% of Income	Aug 14	% of Income	Sep 14	% of Income	Jul - Sep 14	% of Income
Ordinary Income/Expense								
Income								
Landscaping Services	4,598	99%	6,948	87%	3,978	100%	15,524	93%
Retail Sales	28	1%	165	2%	0	0%	193	1%
Service	0	0%	900	11%	0	0%	900	5%
Total Income	4,626	100%	8,013	100%	3,978	100%	16,617	100%
Cost of Goods Sold								
Cost of Goods Sold	544	12%	968	12%	513	13%	2,025	12%
Total COGS	544	12%	968	12%	513	13%	2,025	12%
Gross Profit	4,081	88%	7,046	88%	3,465	87%	14,592	88%
Expense								
Payroll Expenses	11,183	242%	11,211	140%	11,128	280%	33,522	202%
Automobile	102	2%	131	2%	49	1%	281	2%
Bank Service Charges	26	1%	26	0%	26	1%	77	0%
Delivery Fee	25	1%	85	1%	0	0%	110	1%
Depreciation	0	0%	0	0%	575	14%	575	3%
Insurance	100	2%	100	1%	100	3%	300	2%
Interest Expense	84	2%	78	1%	73	2%	235	1%
Job Expenses	439	9%	-220	-3%	0	0%	219	1%
Mileage Reimbursement	0	0%	0	0%	0	0%	0	0%
Miscellaneous	0	0%	847	11%	0	0%	847	5%
Office Supplies	270	6%	0	0%	0	0%	270	2%
Repairs	0	0%	0	0%	75	2%	75	0%
Utilities	238	5%	261	3%	232	6%	731	4%
Total Expense	12,467	270%	12,519	156%	12,256	308%	37,242	224%
Net Ordinary Income	-8,386	-181%	-5,473	-68%	-8,791	-221%	-22,650	-136%
Net Income	-8,386	-181%	-5,473	-68%	-8,791	-221%	-22,650	-136%

Now that you have completed Chapters 2 and 3, you see how easily Quick-Books Accountant creates the two financial reports—the balance sheet and the income statement—most commonly used to communicate accounting information to external users. In Chapter 4, you will continue your brief overview of QuickBooks Accountant by creating a statement of cash flows.

Chapter 3 Questions

1 List at least three of the preset formats that QuickBooks Accountant provides for an income statement.

2 Identify the different periods of time that QuickBooks Accountant provides for an income statement.

3 Describe the steps necessary to create an income statement for a period other than one ending on the computer's current system date.

4 Describe the steps necessary to generate an income statement in QuickBooks Accountant.

5 Describe the steps necessary to create a standard income statement.

6 Describe the steps necessary to modify an income statement so that it includes comparative information.

7 How does QuickZoom help you further investigate an income statement?

8 How could a manager use QuickZoom to access underlying information as reported in an income statement?

9 List five report modification features of QuickBooks Accountant that can be applied to an income statement.

10 How would you modify an income statement to include a column describing the percentage relationship between expenses and total revenues?

Chapter 3 Matching

Select the letter of the item below that best matches the definitions that follow. Use the text or QuickBooks Accountant Help to complete this assignment.

a. Date formats

b. Profit & Loss Standard report

c. % of Income

d. QuickZoom

e. Without Cents

f. Divided by 1000

g. Previous Period $ Change

h. Previous Period % Change

i. To date

_____ The end of the reporting period.

_____ When selected in the Modify Report window, this check box requires QuickBooks Accountant to report amounts in thousands.

_____ Adds a subcolumn to a Profit & Loss report that calculates the relative percentage change in each item from a previous period.

_____ The beginning of the reporting period.

_____ A financial statement reporting the revenues and expenses of a business for a specific accounting period.

_____ Adds a subcolumn to a Profit & Loss report that calculates the amount of change in each item from a previous period.

_____ A preference option that specifies whether years in date fields are shown as two digits or four digits.

_____ A feature in QuickBooks Accountant that allows you to view the transaction details underlying amounts in a report.

_____ When selected in the Modify Report window, this check box requires QuickBooks Accountant to round amounts to the nearest whole dollar.

j. From date

_____ When selected in the Modify Report window, this check box requires Quick-Books Accountant to add a column representing the percentage of each item compared to total revenues.

Chapter 3 Assignments

1   *Preparing an Income Statement for Larry's Landscape & Garden Supply*

Scott has asked you to help him prepare a new income statement. Include your name in the Extra Footer Line of all reports printed. Use the file from your chapter work.

a. First, he asks you to prepare and print an income statement that includes operating information for September 2014. He wants the income statement to include amounts (without cents) and columns reflecting the dollar change and percentage change between periods. (***Hint:*** Set the dates to reflect September only, and be sure the Previous Period box, $ Change, and % Change boxes are also checked in the Modify Report window.) He asks you to change the title to "Comparative Income Statements." Finally, he wants you to format the page layout to the left; collapsed; without a reference to the date prepared, time prepared, or report basis; and printed in portrait orientation. Memorize the report as September Income Statement in your previously created group for use later.

b. Next, Scott asks you to prepare and print a standard income statement for Larry's Landscape & Garden Supply for the month of August 2014 in a collapsed format. Change other formatting options like you used in the chapter so that this report is different from what you used in Assignment 1a.

2   *Investigating the Larry's Landscape & Garden Supply Income Statement Using QuickZoom*

Create and memorize a standard income statement created for the month of February 2014. Investigate the $1,885.00 of Fountain & Garden Lighting income. Examine the invoice used to record this income.

a. Which customer was billed for these services?

b. Which invoice number was used to bill this customer?

c. Is this invoice paid? If so, when was it paid?

3   *Modifying an Income Statement*

Use the income statement you memorized in Assignment 1a above by changing the To/From dates to 3/1/14 and 3/31/14 respectively and then memorize and print this report.

Chapter 3 Cases

Chapter 3 Case Problem 1

SIERRA MARINA

Meagan Casey, sole proprietor and owner of Sierra Marina (see Chapter 2 Case Problem 1), requires some additional financial reports.

Requirements:

Prepare, memorize, and print the following reports using Meagan's Sierra Marina QuickBooks Accountant file. (Use the file you restored in Chapter 2 or restore this file from the Data Files CD. Be sure to include your name in the Extra Footer Line of each report where possible.)

1   A standard Profit & Loss Report for the month of July 2014.

2   A standard Profit & Loss Report for the month of July 2014 without cents, formatted with a left layout, with the title "Income Statement," and with a % of Income column.

3   A report of those transactions recorded in July 2014 that affected the rental income—Personal Watercraft account. (*Hint:* From your income statement already prepared, double-click the rental income—Personal Watercraft account.)

4   Modify the income statement that you created in Step 2 to be a comparative income statement (like you did in the chapter) for July and August 2014 with the title "Comparative Income Statement."

Chapter 3 Case Problem 2
JENNINGS & ASSOCIATES

As you learned in Chapter 2, Kelly Jennings prepared a balance sheet to submit to her banker with her application for a business loan. When she delivered the balance sheet to the banker, he told her that he also needed information about her operations. In other words, her banker needed an income statement.

corporation

Kelly asks you to help her prepare, memorize, and print three versions of the income statement, one of which she will include with her application. She gives you a QuickBooks Accountant file named Kelly Jennings.qbw. Include your name in the Extra Footer Line of all reports printed.

service

Requirements:

1   A collapsed standard Profit & Loss Report for the month of January 2015.

2   A collapsed standard Profit & Loss Report for the month of January 2015 without cents, formatted with a left alignment and with the title "Income Statement."

3   Modify the income statement you prepared for Step 2 by adding a % of Income column.

Chapter 3 Case Problem 3
JASON GALAS ATTORNEY AT LAW PC

Jason Galas (see Chapter 2 Case Problem 3) requires some additional financial reports.

Requirements:

Prepare and print the following reports using the Jason Galas Attorney at Law PC file. (Use the file you updated in Chapter 2 or restore this file from the Data

Files CD. Be sure to include your name in the Extra Footer Line of each report where possible.)

1 Prepare a new standard Profit & Loss Report for the month of January 2012 formatted without cents and without the date prepared, time prepared, or report basis fields. Memorize as Income Statement 1 in a group with your name.

2 Prepare a new standard Profit & Loss Report for the month of February 2012 without cents, formatted with a left alignment and with the title "Income Statement." Format without cents and without the date prepared, time prepared, or report basis fields. Memorize as Income Statement 2 in a group with your name.

3 Modify the income statement you prepared in 2 above by adding a previous period, $ change, and % column. Memorize as Income Statement 3 in a group with your name.

4 Prepare a Transaction Detail by Account report of those transactions recorded in February that affected the payroll expense account. Format without the date prepared, time prepared, or report basis fields. Memorize as Payroll Detail February 2012 in a group with your name.

Preparing a Statement of Cash Flows Using QuickBooks Accountant

4

Student Learning Outcomes

Upon completion of this chapter, the student will be able to:

- Create and customize a statement of cash flows for a specified period
- Investigate the detail underlying statement of cash flow items
- Format and print a statement of cash flows

Case: Larry's Landscaping & Garden Supply

One of the main financial statements used by businesses is the statement of cash flows. Your previous experience with this statement has not always been good, so the thought of a computer program preparing this one for you is quite enticing. You recall that this statement reports cash flow from operating, investing, and financing activities for a specific period.

Once again, as a part of your training with QuickBooks Accountant, Scott asks you to work with him while he prepares a statement of cash flows for the period September 1, 2014, through November 30, 2014.

Creating a Statement of Cash Flows

Unlike the balance sheet and the income statement, the statement of cash flows in QuickBooks Accountant is presented in only one format, although it can be modified after it is created. (Another report for cash flows, not addressed in this text, is called Forecast; it projects future cash flows based on the current period's cash flow.) Scott decides to create the statement of cash flows and modify it later.

Video Demonstration

DEMO 4A - Creating a statement of cash flows

To create a statement of cash flows:

1 Open the Larry's Landscaping & Garden Supply file you used in Chapter 3.

2 From the Report Center, click **Company & Financial**, and then double-click **Statement of Cash Flows**. *Remember*, this is not clicking the Reports menu item; it's clicking **Company & Financial** from the Report Center.

3 Change the From date to **9/1/14** and the To date to **11/30/14**, and then click **Refresh**.

4 Select **Customize Report** and then select the **Header/Footer tab**, and uncheck the **Date Prepared** and **Time Prepared** check boxes, then click **OK**.

5 Scroll down this report and notice the three sections: operating activities, investing activities, and financing activities (see Figure 4.1). Observe that the net cash increase for the period is reported at the bottom of the statement. It is then added to the cash at the beginning of the period to yield cash at the end of the period.

Figure 4.1

Statement of Cash Flows

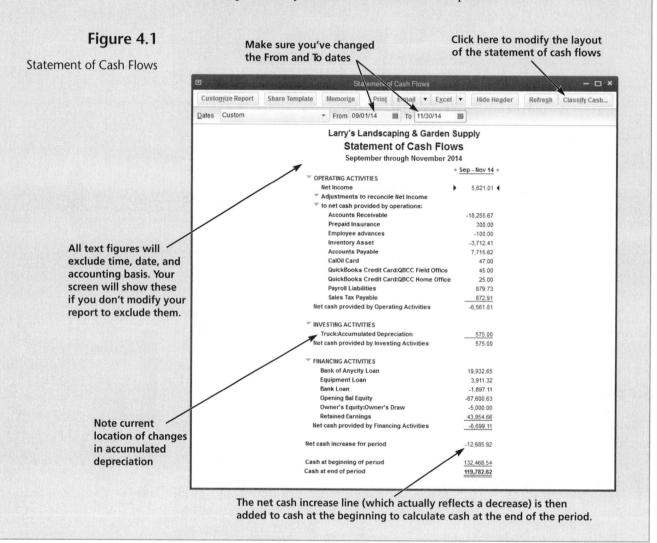

In your examination of the Statement of Cash Flows, you notice in the operating activities section that several adjustments are made to reconcile net income to net cash provided by operations. Scott points out that one of the more common adjustments should be depreciation expense, since it reduces income but does not use cash. However, depreciation is not shown in this reconciliation. Instead, Scott finds that changes in accumulated depreciation (which, of course, usually result from depreciation expense) are shown in the investing activities section of the statement. He knows that investing activities normally include purchases or sales of long-term assets such as land, buildings, or equipment, but Larry's did not have these types of activities during the current period.

Scott says: "We need to modify this statement's layout to properly reflect changes in accumulated depreciation as adjustments to net income in the operating activities section, not as line items in the investing activities section." To do this, he uses the Classify Cash button on the Statement of Cash Flows window.

To modify the layout of the statement of cash flows:

1 Click **Classify Cash** to open the Preferences window with the Reports & Graphs icon selected and the Company Preferences tab selected, as shown in Figure 4.2.

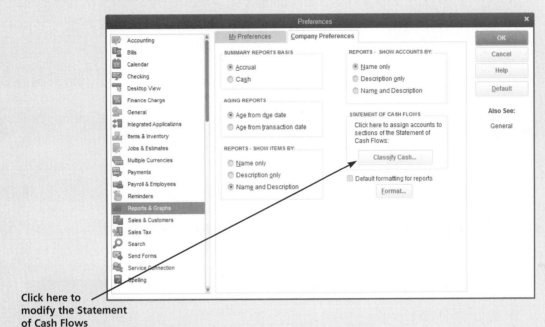

Figure 4.2

Company Preferences

Click here to modify the Statement of Cash Flows

2 Click **Classify Cash** in the Preferences window to view the Classify Cash window.

3 Click in the Operating column next to **Truck: Accumulated Depreciation** to move the change in depreciation from an investing activity to an operating activity as shown in Figure 4.3. Now click **OK** in the Classify Cash window.
Trouble? If you accidentally click in the wrong column, simply click the correct column for the item you accidentally reclassified.

4 Click **OK** in the Preferences window to close it. Note how the report has been adjusted to reflect changes in depreciation (depreciation expense) as an adjustment to operating activities and not an investing activity (see Figure 4.4).

Figure 4.3

Classify Cash
Window for
Modifying the
Statement of
Cash Flows Layout

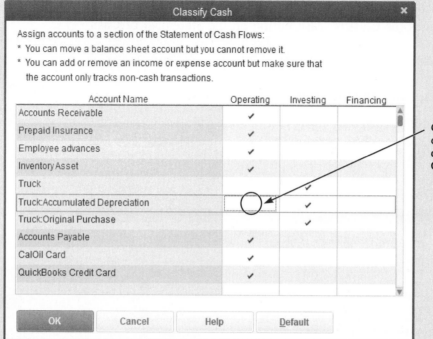

Click here to reclassify
changes in accumulated
depreciation to
Operating Activities

Figure 4.4

Statement of Cash Flows after
Changes in Types of Accounts

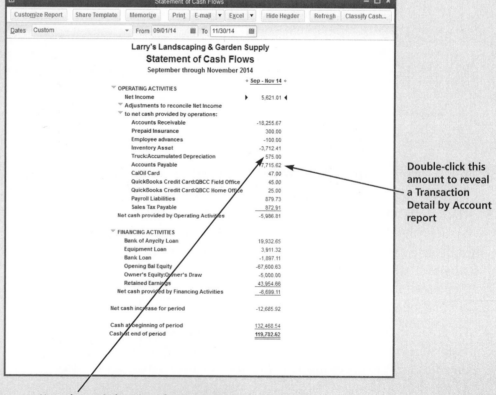

Double-click this
amount to reveal
a Transaction
Detail by Account
report

Note change in location of Depreciation

"How about modifying the Statement of Cash Flows to reflect comparative amounts like prior years? Isn't there a previous year comparative report available like we saw for the income statement?" you ask.

"Well, no." Scott explains. "Not only is there no present comparative report in QuickBooks Accountant, but there is no way to modify the report to show percentage changes or year-to-date amounts like we can do for the income statement. Maybe in the next version."

Using QuickZoom with the Statement of Cash Flows

You then ask about the QuickZoom feature you found so helpful in examining information on the income statement. Scott responds with a big smile. "Let's check it out!"

To use QuickZoom with the statement of cash flows:

1 Double-click the **7,715.62** amount in Figure 4.4 on the report reflecting changes in Accounts Payable and then click **OK** in the Collapsing and Expanding Transactions warning window. You have now opened a Transaction Detail by Account window as shown in Figure 4.5.

Double-click here to view the detail of this transaction

Figure 4.5

Transaction Detail for Accounts Payable in the Statement of Cash Flows

2 Double-click the **Bayshore Water** bill dated 09/04/14 as shown in Figure 4.5.

3 Close both the bill and the Transaction Detail by Account window. Do not memorize the Transaction Detail by Account window.

4 Do not close the revised Statement of Cash Flows.

You have now seen that the QuickZoom feature works for the balance sheet, income statement, and statement of cash flows. However, the QuickZoom feature in the statement of cash flows does not necessarily provide much help. In the case just described, the accounts payable amount in the statement of cash flows reflects the changes in accounts payable—here an increase, which needs to be added to net income in order to reconcile with cash provided by operating activities. It is therefore the change (in this case, an increase) that is being analyzed, not the underlying transactions.

Formatting and Printing the Statement of Cash Flows

Scott would like to print this statement of cash flows in a format without cents.

To modify and print the statement of cash flows:

1   Click **Customize Report** on the report button bar, and then click the **Fonts & Numbers** tab.

2   Click in the **Without Cents** check box, and then click **OK** to close the window.

3   Click **Print** on the report button bar to reveal the Print Reports window.

4   Click **Print** in the Print Reports window to print the report.

5   Close all remaining windows. Memorize the revised Statement of Cash Flows report in your report group.

You've now seen how easily all three of the key financial statements—the balance sheet, income statement, and statement of cash flows—can be created, modified, and printed from within QuickBooks Accountant. In Chapter 5, you will complete your overview of QuickBooks Accountant by creating supporting reports for accounts receivable, inventory, and accounts payable.

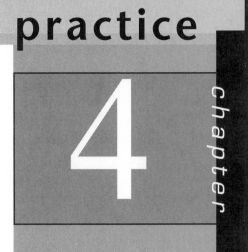
Chapter 4 Questions

1 List the reports available for reporting cash flows.

2 Describe the steps necessary to create a statement of cash flows.

3 What additional steps are necessary to create a statement of cash flows for a period other than the one ending on the computer's current system date?

4 Identify three different periods of time that QuickBooks Accountant provides for a statement of cash flows.

5 List the three sections of the statement of cash flows.

6 Describe the statement of cash flow operating section created by QuickBooks Accountant.

7 Describe the one adjustment necessary to reconcile net income to cash provided by operations that was not initially a part of the statement of cash flows until you made some changes in the reports layout.

8 Describe the steps necessary to make changes in the statement of cash flows report layout in order to properly reflect the adjustments needed to reconcile net income with cash provided by operations.

9 Describe how the QuickZoom feature of QuickBooks Accountant does or does not provide the same help in the statement of cash flows as it does in the income statement.

10 Describe the steps necessary to format and print a statement of cash flows whose header differs from that of the software default of this statement.

Chapter 4 Matching

Select the letter of the item below that best matches the definitions that follow.
Use the text or QuickBooks Accountant Help to complete this assignment.

a. Statement of cash flows   _____ The beginning of the reporting period.

b. Classify Cash   _____ When selected in the Modify Report window, this check box requires QuickBooks Accountant to round amounts to the nearest whole dollar.

c. Depreciation expense   _____ A feature in QuickBooks Accountant that allows you to view the transaction details underlying amounts in a report.

d. QuickZoom   _____ A financial report describing the change in cash during an accounting period.

e. Included in the operating activities section of the statement of cash flows   _____ The end of the reporting period.

f. Included in the investing activities section of the statement of cash flows   _____ Increases in long-term debt.

g. Included in the financing activities section of the statement of cash flows   _____ Button selected to correct QuickBooks Accountant's method of accounting for changes in accumulated depreciation.

h. From date   _____ Increases in equipment.

i. To date

j. Without Cents

_____ Net income.

_____ An adjustment to net income in the operating activities section of the statement of cash flows.

Chapter 4 Assignment

1 *Preparing a Statement of Cash Flows for Larry's Landscaping & Garden Supply*

Scott has asked you to prepare and print a customized statement of cash flows for the month of September 2014. He wants the statement to include amounts (without cents) with a left page layout. (*Hint:* Be sure accumulated depreciation is classified correctly.) Include your name in the Extra Footer Line of all reports printed.

Chapter 4 Cases

Chapter 4 Case Problem 1

SIERRA MARINA

Meagan Casey owns Sierra Marina and is proud of her business's success. After entering past transactions as described in Chapter 2 Case Problem 1, Meagan needs your help in preparing some basic financial reports related to Sierra Marina's cash flow.

Requirements:

Prepare, memorize, and print the following reports using Meagan's Sierra Marina QuickBooks Accountant file. (Use the file you restored in the previous chapter or restore this file from the Data Files CD, and be sure to include your name in the Extra Footer Line of each report where possible. Also don't forget to reclassify changes in accumulated depreciation like you did in the chapter.)

1 A statement of cash flows for the month of July 2014 without cents and formatted with a left layout.

2 A report of those transactions recorded in July 2014 that affected the Accounts Receivable account. (*Hint:* From the statement of cash flows just created, double-click the **Accounts Receivable** account.)

Chapter 4 Case Problem 2

JENNINGS & ASSOCIATES

Continuing your work from Chapter 3, Kelly has asked you to prepare two versions of the statement of cash flows, one of which she will include with her application. Open the Kelly Jennings.qbw file. Include your name in the Extra Footer Line of all reports printed.

Requirements:

1 Prepare a statement of cash flows for the period 1/1/15 to 1/31/15. (*Hint:* Be sure accumulated depreciation accounts are properly classified.)

2 Prepare a statement of cash flows for the same period, 1/1/15 to 1/31/15, but without cents and with a right page layout.

Chapter 4 Case Problem 3

JASON GALAS ATTORNEY AT LAW PC

Jason Galas (see Chapter 2 Case Problem 3) requires some additional financial reports.

sole proprietorship

Requirements:

Prepare and print the following reports using the Jason Galas Attorney at Law PC file. (Use the file you updated in Chapter 3 or restore this file from the Data Files CD. Be sure to include your name in the Extra Footer Line of each report where possible.)

service

1 Prepare a new statement of cash flows for the period 1/1/12 to 1/31/12 without the date prepared or time prepared fields. Memorize as SCF 1 in a group with your name.

2 Prepare a new statement of cash flows for the period 2/1/12 to 2/29/12 with a right page layout formatted without cents and without the date prepared, time prepared, or report basis fields. Memorize as SCF 2 in a group with your name.

5

Creating Supporting Reports to Help Make Business Decisions

Case: Larry's Landscaping & Garden Supply

You arrive at work, and two phones are ringing. As Scott hangs up from one call and is about to answer another, he quickly explains what's happening: He's thinking about expanding the business and needs to borrow from the bank, and they are requesting up-to-the-minute information. You quickly answer a phone and write down the banker's request for some information on inventory. As you hang up from the call, Scott asks you to come into his office. You compare notes—he has requests for information on accounts receivable and accounts payable. You show him your note requesting inventory numbers.

Scott has shown you that QuickBooks Accountant can easily generate transaction reports, but you can see that the banker's requests require more detailed information. You remember from your accounting course that accountants frequently use what are called supporting schedules—reports that provide the underlying details of an account. You ask Scott if QuickBooks Accountant can help. He smiles and says, "You bet. QuickBooks Accountant calls these schedules 'reports,' but they are the same thing. Let's get to work."

Creating and Printing an Accounts Receivable Aging Report

Video Demonstration

DEMO 5A - Creating other useful reports

You know from your accounting course that accounts receivable are amounts due from customers for goods or services they have received but for which they have not yet paid. QuickBooks Accountant provides several preset accounts receivable reports that anticipate the information managers most often need.

The banker wants information on a particular customer's past due account balance, and she wants to know the total amount due from customers as of today.

Scott tells you that the best way to get information on past due accounts is to create a schedule that QuickBooks Accountant calls an "Accounts Receivable

Aging report," but what you learned in your accounting course is usually called an "accounts receivable aging schedule." You remember that an aging schedule is a listing of how long each receivable has been uncollected.

To create an Accounts Receivable Aging report:

1 Open the Larry's Landscaping & Garden Supply QuickBooks Accountant file you used in Chapter 4.

2 From the Report Center, click **Customers & Receivables**, and then double-click **A/R Aging Summary** under the title A/R Aging.

3 Change the report date to **11/30/14**, and then click the **Collapse** button to see the company A/R Aging Summary, as shown in Figure 5.1.

The number of days past the due date

Figure 5.1

A/R Aging Summary

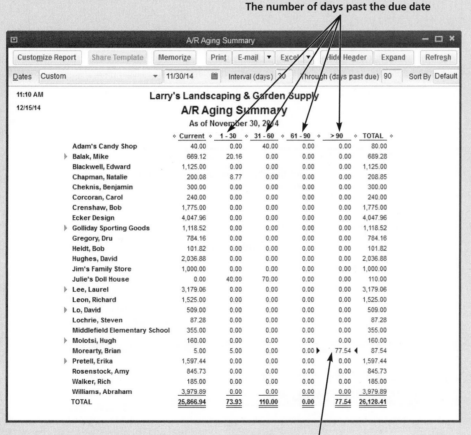

Double-click here for more information on this account

You can see that this report gives Scott an up-to-date listing of customers and their balances. It tells him how long each receivable has been uncollected so he can take appropriate action.

You ask Scott the name of the customer about whom the banker requested information. He says the customer's name is Brian Morearty and that the banker wants to know the status of his account and his payment history. He says that, as you have done with other reports, you can use QuickZoom to gather this information.

To investigate a particular receivable on an Accounts Receivable Aging report:

1   Double-click the **77.54** balance owed by Brian Morearty.

2   An A/R Aging QuickZoom report appears (see Figure 5.2). This report indicates that invoice 23, dated 5/5/14, was due 5/5/14 and is presently 209 days late.

Figure 5.2

A/R Aging QuickZoom Report

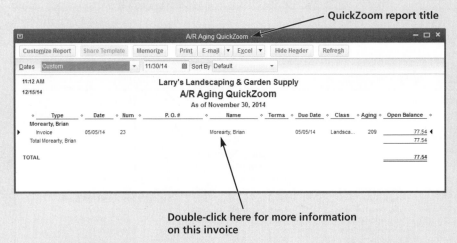

QuickZoom report title

Double-click here for more information on this invoice

3   Double-click this invoice to investigate further. Invoice 23 appears (see Figure 5.3). Invoice 23 describes the items sold, their description, quantity, and sales price.

Figure 5.3

Invoice

Clicking the Transaction tab will reveal more history on this invoice

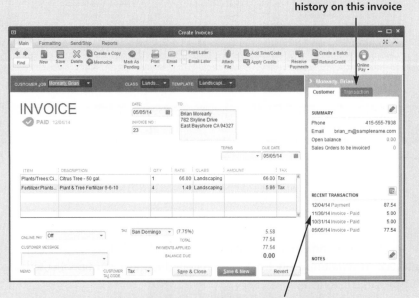

Note that after 11/30/14 this invoice was paid.

4 Click the **Transaction** tab as shown in Figure 5.3 and then click the blue text Payment next to the 12/04/14 date. The customer payment of this invoice appears (see Figure 5.4). Observe that a $87.54 check was received on 12/4/14. Of this payment, $77.54 was applied to pay off invoice 23. The balance of the $87.54—$10.00—was applied to other transactions.

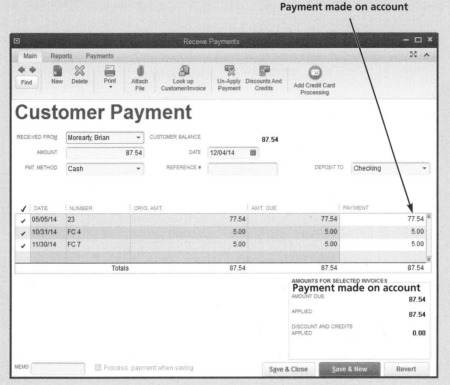

Figure 5.4

Customer Payment Window

5 Close all open windows without memorizing any reports.

Scott has copied down the information the banker requested—As of 11/30/14, Invoice 23 to Brian Morearty was 209 days old but was paid on 12/4/14. He is now ready to fulfill the banker's other request.

Creating and Printing a Customer Balance Summary

Scott says that the banker's request for the total amount due from customers as of today is easy to fulfill because QuickBooks Accountant has a built-in feature that prepares a customer balance summary. He can provide the banker this information with only a few clicks of the mouse.

To create a Customer Balance Summary:

1   From the Report Center, click **Customers & Receivables** and then double-click **Customer Balance Summary** located under the Customer Balance title. Change the To date to 11/30/14 and click the **Collapse** button. (see Figure 5.5).

Figure 5.5

Customer Balance Summary

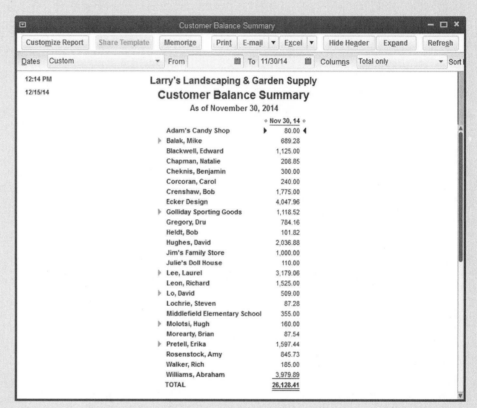

2   Notice that this is exactly the information the banker has requested—a list of the total amounts each customer owes Larry's Landscaping & Garden Supply as of 11/30/14. When you have finished viewing this report, close this window.

Scott prints this report for the banker and asks you to fax it. He's ready to handle the second request.

Creating and Printing an Inventory Valuation Summary Report

Scott asks you about the request you took over the phone. You show him your notes; you spoke to Kim Hui, one of the company's potential investors. He stopped by the other day and noticed a lot of inventory in the store and wondered what kind of inventory we maintained.

He suggests that you use QuickBooks Accountant to show, via an Inventory Valuation Summary report, just exactly what inventory you have.

To create an Inventory Valuation Summary:

1 From the Report Center, click **Inventory**, and then double-click **Inventory Valuation Summary** located under the Inventory Valuation title. Set the report date to **12/15/14**. The Inventory Valuation Summary appears (see Figure 5.6). Resize the columns as necessary to view this report.

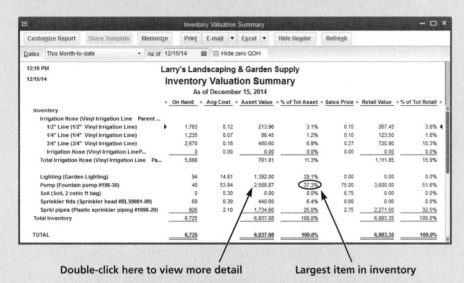

Figure 5.6

Inventory Valuation Summary

Double-click here to view more detail   Largest item in inventory

2 Scroll around this report to familiarize yourself with its contents. It describes the inventory on hand as of 12/15/14.

Scott decides to investigate inventory activity from October through today.

To view the underlying documentation of the Inventory Valuation Summary:

1 Double-click item **Pump**, representing 37.3% of the cost of inventory on hand. An Inventory Valuation Detail appears. By default, this report shows activity for the month to date as of 12/15/14. But Scott wants to know the *total* inventory on hand and to see activity for the quarter. To find this information, you need to change the From date to 10/1/14.

2 Type **10/1/14** in the From box, and then click **Refresh**. A new Inventory Valuation Detail report appears. Scroll down this report and view transactions for the quarter involving the Pump item (see Figure 5.7).

Note that this report shows a beginning inventory of 47, purchases of 11, and sales of 10 for an ending inventory quantity of 48.

Figure 5.7

Inventory Valuation Detail

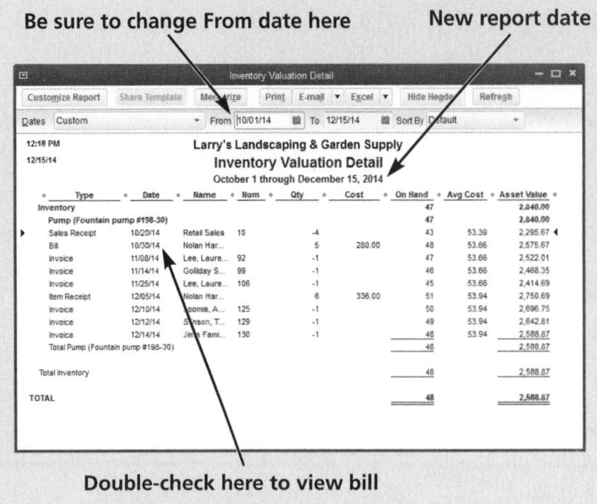

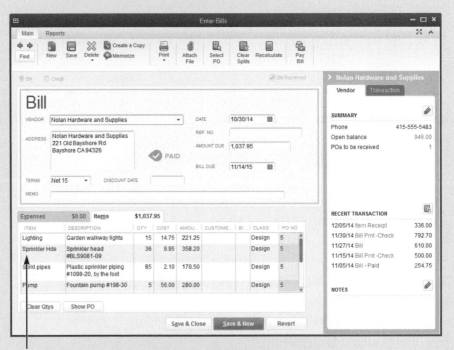

Be sure to change From date here   New report date

Double-check here to view bill

You ask Scott if QuickZoom lets you view the actual invoices. "Sure does," he says. "Let's look at one."

To view an actual bill:

1 Double-click anywhere in the row containing information on the bill from Nolan Hardware and Supplies. The bill appears as shown in Figure 5.8 on the following page. Adjust your window size and scroll down the invoice to locate the pump purchase activity.

Figure 5.8

Bill for Inventory Purchase

This bill was for a variety of items one of which was the 5 pumps reflected in the previous inventory report.

2 After you examine this bill, close all open windows. Do not memorize any reports.

Scott retrieves the Inventory Valuation Summary and prints it for Kim. He notes that this item was purchased for Nolan Hardware and Supplies, which has a fairly large past due account. Scott makes a note to contact this customer and find out what is going on, and he asks you to mail this report to Kim when you have a chance. He's now ready to fulfill the last request.

Creating, Printing, and Analyzing an Accounts Payable Aging Report

The last request to which you and Scott need to respond is from Juan Gomez, who handles all inventory purchase orders, pays bills, and monitors accounts payable. He wants two reports so he can plan next month's cash flow.

You quickly ask if QuickBooks Accountant handles accounts payable aging the same way it handles accounts receivable aging. Scott smiles. "You catch on fast," he says. "Let's start with an Accounts Payable Aging report. It provides the detail Juan needs. Then we'll print him a Vendor Balance Summary."

To create an Accounts Payable Aging report:

1   From the Report Center, click **Vendors & Payables**, and then double-click **A/P Aging Summary** under the title A/P Aging. Change the report date to **11/30/14** and then click **Refresh**. The A/P Aging Summary report appears (see Figure 5.9).

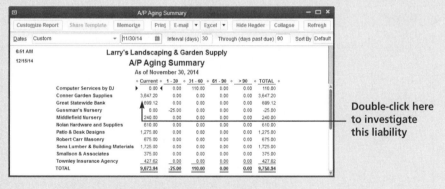

Figure 5.9

Accounts Payable Aging Summary

2   Scroll through the A/P Aging Summary. If necessary, change the column widths so the entire report displays on your screen.

After Scott prints this report for Juan, you look it over. You notice a large balance due to Conner Garden Supplies. You suggest using QuickZoom to investigate it further. Scott and you both decide to investigate this liability to whom Larry's Landscape & Garden Supply owes $3,647.20.

To analyze a specific liability:

1   Double-click the balance of **3,647.20**. An A/P Aging report appears (see Figure 5.10).

Figure 5.10

A/P Aging QuickZoom Report

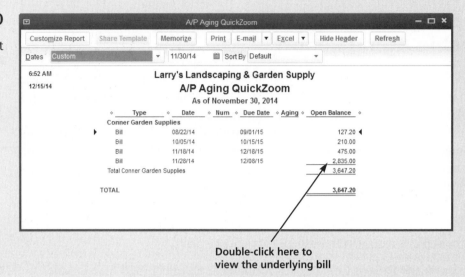

Double-click here to view the underlying bill

2   Double-click the **2,835.00** amount. The details of this bill appear (see Figure 5.11). Notice that this bill documents sprinkler piping items purchased.

Figure 5.11

Specific Bill

3   When you have finished viewing this bill, close all open windows. Do not memorize any reports.

Creating and Printing a Vendor Balance Summary

The final supporting report for Juan is a Vendor Balance Summary. This report is also a preset report available from the QuickBooks Accountant Reports menu. It will summarize for Juan all of the unpaid balances due to vendors and will be valuable information for his cash planning.

To create and print a Vendor Balance Summary:

1 From the Report Center, click **Vendors & Payables**, and then double-click **Vendor Balance Summary**. In the Dates section of the Report tool bar select **All**. The Vendor Balance Summary appears (see Figure 5.12). Notice that the vendors are listed alphabetically.

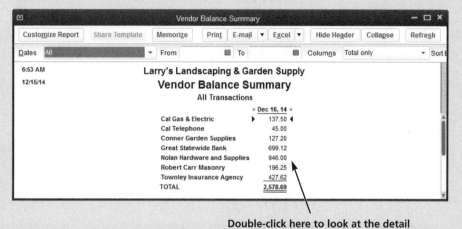

Figure 5.12

Vendor Balance Summary

Double-click here to look at the detail supporting the liability

2 To investigate, Scott suggests you look further into the Nolan Hardware balance. Double-click the **946.00** balance to reveal the Vendor Balance Detail report shown in Figure 5.13.

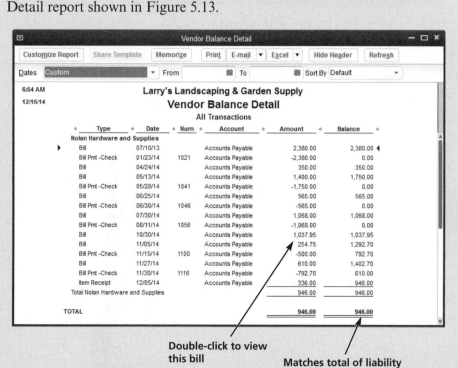

Figure 5.13

Vendor Balance Detail Report

Double-click to view this bill

Matches total of liability

3   Double-click the **1,037.95** amount to reveal the paid bill as shown in Figure 5.14.

Figure 5.14

Payment of Bill

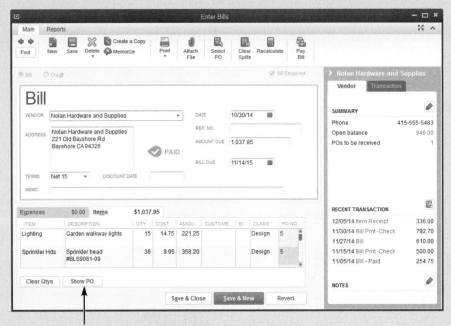

**Click here to view purchase order which
ordered these items, creating this liability**

4   Click the **Show PO** button to view the purchase order generated to order these items (see Figure 5.15).

Figure 5.15

Purchase Order Used to
Order Items

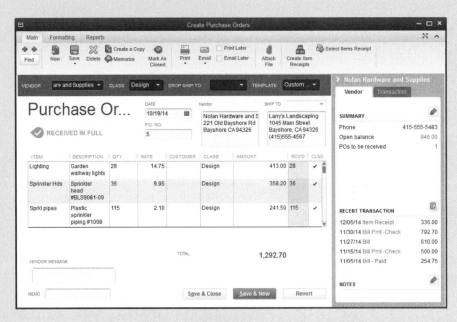

5   Close the purchase order, and then click the **Reports** tab and then the **Transaction History** button and scroll to the bottom of the window to reveal the bill's history; see Figure 5.16.

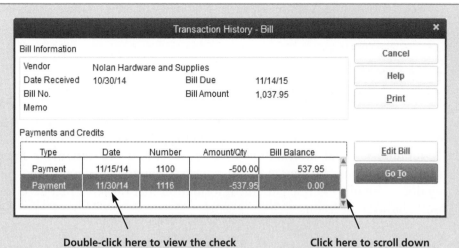

Figure 5.16

Transaction History

Double-click here to view the check   **Click here to scroll down**

6 Scroll down the Payments and Credits section and then double-click the payment on 11/30/14 to view the related check used to pay this bill. See Figure 5.17, Bill Payment (Check No. 1116).

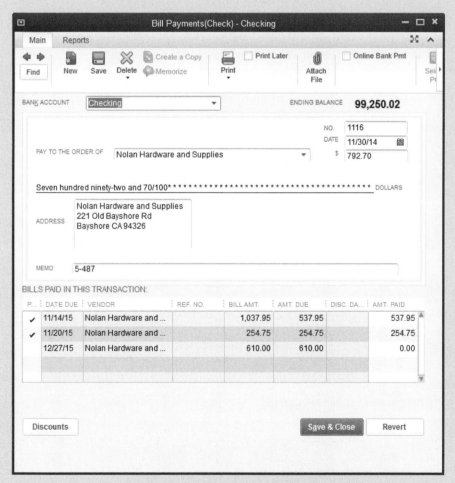

Figure 5.17

Bill Payment

7 When you finish viewing this report, close all windows and do not memorize any reports.

Scott prints the Vendor Balance Summary for Juan, and looks at you. "Yes, I'll deliver this one too," you volunteer good naturedly.

End Note

As you gather the reports and set out to deliver them, you are struck by how easily and quickly Scott has been able to respond to the managers' requests. Within a short time, QuickBooks Accountant has generated accurate, up-to-the-minute financial information to help Scott and his staff make important business decisions. The many preset reports—summaries, details, and supporting documentation—anticipate the information that owners often need to make sound business decisions.

Chapter 5 Questions

1 Which menu in QuickBooks Accountant provides you access to supporting reports?

2 What information does an Accounts Receivable Aging report provide?

3 What types of transactions might appear in a QuickZoom report created from an Accounts Receivable Aging report? Give two examples.

4 How might the payment history of an account receivable help you analyze the Accounts Receivable Aging report?

5 What information does an Inventory Valuation Summary provide?

6 What types of transactions might appear in a QuickZoom report created from an Inventory Summary? Give two examples.

7 What information does an Accounts Payable Aging report provide?

8 What types of transactions might appear in a QuickZoom report created from an Accounts Payable Aging report?

9 What options can you choose from the Print Reports dialog box to help you print a report?

10 How can you create a supporting report for a date other than the system date? Describe a situation for which you would want to do this.

Chapter 5 Matching

Select the letter of the item below that best matches the definitions that follow. Use the text or QuickBooks Accountant Help to complete this assignment.

a. Accounts Receivable Aging report   _____ A report that describes how much the company owes to a vendor and is organized by date due.

b. Vendor Balance Detail report   _____ A feature in QuickBooks Accountant that allows you to view the transaction details that underlie amounts in a report.

c. Inventory Valuation Detail report   _____ A document used to bill a customer for goods or services.

d. Customer Balance Summary report   _____ A report that describes how much is owed to a company by customers and is organized by date due.

e. Inventory Valuation Summary report   _____ A document used to remit amounts to vendors for bills received.

f. Accounts Payable Aging report   _____ A report that describes inventory on hand as of a particular date.

g. Invoice   _____ A report that describes inventory transactions for a particular inventory item over a specified period of time.

h. Vendor Balance Summary report   _____ A report that describes bills received/payments made from/to a particular vendor over a specified period of time.

i. Bill payment check   _____ A report that describes how much each customer owes a company as of a particular date.

j. QuickZoom   _____ A report that describes how much each vendor is owed as of a particular date.

Chapter 5 Assignments

sole proprietorship

1 *Creating Supporting Reports for Larry's Landscaping & Garden Supply*

Remember to include your name in the Extra Footer Line of all reports printed. Scott wants you to help him provide supporting reports. Create the reports Scott has requested, and write down the answers to the following questions:

a. Create and print a Customer Balance Summary as of 9/30/14. What is the amount of the largest customer receivable and what is the customer's name? What invoice supports that receivable? What was purchased on that invoice? Has the customer made any payments on that invoice?

b. Create and print a collapsed A/R Aging Summary report as of 10/31/14. Describe all past due invoices greater than 90 days old. What was the date of each invoice? What was purchased on each invoice?

c. Create and print an A/P Aging Summary report as of 4/30/14. What is the largest vendor liability? What bill makes up this liability? What is the nature of this bill? When was it due?

d. Create and print an Inventory Valuation Summary as of 9/30/14. What is the item with the largest on-hand quantity? What was its cost and retail value?

2 *Creating More Supporting Reports for Larry's Landscaping & Garden Supply*

Scott wants you to help him provide more supporting reports. Create the reports he has requested, and write down the answers to the following questions:

a. Create and print a collapsed Customer Balance Summary as of 8/31/14 and examine the QuickZoom reports for David Lo. How much was this customer billed on 4/11/14? How much is owed on this invoice as of 8/31/14?

b. Create and print a collapsed A/R Aging Summary report as of 7/31/14 and examine the QuickZoom reports for Edward Blackwell. What invoices are represented by this receivable? For what was Blackwell invoiced? What are the terms of these invoices?

c. Create and print an A/P Aging Summary report as of 5/31/14 and examine the QuickZoom reports for Computer Services by DJ. What bill is represented by this payable? What was Larry's Landscape & Gardening Supply billed for? What are the terms of this invoice?

d. Create and print an Inventory Valuation Summary as of 8/31/14. How many pumps were on hand at that date? What was their average cost per unit?

Chapter 5 Cases

Chapter 5 Case Problem 1

SIERRA MARINA

Meagan Casey, the sole proprietor and owner of Sierra Marina, would now like you to help her prepare some basic financial reports related to the company's accounts receivable and payable.

Requirements:

Prepare, memorize, and print the following reports using Meagan's Sierra Marina QuickBooks Accountant file. (Use the file you restored in the previous chapter or restore this file from the Data Files CD. Be sure to include your name in the Extra Footer Line of each report where possible.)

1. A/R Aging Summary as of August 31, 2014.
2. A/P Aging Summary as of August 31, 2014.

Chapter 5 Case Problem 2

JENNINGS & ASSOCIATES

Kelly Jennings created financial reports and submitted them to her banker to secure a loan. Today Kelly received a phone call from her banker, who told her that the balance sheet she submitted requires further explanation. He'd like to see some documentation to support her company's balances of receivables, inventory, and payables.

Requirements:

Kelly asks you to prepare and print three supporting reports using her Quick-Books Accountant file, Kelly Jenning.qbw.

1. Prepare an Accounts Receivable Aging Summary report for January 31, 2015. Print this report. Write a brief paragraph in which you explain the status of the two largest balances—that is, how old they are, what was sold, and so on.

2. Prepare an Accounts Payable Aging Summary report for January 31, 2015. Print this report. Write a brief paragraph in which you explain, as before, the status of the two largest balances.

3. Prepare an Inventory Valuation Summary for January 31, 2015. Print this summary. Drill down from this report and then write a brief paragraph in which you describe the most recent purchase of film. Be sure to include the date, vendor, amount, and cost per unit.

Chapter 5 Case Problem 3

JASON GALAS ATTORNEY AT LAW PC

Jason Galas (see Chapter 2 Case Problem 3) requires some additional financial reports.

Requirements:

Prepare and print the following reports using the Jason Galas Attorney at Law PC file. (Use the file you updated in Chapter 4 or restore this file from the Data Files CD. Be sure to include your name in the Extra Footer Line of each report where possible.)

1   Prepare and print an Accounts Receivable Aging Summary report for January 31, 2012, with a right page layout formatted without cents and without the date prepared or time prepared fields. Memorize as AR Aging in a group with your name. Then write a brief paragraph in which you explain the status of the largest balance—that is, how old it is, what was sold, and so on.

2   Prepare and print an Accounts Payable Aging Summary report for January 31, 2012, with a left page layout formatted without cents and without the date prepared or time prepared fields. Memorize as AP Aging in a group with your name. Then write a brief paragraph in which you explain, as before, the status of the largest balance—that is, how old it is, what was purchased, and so on.

Creating a QuickBooks Accountant File to Record and Analyze Business Events

part

2

In this Part, you will:
- Set Up Your Business's Accounting System
- Enter Cash-Oriented Business Activities
- Enter Additional Business Activities
- Enter Adjusting Entries
- Perform Budgeting Activities
- Generate Reports of Business Activities

Part 2 is designed to teach you how to use QuickBooks Accountant in conjunction with the accounting methods and concepts learned in your introductory accounting course. This part is divided into six chapters, each with its own set of questions, assignments, and case problems. You'll follow the adventures of Donna and Karen at Wild Water Sports, who have hired you to help them set up their business in QuickBooks Accountant, capture various business transactions, make adjusting entries, set up and use budgets, and generate key business reports. You'll use QuickBooks Accountant EasyStep Interview to establish accounts, customers, vendors, items, and employees and then record business transactions using key source documents such as sales receipts, invoices, bills, deposit forms, and checks. You will learn how to create journal entries in QuickBooks Accountant to accrue revenues and expenses, adjust deferred assets and liabilities, and record depreciation of long-lived assets. Finally, you'll learn how QuickBooks Accountant's budgeting and reporting process can help Wild Water Sports plan and control their business activities.

Setting Up Your Business's Accounting System

Upon completion of this chapter, the student will be able to:

- Create a new company file using the EasyStep Interview
- Set up company preferences
- Set up company items
- Set up customers, vendors, and accounts
- Set up payroll and employees
- Create a backup file

Case: **Wild Water Sports, Inc.**

Donna Chandler and her best friend Karen Wilson have been water sports enthusiasts since they were 6 years old. They would spend a good portion of each summer vacation wakeboarding and skiing the lakes and reservoirs of Central Florida. After high school, both went their separate ways. Donna went off to a four-year college and then a career in real estate, while Karen attended a local community college and began a career in small business accounting.

They became reacquainted at their 10-year high school reunion, reminiscing about their fun-filled weekends and summers with boats and friends. They pondered how they could mix their careers and their fun and love of boating into a business. Both vowed to keep in touch. Later that year, Donna called with a plan. She had run into a business investor, Ernesto Martinez, who had opened a retail boat dealership in Orlando, Florida, but didn't have the time to mind the details. Donna figured she could handle the marketing and sales if Karen could handle the day-to-day business operations. Wild Water Sports was born.

The company has some existing cash, receivables, inventory, equipment, and liabilities. The plan is for Karen and Donna to make an investment by purchasing common stock in the existing company. As a result, each will have a one-third interest in the corporation with the remaining third belonging to Ernesto.

Karen knew she would need some help with the daily accounting records, and she chose QuickBooks Accountant to replace the manual accounting system currently in place. She contacted an employment agency to find a part-time accountant. You answered her call as a student who could use some spending money and had completed a basic accounting course, and you were hired the same day.

Your job will be to work with Karen to establish and maintain accounting records for Wild Water Sports using QuickBooks Accountant. The company will open its doors for business under new ownership in January but needs to set up accounts, items, customers, vendors, and employees before it gets started. The company rents its showroom and service bays from a former auto dealership. It plans to sell top-of-the-line ski-boats from Malibu, Tige, and MB Sports. It also plans to service boats by providing engine repair, engine service, and boat cleaning.

You agree to meet with Karen the next day to get started.

Creating a New Company File Using the EasyStep Interview

When you return to Karen's office, she's already purchased a new computer, the QuickBooks Accountant software, Microsoft's Office suite, and supplies. The software is loaded and ready to go. Karen explains that you have two choices to begin setting up the company. QuickBooks Accountant has a built-in EasyStep Interview that can guide you through the company setup process, or you can skip the interview and set up the company yourself. Given this is your first time setting up a company in QuickBooks Accountant, you opt for the interview, which is accessed using the Advance Setup feature. The EasyStep Interview process provides a step-by-step guided series of questions that you can answer to help you choose various QuickBooks Accountant features. The alternative process requires you to enter basic company information, establish a set of accounts, provide sales tax information, and determine a file name.

"Starting with the interview is probably a good idea," Karen says. "Besides, no matter which method you start with, you can always change the decisions you make during setup later."

Video Demonstration

DEMO 6A - Starting a new company

To create a new company file:

1   Start QuickBooks Accountant. Close any previously created company if one appears.

2   Click **New Company** from the File menu. The QuickBooks Setup window appears.

3   Click the **Detailed Start** button.

4   Type the information provided in Figure 6.1.

5   Click **Next**.

6   Scroll down the listing of industries, and select **Retail Shop or Online Commerce** as shown in Figure 6.2.

7   Click **Next**.

8   Select the **Corporation** option button and then click **Next**.

9 Select **January** in the My fiscal year starts in text box and then click **Next**.

10 Do not enter a password, and then click **Next** two times.

Figure 6.1

Starting the EasyStep Interview

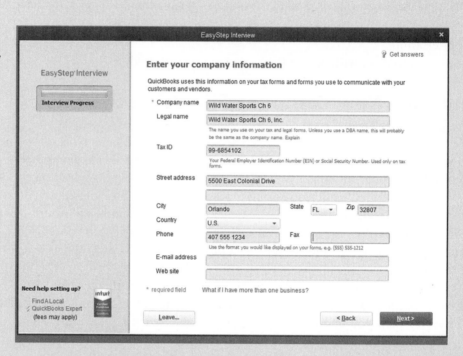

Figure 6.2

Selecting Your Industry

Select Retail Shop or Online Commerce

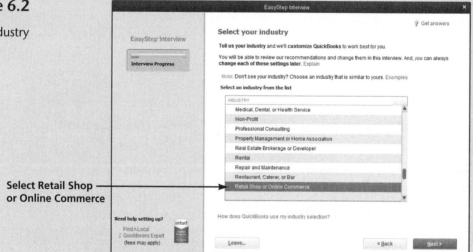

11 Click the **Drop-down Arrow** in the Save in text box to specify where you want your data file saved. Note that in this example the file was saved in a folder called QuickBooks Accountant, as shown in Figure 6.3. Click **Save**. This will take a minute or so.

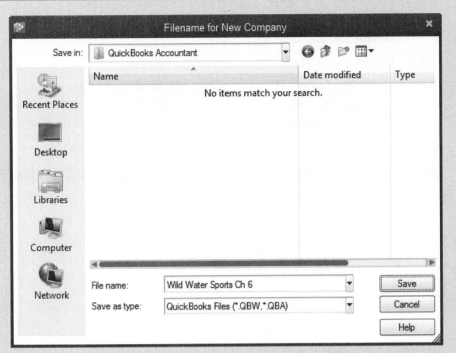

Figure 6.3

Saving Your Data File

12 When EasyStep Interview returns, click **Next**, and then select **Both services and products** since Wild Water Sports will be selling and servicing boats, and then click **Next** to move to the next window. If a "Customizing QuickBooks for your business" window appears, close it and continue.

13 Select **Record each sale individually** and then click **Next**.

14 Select **Yes** when asked if you charge sales tax and then click **Next**.

15 Select **No** when asked if you want to create estimates and then click **Next**.

16 Select **Yes** when asked if you want to track sales orders before you invoice customers and then click **Next**.

17 Select **No** when asked if you want to use billing statements and then click **Next**.

18 Select **No** when asked if you want to use progress invoicing and then click **Next**.

19 Select **Yes** when asked if you want to keep track of bills and then click **Next**.

20 Select **Yes** when asked if you want to track inventory and then click **Next**.

21 Select **Yes** when asked if you want to track time and then click **Next**.

22 Select **Yes** when asked if you have employees, check **We have W-2 employees**, and then click **Next**.

23 Click **Next** to set up your chart of accounts.

24 Select **Use today's date or the first day of the quarter or month**, and then click the calendar icon to select **1/1/2016** as the start date as shown in Figure 6.4. Click **Next** to continue.

Figure 6.4

Choosing Your Start Date

Click here to reveal Calendar

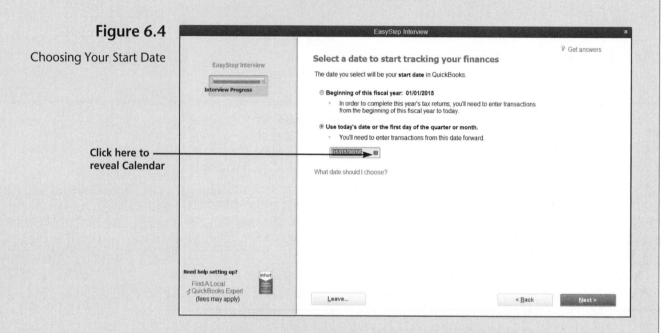

25 Click **Next** to continue and accept the given income and expense accounts.

26 Click **Go to Setup** to end the EasyStep Interview.

27 Before you start the set-up process, you need to establish some preferences. Click **Start Working**.

28 Collapse the My Shortcuts pane.

29 Close the What's New button by clicking the **X** next to the What's New button.

"That wasn't too bad," you comment. "QuickBooks Accountant seems pretty thorough in getting you started."

"That they are," Karen replies. "But we still have a long way to go before we can start entering transactions for January. We need to set up preferences, customers, vendors, employees, et cetera."

Set Up Company Preferences

"In QuickBooks Accountant," Karen explains, "preferences provide a way for turning certain features on or off, changing the look of the QuickBooks Accountant desktop, and customizing how QuickBooks Accountant performs."

Video Demonstration

DEMO 6B - Setting preferences

To set up preferences:

1 Click the **Edit** menu, and then click **Preferences**.

2 Scroll to the top of the preferences list and click **Accounting**.

3 Click the **Company Preferences** tab, and then check **Require accounts** if it is not already checked. Also make sure the **Use account numbers** check box is unchecked. Uncheck the two **Date Warnings** check boxes.

4 Click **Checking** from the preferences list, and click **Yes** if asked whether you want to save your changes.

5 Click the **My Preferences** tab, and then check all the boxes specifying default accounts to be used for different processes. Select <**Add New**> from the drop-down text box as shown in Figure 6.5 to add a new bank account.

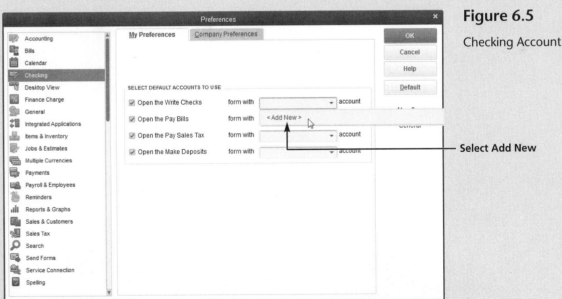

Select Add New

Figure 6.5

Checking Account Preferences

6   Type **Bank of Florida** as the Account Name making sure the Account Type is Bank as shown in Figure 6.6 below.

Figure 6.6

Adding a New Account

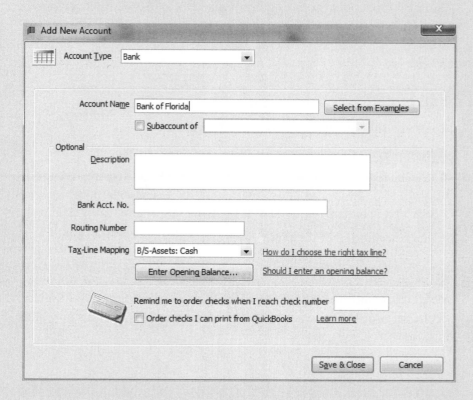

7   Click the **Enter Opening Balance** button, type **25000** in the Statement Ending Balance text box and **12/31/15** in the Statement Ending Date text box, and then click **OK**.

8   Click **Save & Close** to add the new bank account.

9   Select **Bank of Florida** default accounts to use for all the events specified.

10   Click **Desktop View** from the preferences list, and click **Yes** when asked if you want to save your changes.

11   Select the **Multiple Windows** option, and make sure the **Show Home page when opening a company file** and **Switch to colored icons/light background on the Top Icon Bar** check boxes are checked.

12   Click **General** from the preferences list, and click **Yes** if asked whether you want to save your changes.

13   Check all the items shown in Figure 6.7.

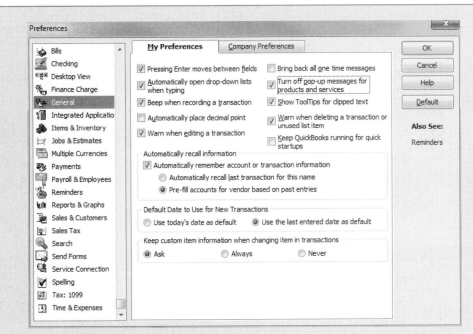

Figure 6.7

General Preferences

14 Click the **Company Preferences** tab, and uncheck the **Always show years as 4 digits** box.

15 Click **Reminders** from the preferences list, and click **Yes** when asked if you want to save your changes.

16 Click **OK** if you see a warning message.

17 Click the **Company Preferences** tab, and choose the **Don't Remind Me** option button for all the reminders as shown in Figure 6.8.

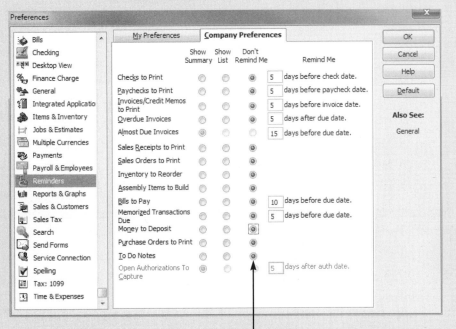

Figure 6.8

Reminders

18 Click **Reports & Graphs** from the preferences list, and click **Yes** when asked if you want to save your changes.

19 Click the **My Preferences** tab, and choose the option to **Refresh automatically**.

20 Click **OK** to close the Preferences window.

21 Click the **View** menu and then click **Top Icon Bar**. Then right-click the Icon Bar and then select **Customize Icon Bar**.

22 Click **Client Review** from the list of Icon Bar Content and then click the **Delete** button.

23 Follow the same procedure to delete all icons and space separators except Accountant, Home, Customers, Vendors, Employees, and Reports.

24 Click **OK** to close the Customize the Icon Bar window and then click **Home.** Your window should now look like Figure 6.9. You may have to resize the home window, but the menu items, icon bar, and home window should look similar to the figure. (*Note:* This screen shot was taken with the Windows 7 operating system using QuickBooks Accountant 2015.)

Figure 6.9

Desktop View of QuickBooks Accountant 2015 as Modified

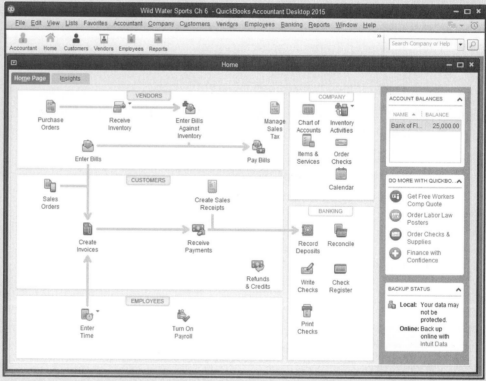

"Why did we choose not to use account numbers?" you ask. "Why just use account names?"

Karen explains that some small businesses use account numbers to help manage their accounting systems. Certain account sequences are followed. For example, assets are commonly assigned numbers beginning with a 1, liabilities with a 2, equities with a 3, revenues with a 4, and expenses with a 5. QuickBooks Accountant will assign all assets a 1000–1999 account number depending on the asset type. Liabilities will be assigned a 2000–2999 number, and so forth. There is no requirement in QuickBooks Accountant for account numbers, but Karen has decided not to use them because she believes account names are more descriptive than account numbers.

You've accomplished quite a bit by telling QuickBooks Accountant that you collect sales tax and use the payroll features, accounts, accrual-based reports, and the like. In addition, you've set certain "look and feel" features of QuickBooks Accountant to facilitate your navigation. Now it's time to specifically address income and expense accounts and items.

Set Up Company Items

Video Demonstration

DEMO 6C - Setting up new inventory and service items

Karen explains that it's now time to set up items. In QuickBooks Accountant, an *item* is anything that your company buys, sells, or resells in the course of business, such as products, shipping and handling charges, discounts, and sales tax (if applicable). You can think of an item as something that shows up as a line on an invoice or other sales form.

Items help you fill out the line item area of a sales or purchase form quickly. When you choose an item from your Item List, QuickBooks Accountant fills in a description of the line item and calculates its amount for you. QuickBooks Accountant provides 11 different types of items. Some—such as the service item or the inventory part item—help you record the services and products your business sells. Others—such as the subtotal item or discount item—are used to perform calculations on the amounts in a sale.

She suggests that you now set up some new service items and inventory part items. For Wild Water Sports, service items will be such things as changing engine oil and filter, engine tune-ups, and 20-hour service checks. Inventory part items will include boats and parts for repairs.

To set up items, Karen and Donna had to agree on prices for common service items, hourly service rates for nonstandard repairs, and pricing for products to be sold. They also had to set up item names and descriptions. One item they both notice is used for consignment sales, which they don't plan on doing, so they both agree to remove that item from the list. They must also edit the sales tax item to specify a tax rate and vendor.

"QuickBooks Accountant has a feature that allows us to enter multiple items at one time, which is a great time saver," says Karen. "I'll show you how it works."

To set up multiple items:

1   Click **Items & Services** from the Company section of the home page. This opens the Item List window. Karen has decided you will set up specific service items and specific inventory items for Wild Water Sports. (*Note:* You may have to resize the columns by clicking in between each column title and dragging to the right or left.)

2   Select the **Consignment Item** from the Item List.

3   Click the **Item** button in the lower left corner of the Item List window, and then select **Delete Item**.

4   Click **OK** to confirm.

5 Click the **Item** button again, and then select **Add/Edit Multiple Items** (see Figure 6.10).

Figure 6.10

Adding Multiple Items

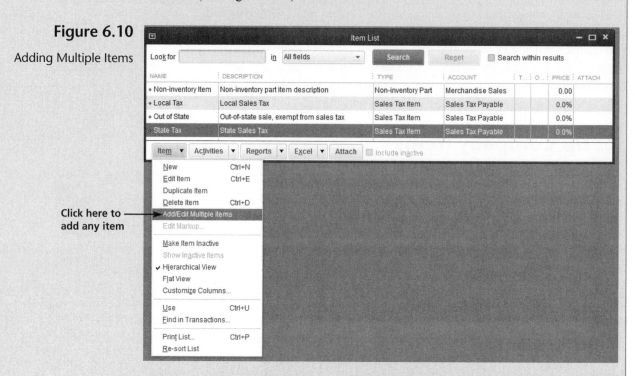

Click here to add any item

6 Select **Service Items** from the List drop-down list.

7 Click the **Customize Columns** button.

8 Click **Subitem of** from the Chosen Columns list.

9 Click the **Remove** button.

10 Now click **Sales Description** from the Available Columns list.

11 Click the **Add** button. With Sales Description selected, click the **Move Up** button so that Sales Description appears just after Item Name. Your window should look like Figure 6.11.

Figure 6.11

Customizing Columns

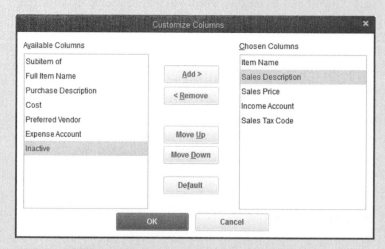

12 Click **OK** to close the Customize Columns window.

13 Type **20-Hour Service** in the space below the Item Name column and then press [**Tab**]. Click **OK** if a Time Saving Tip window appears.

14 Type **Labor charge for 20-hour service check** in the Sales Description column and then press [**Tab**].

15 Type **175** as the Sales Price and then press [**Tab**].

16 Type **Service** as the Income Account and then press [**Tab**].

17 Click **Setup** in the Account Not Found window.

18 Select **Income** in the Account Type drop-down list and then click **Save & Close**.

19 Select **Tax** as the Sales Tax Code and then press [**Tab**].

20 Type **Engine Service** as a new item in the Item Name column below 20-Hour Service and then press [**Tab**].

21 Type **Labor charge for changing engine oil and filter** in the Sales Description column and then press [**Tab**].

22 Type **125** in the Sales Price column and then press [**Tab**].

23 Select **Service** in the Income column and then press [**Tab**].

24 Select **Tax** in the Sales Tax Code column and then press [**Tab**]. Your window should look like Figure 6.12.

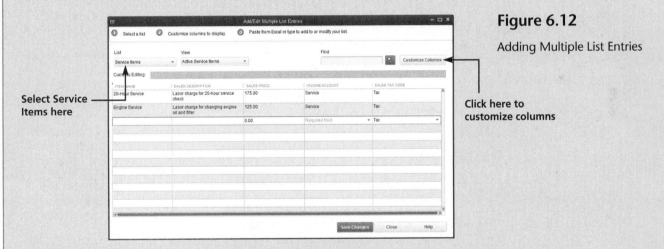

Figure 6.12

Adding Multiple List Entries

25 Click below the Engine Service item you just added in the Add/Edit Multiple List Entries window. Using the same process just illustrated add the following items:

Item Name	Sales Description	Sales Price	Income Account	Sales Tax Code
Engine Tune-Up	Labor charge for engine tune-up	$250.00	Service	Tax
Diagnostic Service	Labor charge for diagnostic service	$ 85.00	Service	Tax

26 Once you've entered all the service items above click **Save Changes** and then click **OK**. Now, it is time to enter new inventory parts.

27 Select **Inventory Parts** from the List drop-down list.

28 Click the **Customize Columns** button.

29 Click **Subitem of** from the Chosen Columns list.

30 Click the **Remove** button. In addition remove Total Value, Preferred Vendor, Max, and Manufacturer's Part Number columns.

31 Now click **Purchase Description** from the Available Columns list.

32 Click the **Add** button.

33 Click the **Purchase Description** column title and then click the **Move Up** button multiple times until the Purchase Description column title appears below the Item Name column title. In addition add the As Of Date column to the end of the list.

34 Click **OK** to close the Customize Columns window.

35 Type **MS LXi** as the Item Name and then press [**Tab**].

36 Type **Malibu Sunsetter LXi** as the Purchase Description and then press [**Tab**].

37 Type **48000** in the Cost column and then press [**Tab**]. (*Note:* All merchandise is marked up 25% of cost; thus, all merchandise cost is 80% of the sales price.)

38 Type **60000** as the Sales Price and then press [**Tab**].

39 Type **Cost of Goods Sold** as the COGS Account if it is not already present, and then press [**Tab**].

40 Select **Merchandise Sales** as the Income Account and then press [**Tab**].

41 Select **Inventory Asset** as the Asset Account if it is not already present, and then press [**Tab**].

42 Type **0** as the Reorder Point, and then press [**Tab**].

43 Select **Tax** as the Sales Tax Code and then press [**Tab**].

44 Type **1** in the Qty On Hand column and then type **12/31/15** as the As Of Date.

45 Press [**Tab**] to set up another inventory part item. Click **Add** whenever the Check Spelling on Form window appears as long as you've correctly typed the part name. If a warning window about dates appears, you can either ignore it or change preferences as instructed.

46 Continue this process for the remaining inventory part items listed next. Be sure to specify **12/31/15** in the As of text box for all items added, Tax as the Tax Code, Cost of Goods Sold as the COGS Account, 0 as the Reorder Point, and Merchandise Sales as the Income Account.

Item Name	Description	Cost	Sales Price	On Hand
MS LX	Malibu Sportster LX	$41,600	$52,000	1
MS LSV	Malibu Sunscape LSV	$52,000	$65,000	2
MV	Malibu Vride	$38,400	$48,000	2
MW VLX	Malibu WakeSetter VLX	$45,600	$57,000	1
MW XTI	Malibu WakeSetter XTI	$56,000	$70,000	1

47   Your window should now look like Figure 6.13. Click **Save Changes** after you've entered all five additional inventory items. Click **Close** to close the Add/Edit Multiple List Entries window.

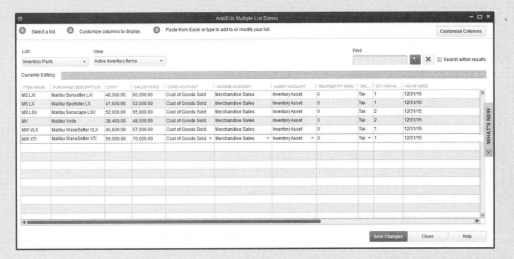

Figure 6.13   View of Add/Edit Multiple List Entries Window

"Don't you agree that entering multiple items at a time is much more efficient than entering them one at a time?" says Karen.

"I do," you respond. "But we didn't enter a sales description. We only entered a purchase description. Won't that cause problems later?"

"Yes, that's a good point." Karen answers. "I'll show you how to edit the items using the same multiple entry format."

To edit multiple items:

1   Open the Item List window again by clicking **Items & Services** from the Company section of the home page.

2   Click the **Item** button and then select **Add/Edit Multiple Items**.

3   Select **Inventory Parts** from the List drop-down text box.

4   Click the **Customize Columns** button.

5   Click **Sales Description** from the list of Available Columns.

6   Click the **Add** button to move Sales Description to the list of Chosen Columns.

7   With Sales Description selected click the **Move Up** button 10 times to move it just below the Item Name column.

8   Click **OK** to close the Customize Column window.

9   Click in the **Item Name** column title until the arrow points up, meaning sort inventory items by Item Name from A to Z. Now click and drag the mouse to select the text **Malibu Sunscape LSV** from the purchase description of item MS LSV then **right-click** and click **Copy**.

10 Click in the sales description text box for item MS LSV then **right-click** and click **Paste**.

11 Continue this process to copy the purchase description you had previously entered to the sales description column. Resize the columns so all the data fits into your window. Upon completion of this process your window should now look like Figure 6.14.

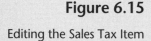

ITEM NAME ▲	SALES DESCRIPTION	PURCHASE DESCRIPTION	COST	SALES P...	COGS ACCOUNT	INCOME ACCOUNT
MS LSV	Malibu Sunscape LSV	Malibu Sunscape LSV	52,000.00	65,000.00	Cost of Goods Sold	Merchandise Sales
MS LX	Malibu Sportster LX	Malibu Sportster LX	41,600.00	52,000.00	Cost of Goods Sold	Merchandise Sales
MS LXi	Malibu Sunsetter LXi	Malibu Sunsetter LXi	48,000.00	60,000.00	Cost of Goods Sold	Merchandise Sales
MV	Malibu Vride	Malibu Vride	38,400.00	48,000.00	Cost of Goods Sold	Merchandise Sales
MW VLX	Malibu WakeSetter VLX	Malibu WakeSetter VLX	45,600.00	57,000.00	Cost of Goods Sold	Merchandise Sales
MW XTI	Malibu WakeSetter XTI	Malibu WakeSetter XTI	56,000.00	70,000.00	Cost of Goods Sold	Merchandise Sales

Figure 6.14 Partial View of Add/Edit Multiple List Entries Window

12 Click **Save Changes**, click **OK**, and then click **Close**.

Karen explains that you have one more item to enter and then need to print a list of items.

1 From the Item List, double-click the **State Tax** item.

2 Type **6.5%** as the Tax Rate.

3 Type **Florida Department of Revenue** as the Tax Agency show that your window looks like Figure 6.15.

Figure 6.15

Editing the Sales Tax Item

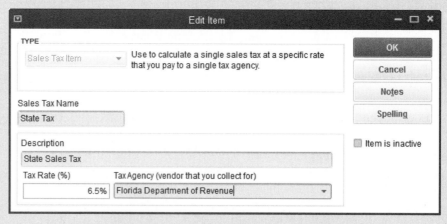

4 Click **OK** and then click the **Set Up** button.

5 Type **1379 Blountstown Hwy, Tallahassee, FL 32804-2716** in the Billed From box in the Address Details section.

6 Click **OK** twice to accept the modifications for this new vendor and sales tax item.

7 Prepare this window for printing by clicking the **Reports** button at the bottom of the window and then selecting **Item Listing**.

8 Click the **Customize Report** button.

9 Click the **Display** tab, and then uncheck **Sales Tax Code, Quantity on Purchase Order, Quantity on Sales Order, Reorder Point,** and **Preferred Vendor**.

10 Click the **Header/Footer** tab, and then uncheck **Subtitle, Date Prepared,** and **Time Prepared**.

11 Click **OK**.

12 Click the **Print** button on the top of the Reports window, select Report from the list, and then, choose **Landscape** orientation, and then click **Print**. Your printout should look like Figure 6.16.

13 Close both the Item Listing report and the Item List window. Memorize this report into a report group with your name like you have done in the previous chapters.

Item	Description	Type	Cost	Price	Quantity On Hand
20-Hour Service	Labor charge for 20 hour service check	Service	0.00	175.00	
Diagnostic Service	Labor charge to diagnostic service	Service	0.00	85.00	
Engine Service	Labor charge for changing engine oil and filter	Service	0.00	125.00	
Engine Tune-Up	Labor charge for engine tune-up	Service	0.00	250.00	
MS LSV	Malibu SunScape LSV	Inventory Part	52,000.00	65,000.00	2
MS LX	Malibu Sportster LX	Inventory Part	41,600.00	52,000.00	1
MS LXi	Malibu Sunsetter LXi	Inventory Part	48,000.00	60,000.00	1
MV	Malibu Vride	Inventory Part	38,400.00	48,000.00	2
MW VLX	Malibu WakeSetter VLX	Inventory Part	45,600.00	57,000.00	1
MW XTI	Malibu WakeSetter XTI	Inventory Part	56,000.00	70,000.00	1
Non-inventory Item	Non-inventory part item description	Non-inventory Part	0.00	0.00	
Local Tax	Local Sales Tax	Sales Tax Item	0.00	0%	
Out of State	Out-of-state sale, exempt from sales tax	Sales Tax Item	0.00	0%	
State Tax	State Sales Tax	Sales Tax Item	0.00	6.5%	

Figure 6.16 Item Listing

"We are well on our way to getting this company set up," Karen explains.

"Should we save our work?" you ask.

"Funny you should mention that," Karen responds. "QuickBooks Accountant automatically saves every event you record. In fact, QuickBooks Accountant doesn't even have a Save or Save As feature like most other software."

"Shouldn't we at least make a copy of the file in case something happens to this one?" you inquire.

"Good point," Karen says. "Once we're set up we can use the QuickBooks Accountant backup procedure to save a copy."

Karen explains that it's now time to enter our existing customers and vendors into QuickBooks Accountant and to establish beginning balances.

Set Up Customers, Vendors, and Accounts

Donna has met with Ernesto and has determined he did have some outstanding balances from a few customers and also owed some vendors for purchases made in the previous months. He has an existing bank account and a MasterCard credit card account for the business. He also owned some equipment and a related note payable.

job costing

Karen has also decided to use QuickBooks Accountant's job tracking feature to follow service-related efforts for customers. The firm plans to market its service program to existing customers and will need to track costs for each job as well as bill customers based on hours worked and materials used for each job.

Karen has gathered the information she needs and is ready for you to input it into the system.

To set up existing customers:

1 Click **Customers** from the Customer section of the home page. This opens the Customer Center window.

2 Click **New Customer & Job**, and then click **Add Multiple Customer: Jobs** from the shortcut menu.

3 Click the **Customize Columns** button.

4 Remove all columns from the Chosen Columns list except Name and Company Name.

5 Add columns Customer Balance and Opening Balance as of Date so that you now have four items listed in the Chosen Columns section of the Customize Columns window and then click **OK**.

6 Type **Orlando Water Sports** in the Name and Company Name columns.

7 Type **48300** in the Customer Balance column.

8 Type **12/31/15** in the Opening Balance as of Date column.

9 Your window should look like Figure 6.17.

Figure 6.17

Adding a New Customer

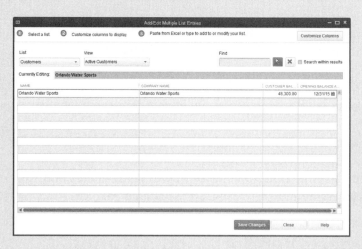

10 Continue this process for the remaining customers listed below. Once again, be sure to type the date 12/31/15 in the Opening Balance as of Date for all customers.

Name/Company Name	Customer Balance
Buena Vista Water Sports	$33,000
Walking on Water	$15,000

11 Click **Save Changes** in the Add/Edit Multiple List Entries window. Click **OK** to acknowledge that 3 customer records have been saved and then click **Close**. Select **All** from the Date drop-down list to view all invoices. Resize the window and various columns so that all information is displayed. Your Customer Center should now look like Figure 6.18. Close this window after viewing the updated Customer Center.

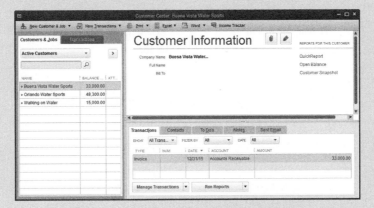

Figure 6.18

Updated Customer Center

12 Click the **Reports** icon from the Icon Bar to open the Reports Center. Click the **Standard** tab and then click **Customers & Receivables,** scroll down the page, and then select Customer Balance Summary in the Customer Balance section as shown in Figure 6.19.

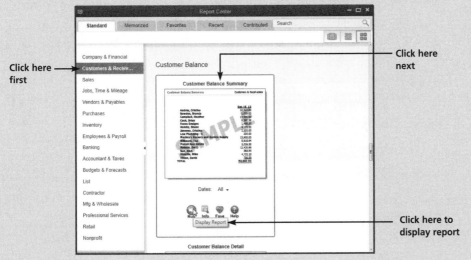

Figure 6.19

Reports Center

13 Click the **Run** icon shown below the Customer Balance Summary report. Type **12/31/15** as the From and To dates.

14 Click the **Customize Report** button.

15   Click the **Header/Footer** tab and then uncheck **Subtitle, Date Prepared,** and **Time Prepared**.

16   Click **OK** to close the Modify Report window.

17   Click the **Print** button on the top of the Reports window and then select **Report**.

18   Choose the printer you want to print to, choose **Portrait** orientation, and click **Print**. Your printout should look like Figure 6.20.

Figure 6.20

Customer Balance Summary

Wild Water Sports Ch 6
Customer Balance Summary

	Dec 31, 15
Buena Vista Water Sports	33,000.00
Orlando Water Sports	48,300.00
Walking on Water	15,000.00
TOTAL	**96,300.00**

19   Close the Customer Balance Summary window.

20   Memorize this report into a report group with your name like you have done in previous chapters.

21   To print a customer contact list, scroll down the list of reports shown in the Customers & Receivables section of the Report Center, click **Customer Contact List,** then click the **Run** icon.

22   Remove the Subtitle, Date Prepared, and Time Prepared fields as you've done previously.

23   Click the **Display** tab and remove the Bill to and Fax columns and then click **OK**.

24   Click the **Print** button on the top of the Reports window and then click **Report**.

25   Choose the printer you want to print to, choose **Portrait** orientation, and then click **Print**. Your printout should look like Figure 6.21.

Wild Water Sports Ch 6
Customer Contact List

Customer	Primary Contact	Main Phone	Balance Total
Buena Vista Water Sports			33,000.00
Orlando Water Sports			48,300.00
Walking on Water			15,000.00

Figure 6.21 Customer Contact List

26   Close the Customer Contact List window and memorize the report. Then close the Report Center and Customer Center.

"That will be fine for now, and as we add new customers, we'll follow the same process," Karen explains. "As you can see, we have several options for printing a list of customers. The Customer Balance Summary prints only the names of customers with outstanding balances at the dates we specified. The Customer Contact List prints all customers with the addresses and phone numbers we provided. Now let's set up Malibu Boats as our only current vendor."

To set up an existing vendor:

1   Click **Vendors** from the Vendor section of the home page. This opens the Vendor Center window.

2   Click **New Vendor** and then select **New Vendor** from the drop-down list.

3   Type **Malibu Boats** in the Vendor Name text box and Company Name text box.

4   Type **76000** in the Opening Balance text box.

5   Type **12/31/15** in the As of text box. Your screen should look like Figure 6.22.

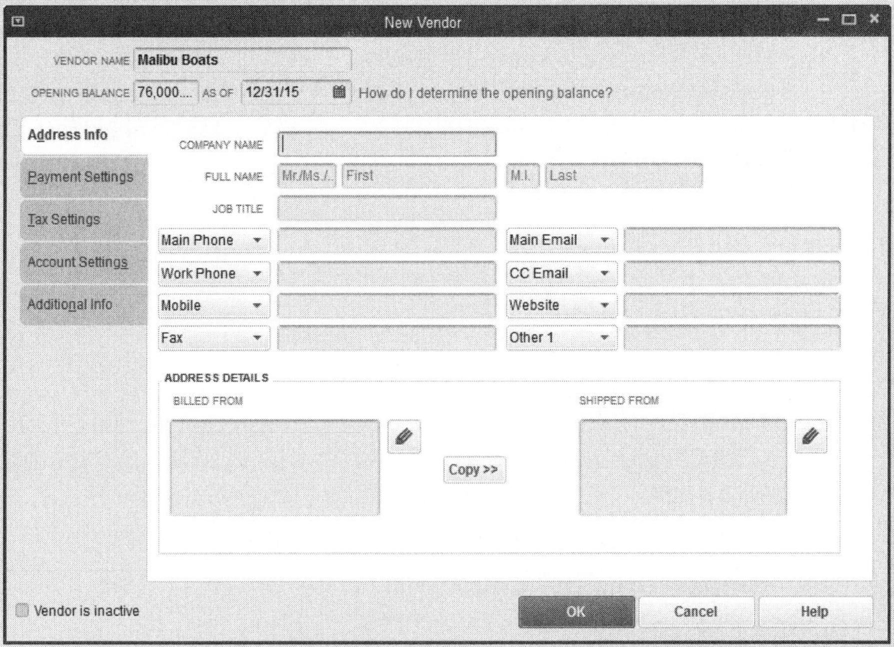

Figure 6.22

New Vendor

6   Click the **Payment Settings** tab and note that if credit terms or credit limits were provided, you would enter them here. Click **OK** to finish adding a new vendor. Close the Vendor Center.

7   Open the Report Center, click **Vendors & Payables**, and then double-click **Vendor Balance Summary**.

8 Type **01/01/16** as the From and To dates.

9 Click the **Customize Report** button.

10 Click the **Header/Footer** tab, and then uncheck **Subtitle, Date Prepared,** and **Time Prepared**.

11 Click **OK** to close the Modify Report window.

12 Click the **Print** button on the top of the Reports window and then select **Report**.

13 Choose the printer you want to print to, choose **Portrait** orientation, and then click **Print**. Your printout should look like Figure 6.23.

Figure 6.23

Vendor Balance Summary

Wild Water Sports Ch 6
Vendor Balance Summary

	Jan 1, 16
Malibu Boats	76,000.00
TOTAL	**76,000.00**

14 Memorize and then close the Vendor Balance Summary window.

15 To print a vendor contact list, double-click **Vendor Contact List** from the Reports Center.

16 Click **Customize Report** and then click **Display**. Include only the Vendor, Bill from, and Balance Total fields. Remove Subtitle, Date Prepared, and Time Prepared fields as you've done before.

17 Click **OK** and then click the **Print** button on the top of the Reports window and then click **Report**.

18 Choose the printer you want to print to, choose **Landscape** orientation, and then click **Print**. Your printout should look like Figure 6.24.

Wild Water Sports Ch 6
Vendor Contact List

Vendor	Bill from	Balance Total
Florida Department of Revenue	Florida Department of Revenue 1379 Blountstown Hwy Tallahassee, FL 32804-2716	0.00
Malibu Boats		76,000.00

Figure 6.24 Vendor Contact List

19 Close the Vendor Contact List window and memorize this report.

20 Close the Report Center and Vendor Center windows.

Karen explains that although Malibu Boats is the only vendor she needs to add at this time, later she'll be adding more vendors "on the fly" as she enters transactions for January. Now she suggests you complete the setup process by adding some new accounts to establish the company's credit card and long-term liability as well as its fixed asset balances as of 12/31/15. (*Note:* Fixed asset acquisition, depreciation, and disposition are addressed in Chapter 12.)

To create and modify accounts:

1 Click **Chart of Accounts** from the Company section of the home page.

2 Click the **Account** button, and select **New**.

3 Select **Credit Card** from the list and then click **Continue**.

4 Type **MasterCard** in the Account Name text box.

5 Click the **Enter Opening Balance** button.

6 Type **1000** in the Statement Ending Balance text box.

7 Type **12/31/15** in the Statement Ending Date text box and then click **OK**. Your screen should look like Figure 6.25.

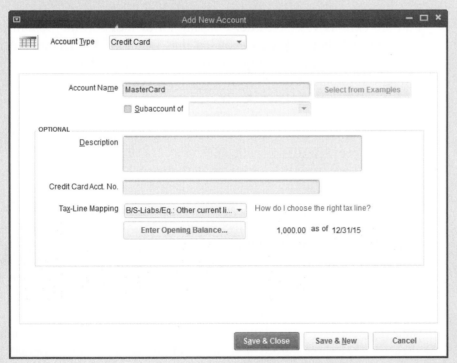

Figure 6.25

Establishing a Credit Card Account

8 Click **Save & New** to enter another account.

9 Select **Long-Term Liability** from the Account Type drop-down list.

10 Type **Loan Payable** in the Account Name text box.

11 Click the **Enter Opening Balance** button.

12 Type **383800** in the Opening Balance text box and **12/31/15** in the As of text box and then click **OK**.

13   Click **Save & Close**.

14   Select **Furniture and Equipment** from the Chart of Accounts, click the **Account** button, and then click **Edit Account**.

15   Click the **Enter Opening Balance** button, type **75000** in the Opening Balance text box and **12/31/15** in the As of text box, and then click **OK**.

16   Click **Save & Close**.

17   Select **Accumulated Depreciation** from the Chart of Accounts, click the **Account** button, and then click **Edit Account**.

18   Click the **Enter Opening Balance** button, type **–7500** in the Opening Balance text box and **12/31/15** in the As of text box, and then click **OK**.

> *Trouble?* Be sure to enter this amount as a negative number. If you don't, your trial balance will be out of balance. Accumulated depreciation is a contra-asset account that has a normal credit balance.

19   Click **Save & Close**.

20   Close the Chart of Accounts window.

You are curious whether, after entering all of these opening balances, the accounts are in balance. Karen explains that QuickBooks Accountant establishes an Opening Balance Equity account that is used to balance all the assets and liabilities established via this opening balances effort *except* for Accounts Receivable and Accounts Payable. The beginning accounts receivable balances were assigned to an account called Uncategorized Income on 12/31/15, and all beginning accounts payable balances were assigned to an account called Uncategorized Expenses as of the same date.

"But aren't we mostly concerned with balances beginning 1/1/16?" you question.

Karen points out that QuickBooks Accountant will automatically close these accounts to Retained Earnings as of 1/1/16. She does suggest, however, that you recategorize the retained earnings balance as of 1/1/16 to be part of the Opening Balance Equity account. She also suggests that it might make sense to transfer the resulting balance in the Opening Balance Equity account to the Common Stock account, because that is the basis the company will use for Karen and Donna's new investment in the company.

She enlightens you by explaining the arrangement that she and Donna have with Ernesto. The three agreed that the Opening Balance Equity (assets minus liabilities) was $100,000. Donna and Karen will each be purchasing stock in the company on January 1 for $100,000, thus giving the company a value of $300,000. Each stockholder—Ernesto, Donna, and Karen—will have a one-third interest in the company.

"Are we sure that our opening balance effort yielded an Opening Balance Equity of $100,000?" you ask.

"We'll check while we make the adjustments for the opening equity we just spoke of," Karen responds. "First let's look at a trial balance as of 1/1/16, which will give us the account balances as of that date."

To view opening balances and recategorize the opening balance equity and uncategorized account balances:

1 Open the Report Center, select **Accountant & Taxes,** and then double-click **Trial Balance**.

2 Change the To and From dates to **01/01/16** to view the trial balance shown in Figure 6.26.

Wild Water Sports Ch 6
Trial Balance
As of January 1, 2016

	Jan 1, 16	
	Debit	Credit
Bank of Florida	25,000.00	
Accounts Receivable	96,300.00	
Inventory Asset	372,000.00	
Accumulated Depreciation		7,500.00
Furniture and Equipment	75,000.00	
Accounts Payable		76,000.00
MasterCard		1,000.00
Loan Payable		383,800.00
Opening Balance Equity		79,700.00
Retained Earnings		20,300.00
TOTAL	568,300.00	568,300.00

Figure 6.26

Trial Balance

3 Close the Trial Balance window and then close the Reports Center window. (No need to memorize this report since you didn't make any changes to the standard trial balance report.)

4 Select **Chart of Accounts** from the Company section of the home page.

5 Double-click the **Opening Balance Equity** account to use the register.

6 If necessary, scroll down the account until an empty row can be seen.

7 Type **01/01/16** in the date column in the first open row available.

8 Type **20300** in the increase column of that same row.

9 Select **Retained Earnings** from the Account drop-down list.

10 Click **Record**.

11 Click **OK** if asked whether you really want to make an adjustment to this account.

12 Type **01/01/16** in the date column in the next open row available if it is not already there.

13 Type **100000** in the decrease column of that same row.

14 Select **Capital Stock** from the Account drop-down list.

15 Click **Record**. Your screen should now look like Figure 6.27.

Figure 6.27

Opening Balance Equity Account Register

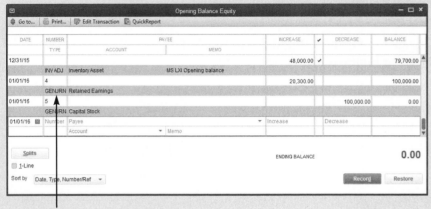

Double-click here to reveal journal entry

16 Double-click **GENJRNL** under the number 5 to reveal the general journal entry that was created when you adjusted the Opening Balance Equity account as shown in Figure 6.28. Close the Assigning Numbers to Journal Entries window.

Figure 6.28

General Journal Entry

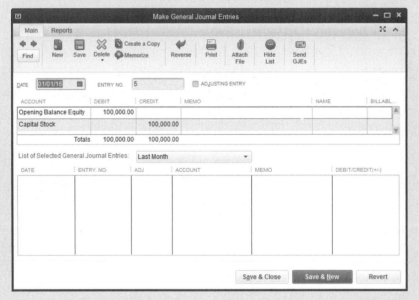

17 Close the **Opening Bal Equity** and the **Make General Journal Entries** windows.

18 The Opening Balance Equity and Retained Earnings accounts should now be zero, and the Capital Stock account should be $100,000. Your Chart of Accounts should now look like Figure 6.29.

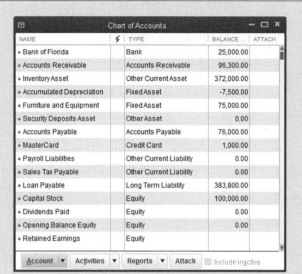

Figure 6.29

Chart of Accounts after Adjustments

"Much better," you proclaim.

Karen suggests you print this Chart of Accounts for later reference.

To print the Chart of Accounts:

1 Prepare this window for printing by clicking the **Reports** button at the bottom of the window and then selecting **Account Listing**.

2 Click the **Customize Report** button.

3 Click the **Header/Footer** tab, and then uncheck **Subtitle**, **Date Prepared**, and **Time Prepared**.

4 Click the **Display** tab, and then uncheck **Tax Line** and **Description** to remove those columns from your report.

5 Click **OK**.

6 Click the **Print** button on the top of the Reports window, choose **Portrait** orientation, and then click **Print**. Alternatively, you can access this list by clicking the **Reports** menu, then **List**, and then **Account Listing**.

7 Close both the Account Listing report and the Chart of Accounts window. Be sure to memorize the Accounting Listing report.

Karen points out the opening equity balance in the accounts listing is, in fact, the $100,000 they expected. Her stock purchase and Donna's stock purchase will occur in the first few days of January. All that's left in the company creation process is setting up payroll and adding employees.

Set Up Payroll and Employees

"Now it's time to establish information about our employees in QuickBooks Accountant," Karen says. "QuickBooks Accountant has some very nice payroll features that will help us track employee information, prepare payroll tax reports, and account for our employee cost."

"Will it calculate payroll withholding for federal and state taxes?" you ask.

"It will if we purchase a payroll tax table service from Intuit," Karen answers, "but we decided not to do that."

First, we must set up QuickBooks Accountant so that it knows we want to compute payroll manually. As you will see, this is not a straightforward proposition. QuickBooks Accountant makes you do some fairly strange things to begin a manual payroll, and none is intuitive or easy to discover. To get started, we use the Help menu.

To set up payroll:

1 First, note that the home page lists only two icons (Enter Time and Turn On Payroll) in the Employee section. Now press the F1 key to start QuickBooks Accountant Help.

2 Type **process payroll manually** in the text box, then press the **Enter** key.

3 Click the text **Process payroll manually (without a subscription to Quick-Books Payroll)**. Your screen should look like Figure 6.30.

Figure 6.30

Using QuickBooks Accountant Help to Set Up Manual Payroll

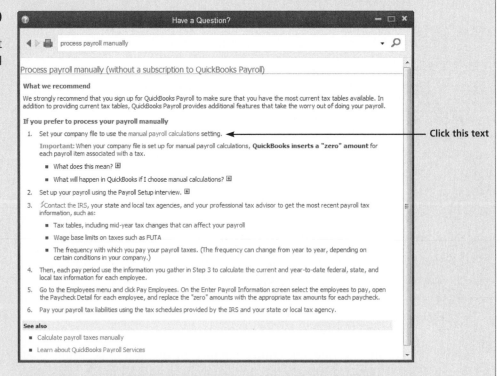

4 Click the text **manual payroll calculations**.

5 Click the text **Set my company file to use manual calculations**.

6 Click **OK** and then close the Have a Question? windows. Notice that the home page now contains new icons that will allow you to process payroll as shown in Figure 6.31 below.

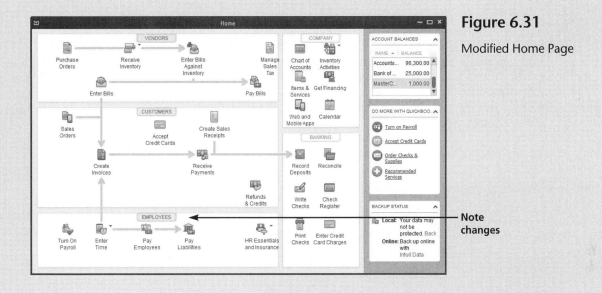

Figure 6.31

Modified Home Page

Note changes

Now it's time to enter payroll details for January. Karen explains that, during the month of January, she and Donna will work full time as salaried employees. Ryder and Pat, sales staff and service technicians, will work occasional days until the end of the month when the business is more established. For the first few weeks, most of their work will be setting up the business, passing out marketing flyers, and trying to sell boats. Later in the month, they will begin servicing some boats.

For each employee you'll need to add personal, address and contact, and tax information. In doing so, Karen points out, you'll also be setting up payroll tax items such as salary and hourly as well as identifying how often your employees are paid (monthly in this case). You'll also be identifying each employee's salary or hourly rate, taxes to be withheld, state worked, filing status, tax rates (e.g., unemployment), and tax payees (e.g., Florida Department of Revenue) to whom state taxes are paid. Karen then explains that the best way to get started is to use QuickBooks Accountant Payroll Setup.

Video Demonstration

DEMO 6F - Setting up payroll after setting manual payroll calculations

To set up payroll:

1 Click **Payroll Setup** from the Employees menu.

2 Click the **Continue** button after reading each window until you get to the Add New window.

3 Make sure that only the **Salary** and **Hourly wage and overtime** check boxes are checked in the Add New window and then click **Finish**.

4 Click **Continue** to accept the Compensation list provided.

5 Click **Continue** again, check the **My company does not provide insurance benefits** check box, then click **Continue** again and then click **Finish**.

6 Proceed in the same manner through the payroll setup process, as the company does not provide retirement benefits and paid time off or have any special additions and deductions.

7 Click **Continue** when you get to the Set up your employees section.

8 Enter the information for Donna Chandler as shown in Figure 6.32.

Figure 6.32

Personal Information for
Donna Chandler

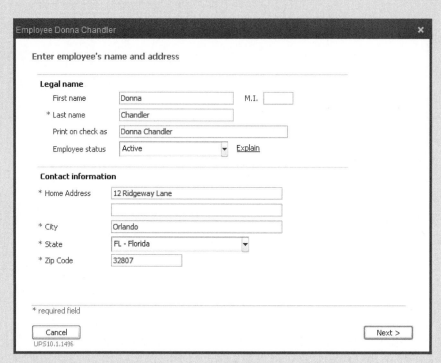

9 Click **Next** and then enter the hiring information for Donna Chandler as shown in Figure 6.33.

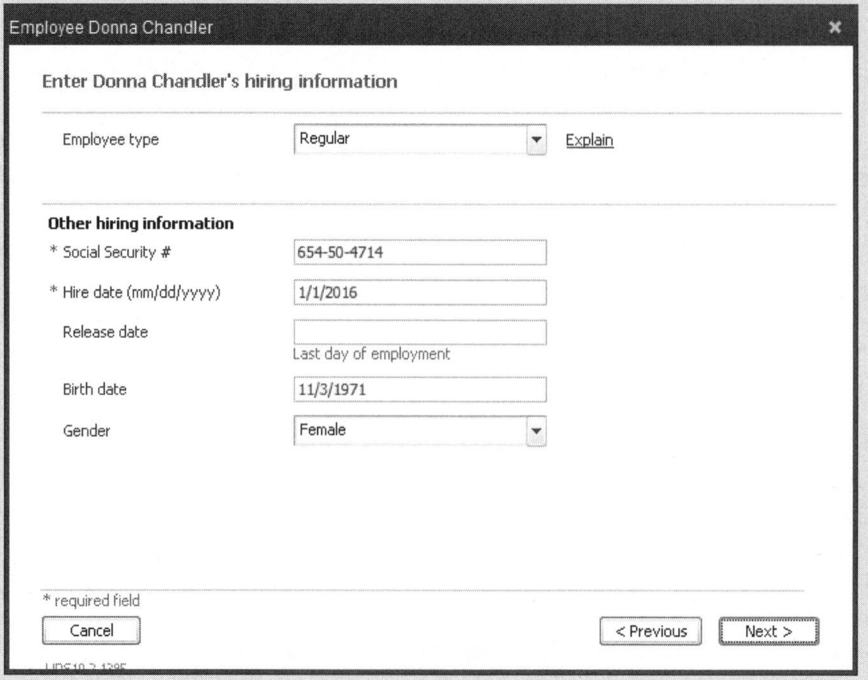

Figure 6.33

Hiring Information for
Donna Chandler

10 Click **Next** and then enter the compensation information for Donna Chandler as shown in Figure 6.34.

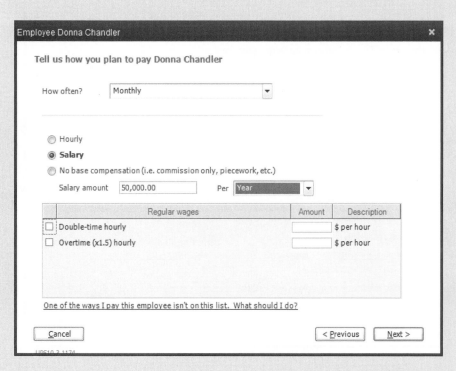

Figure 6.34

Compensation Information for Donna Chandler

11 Click **Next** two times and then enter the subject to tax information for Donna Chandler as shown in Figure 6.35.

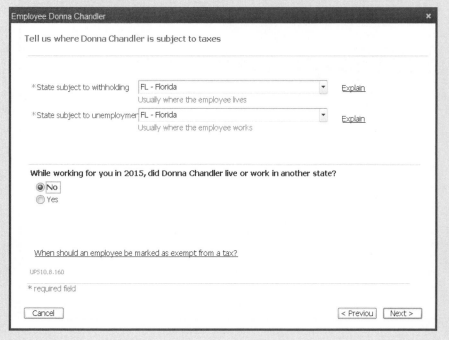

Figure 6.35

Subject to Tax Information for Donna Chandler

12 Click **Next** and then enter the federal tax information for Donna Chandler as shown in Figure 6.36.

Figure 6.36

Federal Tax Information for Donna Chandler

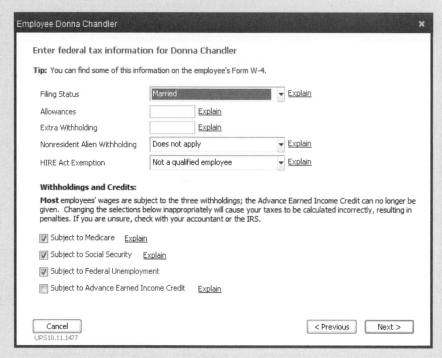

13 Click **Next** and then enter the state tax information for Donna Chandler as shown in Figure 6.37.

Figure 6.37

State Tax Information for Donna Chandler

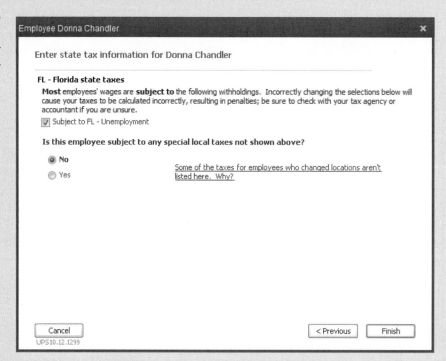

14 Click **Finish** to finish adding Donna to the payroll system. Click **Continue** to carry on the payroll setup process.

15 Click **Continue** two more times to accept the tax items set up for you.

16 Click **Edit** and then click **Next**, then type **2.7%** as the FL—Unemployment Company Rate and then click **Finish**.

17 Click **Continue** and then set the Payee to FL Dept of Revenue and the Deposit Frequency to Quarterly for all tax payments. Click **Next**.

18 Type **6854102** as the FL Dept of Revenue UT Acct No and then click **Finish**.

19 Click **Continue** twice and then click **2016** if you are asked when you will start processing payroll in QuickBooks Accountant. If asked, select **No** to a question about whether your company issued paychecks this year.

20 Click **Continue** and then click **Go to the Payroll Center** to finish the payroll setup process.

You note that Donna Chandler is now set up as an employee for the company and that payroll is ready to go, but you still have more employees to enter. Karen suggests that you add one employee for now, perhaps Ryder Zacovic, an hourly employee. You respond that you are up to the task.

To add Ryder as an employee:

1 Click **New Employee**. A New Employee window appears.

2 Be certain that the Personal tab is selected. Then, fill in the form with the following information:
   Name: Mr. Ryder Zacovic
   Social Security number: 556-74-6585
   Gender: Male
   Date of Birth: 02/19/85

3 Click the **Address and Contact** tab and then type **1554 Rose Avenue Apt. #4, Orlando, FL 32804** in the Home Address section.

4 Click the **Payroll Info** tab.

5 Select **Monthly** as the Pay Frequency.

6 Select **Hourly** as the Item Name in the Earnings section.

7 Type **15** as the Hourly/Annual Rate in the Earnings section.

8 Click the **Taxes** button and enter the following information in the Federal tab: Ryder is single and subject to Medicare, Social Security, and Federal Unemployment Tax.

9 Click the **State** tab and identify Ryder as working in Florida (FL) and subject to Florida (FL) withholding.

10 Click **OK** two times to finish entering Ryder as a new employee.

11 Click **Leave As Is** when asked if you want to set up other payroll information and then close the Employee Center window and click **Home** to return to the Home window.

12 Click the **Reports** menu, click **List**, and then click **Employee Contact List**.

13 Click the **Customize Report** button.

14 Click the **Header/Footer** tab, and then uncheck **Date Prepared** and **Time Prepared**.

15 Click the **Display** tab, and then uncheck **Main Phone** from the list of columns.

16 Click **OK** to close the Modify Report window.

17 If necessary, resize the remaining columns of the report to fit it onto one page.

18 Click the **Print** button on the top of the Reports window and then click **Report**.

19 Choose the printer you want to print to, choose **Portrait** orientation, and then click **Print**. Your printout should look like Figure 6.38.

20 Close the Employee Contact List window memorizing this report.

21 Close the Employee Center window.

Figure 6.38

Employee Contact List

Wild Water Sports Ch 6
Employee Contact List

Employee	SS No.	Address	Gender
Donna Chandler	654-50-4714	12 Ridgeway Lane Orlando, FL 32807	Female
Ryder Zacovic	556-74-6585	1554 Rose Avenue Apt. #4 Orlando, FL 32804	Male

You have now finished setting up new company files, establishing company preferences, and setting up company items, customers, vendors, accounts, and employees.

Your final task is to view a transactions by date report and back up your data file for safekeeping.

Viewing Transactions and Backing Up Your Company File

"It's always important to view a Transactions List by Date Report to verify that all business events recorded are present in the period of time you expected them," Karen says. "Let's create such a report."

To create and print a Transactions by Date Report:

1 Click the **Reports** menu and then select **Accountant & Taxes**.

2 Click **Transactions List by Date**.

3 Click **Customize Report** and then click the **Display** tab.

4 Uncheck **Adj.** column and set the From and To dates to **12/31/15** and **01/01/16** respectively.

5 Click the **Header/Footer** tab and remove the **Date Prepared** and **Time Prepared** header information and then click **OK**.

6 Resize column widths so that all data in each is clearly visible.

7 Memorize this report into your Group, then click **Print** and then click **Report**.

8 Select **Landscape** orientation and check the Fit report to 1 page wide. Your printed report should look like Figure 6.39.

Wild Water Sports Ch 6
Transaction List by Date
December 31, 2015 through January 1, 2016

Type	Date	Num	Name	Memo	Account	Clr	Split	Debit	Credit
Dec 31, '15 - Jan 1, 16									
Deposit	12/31/15			Account Opening Balance	Bank of Florida	X	Opening Balance Equity	25,000.00	
Inventory Adjust	12/31/15			MW XTI Opening balance	Opening Balance Equity	X	Inventory Asset		56,000.00
Inventory Adjust	12/31/15			MW VLX Opening balance	Opening Balance Equity	X	Inventory Asset		45,600.00
Inventory Adjust	12/31/15			MV Opening balance	Opening Balance Equity	X	Inventory Asset		76,800.00
Inventory Adjust	12/31/15			MS LSV Opening balance	Opening Balance Equity	X	Inventory Asset		104,000.00
Inventory Adjust	12/31/15			MS LX Opening balance	Opening Balance Equity	X	Inventory Asset		41,600.00
Inventory Adjust	12/31/15			MS LXi Opening balance	Opening Balance Equity	X	Inventory Asset		48,000.00
Invoice	12/31/15		Walking on Water	Opening balance	Accounts Receivable	X	Uncategorized Income	15,000.00	
Invoice	12/31/15		Buena Vista Water Sports	Opening balance	Accounts Receivable	X	Uncategorized Income	33,000.00	
Invoice	12/31/15		Orlando Water Sports	Opening balance	Accounts Receivable	X	Uncategorized Income	48,300.00	
Bill	12/31/15		Malibu Boats	Opening balance	Accounts Payable	X	Uncategorized Expenses		76,000.00
Credit Card Char...	12/31/15			Account Opening Balance	MasterCard	X	Opening Balance Equity		1,000.00
General Journal	12/31/15	1		Account Opening Balance	Loan Payable	X	Opening Balance Equity		383,800.00
General Journal	12/31/15	2		Account Opening Balance	Furniture and Equipment	X	Opening Balance Equity	75,000.00	
General Journal	12/31/15	3		Account Opening Balance	Accumulated Depreciation	X	Opening Balance Equity		7,500.00
General Journal	01/01/16	4			Opening Balance Equity		Retained Earnings		20,300.00
General Journal	01/01/16	5			Opening Balance Equity		Capital Stock	100,000.00	
Dec 31, '15 - Jan 1, 16									

Figure 6.39 Printed Transaction List by Date Report

9 Close all windows.

"It is also very important to keep a backup of your company file just in case your computer hard drive crashes or your data file gets corrupted or destroyed," Karen explains. She goes on to explain that some business users save their files to USB drives.

To back up and restore a file to an external disk using QuickBooks Accountant Backup procedures:

1 Click **Backup Company** and then select **Create Local Backup** from the File menu.

2 Choose the **Local backup** option and then click **Next**.

3 Choose a location to which you would like to back up your file. In Figure 6.40, we chose to back up the file to an external drive defined as Drive J in a folder we called My QuickBooks Accountant Backups. Click **Browse** to locate the drive and location where you would like to back up your file.

Figure 6.40

Backing Up to an External Drive

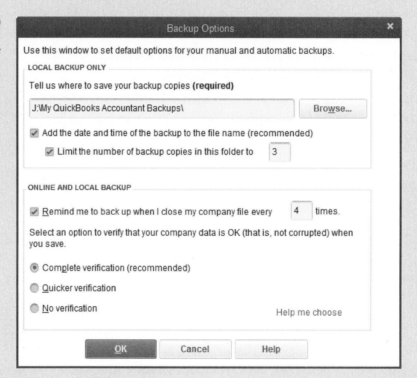

4 Click **OK**, click **Next**, and then click **Save** to begin the backup process.

5 Click **OK** again when QuickBooks Accountant informs you that your file has been backed up successfully. Choose **No Thanks** if a message pops up asking you to try the Online Solution.

6 To restore that same file from the external drive to your hard drive, choose **Open or Restore Company** from the QuickBooks Accountant File menu.

7 Choose the **Restore a backup copy** option and then click **Next**.

8 Choose the **Local backup** option and then click **Next**.

9 Identify the location of your backup file and then click **Open**.

10 Click **Next** to identify where the company file will be restored.

11 Once you've identified the location where the company file will be restored, click **Save**. Figure 6.41 shows an example where a backup file is being restored to a folder on a computer's hard drive.

12 Click **OK** when QuickBooks Accountant informs you that your file has been restored successfully.

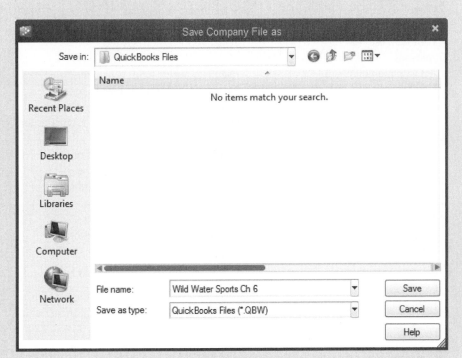

Figure 6.41

Restoring a QuickBooks Accountant File

"USB drives are ideal," you point out. Karen suggests that the two of you back up and restore a file for practice.

End Note

Karen thanks you for your patience in helping to create a QuickBooks Accountant file for Wild Water Sports. You've created a new company and have also set up company preferences, company items, customers, vendors, accounts, and employees. Next, you'll begin recording business transactions.

Business Events Summary

Business Event	Process Steps	Page
New Company		
Create new company	Use EasyStep Interview	91
Set up company preferences	Select Edit menu, then Preferences	95
Customers		
Create customer	New Customer & Job from Customer Center	106
Print customer list	Customer Contact List from Reports Center	108
Vendors		
Create vendor	New Vendor from Vendor Center	109
Print vendor list	Vendor Contact List from Reports Center	110
Items		
Create service/inventory items	Select Items & Services	99
Set up sales taxes	Sales tax from Item List	104
Print item list	Select Reports, Item Listing	105
Employees		
Activate manual payroll	Use F1 to access help	116
Set up payroll	Payroll Setup from Employees menu	117
Create employee	New Employee from Employee Center	121
Print employee list	Employee Contact List from Reports Center	122
Accounts		
Create account	Chart of Accounts from Home page	111
Set up beginning balances	Enter Opening Balance in Account	111
Print account list	Reports menu: List: Account Listing	115
Other		
Trial balance	Accountant & Taxes in Reports Center	113
Recategorize opening balances	Use Opening Bal Equity account	113
Back up company file	Save Copy or Backup from File menu	124

Chapter 6 Questions

1   Describe the EasyStep Interview process to create a new QuickBooks Accountant company file.

2   What is the purpose of setting preferences in QuickBooks Accountant?

3   Do all businesses use account numbers?

4   Give examples of service items and inventory part items used by Wild Water Sports.

5   Why did Wild Water Sports choose to use QuickBooks Accountant's job tracking feature?

6   Explain the process of establishing new accounts for fixed assets that will be depreciated like equipment. Why is accumulated depreciation set up with a negative beginning balance?

7   What happens when you first establish beginning balances for Accounts Receivable and Accounts Payable?

8   Describe the process for telling QuickBooks Accountant you want to manage payroll manually.

9   When creating a new employee during the payroll setup process, what information is provided in the Payroll and Compensation Info tab?

10   Why is it important to back up your QuickBooks Accountant file?

Chapter 6 Matching

Select the letter of the item below that best matches the definitions that follow. Use the text or QuickBooks Accountant Help to complete this assignment.

a. EasyStep Interview

b. Items

c. Service items

d. Inventory part items

e. Customer

f. Vendor

g. Opening balance

h. Job

i. Fixed asset

j. Trial balance

_____ Anyone who pays you.

_____ Anyone you pay except employees.

_____ Anything that your company buys, sells, or resells in the course of business.

_____ This QuickBooks Accountant setup process walks you through the setup procedure and helps you tailor QuickBooks Accountant to suit your business.

_____ Items representing services you sell.

_____ Items representing products you sell.

_____ In traditional accounting, a document that adds up all the debits and credits so that mistakes can be traced if debits don't equal credits.

_____ Property used in a productive capacity that will benefit your business for longer than one year.

_____ An optional way to keep track of larger orders, such as those placed by different departments within the same organization.

_____ The amount of money in, or the value of, an account as of the start date of your records in QuickBooks Accountant.

Chapter 6 Exercises

Chapter 6 Exercise 1
CREATE A NEW COMPANY

Having just completed your second year of college studying business and accounting, you are looking for summer employment when you run across an ad from a Jessica Gil, a local CPA, who is in need of part-time help. After an hour-long interview you get the job and are anxious to apply your newfound knowledge in accounting to help a business gain success. Jessica has just taken on a new client, Boston Catering, a catering firm located in Cambridge, Massachusetts, that provides catering services to businesses in the Cambridge and Boston area. So far they have been manually keeping their accounting records but wish to convert to QuickBooks Accountant starting July 1, the beginning of their fiscal year. Jessica would like you to spearhead this effort by creating a QuickBooks Accountant file containing their existing customers, vendors, and employees and then entering their business events in July.

The company's federal tax ID is 99-2158715 and state tax ID is 4513-41. They are located at 305 Hampshire Street, Cambridge, MA 02139 with a phone number 617-555-2806. The company is organized as a corporation and sells both services and products. They do not sell products online, do charge sales tax of 5% on all items which is paid to the Massachusetts Department of Revenue, but do not create estimates and do not use sales receipts because all products and services are invoiced. Statements and progress invoices are not used but they do wish to use QuickBooks Accountant to manage the bills they owe. They do not print checks but do keep track of inventory (change standard inventory account to food inventory) and accept credit cards. Customers of this catering business are billed a fixed fee, but the company wants to keep track of hourly employees' hours so they have chosen to track time in QuickBooks Accountant. They will need a chart of accounts and will starting using QuickBooks Accountant 7/1/2010.

The company's existing bank account is with Bank of America in Cambridge. The 6/30/2010 statement reveals an ending balance of $8,345. You decide to use the following income and expense accounts:

Account Name	Type
Bar Sales	Income
Catering Sales	Income
Bar Purchases	Cost of Goods Sold
Food Purchases	Cost of Goods Sold
Restaurant Supplies	Cost of Goods Sold
Advertising and Promotion	Expense
Bank Service Charges	Expense
Depreciation Expense	Expense
Insurance Expense	Expense
Payroll Expenses	Expense
Professional Fees	Expense
Rent Expense	Expense
Telephone Expenses	Expense
Uniforms	Expense
Utilities	Expense

Any additional accounts already present in your file are to remain as is except for the Inventory Asset account which should be changed to Food Inventory. You decide to not sign up for an account at intuit.com and to set up preferences exactly as you did in Chapter 6. Create a new company using QuickBooks Accountant's EasyStep Interview. Use Boston Catering Ch 6 Ex 1 as the Company Name. The company is in the general service based industry. Each sale is recorded individually, using the U.S. dollar. They have W-2 employees. (*Hint:* be sure to set up your sales tax item information now for use in later exercises.)

Print an Account Listing report after removing the description and tax lines and then create a backup file with the name Boston Catering Ch 6 Ex 1 (Backup).

Chapter 6 Exercise 2
ADD CUSTOMERS

You must have completed Exercise 1 in this chapter to complete this exercise.

Restore the backup file you created in Exercise 1. Change the company name to Boston Catering Ch 6 Ex 2. Add the following customers to your file:

	MA General Hospital	Fidelity Investments	John Hancock
Address	55 Fruit St.	1 Devonshire St.	601 Congress St.
City	Boston	Boston	Boston
State	MA	MA	MA
Zip	02114	02109	02210
Phone	617-555-2000	617-555-1000	617-555-3000
Beginning Balance	$7,000	$8,000	$9,000
Terms	Net 30	Net 30	Net 30
Sales Tax Item	Sales Tax 5%	Sales Tax 5%	Sales Tax 5%

Print a Customer Balance Summary report as of 6/30/10.

Chapter 6 Exercise 3
ADD VENDORS

You must have completed Exercise 1 in this chapter to complete this exercise.

Restore the backup file you created in Exercise 1. Change the company name to Boston Catering Ch 6 Ex 3. Add the following vendors to your file.

	Sanford Winery	Fiddlehead Cellars	US Food Service
Address	5010 Santa Rosa Rd.	1597 East Chestnut Ave.	One Technology Dr.
City	Lompoc	Lompoc	Peabody
State	CA	CA	MA
Zip	93436	93436	01960
Phone	805-555-5900	805-555-0204	978-555-5100
Beginning Balance	$2,000	$3,000	$4,000
Terms	Net 30	Net 30	Net 30

Print a Vendor Balance Summary report as of 6/30/10.

Chapter 6 Exercise 4

ADD ITEMS

You must have completed Exercise 1 in this chapter to complete this exercise.

Restore the backup file you created in Exercise 1. Change the company name to Boston Catering Ch 6 Ex 4. Add the following items to your file:

#	Type	Description	Vendor	Cost	Price /Unit	Income Account	Quantity
A100	Service	Appetizers Heavy	-	-	$18	Catering Sales	-
A200	Service	Appetizers Light	-	-	$12	Catering Sales	-
S100	Service	Spring Supper	-	-	$35	Catering Sales	-
S200	Service	Summer Supper	-	-	$40	Catering Sales	-
S300	Service	Fall Supper	-	-	$65	Catering Sales	-
S400	Service	Winter Supper	-	-	$50	Catering Sales	-
D100	Service	Desserts	-	-	$ 6	Catering Sales	-
P100	Service	Pastries	-	-	$ 5	Catering Sales	-
W100	Inventory Part	Sanford Chardonnay	Sanford Winery*	$45	$60	Bar Sales	25
W200	Inventory Part	Fiddlehead Pinot Noir	Fiddlehead Cellars*	$50	$65	Bar Sales	30

*You will need to add these vendors to complete this assignment.

Print an Item Listing report.

Chapter 6 Exercise 5

ADD EMPLOYEES

You must have completed Exercise 1 in this chapter to complete this exercise.

Restore the backup file you created in Exercise 1. Change the company name to Boston Catering Ch 6 Ex 5. You will need to create two new payroll items: Salary and Hourly, which both track to a Payroll Expense account. Payroll is paid monthly at the end of the month. All employees are subject to Medicare, Social Security, and Federal Unemployment federal taxes and state unemployment taxes which are paid quarterly. The company's state tax ID is 4513-41. All state taxes are paid to the Massachusetts Department of Revenue quarterly. The company's state unemployment tax rate is 3%. The company is also subject to a workforce training fund tax of .01%. (**Note:** use this information even if the QuickBooks Accountant software warns you about account numbers and payees.) Make sure you set up your company file to use manual calculations and then add the following employees:

	Nathan Chambers	Kyle Hain	Amy Casey
Address	One Leighton St.	101 Canal St. #9	1449 Main St. #30
City	Cambridge	Boston	Waltham
State	MA	MA	MA
Zip	02141	02114	02451
Phone	617-555-9822	617-555-0905	617-555-1234
SS#	154-74-8745	541-84-7312	641-87-9825
Earnings	$50,000/year	$16/hour	$18/hour
Filing Status	Single	Single	Married
Type	Regular	Regular	Regular

Print an Employee Contact List report with phone number.

Chapter 6 Exercise 6

ADD ACCOUNTS AND SET OPENING BALANCES

You must have completed Exercise 1 in this chapter to complete this exercise.

Restore the backup file you created in Exercise 1. Change the company name to Boston Catering Ch 6 Ex 6. Add accounts and set opening balances so that your chart of accounts looks like the following as of 6/30/10. (Use information from the previous exercises for details of accounts receivable, inventory, and accounts payable.)

Description	Dr.	Cr.
Bank of America	8,345	
Accounts Receivable	24,000	
Prepaid Insurance	3,000	
Inventory Asset	2,625	
Furniture and Equipment	62,030	
Accumulated Depreciation		2,030
Accounts Payable		9,000
Note Payable		50,000
Opening Balance Equity		23,970
Retained Earnings		15,000
Total	100,000	100,000

Make journal entries as of 7/1/10 to adjust retained earnings to zero and capital stock to 38,970. Print the Account Listing report as of 7/1/10.

Chapter 6 Assignments

Chapter 6 Assignment 1

ADDING MORE INFORMATION: WILD WATER SPORTS

Restore the file Wild Water Sports Ch 6A (Backup) found on the text CD or download it from the text web site. Add a new income type account titled "Part Sales." Add a new other current asset account titled "Inventory Parts." Change the title of the existing Inventory Asset account to Inventory Boats. Change the title of the existing Merchandise Sales account to Boat Sales.

corporation

merchandising

Add the following service items:

Item Name	Description	Rate	Tax Code	Account
Cleaning	Labor charge for cleaning boat	$75.00	Tax	Service
Painting & Body Repairs	Labor charge for painting and repairs	$80.00	Tax	Service

Add the following inventory parts. (Use Cost of Goods Sold for the COGS Account for all items.)

Item Name & Description	Sales Price	Tax Code	Income Account	Asset Account	Cost	On Hand
Engine Oil	$ 5.00	Tax	Part Sales	Inventory Parts	$ 4.00	0
Oil Filter	$ 15.00	Tax	Part Sales	Inventory Parts	$ 12.00	0
Tune-Up Parts	$250.00	Tax	Part Sales	Inventory Parts	$200.00	0
Air Filter	$ 35.00	Tax	Part Sales	Inventory Parts	$ 28.00	0

Add the following customers:

Customer/Company Name	Balance Due
Freebirds	$0
Florida Sports Camp	$0

Add the following vendors:

Vendor/Company Name	Address	Phone	Balance Owed
MB Sports	280 Air Park Road, Atwater, CA 95301	209-357-4153	$0
Tige Boats	6803 US Hwy 83 N., Abilene, TX 79601	325-676-7777	$0

Add the following employees:

Employee Data	Karen Wilson	Pat Ng
Social Security number	654-85-7844	125-95-4123
Gender	Female	Male
Salary	$50,000 per year	n/a
Hourly Wage	n/a	$18 per hour
Filing Status	Single	Single
Taxes	Subject to Medicare, Social Security, FUTA, and all applicable state taxes	Subject to Medicare, Social Security, FUTA, and all applicable state taxes
Filing State	Florida	Florida
Pay Period	Monthly	Monthly

Create, memorize, and print the following as of 1/1/16 (similar to what you did in the chapter):

a. Customer Balance Summary

b. Customer Contact List (include Customer Name and Balance Total columns only)

c. Vendor Balance Summary

d. Vendor Contact List (include only Vendor, Bill from, and Balance Total columns)

e. Employee Contact list

f. Account Listing (Account, Type, and Balance Total only)

g. Item Listing (list only Item, Description, Type, Cost, Quantity On Hand, and Price)

h. Trial Balance

Chapter 6 Assignment 2

CREATING A NEW COMPANY: CENTRAL COAST CELLULAR

Van Morrison would like to use QuickBooks Accountant for his new company, Central Coast Cellular. You choose to use QuickBooks Accountant EasyStep Interview. The company's federal tax ID is 77-9418745. The company is located at 950 Higuera St., San Luis Obispo, CA 93401. The company's phone number is 805-555-9874, and its fiscal and tax year begins in January 2014. The company's main business is cellular phone sales and rentals (which will not be done online), but it also earns revenue by consulting with customers on alternative cellular phone plans. Choose Professional Consulting as the Industry for this company. The company is organized as a sole proprietorship selling both products and services. Sales tax at 8% is collected on all products and services and then paid to the State Board of Equalization. (***Hint:*** Be sure to create a tax item.) No estimates are used, but sales receipts are used to record cash sales and invoices to record credit sales. Customer billing statements may be used to remind customers of monthly balances owed. Progress billing is not used, but Van wants to keep track of bills that he owes. All checks are handwritten, inventory needs to be tracked, and credit cards are accepted. Van does plan on keeping time records for his hourly W-2 employees. He will use accounts (but not account numbers) starting on 1/1/14, at which time he plans to establish a checking account with a local bank. In addition to the recommended income and expense accounts, Van would like to have a Product Sales (Type: Income) account.

Change the preferences in QuickBooks Accountant as follows: Set QuickBooks Accountant to move between fields after pressing the Enter key. Set dates to a two-digit year format. Enable reports and graphs to refresh automatically. Enable manual payroll features.

Set up the following customers:

- Tribune, 3825 S. Higuera St., San Luis Obispo, CA 93401, 805-781-7800, Terms: Net 30, Contact: Sara Miles, Subject to state sales taxes.

- City of San Luis Obispo, 990 Palm Street, San Luis Obispo, CA 93401, 805-781-7100, Terms: Net 30, Contact: Robert Preston, Subject to state sales taxes.

- Sterling Hotels Corporation, 4115 Broad Street, Suite B-1, San Luis Obispo, CA 93401, 805-546-9388, Terms: Net 30, Contact: Monica Flowers, Subject to state sales taxes.

Set up the following vendors:

- Verizon Communications, 1255 Corporate Drive, Irving, TX 75038, 972-507-5000, Terms: Net 30, Contact: Francisco Rojas.

- Nokia Mobile Phones, 23621 Park Sorrento Road, Suite 101, Calabasas, CA 91302, 818-676-6000, Terms: Net 30, Contact: Brandy Parker.

- Ericsson, Inc., 740 East Cambell Road, Richardson, TX 75081, 972-583-0000, Terms: Net 30, Contact: Monty Python.

- Employment Development Department (EDD).

Set up the following employees using the company's federal and state tax ID 779-4187-4 All employees are paid semi-monthly and subject to Social Security, FUTA, Medicare, CA state withholding, SUI (CA Unemployment Company Rate: 3%), SDI, and California's Employment Training Taxes payable to the Employment Development Department (EDD). The California wage plan code for all employees is U (Voluntary DI, State UI Plan). Payroll taxes are paid quarterly.

- Name: Mr. Jay Bruner, Address: 552 Olive St., San Luis Obispo, CA 93401, Phone: 805-555-7894, SSN 578-94-3154, Start date: 1/1/14, Salary: $36,000 per year, Filing status: Single.

- Name: Mr. Alex Rodriguez, Address: 1480 Monterey St., San Luis Obispo, CA 93401, Phone: 805-555-1579, SSN 487-98-1374, Start date: 1/1/14, Salary: $48,000 per year, Filing status: Married with two incomes.

- Name: Ms. Megan Paulson, Address: 400 Beach St., San Luis Obispo, CA 93401, Phone: 805-555-4489, SSN 547-31-5974, Start date: 1/1/14, Hourly: $12 per hour, Filing status: Married with one income.

Modify the existing chart of accounts to include an Accounts Receivable account and a checking account.

Set up the following items:

- Consulting Services: Type: Service, Rate: $95, Taxable, and using income account: Consulting Income.

- Inventory Part: Item name/description: Nokia 8290, Cost: $150, Preferred vendor: Nokia Mobile Phones, Sales price: $225, Taxable, and using income account: Product Sales.

- Inventory Part: Item name/description: Nokia 8890, Cost: $175, Preferred vendor: Nokia Mobile Phones, Sales price: $250, Taxable, and using income account: Product Sales.

- Inventory Part: Item name/description: Nokia 3285, Cost: $200, Preferred vendor: Nokia Mobile Phones, Sales price: $300, Taxable, and using income account: Product Sales.

- Inventory Part: Item name/description: Ericsson LX588, Cost: $50, Preferred vendor: Ericsson, Inc., Sales price: $85, Taxable, and using income account: Product Sales.

- Inventory Part: Item name/description: Ericsson T19LX, Cost: $75, Preferred vendor: Ericsson, Inc., Sales price: $100, Taxable, and using income account: Product Sales.

Print the following as of 1/1/14.

a. Customer Contact List (include only the columns for Customer, Bill to, Contact, and Phone; print in landscape orientation).

b. Vendor Contact List (include only the columns for Vendor, Bill from, Contact, and Phone; print in landscape orientation).

c. Employee Contact List (include only the columns for Employee, SSN, Phone, and Address; print in portrait orientation).

d.   Account Listing (include only the columns for Account, Type, and Balance Total).

e.   Item Listing (list only Item, Description, Type, Cost, Price, and Quantity On Hand).

Chapter 6 Assignment 3

CREATING A NEW COMPANY: SANTA BARBARA SAILING

Rob Dutton, an old friend from your high school days, has just purchased Santa Barbara Sailing Center and is getting ready to start business July 1, 2015. He purchased the corporation from its previous owner for $50,000 and assumed the company's existing long-term debt of $264,900. In return, he now owns 100% of the outstanding capital stock. The company owns several sailboats, which it charters and rents to the public and businesses in town. As of 6/30/15, these boats had an estimated value of $300,000. There is an existing company bank account at Coast Hills Federal Credit Union, and there are existing customer receivable balances and vendor accounts payable balances that are expected to be collected/paid in the near future. The only remaining asset owned by the company is some furniture and equipment valued at $2,450. Rob has asked you to help him set up QuickBooks Accountant to account for and report on his business activities for the bank's information.

easy step

service

corporation

Company Information

*   Company name: Santa Barbara Sailing Center

*   Legal name: Santa Barbara Sailing Center, Inc.

*   Tax ID: 99-9851206

*   Address: 133 Harbor Way, Santa Barbara, CA 93109

*   Phone: (805) 962-2826

*   Industry: Rental

*   Company Organization: Corporation

*   Fiscal Year Starts: July

*   Services only, sales tax at 8%, without estimates, and statements, some corporate customers are invoiced but no progress invoicing, keep track of bills you owe, keep track of time, they have W-2 employees, use 7/1/15 as the first day of the quarter (since they are a calendar year company starting business 7/1/15).

*   Existing bank account name "Checking," account number 122541584 with a balance of $10,000 on 6/30/15.

*   Income and expense accounts: accept recommended accounts

Preferences

*   Accounting: Require accounts but no account numbers. Turn off date warnings.

*   Checking: Use the checking account as the default to write checks, pay bills, pay sales tax, and make deposits.

- Desktop View: Use multiple windows and show home page when opening a company file.

- General: Check the **Pressing Enter moves between fields** check box in addition to the default settings. Uncheck the **Always show years as 4 digits** check box.

- Sales Tax: Add sales tax item; Type: Sales Tax Item; Sales Tax Name: Tax; Description: Sales Tax; Tax Rate: 8%; Tax Agency: State Board of Equalization. Quick Add the vendor and then set your most common sales tax item to Tax.

Item Information

- Type: Service, Item Name: CAT 28, Sales Description: Catalina 28, Sales Price: $220 per day, Account: Rental Income

- Type: Service, Item Name: CAT 32, Sales Description: Catalina 32, Sales Price: $275 per day, Account: Rental Income

- Type: Service, Item Name: CAT 42, Sales Description: Catalina 42, Sales Price: $465 per day, Account: Rental Income

- Type: Service, Item Name: CAT 50, Sales Description: Catalina 50, Sales Price: $560 per day, Account: Rental Income

Customer Information

- Customer Name: SBMED, Opening Balance as of 6/30/15: $1,485, Company Name: Santa Barbara Medical, Address: 470 South Patterson, Santa Barbara, CA 93111, Terms: Net 30, Credit limit: $25,000

- Customer Name: RAY, Opening Balance as of 6/30/15: $8,465, Company Name: Raytheon, Address: 7418 Hollister Ave., Goleta, CA 93117, Terms: Net 30, Credit limit: $20,000

Vendor Information

- Vendor Name: Catalina, Opening Balance as of 6/30/15: $7,500, Company Name: Catalina Yachts, Address: 21200 Victory Blvd., Woodland Hills, CA 91367, Terms: Net 30, Credit limit: $50,000

Other Account Information

- Furniture & Equipment (Fixed Asset) opening balance at 6/30/15: $2,450

- Boats (new Fixed Asset) opening balance at 6/30/15: $300,000

- Accumulated Depreciation (Fixed Asset) opening balance at 6/30/15: $0

- Loan Payable (Long-Term Liability) opening balance at 6/30/15: $264,900

Payroll and Employee Information

- Payroll is calculated manually. The company does not provide insurance benefits, retirement benefits, paid time off, or have any special additions and deductions. All employees are subject to CA withholding, CA unemployment, Medicare, Social Security, federal unemployment, CA employment training, and CA disability taxes. The California wage plan code for all employees is U (Voluntary DI, State UI Plan). Payroll taxes are paid quarterly.

- Employee Name: Rob Dutton, Social Security number: 239-09-7466, Gender: Male, Address: 1044 Padre St., Santa Barbara, CA 93105. Hire date 7/1/15. Payroll Item: Regular, which represents an annual salary of $65,000 recorded to the Payroll Expenses account and paid semi-monthly. Filing Status: Single. Wage Plan Code = P (Personal Income Tax Purposes Only).

- Employee Name: Jeanne Winestock, Social Security number: 222-32-0298, Gender: Female, Address: 4678 Berkeley Rd., Goleta, CA 93117. Hire date 7/1/15. Payroll Item: Staff Hourly, which represents a regular hourly salary of $18 per hour recorded to the Payroll Expense account and paid semi-monthly. Filing Status: Married, one income. Wage Plan Code = P (Personal Income Tax Purposes Only).

- CA Unemployment tax rate is 3.4%, CA Employment Training Tax is 0.1%, CA Disability Employee Tax Rate is 1.0%. CA taxes are paid to the EDD quarterly (Acct. No. 203-8232-1). Federal taxes are paid to the U.S. Treasury quarterly.

Use the EasyStep Interview to create Santa Barbara Sailing Center's QuickBooks Accountant file. Reclassify Opening Balance Equity, Uncategorized Income, and Uncategorized Expense as Capital Stock. Print the following reports as of 7/1/15 without a Subtitle, Date Prepared, or Time Prepared reference. Place your name in the Extra Footer Line and print with a Landscape orientation.

a. Customer Contact List (Customer, Company, Balance Total, City, and State columns only)

b. Vendor Contact List (Vendor, Bill from, and Balance Total columns only)

c. Employee Contact List (Employee, SS No., Address, and Gender columns only)

d. Item List (Item, Description, Type, Price, and Sales Tax Code columns only)

e. Trial Balance

Chapter 6 Assignment 4
CREATING A NEW COMPANY: DRONE CITY

You have decided that the drone sales and rental business is ripe for expansion in the Pacific Northwest and have just opened for business January 1, 2017, doing business as a sole proprietor with the name Drone City. You've decided to use QuickBooks Accountant to account for and report on your business activities. You plan to lease a facility at 56 Waterview Way #44, Seattle, WA 98144. You've applied for and received a tax ID (45-6789123) and plan to initially set up your QuickBooks Company as a retail shop.

sole proprietorship

easy step

You plan to sell both services and products and record each sale individually. The sales tax for their location is 6.5%. You do not plan to provide estimates or statements or track sales customer orders. You do plan to invoice customers but not use progress invoicing. You do want to keep track of bills you owe and inventory. You expect to hire two W-2 employees, one salaried and one hourly, and thus need to keep track of time.

You decide to accept the QuickBooks-provided income and expense accounts. You have already opened a bank account with the account name "Checking," but no funds have been deposited. You have not purchased any inventory but have two vendors you've decided to add to QuickBooks: Quadcopters located at 23 Vernon Place, Los Angeles, CA 90017 and Space Age Transport located at 577 Trick Way, Chicago, IL 60601.

You haven't sold any products yet but you do have two prospective customers you've decided to add to QuickBooks: US DOD located at The Pentagon, Arlington, VA 22202 and Amazon, Inc. located at 1516 2nd Ave., Seattle, WA 98101.

You plan to offer consulting services at $200 per hour and plan to purchase two products for inventory. The first is a Quad 1, which will sell for $3,450 and cost $2,700. The second is a Hex Transport, which will sell for $2,800 and cost $2,000.

You've decided to set up QuickBooks with the following preferences:

- Accounting: Require accounts but no account numbers. Turn off date warnings.

- Checking: Use the checking account as the default to write checks, pay bills, pay sales tax, and make deposits.

- Desktop View: Use multiple windows and show home page when opening a company file and switch to color icons/light background in the Top Icon Bar.

- General: Check the **Pressing Enter moves between fields** check box in addition to the default settings. Uncheck the **Always show years as 4 digits** check box.

- Sales Tax: Add Type: Sales Tax Item; Sales Tax Name: Tax; Description: Sales Tax; Tax Rate: 6.5%; Tax Agency: WA Dept. of Revenue. Quick add the vendor and then set your most common sales tax item to Tax.

Be sure you have both a Furniture and Equipment (Fixed Asset) and Accumulated Depreciation (Fixed Asset) account.

Payroll is calculated manually. The company does not provide insurance benefits, retirement benefits, or paid time off, or have any special additions and deductions. Employees must pay federal income, Medicare, and Social Security taxes. The state of Washington has no state income tax. Employers must pay WA unemployment (2.59% rate payable to the Employment Security Department using Ref. 841299-02 1), WA Admin. Fund (.03% rate payable to the Employment Security Department using Ref. 841299-02 1), Medicare, Social Security, and federal unemployment and are paid semi-monthly (twice per month). Payroll taxes are paid quarterly.

You hired two employees on 1/1/17:

- Name: Monica Clinton

- Social Security number: 454-95-0078

- Gender: Female

- Address: 3 West St. #43, Seattle, WA 98445
- Employee type: Regular, Salary $55,000 per year
- Filing Status: Married

- Name: Emily Hain
- Social Security number: 546-87-9011
- Gender: Female
- Address: 399 Ferry Lane, Seattle, WA 98541
- Employee type: Regular, Hourly at $18 per hour
- Filing Status: Single

You decide to use the EasyStep Interview to create the company's QuickBooks file. Once you've created your new company (Drone City), click **View** on the QuickBooks menu and click **Top Icon Bar** to place icons at the top of the QuickBooks menu. Right click the icon bar and select **Customize Icon Bar**. Delete all icons except Accountant, Home, Customers, Vendors, Employees, and Reports.

Place your name in the Extra Footer Line; remove subtitle, date, and time prepared header information; and then print the following with a Landscape orientation.

a. Customer Contact List (Customer, Company, Balance Total, City, and State columns only)

b. Vendor Contact List (Vendor, Bill from, and Balance Total columns only)

c. Employee Contact List (Employee, SS No., Address, and Gender columns only)

d. Item List (Item, Description, Type, Price, Cost, and Sales Tax Code columns only)

e. Account Listing (Account, Type, and Balance Total columns only)

Chapter 6 Cases

Chapter 6 Case 1
FOREVER YOUNG

Sebastian Young played quarterback for the Los Angeles Raiders for the 12 years of his professional football career. As a team leader, Sebastian guided his team to three Super Bowl victories and earned the respect of his teammates, the coaching staff, the press, and fans across the country. Now retired, Sebastian is a guest commentator for a variety of sports talk shows on radio and television. He recently formed a sole proprietorship called Forever Young to promote himself as a motivational speaker to large corporations and organizations. He has hired Cory Walsh to promote and coordinate his appearances and Anne Sunshine to manage the office. Sebastian has contacted some vendors and customers and is about to

sole proprietorship

service

embark on a new business adventure. He has asked you to set up an accounting system for the business and has given you the following information:

Company Information

- Company and legal name: Forever Young
- Tax ID: 94-9723900
- Address: 100 Westwood Blvd., Los Angeles, CA 90024
- Phone: 310-555-2324
- Industry: Professional Consulting
- Company Organization: Sole Proprietor
- Fiscal year starts: January 2015
- Services only, no sales tax, with estimates, with sales receipts and statements, no progress invoicing, keep track of bills you owe, print checks, accept credit and debit cards, keep track of time, has W-2 employees, use 1/1/15 as the first day of the quarter
- Existing bank account: Washington Mutual, bank account name: "Checking," account number: 390093912, opened 1/1/15
- Income and expense accounts: accept recommended accounts

Preferences

- Accounting: Use accounts but do not require account numbers.
- Checking: Use the checking account as the default to write checks, pay bills, pay sales tax, and make deposits.
- Desktop View: Use multiple windows and show home page when opening a company file.
- General: Check the **Pressing Enter moves between fields** check box in addition to the default settings. Uncheck the **Always show years as 4 digits** check box.

Item Information

- Type: Service, Number: 001, Description: Full-Day Seminar, Rate: $10,000, Consulting Income
- Type: Service, Number: 002, Description: Half-Day Seminar, Rate: $6,000, Consulting Income
- Type: Service, Number: 003, Description: One-Hour Presentation, Rate: $2,000, Consulting Income

Customer Information

- Customer Name: Levi, Company Name: Levi Strauss, Address: 100 Market St., San Francisco, CA 94099, Terms: Net 30, Credit limit: $25,000
- Customer Name: Boeing, Company Name: Boeing Aerospace, Address: 139 Boeing Park Dr., El Segundo, CA 90233, Terms: Net 30, Credit limit: $25,000

Vendor Information

*   Vendor Name: Fleet, Company Name: Fleet Promotions, Address: 3099 Wilshire Blvd. #300, Los Angeles, CA 90024, Terms: Net 30, Credit limit: $50,000

*   Vendor Name: Galas, Company Name: Galas & Associates, Address: 37321 Santa Monica Blvd. #100, Los Angeles, CA 90024, Terms: Net 30, Credit limit: $50,000

Account Information

*   Checking account (already created)

*   Accounts receivable (not yet created)

Payroll and Employee Information

*   Payroll is calculated manually.

*   Employee Name: Cory Walsh, Social Security number: 339-09-7466, Gender: Male, Address: 399 Sunset Blvd., Bel Air, CA 90033. Payroll item: Officer Salary, which represents a regular annual salary of $80,000 recorded to the Payroll Expenses account and paid semi-monthly. Filing Status: Single. Hire date 1/1/15.

*   Employee Name: Anne Sunshine, Social Security number: 232-38-0098, Gender: Female, Address: 2983 Olympic Blvd., Los Angeles, CA 90032. Payroll item: Staff Hourly, which represents a regular hourly salary of $20 per hour recorded to the Payroll Expense account and paid semi-monthly. Filing Status: Single. Hire date 1/1/15.

*   State: California, State tax, unemployment, and state disability vendor: Franchise Tax Board, ID number: 930808, Liability account: Payroll Liabilities, California Unemployment tax rate: 3.4%, California Disability tax rate: 1.1%, all employees are subject to the California Training Tax. The California wage plan code for all employees is U (Voluntary DI, State UI Plan). Payroll taxes are paid quarterly.

Requirements:

Use the EasyStep Interview to create Forever Young's QuickBooks Accountant file and then print the following reports as of 1/1/15 without a Subtitle, Date Prepared, or Time Prepared reference. Place your name in the Extra Footer Line and print with a Landscape orientation. (Be sure to keep this QuickBooks Accountant file in a safe place; it will be used as a starting file for this case in Chapter 7.)

1   Customer Contact List

2   Vendor Contact List

3   Employee Contact List

4   Item List

corporation

merchandising

Chapter 6 Case 2

OCEAN VIEW FLOWERS

Ocean View Flowers is in the wholesale distribution and sales industry and is located at 100 Ocean Ave. in Lompoc, CA 93436. Ocean View started business as a corporation on January 1, 2016, and owner Scott Cruz would like you to use QuickBooks Accountant to keep track of its business transactions. Ocean View is a calendar year corporation (for both fiscal and tax purposes) and will need to use the inventory, purchase order, and manual payroll features of Quick-Books Accountant. The company established a bank account, titled Union Checking, at the beginning of the year. In addition, the company filed for federal (91-3492370) and state (234-3289-4) tax ID numbers. All employees are paid semi-monthly but do not earn sick or vacation pay. All of their customers are product resellers and thus no state sales tax is collected. They don't use estimates or progress invoicing, but do use sales receipts, invoices, and statements. They keep track of the bills they owe but don't print checks. They accept checks and credit cards as payment from customers but don't keep detailed records of the time employees work. All state payroll taxes are paid to the Employment Development Department. The state unemployment tax (SUTA) rate is 3.4%, and the state disability tax rate is 1.1%. The company's expected customers, items, and vendors are tabulated as follows:

Customer	Address	Terms	Contact
Valley Florists	101 Main St., Los Angeles, CA 90113	2/10 net 30	Sam Davies
FTD	2033 Lakewood Dr., Chicago, IL 60601	Net 30	Beverly Rose
California Beauties	239 Hyde Street, San Francisco, CA 95114	2/10 net 30	Farrah Faucet
Eastern Scents	938 42nd Street, New York, NY 10054	2/10 net 30	Nick Giovanni
Latin Ladies	209 Zona Rosa, Mexico City, Mexico	2/10 net 30	Juan Valdez

Item Type	Item Name/Description	Cost	Sales Price	Income Account
Inventory part	Almond Puff	$12.00	$24.00	Sales
Inventory part	Calistoga Sun	$ 8.00	$16.00	Sales
Inventory part	Caribbean Pink Sands	$13.00	$26.00	Sales

Vendor	Address	Terms	Contact
Hawaiian Farms	2893 1st Street, Honolulu, HI 05412	Net 30	Mahalo Baise
Brophy Bros. Farms	90 East Hwy 246, Santa Barbara, CA 93101	Net 30	Tim Beach
Princess Flowers	92 West Way, Medford, OR 39282	Net 30	Bonnie Sobieski
Keenan's Pride	10 East Betteravia, Santa Maria, CA 93454	2/10 net 30	Kelly Keenan
Vordale Farms	62383 Lido Isle, Newport, CA 90247	Net 30	Deana Vordale

Ocean View Flowers employees (all of whom are considered regular-type employees) were hired on 1/4/16 and are subject to federal and state taxes and withholdings, state unemployment, state disability, and state employee training taxes. Two wage items are used: Hourly and Salary. The California wage plan code for all employees is U (Voluntary DI, State UI Plan). Payroll taxes are paid quarterly. A list of employees is shown below.

Employee	Address	Social Security #	Compensation	Filing Status
Margie Cruz	2322 Courtney, Buellton, CA 93246	654-85-1254	$12/hour	Single
Kelly Gusland	203 B St., Lompoc, CA 93436	567-78-1334	$15/hour	Single
Stan Comstock	383 Lemon St., Lompoc, CA 93436	126-85-7843	$50,000/year	Married with one income
Marie McAninch	1299 College Ave., Santa Maria, CA 93454	668-41-9578	$60,000/year	Married with two incomes
Edward Thomas	1234 St. Andrews Way, Lompoc, CA 93436	556-98-4125	$70,000/year	Single

Requirements:

Create a new company file for Ocean View Flowers using the EasyStep Interview. Then add the customers, vendors, employees, accounts, items, and other information as just described. (Be sure to keep this QuickBooks Accountant file in a safe place; it will be used as a starting file for this case in Chapter 7.) Print the following as of 1/1/16:

1   Customer Contact List (Customer, Bill to, and Contact fields only)

2   Vendor Contact List (Vendor, Bill from, and Contact fields only)

3   Employee Contact List (Employee, SS No., and Address fields only)

4   Item List (Item, Description, Type, Cost, and Price fields only)

Chapter 6 Case 3
ALOHA PROPERTIES

Aloha Properties is located at 4-356 Kuhio Highway, Suite A-1, Kapaa Kauai, HI 96746. Its phone number is 808-823-8375, and the corporation specializes in Hawaii Vacation Rentals. Its federal tax ID number is 72-6914707, and it plans to start using QuickBooks Accountant as its accounting program on January 1, 2014. It has been in business for two years using a manual accounting system. Aloha hopes that you can help it migrate to QuickBooks Accountant. It is a property rental firm, files Form 1120 each year, and collects a 4% general excise tax (Tax name: HI Sales Tax, Description: Sales Tax) on all rental income, which must be paid to the State of Hawaii Department of Taxation located at P.O. Box 1425, Honolulu, HI 96806-1425. It has chosen to use sales receipts for its cash sales and invoices and statements for its credit sales. The firm would like to use QuickBooks Accountant to keep track of bills it owes but will continue to handwrite checks. It accepts credit and debit cards.

corporation

service

Aloha plans to use QuickBooks Accountant's service invoice format but not use progress invoicing. It also plans to use QuickBooks Accountant's payroll features but to continue calculating payroll manually, because it currently has only two W-2 employees. The firm doesn't prepare estimates and does not track employee time or segments. It does, however, plan to enter bills as received and then enter payments later. Reports are to be accrual based, and Aloha plans to use the income and expense accounts created in QuickBooks Accountant for a property management company. It will be providing services only, no products. Most of its revenue comes from renting properties located on the island of Kauai to individual and corporate accounts. The company's policy is to collect a 50% deposit upon reservation and the balance upon arrival. Some customers (those that have prior credit approval) are invoiced upon arrival with the remaining payment due within 30 days. Deposits are recorded as payments on account, even though revenue is not recorded until customers arrive. Other customers (those without prior credit approval) must pay upon arrival, at which time a sales receipt is generated and the remaining payment is collected. Service items are used, but no inventory is maintained. Existing service items, customers, vendors, and employee information are provided below. (*Note:* Deposits for rentals not yet provided are shown as negative numbers.)

Service Item Name	Description	Income a/c	Rate
Moana Unit #1	Moana Unit #1	Rental Income	$ 2,000
Moana Unit #2	Moana Unit #2	Rental Income	$ 2,500
Moana Unit #3	Moana Unit #3	Rental Income	$ 4,000
Moana Unit #4	Moana Unit #4	Rental Income	$12,000
Villa Kailani Unit #1	Villa Kailani Unit #1	Rental Income	$ 3,000
Villa Kailani Unit #2	Villa Kailani Unit #2	Rental Income	$ 4,500
Villa Kailani Unit #3	Villa Kailani Unit #3	Rental Income	$ 4,200
Villa Kailani Unit #4	Villa Kailani Unit #4	Rental Income	$ 6,000

Customer Name	Balance Due (Deposits) at 12/31/13
Boeing	$ 10,000
General Motors	$ 75,000
Brice Montoya	−$3,000
Sara Rice	−$6,000
Apple Computer	$ 25,000

Vendor Name	Balance Owed
Reilly Custodial	$4,500
Blue Sky Pools	$1,800

Employee Data	Fran Aki	Daniele Castillo
Social Security #	128-85-7413	984-74-1235
Hire date	1/1/12	1/1/12
Salary	$75,000 per year	n/a
Hourly wage	n/a	$20 per hour
Filing status	Married with one income	Single
Taxes	Subject to Medicare, Social Security, FUTA, and all applicable state taxes	Subject to Medicare, Social Security, FUTA, and all applicable state taxes
Filing state	Hawaii	Hawaii

The company owns two properties: Moana located in Princeville and Villa Kailani located in Poipu. As of 12/31/13, it owed $3,875,000 (a 25-year mortgage classified as a long-term liability called Notes Payable) on the two properties for which it originally paid $2,000,000 and $3,000,000 (respectively) several years ago. Of this amount, $500,000 was identified as land, $250,000 as furniture and equipment, and $4,250,000 as buildings. Use Buildings as the fixed asset account name for the buildings. Accumulated depreciation for all fixed assets as of 12/31/13 was $1,200,000.

The company has one checking account, which had a balance of $15,000 on 12/31/13 with the Bank of Hawaii (account name: checking). Its Hawaii with-holding, unemployment, and disability identification number is 8432518452. Its unemployment tax rate is 1.9%, and the disability tax rate is 0.01%. Only two payroll items are used: Salary and Hourly. Federal taxes are paid to the U.S. Treasury, and state taxes are paid to the State of Hawaii Department of Taxation quarterly. All employees are paid monthly.

You've been asked to reclassify the balance in the Opening Balance Equity account as Capital Stock ($10,000) and Retained Earnings ($70,000). You've also been asked to use account names, not numbers, for all accounts.

Use the information provided here to create a new QuickBooks Accountant file for Aloha. (**Hint:** Read the entire case before you begin, establish the new company file accepting the default name provided, and modify preferences as you did earlier in the chapter. Enter all beginning asset, liability, and equity account balances as of 12/31/13. Use journal entry adjustments to close the Opening Balance Equity account so that there is $10,000 in the Capital Stock account and $24,700 in the Retained Earnings account. Change account names and delete accounts not used so they match up with the following trial balance.) After adjustments, the trial balance at 1/1/14 should look like Figure 6.42.

Aloha Properties
Trial Balance
As of January 1, 2014

	Jan 1, 14	
	Debit	Credit
Checking	15,000.00	
Accounts Receivable	101,000.00	
Accumulated Depreciation		1,200,000.00
Buildings	4,250,000.00	
Furniture and Equipment	250,000.00	
Land	500,000.00	
Accounts Payable		6,300.00
Notes Payable		3,875,000.00
Capital Stock		10,000.00
Opening Bal Equity	0.00	
Retained Earnings		24,700.00
TOTAL	5,116,000.00	5,116,000.00

Figure 6.42

Aloha Properties Trial Balance as of January 1, 2014

Requirements:

Once you've entered all the beginning information, print the following reports as of 1/1/14. (Be sure to keep this QuickBooks Accountant file in a safe place; it will be used as a starting file for this case in Chapter 7.)

1 Customer Balance Summary

2 Vendor Balance Summary

3 Employee Contact List (Employee and SS No. only)

4 Account Listing (Account, Type, and Balance Total only)

5 Item Listing (List only Item, Description, Type, and Price)

6 Trial Balance

Cash-Oriented Business Activities

Student Learning Outcomes

Upon completion of this chapter, the student will be able to:

- Record cash-oriented business transactions classified as financing activities, such as owner contributions
- Record cash-oriented business transactions classified as investing activities, such as equipment purchases
- Record cash-oriented business transactions classified as operating activities, such as inventory purchases, sales, and payroll
- Evaluate a firm's performance and financial position

Case: Wild Water Sports, Inc.

You and Karen completed the initial setup of the QuickBooks Accountant program at the beginning of January and are ready to begin recording business transactions for the month. The new company has completed its first month of business, and Ernesto is pleased with the new business relationship he established with Karen and Donna. However, no one knows the extent of their profitability or financial position because none of the accounting events has yet been recorded into QuickBooks Accountant. You had to start the spring semester, and Karen has been busy just keeping the business going.

"I'm brand new to QuickBooks Accountant," you explain. "I know a little about financial accounting and I'm taking a managerial class right now, but I haven't had a course in QuickBooks Accountant or any other computerized accounting program for that matter."

"No problem," Karen says, trying to reassure you. "QuickBooks Accountant is very easy for first-time users to learn, and you'll be pleased with how much it will help the company understand its performance and financial position."

The two of you agree to meet today to review the business transactions that took place in January. Karen agrees to explain the nature of each transaction and how it should be recorded in QuickBooks Accountant. She suggests that the best way to accomplish this is to view each transaction in terms of the three fundamental business activities: financing, investing, and operating.

"I remember studying those concepts in my first accounting course," you comment. "If I remember correctly, financing activities are initiated when money or other resources are obtained from short-term nontrade creditors, long-term creditors, and/or owners. Financing activities are completed when amounts owed are repaid to or otherwise settled with these same creditors and/or owners. Investing activities are initiated when the money obtained from financing activities is applied to nonoperating uses, such as buying investment securities and/or productive assets like equipment, buildings, land, or furniture and fixtures. Investing activities are completed when the investment securities and/or productive assets are sold. Finally, operating activities occur when the money obtained from financing activities and the productive assets obtained from investing activities are applied to either purchase or produce goods and services for sale. These operating activities are substantially completed when goods are delivered or when services are performed."

"Wow, they taught you well!" Karen exclaims. "Let's begin with a few cash-oriented financing activities."

Recording Cash-Oriented Financing Activities

You begin with two financing activities. The first occurred on January 2 when the company received $200,000 from Karen and Donna ($100,000 each) as their purchase of stock in the company.

Video Demonstration

DEMO 7A - Receive cash from stock sales and borrowings

To record the deposit received from Karen and Donna:

1 Start the QuickBooks Accountant program.

2 Restore the Wild Water Sports Ch 7 (Backup) file that you downloaded from the text web site. See "Data Files" in Chapter 1 if you need more information.

3 The newly restored Wild Water Sports Ch 7.qbw file should now be open.

4 Click the **Record Deposits** icon from the Banking section of the home page. The Make Deposits window appears. Note that QuickBooks Accountant has automatically inserted today's date.

5 Enter the information for Karen and Donna's stock purchase as shown in Figure 7.1. Be sure to enter the correct date and add Karen Wilson to the employee list.

6 Click **Save & New** to record the deposit. Do not close the Make Deposits window.

Figure 7.1

Make Deposits Window

Be sure to enter the correct date

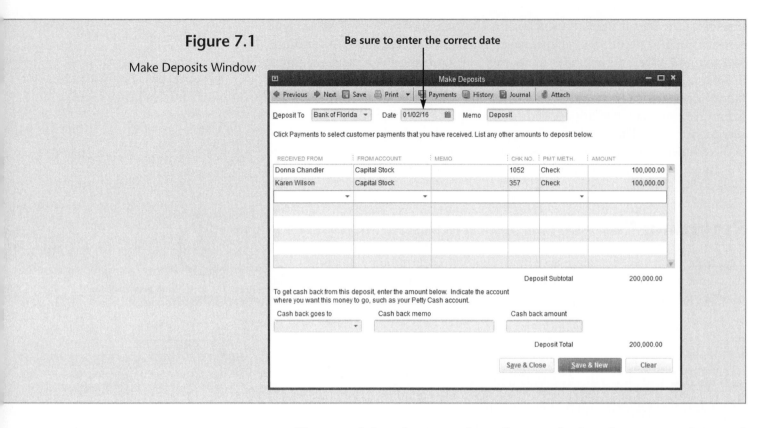

The second deposit was made on January 4 when the company borrowed $250,000 from their bank (Bank of Florida) at 5%, payable in five years.

To record the long-term loan from the Bank of Florida:

1 Select account **Bank of Florida** as the Deposit To account.

2 Type **1/04/16** as the deposit date.

3 Type **Bank of Florida** in the received from text box and then press **[Tab]**.

4 Click **Quick Add** in the Name Not Found window.

5 Click **Other** in the Select Name Type window and then click **OK**.

6 Select account **Loan Payable** as the From account.

7 Type **250000** as the amount and then click **Save & Close**.

You have now recorded two different cash-oriented financing activities: the sale of stock to investors and the borrowing of funds on a long-term basis. Now it's time to look at recording cash-oriented investing activities.

Video Demonstration

DEMO 7B - Investing funds and purchasing furniture

Recording Cash-Oriented Investing Activities

After making the deposits from investors and creditors, the company decided to temporarily invest those funds in a money market account with its bank. By transferring those funds from its checking account to a money market account, the company expected to generate some interest revenue until the funds were needed. To accomplish this transfer, Karen wrote Check No. 1001 on January 8 from the company's checking account with Bank of Florida and deposited the check into their new money market account with ETrade.

"Do we have a general ledger account for this?" you ask.

"No, but we can create one while we record this transaction," Karen answers.

To create a new general ledger account and record the purchase of money market funds:

1   Click the **Write Checks** icon from the Banking section of the home page. The Write Checks window appears.

2   Uncheck the **Print Later** check box if it is checked.

3   Type **1001** in the No. text box.

4   Type **1/8/16** as the date.

5   Type **ETrade** in the Pay to the Order of section of the check, and then press **[Tab]**.

6   Click **Quick Add** in the Name Not Found window.

7   Select **Other** in the Select Name Type window and then click **OK**.

8   Type **300000** as the check amount, and then press **[Tab]** three times or until the cursor is in the account section of the check.

Trouble? Near the bottom of the Write Checks window are two tabs—one labeled Expenses and one labeled Items. The Expenses tab is somewhat misleading because you can type or select any account to appear here, including assets. On the other hand, you use the Items tab to enter inventory acquisitions only. The main difference between them is that the Items tab has a column for quantities purchased and the Expenses tab has a column for an account.

9   In the Expenses tab, select **<Add New>** from the drop-down arrow list of accounts. (*Note:* You may have to scroll up the list to the top to find <Add New>.) An Add New Account: Choose Account Type window should appear.

10 Select **Bank** as the Account Type, and then click **Continue**.

11 Type **Short-Term Investments** as the Account Name. Your screen should look like Figure 7.2.

Figure 7.2

Entering a New General Ledger
Account

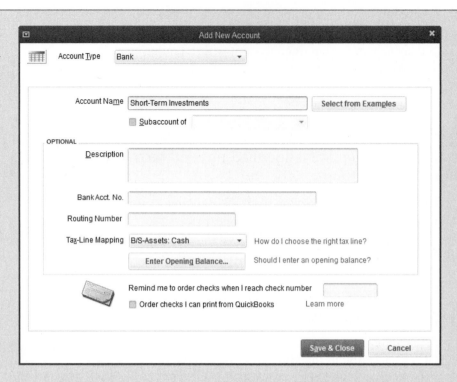

12   Click **Save & Close** to record this new general ledger account. Your Write Checks window should look like Figure 7.3.

Figure 7.3

Writing a Check for a Short-Term
Investment

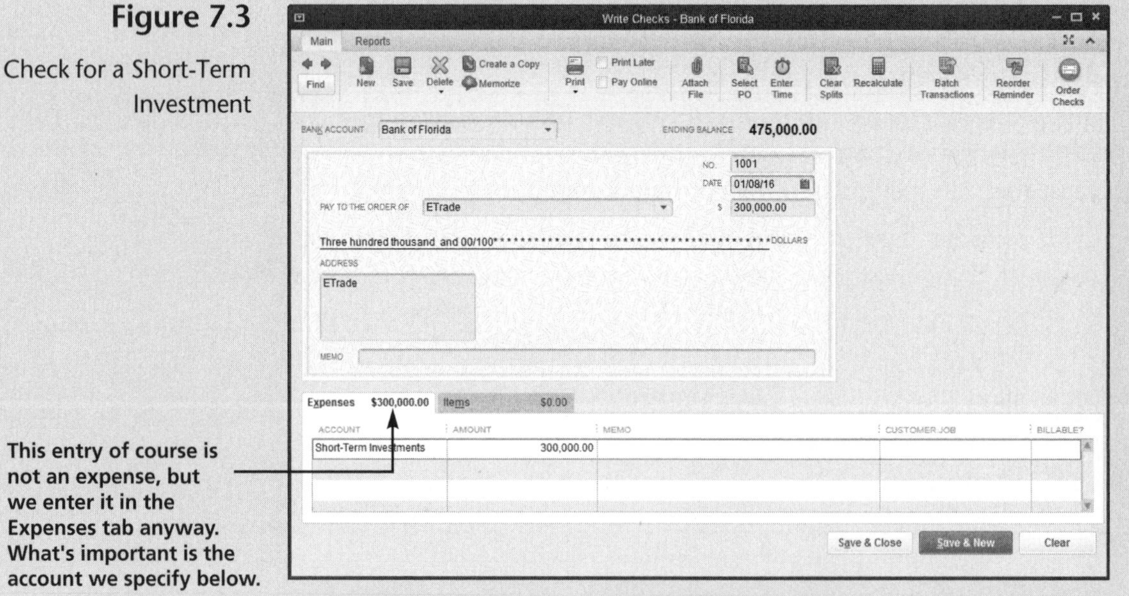

This entry of course is
not an expense, but
we enter it in the
Expenses tab anyway.
What's important is the
account we specify below.

13   Click **Save & New** to record this transaction. Do not close this window.

Wild Water also had other cash-oriented investment activities in January. On January 9, it purchased new office furniture for the sales, marketing, and service staff from the local Staples store and new equipment for the service bays from AJ Marine Equipment.

To record the purchase of furniture and equipment:

1 Type **1002** as the check number (if it is not already there).

   Trouble? If you previously closed the Write Checks window, open it again by clicking the Write Checks icon on the home page.

2 Type **1/9/16** as the date of purchase in the Write Checks window.

3 Type **Staples** in the Pay to the Order of section of the check, and then press **[Tab]**.

4 Click **Quick Add** in the Name Not Found window.

5 Select **Vendor** in the Select Name Type window and then click **OK**.

6 Type **70000** as the check amount, and then press **[Tab]** three times or until the cursor is in the account section of the check.

7 In the Expenses tab, select **Furniture and Equipment** from the drop-down arrow list of accounts.

8 Click **Save & New** to enter another purchase.

9 Type **1003** as the check number (if it is not already there).

10 Type **1/11/16** as the date of purchase in the Write Checks window.

11 Type **AJ Marine Equipment** in the Pay to the Order of section of the check, and then press **[Tab]**.

12 Click **Quick Add** in the Name Not Found window.

13 Select **Vendor** in the Select Name Type window and then click **OK**.

14 Type **100000** as the check amount, and then press **[Tab]** three times or until the cursor is in the account section of the check.

15 In the Expenses tab, select **Furniture and Equipment** from the drop-down arrow list of accounts and then press **[Tab]** twice. Your check should look like Figure 7.4.

16 Click **Save & Close** to complete this process.

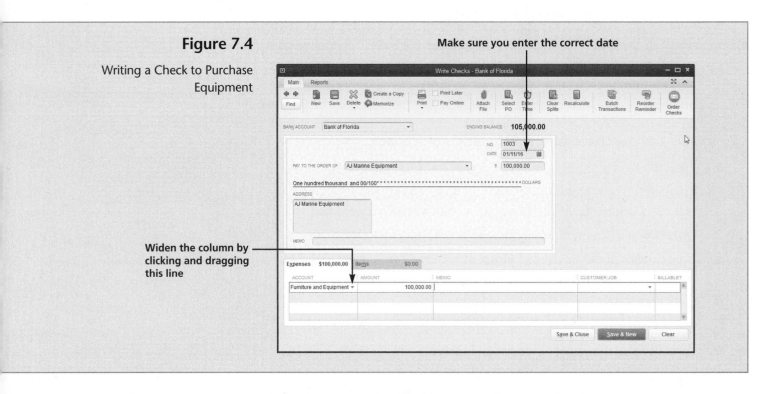

Figure 7.4

Writing a Check to Purchase Equipment

Karen explains that, since Wild Water is using the Accountant version of QuickBooks, they have access to QuickBooks Fixed Asset Manager application, which runs separate from QuickBooks Accountant.

"When the Fixed Asset Manager is started from within QuickBooks Accountant, it can extract information about fixed assets from our company file," she comments. "We can determine depreciation for the assets and post a journal entry back to our QuickBooks Accountant file. Alternatively, we can enter assets directly into the Fixed Asset Manager and send that information back to QuickBooks Accountant."

"Which method are we going to use?" you ask.

"We'll enter the general ledger accounting for the purchase of fixed assets here and then enter the detail behind the purchase later using the Fixed Asset Manager," she answers. (*Note:* This will be explained further in Chapter 12.)

"When is depreciation recorded on fixed assets?" you ask.

"Not until the end of the accounting period, before we create financial statements," Karen responds. "The Fixed Asset Manager can help us do that as well but we have lots to do before that."

Recording Cash-Oriented Operating Activities

Video Demonstration

DEMO 7F - Order, receive, and pay for inventory

Karen explains that Wild Water uses purchase orders to help manage its business activities. She remarks that purchase orders do not usually have an impact on financial statements, but they do play an important role as a control feature in QuickBooks Accountant. So she plans on using them.

"For example," she says, "we ordered two custom boats for two customers in January using purchase orders 4001 and 4002. Let me show you how purchase orders are used in QuickBooks Accountant."

"Are all purchase orders related to customers?" you ask.

"Not necessarily," Karen responds. "Sometimes we order for inventory to have in our showroom, but in these two we were ordering boats for specific customers."

The first boat was an existing inventory item (Malibu WakeSetter XTI sold for $70,000) and was ordered for an existing customer from an existing vendor. The second boat was for a new item (Tige 22v sold for $78,750) and was ordered from an existing vendor but for a new customer. In both transactions, the customer was required to pay a 25% deposit upon order ($17,500.00 and $19,687.50, respectively).

"How do you account for the amounts received?" you ask.

"We treat them just like payments received from customers, but since there is no invoice to allocate them to, we just leave them as credit balances in customers' accounts," Karen answers. "Accounting would normally require you to treat these as unearned revenue and record them as liabilities; however, we make adjustments for credit balances in accounts only if, prior to preparing financial statements, we still have remaining credits in customer accounts."

Karen decides to first show you the purchase orders generated to place the order with the vendors and then how to account for the two deposits on sales.

To create a purchase order:

1   Click the **Purchase Orders** icon from the Vendors section of the home page to open the Create Purchase Orders window.

2   Select **Malibu Boats** from the Vendor drop-down list.

3   Type **1/12/16** as the date.

4   Type **4001** as the P.O. No.

5   Select **MW XTI** as the item, type **1** as the Qty (quantity), and select **Florida Sports Camp** as the customer for which we are ordering the boat. (You'll need to add them as a new customer.) Your purchase order should now look like Figure 7.5.

Note the historical information on the purchase order. Click on the Hide History arrow to hide this information. Once hidden, the arrow will reappear if you want to show this information again.

Figure 7.5

Purchase Order No. 4001

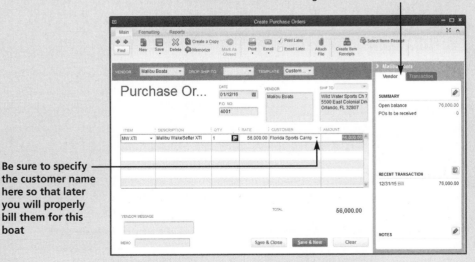

Be sure to specify the customer name here so that later you will properly bill them for this boat

6 Click on the **Hide History** arrow to hide this information and then click **Save & New**. Note that QuickBooks Accountant may identify a word it doesn't know and, before processing this purchase order, a Check Spelling on Form window may appear to verify the spelling of WakeSetter.

7 Add **Tige Boats** to the Vendor drop-down list in the new purchase order form.

8 Type **1/12/16** as the date (if it's not already there).

9 Type **4002** as the P.O. No. (if it's not already there).

10 Select **<Add New>** from the drop-down Item list to display the New Item window.

11 Select **Inventory Part** from the drop-down Type list.

12 Type **T 22v** as the Item Name/Number and **Tige 22v** as the Description for both purchase and sales transactions.

13 Type **63000** as the Cost.

14 Leave Cost of Goods Sold as the COGS Account.

15 Select **Tige Boats** as the Preferred Vendor.

16 Type **78750** as the Sales Price.

17 Leave Tax as the Tax Code.

18 Add **Boat Sales** as a new Income Account.

19 Add Inventory Boats as the Asset Account. The New Item window should look like Figure 7.6.

Figure 7.6

Creating a New Item from a Purchase Order

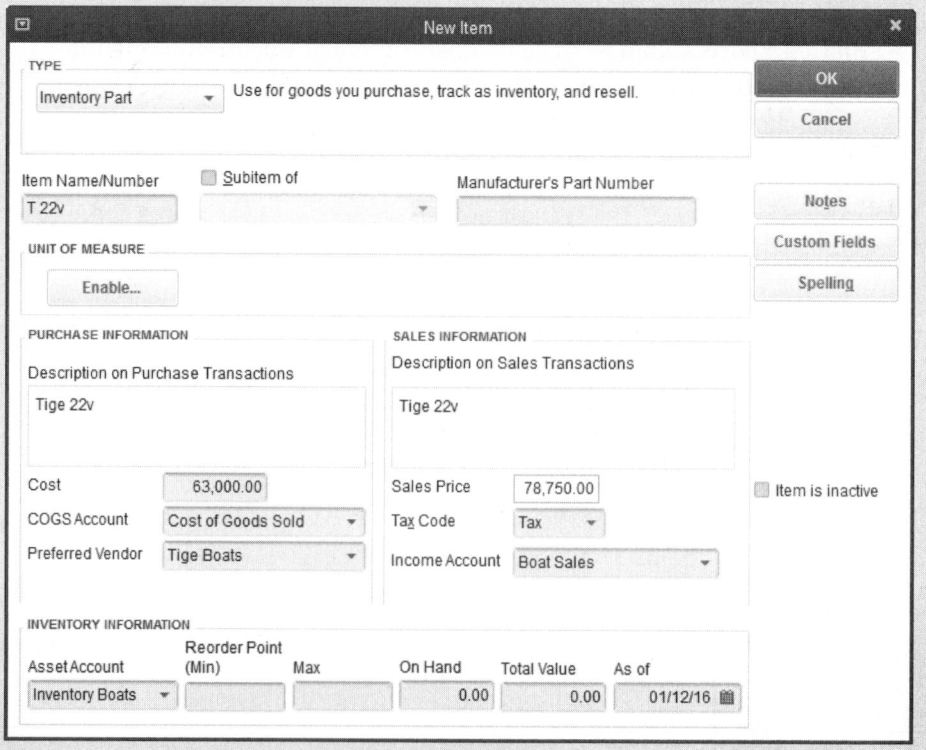

20 Click **OK** to accept this new item and add Tige to the dictionary if necessary.

21 Type **1** as the Qty.

22 Select **<Add New>** from the drop-down Customer list to display the New Customer window.

23 Type **Performance Rentals** as the Customer Name and Company Name.

24 Type **15 Hwy 22, Orlando, FL 32807** as the customer's address.

25 Click **Copy >>** to copy the Bill To address to the Ship To address section. Click **OK** to accept. Your New Customer window should look like Figure 7.7.

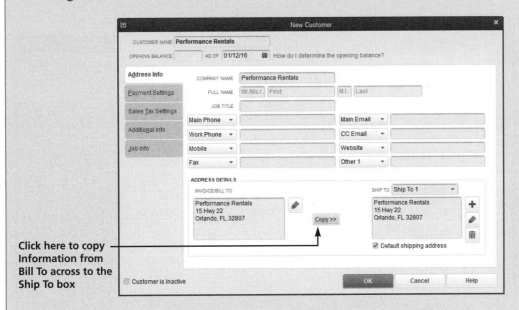

Figure 7.7

Adding a New Customer

Click here to copy Information from Bill To across to the Ship To box

26 Click **OK** to add this new customer.

27 Click **Save & Close** to add this new purchase order.

Karen has shown you how to create purchase orders and now would like to show you how to account for the customers' deposits. Remember, in both cases customers remitted cash to Wild Water Sports, but a sale could not be recorded because the products had not been delivered and thus the earnings process was not complete.

Video Demonstration

DEMO 7D - Receive and deposit cash

To record the receipt of deposits on future sales:

1 Click the **Receive Payments** icon located in the Customers section of the home page.

2 Select **Florida Sports Camp** as the customer from which the first deposit was received.

3 Type **17500** as the amount received.

4 Type the date **1/12/16**.

5 Select **Check** as the payment method.

6 Type **8755** in the Check # text box. Your Receive Payments window should look like Figure 7.8.

Figure 7.8

Receive Payments
Window

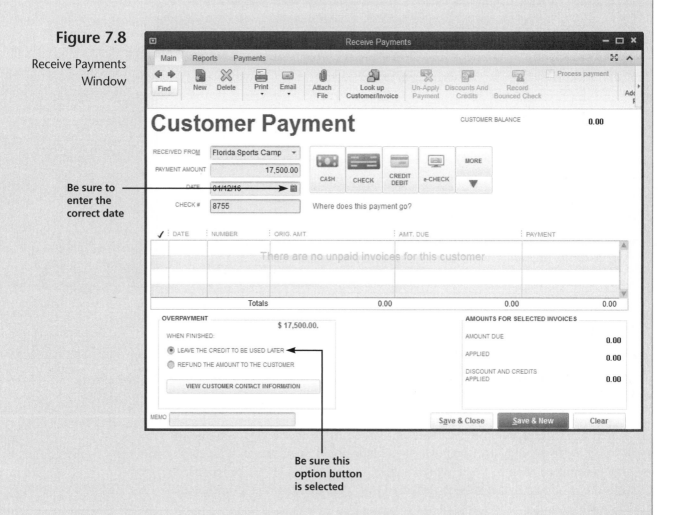

7 Click **Save & New** to record another deposit.

8 Click **OK** to save the credit on the customer's account and not print a credit memo.

9 Select **Performance Rentals** as the customer from which the second deposit was received.

10 Type **19687.50** as the amount received.

11 Type the date **1/12/16**.

12 Select **Credit Debit Card** and then select **MasterCard** as the payment method.

13 Type **2158-6412-9842-9855** as the credit card number and **04/17** as the expiration date and then click **Done**. Your Receive Payments window should look like Figure 7.9.

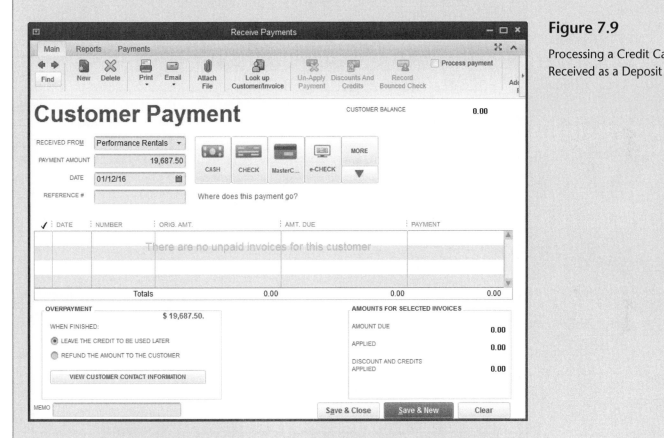

Figure 7.9

Processing a Credit Card Received as a Deposit

14 Click **Save & Close** to exit, and then click **OK** once again to leave this credit balance for the customer.

"Typically, we collect cash from sales on account, such as sales made to customers where we gave them credit terms like net 30," Karen comments. "If you recall when we set up our accounting system on January 1, 2016, we had some customers who owed us money from previous sales. The balances owed were reflected in accounts receivable."

"Do you record those cash collections like we just recorded deposits?" you ask.

"Yes, plus we had some cash sales during January that I'll show you as well," Karen answers. "We had one cash boat sale and one cash boat service during the month, both from new customers."

To record cash collected on account:

1   Click the **Receive Payments** icon located in the Customers section of the home page.

2   Select **Buena Vista Water Sports** from the Received From drop-down list.

3   Type **30000** as the amount received.

4   Type **1/15/16** as the date received.

5   Select **Check** as the payment method and type **65454** as the check number. Your screen should look like Figure 7.10.

Figure 7.10

Receipt of Payments from Customer on Account

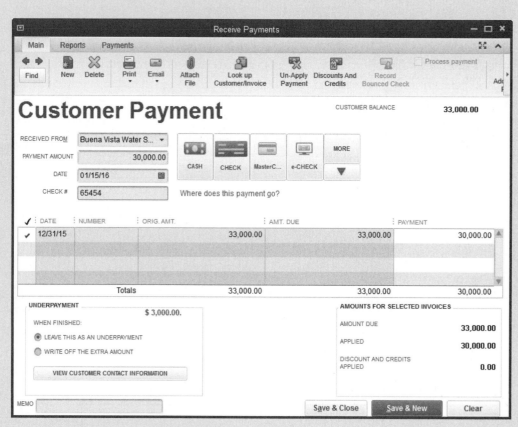

6   Click **Save & Close** to complete this transaction.

Video Demonstration

DEMO 7G - Sell inventory and apply deposits

To record cash sales:

1   Click the **Create Sales Receipts** icon located in the Customers section of the home page.

2   Select **<Add New>** from the Customer:Job drop-down list.

3 Type **Seth Backman** as both the Customer Name and Company Name.

4 Type this customer's Bill To and Ship To address as **140 Fir Ave., Miami, FL 33109**.

5 Click **OK** to accept this new customer.

6 Type **1/16/16** as the date of sale and **6001** as the Sale No.

7 Type **161** as the check number and select **Check** as the payment method.

8 Select **MS LX** from the drop-down list of items.

9 Type **1** as the Qty.

10 Select **State Tax** from the Tax drop-down list if it is not already there.

11 Make sure the Print Later check box is unchecked. Your screen should look like Figure 7.11.

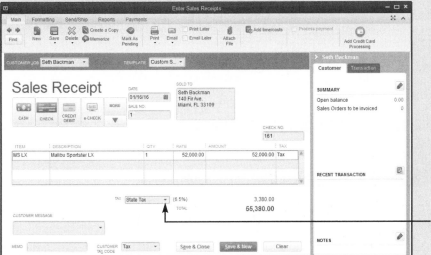

Figure 7.11

Recording Cash Sales with a Sales Receipt

Be sure State Tax is selected here

12 Click the **Hide History** arrow and then click **Save & New** to record another sales receipt. Click **Yes** if asked to have the new tax item appear next time.

13 Select **<Add New>** from the Customer:Job drop-down list.

14 Type **Alisa Hay** as both the Customer Name and Company Name.

15 Type this customer's Bill To and Ship To address as **2999 Dover Blvd., Daytona Beach, FL 32114**.

16 Click **OK** to accept this new customer.

17 Type **1/26/16** as the date of sale and then accept **6002** as the Sale No.

18 Select **Cash** as the payment method.

19 Select **Engine Service** from the drop-down list of items.

20 Type **1** as the Qty.

21 Add **Engine Oil** to the drop-down list of items. (You will need to add Parts Sales as the Income account and Inventory Parts as the Asset account.)

22 Type **5** as the Qty.

23 Click **OK** in the two warning windows that appear. (Since you're recording these transactions after the events have already occurred, your timing may be off from the actual acquisition of inventory items like engine oil and the date you record the receipt of those items.)

24 Add **Oil Filter** to the drop-down list of items.

25 Click **OK** in the warning window that appears.

26 Type **1** as the Qty. Click **OK** in the two warning windows that appear.

27 Select **State Tax** from the Tax drop-down list.

28 Make sure the Print Later check box is unchecked. Your screen should look like Figure 7.12.

Figure 7.12

Recording More Cash Sales with a Sales Receipt

Click and drag here to increase width of column to view all of the items

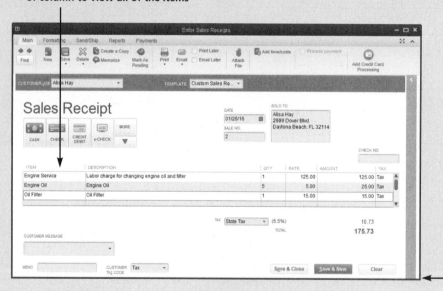

Click and drag here to increase the size of the receipt to view more lines

29 Click **Save & Close**. Click **Yes** to accept tax change.

"Have all of these cash receipt transactions been recorded in our checking account?" you ask.

"No, one of the preferences we specified in the company setup was that all cash receipts like payments on account, advance payments, etc., are to be recorded into an Undeposited Funds account since bank deposits are often made at a different time than cash is actually received," Karen answers. "We've made those deposits now, so let me show you how we record them in Quick-Books Accountant."

To record cash deposits made to banks:

1 Click the **Record Deposits** icon located in the Banking section of the home page. The Payments to Deposit window should appear as shown in Figure 7.13.

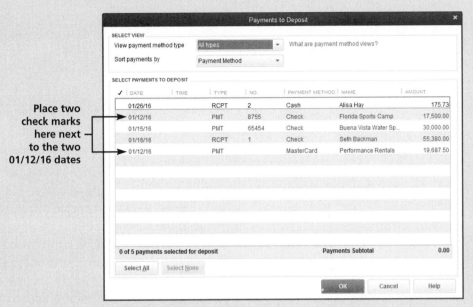

Place two check marks here next to the two 01/12/16 dates

Figure 7.13

Payments to Deposit

2 Click next to the two **1/12/16** dates to place a check next to each, and then click **OK**.

3 Type **1/14/16** as the date of deposit. Your window should look like Figure 7.14. Note the default Deposit To account should be the account Bank of Florida. Note also that the From Account is the Undeposited Funds account, which is where the payments were recorded when first received and accounted for.

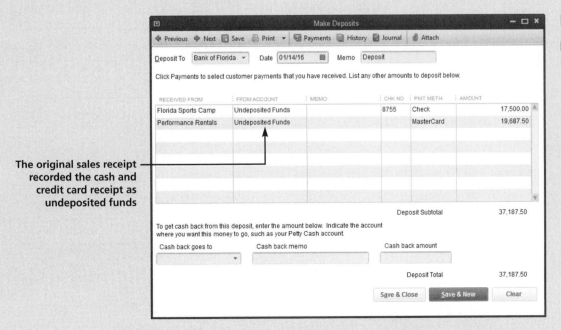

The original sales receipt recorded the cash and credit card receipt as undeposited funds

Figure 7.14

Make Deposits Window

4 Click **Save & New**.

5 Click next to the **1/15/16** and **1/16/16** dates to place a check next to each and then click **OK**.

6 Type **1/16/16** as the date of deposit.

7 Click **Save & New**.

8 Click next to the **1/26/16** date to place a check next to that payment, and then click **OK**.

9 Type **1/28/16** as the date of deposit.

10 Click **Save & Close**.

You have now accounted for the payments received from customers and the bank deposits that reflect amounts deposited to the checking account. Karen explains that the next item on your list is to record the inventory received from purchase order 1001 and the related payment to the vendor.

"When inventory received is related to a purchase order, it's important to do more than just record the check which paid for the inventory," Karen points out. "We also have to close out the purchase order and properly record the receipt of inventory. In this case, we received the two boats ordered under purchase orders 1001 and 1002. Both of these were cash-only purchases in that the vendor did not extend us credit and thus payment was due on receipt. Thus, we'll use the Write Checks process to record these transactions."

Video Demonstration

DEMO 7F - Order, receive, and pay for inventory

To record the receipt and payment of inventory:

1 Click the **Write Checks** icon located in the Banking section of the home page.

2 Select **Malibu Boats** from the Pay to the order of drop-down list. An Open POs Exist window should appear as shown in Figure 7.15.

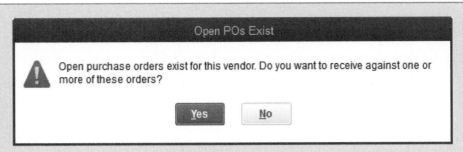

Figure 7.15

Open Purchase Order Warning

3   Click **Yes**. An Open Purchase Orders window should appear as shown in Figure 7.16.

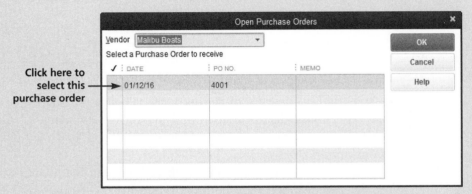

Figure 7.16

Open Purchase Orders for Malibu Boats

4   Click next to the **1/12/16** date to place a check mark on the purchase order 4001 line and then click **OK**. If a Warning window appears then click **OK** and ignore the warning since, although we owe funds to Malibu Boats from a previous purchase, we are not accounting for that payment at this point.

5   Type **1004** as the check number if it is not already present. (You may have to uncheck the Print Later check box.)

6   Type **1/29/16** as the check date. Your window should look like Figure 7.17.

7   Note that, because this transaction was treated as the payment for and receipt of inventory, the transaction is recorded using the Items tab, and the item being received is that item ordered under purchase order 4001 for $56,000. Click **Save & New** to continue.

8   Select **Tige Boats** from the Pay to the order of drop-down list. An Open POs Exist window should appear.

9   Click **Yes**. An Open Purchase Orders window should appear.

10   Click next to the **1/12/16** date to place a check mark on the purchase order 4002 line and then click **OK**.

11   Type **1005** as the check number if it is not already present.

12   Type **1/30/16** as the check date.

13   Click **Save & Close**.

Figure 7.17

Payment for Inventory Received

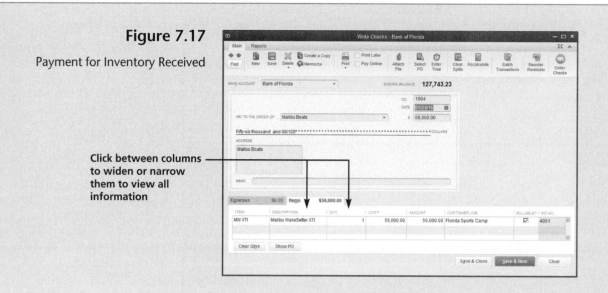

Click between columns to widen or narrow them to view all information

Karen explains that, as a result of paying these vendors for boats received under purchase orders, cash has decreased and inventory has increased. Both customers for whom these boats were ordered were contacted, and they picked up their boats on January 30.

"I'll show you how we record the sales of these boats via the invoice process," Karen says. "Remember that both of these customers remitted their deposits when we placed the order, and thus we only need to collect the remaining 75% balance owed."

"How do we account for the deposits already received?" you ask.

"Recall that, when we received these deposits earlier in January, we credited each of these customers' accounts receivable balances," she answers. "Because of that, we need to use the invoicing process to record the sales first, apply the existing credits, and then separately record the receipt of the balance due on the sale. Let me first show you how to record these two invoices."

Video Demonstration

DEMO 7G - Sell inventory and apply deposits

To record the sales of inventory, application of advanced deposits received, and receipt of payment for the balance due:

1 Click the **Create Invoices** icon located in the Customers section of the home page.

2 Select **Florida Sports Camp** from the Customer:Job drop-down list. A Billable Time/Costs window should appear indicating that this customer has billable costs.

3   Check the **Save this as a preference** check box as shown in Figure 7.18 and then click **OK**.

Figure 7.18

Billable Time/Costs

4   Click the **Items** tab to reveal the information shown in Figure 7.19. Note that this window identifies that an item has been received for Florida Sports Camp and is available for billing. Click next to the **1/29/16** date in the ✓column to place a check mark there, indicating you would like to bill the customer for this item.

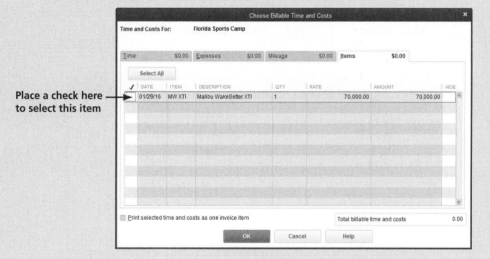

Figure 7.19

Choosing Billable Costs

5   Click **OK**.

6   Type **1/30/16** as the invoice date and **10001** as the Invoice #.

7   Click the **Hide History** arrow, uncheck the **Print Later** and **Email Later** check boxes, and then complete the invoice by adding a Tax Code, a Bill To address, and a Ship To address as shown in Figure 7.20.

Figure 7.20

Invoicing Billable Costs

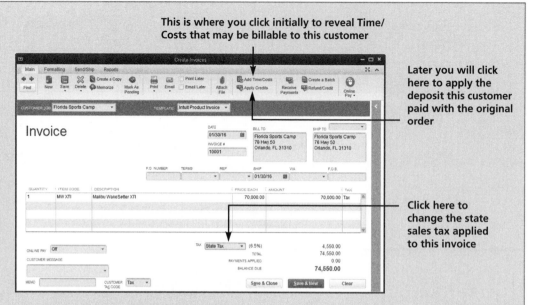

Figure 7.21

Apply Credits Window

8 Click the **Apply Credits** button.

9 Click **Yes** two times to accept the changes you made to the invoice and customer. An Apply Credits window should appear like that shown in Figure 7.21.

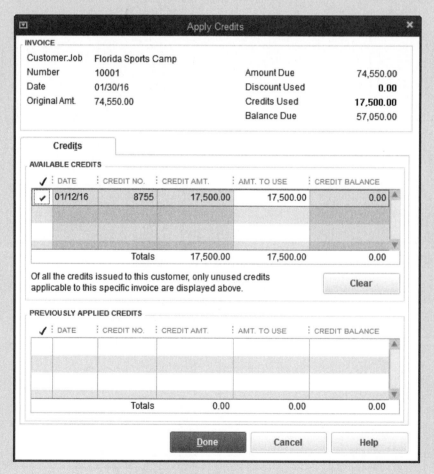

10 Note that the credit balance shown is the deposit we recorded earlier this month and that it is prechecked for application. Click **Done** to apply this credit to the balance owed on the invoice.

11 Click **Save & New** to record this invoice.

12 Select **Performance Rentals** from the Customer:Job drop-down list and then click the **Items** tab.

13 Check the ✓**column** next to the 1/30/16 date.

14 Click **OK**.

15 Click **Apply Credits**, click **Yes** to save your changes, and then click **Done**. You may have to uncheck the **Email Later** check box to proceed.

16 Change the Tax to State Tax.

17 Click **Save & Close**, and then click **Yes** twice as before.

Now that the invoices are recorded, it follows that sales and accounts receivable have been increased, cost of goods sold has been increased, and inventory has been decreased. Wild Water can now record the receipt of full payment from the customers and record the related deposit to their bank account. Florida Sports Camp remitted $57,050.00 as the balance due on their purchase, while Performance Rentals remitted $64,181.25.

To record the payment and deposit of funds from boat sales:

1 Click the **Receive Payments** icon located in the Customers section of the home page.

2 Select **Florida Sports Camp** from the Received From drop-down list.

3 Type **57050.00** as the amount received. (Note that this is the amount shown as due from them.)

4 Type **1/30/16** as the date received.

5 Type Check # **4532**. Your Receive Payments window should look like Figure 7.22.

6 Click **Save & New**.

7 Select **Performance Rentals** from the Received From drop-down list.

8 Type **64181.25** as the amount received. (Note that this is the amount shown as due from them.)

9 Type **1/30/16** as the date received.

10 Type Check # **10885**.

11 Click **Save & Close**.

12 Click **Record Deposits** from the Banking section of the home page.

Figure 7.22

Recording Balance of
Payment Due from
Customer

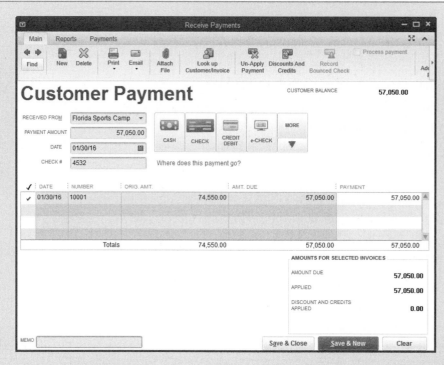

13 Click next to both cash receipts dated **1/30/16** to include them in this deposit, and then click **OK**.

14 Click **Save & Close** to record this deposit.

"Next," Karen comments, "I'd like to show you how Wild Water will pay for monthly expenses and bills. Currently, most of our vendors want us to pay on receipt of their bills, so we've been recording expenses only when we pay the bills. In a couple of months, we will be in a position to ask for credit terms from most of our vendors. In the meantime, we write checks at the end of the month to pay for expenses."

One of their payments was for insurance for the year, which will be treated as prepaid insurance and adjusted prior to preparing financial statements. A second payment represents inventory parts received earlier in the month (oil, air filters, and oil filters used in servicing boats). Still another represents an amount due to Malibu Boats, which was established as a liability when the company was first set up. This payment requires the use of QuickBooks Accountant's bill payment process. The balance of their payments this month relate to expenses already incurred.

"Let's first look at how we pay for expenses and inventory parts," Karen suggests.

Video Demonstration

DEMO 7H - Pay expenses

To record checks written for expenses and inventory parts:

1 Click the **Write Checks** icon in the Banking section of the home page.

2 Type **1006** as the check number if it is not already there.

3 Type **1/31/16** as the check date.

4 Type **Manchester Insurance** in the Pay to the Order of section of the check and then press **[Tab]**.

5 Click **SetUp** in the Name Not Found window.

6 Select **Vendor** from the Select Name Type window, and then click **OK**.

7 Type **Manchester Insurance** in the Company Name text box.

8 Type the vendor's address as **234 Wilshire Blvd., Los Angeles, CA 91335**.

9 Click **OK** in the New Vendor window.

10 Type **22000** as the check amount and then press **[Tab]** three times.

11 Select the **Expenses** tab and then select **<Add New>** from the Account drop-down list.

12 Select the **Other Account Types** option and then select **Other Current Asset** from the drop-down list in the Add New Account window.

13 Click **Continue**.

14 Type **Prepaid Insurance** in the Account section, and then click **Save & Close**.

15 Press **[Tab]** twice. Your window should look like Figure 7.23.

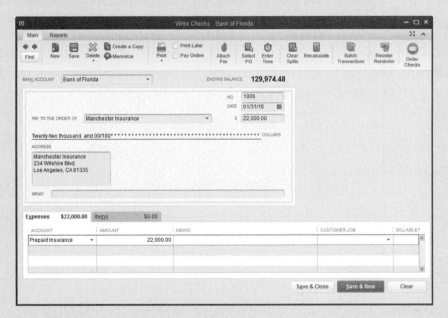

Figure 7.23

Payment for Prepaid Insurance

16 Click **Save & New**.

17 Type **1007** as the check number if it is not already there.

18 Type **1/31/16** as the check date if it is not already there.

19 Type **Chevron** in the Pay to the Order of section of the check, and then press **[Tab]**.

20 Click **SetUp** in the Name Not Found window.

21 Select **Vendor** from the Select Name Type window, and then click **OK**.

22 Type **Chevron** in the Company Name text box.

23 Type the vendor's address as **2389 Peachtree Blvd., Atlanta, GA 30311**.

24 Click **OK** in the New Vendor window.

25 Type **1600** as the check amount and then press **[Tab]**.

26 Click the **Items** tab to make it active.

27 Add **Air Filter** to the Item drop-down list.

28 Type **25** as the Qty.

29 Click in the next line below the air filter you just added.

30 Select **Engine Oil** from the Item drop-down list.

31 Type **150** as the Qty.

32 Click in the next line below the engine oil you just added.

33 Select **Oil Filter** from the Item drop-down list.

34 Type **25** as the Qty and then press **[Tab]**. Your screen should look like Figure 7.24.

Figure 7.24

Payment for Inventory Parts

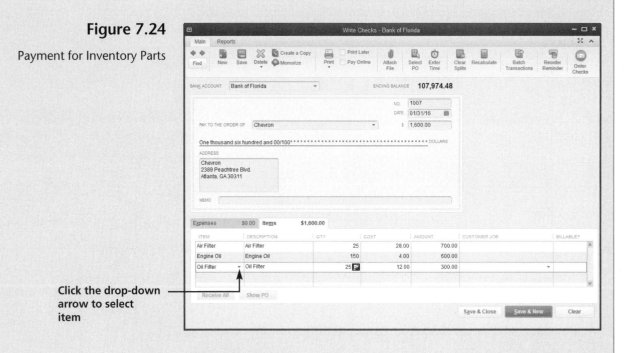

Click the drop-down arrow to select item

35 Click **Save & New**.

36 Type **1008** as the check number if it is not already there.

37 Type **1/31/16** as the check date if it is not already there.

38 Type **Central Florida Gas & Electric** in the Pay to the Order of section of the check and then press **[Tab]**.

39 Click **Quick Add** in the Name Not Found window.

40 Select **Vendor** from the Select Name Type window, and then click **OK**.

41 Type **890** as the amount.

42 Click the **Expenses** tab to make it active.

43 Select **Utilities** from the Account drop-down list and press **[Tab]** twice. Your window should look like Figure 7.25.

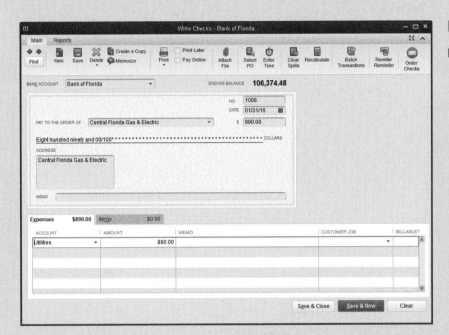

Figure 7.25

Payment of Utilities

44 Click **Save & New**.

45 Type **1009** as the check number if it is not already there.

46 Type **1/31/16** as the check date if it is not already there.

47 Type **Verizon** in the Pay to the Order of section of the check, and then press **[Tab]**.

48 Click **Quick Add** in the Name Not Found window.

49 Select **Vendor** from the Select Name Type window, and then click **OK**.

50 Type **1700** as the amount.

51 Click the **Expenses** tab to make it active.

52 Select **Telephone Expense** from the Account drop-down list.

53 Click **Save & Close**.

"Let's now look at how we pay for bills already established in accounts payable," Karen suggests.

To record checks written to pay bills:

1 Click the **Pay Bills** icon in the Vendor section of the home page. The Pay Bills window should appear as shown in Figure 7.26.

Figure 7.26

Payment of Bills

Click here to select this bill for payment →

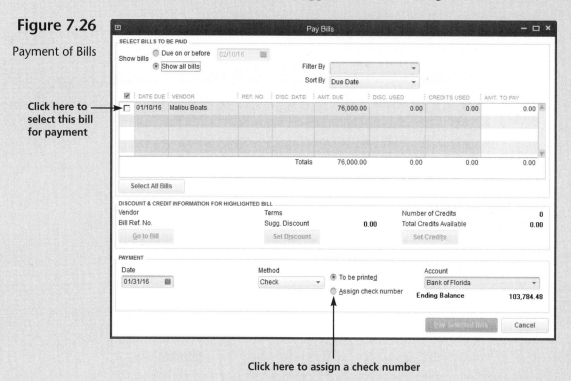

Click here to assign a check number

2 Click next to the **1/10/16** date to select this bill for payment.

3 Click in the **Assign check number** option button.

4 Click **Pay Selected Bills**.

5 Type **1010** as the check number assigned to this payment as shown in Figure 7.27.

Figure 7.27

Assigning Check Numbers

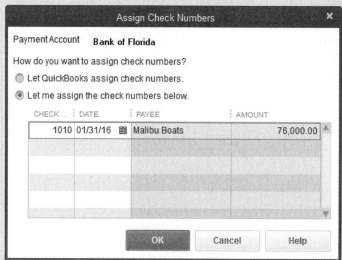

6 Click **OK** and then click **Done**.

Now it's time to calculate payroll. Karen explains that entering information about payroll is a little tricky because Wild Water has decided not to use Quick-Books Accountant's payroll service. To participate at any level would have required a monthly or annual fee and, since Wild Water has so few employees, the company has decided to compute payroll manually.

"Is that why we previously set up Wild Water to calculate payroll manually?" you ask.

"Exactly," Karen answers. "That was a part of the QuickBooks Accountant setup process. Now we are going to enter payroll information for the month of January."

"Wouldn't it be faster to use the payroll service?" you ask.

"Well, yes," she responds, "but, as you'll see, entering payroll withholding and tax information manually isn't that difficult."

"QuickBooks Accountant has a nice time sheet capability, which is how we'll track Ryder's and Pat's time," Karen explains. "It also has a job cost tracking feature so that, when either Ryder or Pat works on a specific boat, their time can be automatically charged to a customer and a specific job for that customer. Time sheets are typically used when a company is trying to keep track of hours worked on specific jobs, but they are not required. Many companies who don't track job costs will only enter the hours for each employee right before processing the payroll. However, in this company's situation, time sheets are very helpful. Before we can enter the employees' time, we must make sure that a customer/job entry is set up. Later, we'll do this during the month as each job is started, but for now we'll enter them after the fact. Two jobs were started in the last couple of days of January, one for Florida Sports Camp and one for Freebirds. Let me show you how to create those jobs entries, both of which are for customers we've already created in QuickBooks Accountant."

Video Demonstration

DEMO 7I - Recording payroll timesheets

To create new jobs for existing customers:

1 Click the **Customers** button in the Customers section of the home page to open the Customer Center.

2 Select **Florida Sports Camp** from the list of customers and jobs.

3 Click the **New Customer & Job** button and then select **Add Job** from the menu options provided as shown in Figure 7.28.

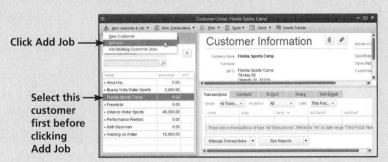

Figure 7.28

Creating a New Job

4 Type **50001** as the Job Name, and then click **OK**.

5 Add **Freebirds** to the list of customers and jobs.

6 Click the **New Customer & Job** button, and then select **Add Job** from the menu options provided.

7 Type **50002** as the Job Name, and then click **OK**.

8 The Customer Center should now reflect the two new jobs added and should look like Figure 7.29.

Figure 7.29

Customer Center Window

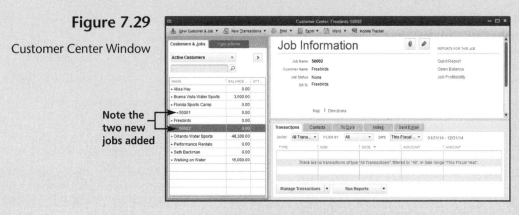

Note the two new jobs added

9 Close the Customer Center window.

With the two new jobs added, Karen explains that you can now enter the hours worked into QuickBooks Accountant's time sheets, which are organized by week.

To complete weekly time sheets for January:

1 Click the **Enter Time** icon from the Employees section of the home page.

2 Select **Use Weekly Time Sheet** from the menu options provided.

3 Click the **Calendar** icon and then click either the right or left arrow to navigate to the month of January 2016 as shown in Figure 7.30.

4 Click the **4** in the January calendar.

5 Select **Ryder Zacovic** from the drop-down name list presented in the weekly time sheet and then click **Yes** to set up this employee to use time data.

6 Choose **Hourly** from the Payroll Item drop-down list.

7 Type **6** and **4** as the hours worked on M 1/4/16 and Tu 1/5/16, respectively.

8 Click the **Billable** column (the far right column), which will uncheck the billable check box and so indicate that this line is not billable. Your screen should look like Figure 7.31.

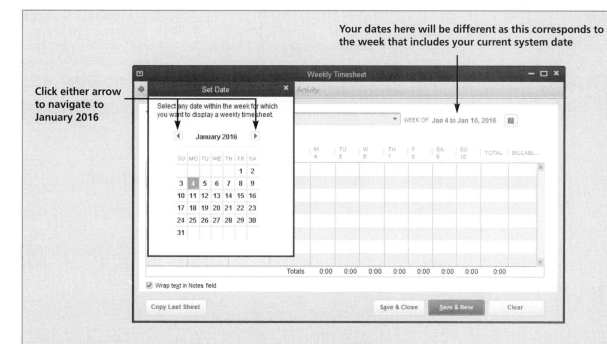

Figure 7.30

Setting Time
Sheet Date

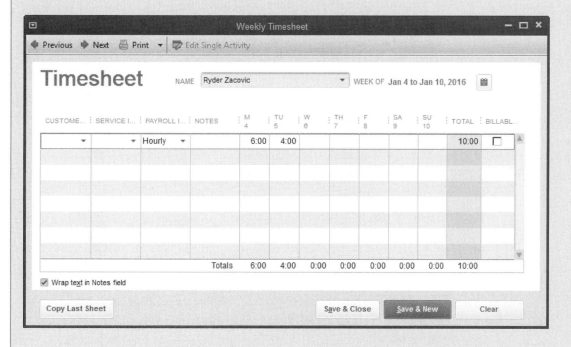

Figure 7.31

Time Sheet for Ryder
Zacovic for the Week
Beginning 1/4/16

9 Click the **Next** button. (*Note:* This creates a new time sheet for the next week for the current employee.)

10 Choose **Hourly** from the Payroll Item drop-down list.

11 Type **8**, **6**, and **4** as the hours worked on M 1/11/16, W 1/13/16, and F 1/15/16.

12 Click the **Billable** column (the far right column) to indicate that this line is not billable.

13 Click the **Next** button.

14 Use the same process to record hourly nonbillable hours for Ryder Zacovic of 8 hours each day on M 1/18/16, W 1/20/16, and F 1/22/16. Then click **Next**.

15 Select **50002** as the Customer:Job from the drop-down list in the first column's first row.

16 Select **20 Hour Service** as the Service Item.

17 Select **Hourly** as the Payroll Item.

18 Type **3** in the W 27 column to record 3 hours worked on Wednesday 1/30/16.

19 Leave the Billable column checked.

20 Select **50002** as the Customer:Job from the drop-down list in the first column's second row.

21 Add **Painting & Body Repairs** as a Service Item.

22 Select **Hourly** as the Payroll Item.

23 Type **4** in the W 27 column to record 4 hours worked on Wednesday 1/30/16.

24 Leave the Billable column checked.

25 Select **Hourly** as the Payroll Item in the third row.

26 Type **1** in the W 27 column to record 1 hour worked on Wednesday 1/27/16.

27 Click in the **Billable** column to uncheck the box. Your screen should look like Figure 7.32.

Figure 7.32

Time Sheet for Ryder Zacovic for the Week of Jan 25 to Jan 31, 2016

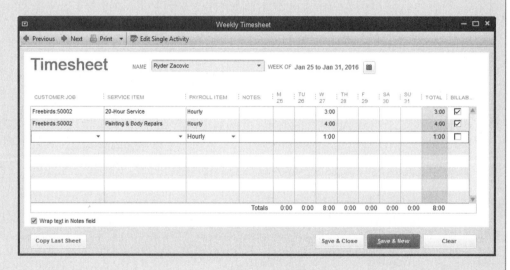

28 Click **Save & New** to enter hours for another employee and then change the Week Of to Jan 4 to Jan 10, 2016.

29 Add **Pat Ng** as an employee and then select him from the Name drop-down list.

30 Click **Yes** to set up this employee to use time data.

31 Use the process you have learned to enter the following time data on time sheets for Pat Ng (all times use the Hourly Payroll Item). Note, you'll have to add Cleaning as a new Service Item.

Date	Hours	Customer:Job	Service Item	Billable ?
1/4/16	6	n/a	n/a	No
1/5/16	4	n/a	n/a	No
1/11/16	2	n/a	n/a	No
1/13/16	4	n/a	n/a	No
1/15/16	6	n/a	n/a	No
1/18/16	8	n/a	n/a	No
1/20/16	8	n/a	n/a	No
1/22/16	8	n/a	n/a	No
1/26/16	6	50001	Engine Tune-Up	Yes
1/26/16	1	50001	Cleaning	Yes
1/26/16	1	n/a	n/a	No

32 When you've entered all the hours for Ryder and Pat, click **Save & Close** to close the Weekly Time sheet window.

"That takes care of January's hourly time sheets, but now we have to process payroll for those time sheets and for our two salaried employees," Karen remarks.

To process payroll for January:

1. Click **Pay Employees** from the Employees section of the home page.

2. Click **No** if the QuickBooks Accountant Payroll Service window appears.

3. Type **1/31/16** in the Pay Period Ends text box and then press **[Tab]**.

4. Click **Yes** to refresh the data for time-card employees.

5. Type **1/31/16** in the Check Date text box and then press **[Tab]**.

6. Select **Bank of Florida** in the Bank Account text box.

7. Resize the columns if need be to view all columns, and then click **Check All**. Your window should look like Figure 7.33.

8. Click the **Continue** button in the lower right-hand corner of your window.

   Trouble? If the window doesn't show all of the information you were expecting, just double-click the title bar of that window so that it enlarges to the maximum size of your screen.

9. Verify the number of hours for both hourly employees to make sure you have accounted for all hours specified in the schedule provided. In this case, the Review and Create Paychecks window indicates 54 hours for Pat Ng and 60 hours for Ryder Zacovic.

10. Click the text **Donna Chandler** in the Employee column. Enter information for Donna Chandler's paycheck from Figure 7.34. Be sure to put

Figure 7.33

Selecting Employees to Pay

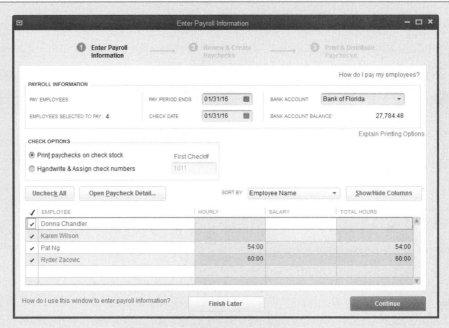

Figure 7.34

Payroll Information for Donna Chandler

If a company doesn't use time sheets, you would place hours worked (for hourly employees) here

Check this box

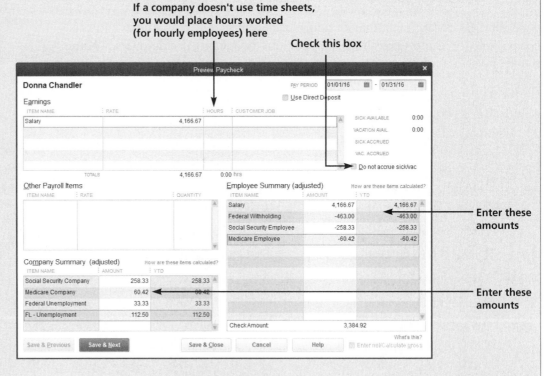

employee amounts as negative numbers and company amounts as positive numbers.

11 Verify the net check amount on your screen with the net check amount in Figure 7.34, and then click **Save & Next**.

12 Continue the payroll process based on the following payroll information. Click **Save & Next** after entering each of the following employees' payroll information:

Item	Karen	Pat	Ryder
Earnings	4,166.67	972.00	900.00
Federal Withholding	−710.00	−133.16	−123.30
Social Security Employee	−258.33	−60.26	−55.80
Medicare Employee	−60.42	−14.09	−13.05
Social Security Company	258.33	60.26	55.80
Medicare Company	60.42	14.09	13.05
Federal Unemployment	33.33	7.78	7.20
FL Unemployment Company	112.50	26.24	24.30
Check Amount	3,137.92	764.49	707.85

13 Click **Save & Close** after entering the last paycheck.

14 Select the **Handwrite & Assign check numbers** option button located in the Paycheck Options section of the Review and Create Paychecks window.

15 Type **1011** as the First Check #.

16 Click **Continue** and then click the **Create Paychecks** button located in the lower right-hand corner of the window.

17 Click **Close** without printing paychecks.

"How did you determine the withholding amounts and the other tax items?" you ask.

"Withholding amounts came from the payroll tax withholding tables I downloaded from the Internal Revenue Service web site at http://www.irs.gov," says Karen. "The others were provided by our local CPA, as follows: Social Security is 6.2% of earnings, Medicare is 1.45% of earnings, and federal unemployment is 0.8% of earnings, while state unemployment is 2.7% of earnings." (See Appendix 1: Payroll Accounting.)

Karen further explains that, since the hourly employees' time was recorded on time sheets, she did not need to enter hours on each employee's paycheck. However, if her company didn't use time sheets then we would enter hours worked by hourly employees in each Preview Paycheck window.

"What about the two customer jobs we charged for Ryder's and Pat's time?" you ask. "Don't we have to bill the customers for the time charged?"

"Yes," Karen answers. "You are quite perceptive. As it turns out, both of these jobs were completed and the boats were picked up by the customers. Had they not been completed, we would wait to bill them until they were complete. Let me show you the process for generating a sales receipt based on time recorded via the payroll system. This should look familiar since we have already invoiced customers for boats purchased on their behalf. In those cases, when we generated an invoice to a particular customer who had unbilled costs, Quick-Books Accountant reminded us of that fact and hence we billed the customer."

"How do we know when to create an invoice and when to create a sales receipt?" you ask.

"Good question," Karen answers. "Invoices are used in two cases. If we've received advance payments (deposits) from a customer, we must create an invoice in order to apply his or her credit balance in accounts receivable.

Invoices are also used whenever we bill a customer and don't receive cash payment at the same time. Thus, sales receipts are always used when we want to bill a customer for time or costs incurred or product sales, and we collect full payment at the same time."

Video Demonstration

DEMO 7J - Billing customers

To bill customers for time recorded via the payroll system:

1 Click the **Create Sales Receipts** icon in the Customers section of the home page.

2 Click job **50001**, located under the customer name Florida Sports Camp.

3 Click the **Time** tab, and then click **Select All** to place a check next to the time charged by Pat Ng to this job. Your screen should look like Figure 7.35.

Figure 7.35

Click the Time tab to view time charged to this customer

Billable Time and Costs

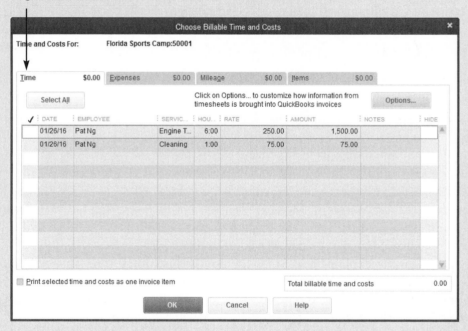

4 Click **OK**.

5 Type **1/31/16** as the sales receipt date.

6 Type **6003** as the sale number.

7 Uncheck the **Email Later** check box and then click **Save & New**.

8 Click job **50002** located under the customer name Freebirds.

9 Click the **Time** tab, and then click **Select All** to place a check next to the time charged by Ryder Zacovic to this job.

10 Click **OK**.

11 Type **1/31/16** as the sales receipt date.

12   Type **6004** as the sale number.

13   Type **1000 Boomer St., Tallahassee, FL 32303** in the Sold To section of the sales receipt under the Freebirds name. Select **State Tax** as the Tax item. Your screen should look like Figure 7.36.

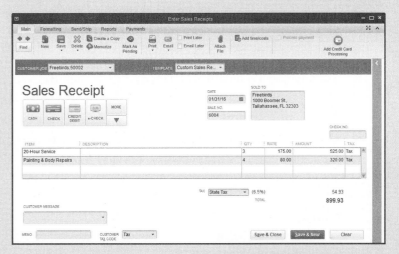

Figure 7.36

Sales Receipt for Freebirds

14   Uncheck the **Email Later** check box and then click **Save & Close**.

15   Click **Yes** in the Name Information Changed window to preserve your changes.

"Did we deposit funds collected from those two transactions?" you ask.

"No," Karen answers. "We didn't deposit them until the next month. Thus, they will stay in the Undeposited Funds account until we do."

You've now recorded many operating activities including cash sales, purchase orders, writing checks, and processing payroll, and you'd like to know how the business did for the month.

Evaluate a Firm's Performance and Financial Position

The best way to evaluate a firm's performance and financial position at this point is to generate an income statement and a balance sheet as of January 31, 2016. Karen suggests that you apply what you learned from past experience with QuickBooks Accountant to create and print a standard income statement and a standard balance sheet for January.

To prepare a standard income statement and a balance sheet for January:

1 Click the **Report Center** icon from the icon toolbar and then click the **Standard** tab.

2 Double-click the **Profit & Loss Standard** view under the Profit & Loss section.

3 Change the From date to **1/1/16**.

4 Change the To date to **1/31/16**, and then click **Refresh**. Remove the Date Prepared, Time Prepared and Report Basis fields from the header as you have done before.

5 Click the **Print** button from the toolbar, select **Report**, and then click **Print** in the Print Reports window. Your report should look like Figure 7.37.

Figure 7.37

Income Statement for January 2016

Wild Water Sports Ch 7
Profit & Loss
January 2016

	Jan 16
Ordinary Income/Expense	
Income	
Boat Sales	200,750.00
Part Sales	40.00
Service	2,545.00
Total Income	203,335.00
Cost of Goods Sold	
Cost of Goods Sold	160,632.00
Total COGS	160,632.00
Gross Profit	42,703.00
Expense	
Payroll Expenses	11,343.22
Telephone Expense	1,700.00
Uncategorized Expenses	0.00
Utilities	890.00
Total Expense	13,933.22
Net Ordinary Income	28,769.78
Net Income	**28,769.78**

6 Close the Profit & Loss report window, memorize the report in a group with your name, and then minimize the Report Center.

7 Expand the Report Center and then double-click the **Balance Sheet Standard** view from the Balance Sheet & Net Worth section.

8 Change the As of date to **1/31/16**, and then click **Refresh**. Remove the Date Prepared, Time Prepared, and Report Basis fields from the header as you have done before.

9 Click the **Print** button from the toolbar, select **Report**, and then click **Print** in the Print Reports window. Your report should look like Figure 7.38.

Wild Water Sports Ch 7
Balance Sheet
As of January 31, 2016

	Jan 31, 16
ASSETS	
Current Assets	
Checking/Savings	
Bank of Florida	19,789.30
Short-Term Investments	300,000.00
Total Checking/Savings	319,789.30
Accounts Receivable	
Accounts Receivable	66,300.00
Total Accounts Receivable	66,300.00
Other Current Assets	
Inventory Boats	330,400.00
Inventory Parts	1,568.00
Prepaid Insurance	22,000.00
Undeposited Funds	2,577.31
Total Other Current Assets	356,545.31
Total Current Assets	742,634.61
Fixed Assets	
Accumulated Depreciation	-7,500.00
Furniture and Equipment	245,000.00
Total Fixed Assets	237,500.00
TOTAL ASSETS	980,134.61
LIABILITIES & EQUITY	
Liabilities	
Current Liabilities	
Credit Cards	
MasterCard	1,000.00
Total Credit Cards	1,000.00
Other Current Liabilities	
Payroll Liabilities	3,348.04
Sales Tax Payable	13,216.79
Total Other Current Liabilities	16,564.83
Total Current Liabilities	17,564.83
Long Term Liabilities	
Loan Payable	633,800.00
Total Long Term Liabilities	633,800.00
Total Liabilities	651,364.83
Equity	
Capital Stock	300,000.00
Net Income	28,769.78
Total Equity	328,769.78
TOTAL LIABILITIES & EQUITY	980,134.61

Figure 7.38

Balance Sheet

10 Close the Balance Sheet report window and memorize the report in a group with your name.

"Is there a way for us to see what transactions made up these balances?" you ask.

"Yes," Karen responds. "We'll print a Transaction List by Date report, which will show us every transaction recorded in chronological order. It will include the type of transaction, the date it was recorded, a number reference (check number, invoice number, etc.), the name of the entity (vendor name, customer name, employee name, etc.), the balance sheet account affected (checking, accounts receivable, undeposited funds, etc.), other accounts affected (inventory, revenue, expenses, etc.), and the amount. Let me show you how to create this report."

To prepare a Transaction List by Date report for January:

1 Click the **Accountant and Taxes** section in the Report Center.

2 Double-click the **Transaction List by Date** view from the Account Activity section of Accountant and Taxes.

3 Type **1/1/16** in the From text box.

4 Type **1/31/16** in the To text box.

5 Click the **Refresh** button. Edit the report to remove the date prepared and time prepared information. Your window should look like Figure 7.39.

Figure 7.39

Transaction List by Date for January 2016

Wild Water Sports Ch 7
Transaction List by Date
January 2016

Type	Date	Num	Adj	Name	Memo	Account	Clr	Split	Debit	Credit
Jan 16										
General Journal	01/01/16	4				Opening Balance E...		Retained Earn...		20,300.00
General Journal	01/01/16	5				Opening Balance E...		Capital Stock	100,000.00	
Deposit	01/02/16				Deposit	Bank of Florida		-SPLIT-	200,000.00	
Deposit	01/04/16				Deposit	Bank of Florida		Loan Payable	250,000.00	
Check	01/08/16	1001		ETrade		Bank of Florida		Short-Term In...		300,000.00
Check	01/09/16	1002		Staples		Bank of Florida		Furniture and...		70,000.00
Check	01/11/16	1003		AJ Marine Equipment		Bank of Florida		Furniture and...		100,000.00
Payment	01/12/16	8755		Florida Sports Camp		Undeposited Funds	✓	Accounts Re...	17,500.00	
Payment	01/12/16			Performance Rent...		Undeposited Funds	✓	Accounts Re...	19,687.50	
Deposit	01/14/16				Deposit	Bank of Florida		-SPLIT-	37,187.50	
Payment	01/15/16	65454		Buena Vista Wate...		Undeposited Funds	✓	Accounts Re...	30,000.00	
Sales Receipt	01/16/16	1		Seth Backman		Undeposited Funds	✓	-SPLIT-	55,380.00	
Deposit	01/16/16				Deposit	Bank of Florida		-SPLIT-	85,380.00	
Sales Receipt	01/26/16	2		Alisa Hay		Undeposited Funds	✓	-SPLIT-	175.73	
Deposit	01/28/16				Deposit	Bank of Florida		Undeposited ...	175.73	
Check	01/29/16	1004		Malibu Boats		Bank of Florida		-SPLIT-		56,000.00
Check	01/30/16	1005		Tige Boats		Bank of Florida		Inventory Boa...		63,000.00
Invoice	01/30/16	10001		Florida Sports Camp		Accounts Receiva...		-SPLIT-	74,550.00	
Invoice	01/30/16	10002		Performance Rent...		Accounts Receiva...		-SPLIT-	83,868.75	
Payment	01/30/16	4532		Florida Sports Camp		Undeposited Funds	✓	Accounts Re...	57,050.00	
Payment	01/30/16	10885		Performance Rent...		Undeposited Funds	✓	Accounts Re...	64,181.25	
Deposit	01/30/16				Deposit	Bank of Florida		-SPLIT-	121,231.25	
Check	01/31/16	1006		Manchester Insura...		Bank of Florida		Prepaid Insur...		22,000.00
Check	01/31/16	1007		Chevron		Bank of Florida		-SPLIT-		1,600.00
Check	01/31/16	1008		Central Florida Gas...		Bank of Florida		Utilities		890.00
Check	01/31/16	1009		Verizon		Bank of Florida		Telephone Ex...		1,700.00
Bill Pmt -Check	01/31/16	1010		Malibu Boats	Opening bal...	Bank of Florida		Accounts Pa...		76,000.00
Paycheck	01/31/16	1011		Donna Chandler		Bank of Florida		-SPLIT-		3,384.92
Paycheck	01/31/16	1012		Karen Wilson		Bank of Florida		-SPLIT-		3,137.92
Paycheck	01/31/16	1013		Pat Ng		Bank of Florida		-SPLIT-		764.49
Paycheck	01/31/16	1014		Ryder Zacovic		Bank of Florida		-SPLIT-		707.85
Sales Receipt	01/31/16	6003		Florida Sports Cam...		Undeposited Funds		-SPLIT-	1,677.38	
Sales Receipt	01/31/16	6004		Freebirds:50002		Undeposited Funds		-SPLIT-	899.93	
Jan 16										

Trouble? On occasion, you might accidentally enter the wrong date for a transaction (e.g., accepting the default date, which might be before January 2016 or after January 2016). If you're pretty sure you entered a transaction but don't see it on your transactions list, it is likely that dates are your problem. To verify this, try entering 1/1/06 as the From date and 12/31/20 as the To date. If your missing transaction appears, double-click it to correct the date and you'll be good to go!

6 Close the Report window and then memorize the report in a group with your name, and then close the Report Center window.

"Not bad for our first month," Karen comments. "But we need to pay off some of the debt acquired with the company acquisition. Plus, we can't forget that some costs such as interest and depreciation expenses have not been accrued or paid, so this information is not complete."

End Note

The two of you decide to quit for the day because you've accomplished quite a lot. You've recorded the firm's financing, investing, and operating activities for the month of January, which included processing purchase orders, receiving inventory, paying for inventory and other bills, recognizing cash sales, and writing checks, including some for payroll. Next up are February transactions and a few noncash activities.

Business Events Summary

Business Event	Process Steps	Page
Financing Activities:		
Receive cash from the sale of stock	Record deposits from Banking section	147
Receive cash from borrowings	Record deposits from Banking section	148
Investing Activities:		
Invest funds	Write checks from Banking section	149
Purchase furniture and equipment	Write checks from Banking section	151
Operating Activities:		
Order inventory	Purchase order from Vendor section	153
Receive cash as a deposit on future sales	Receive payments from Customer section	156
Receive cash on account	Receive payments from Customer section	158
Receive cash from cash sales	Create sales receipts from Customer section	158
Deposit cash	Record deposits from Banking section	161
Receive and pay for inventory	Write checks from Banking section	162
Sell inventory and apply deposit	Create invoices from Customer section	164
Pay expenses	Write checks from Banking section	168
Pay for inventory parts	Write checks from Banking section	168
Pay bills	Pay bills from Vendor section	172
Create new jobs	Add job from Customer section	173
Enter employee hours	Enter time from the Employees section	174
Process payroll and pay employees	Pay employees from the Employees section	177
Bill customers for billable hours	Create sales receipts from Customers section	180
Evaluate a firm's financial performance	Report center from the icon toolbar	181

Chapter 7 Questions

1 Compare and contrast operating, investing, and financing activities.

2 Describe some of the financing activities you recorded for Wild Water in January.

3 Describe some of the investing activities you recorded for Wild Water in January.

4 Describe some of the operating activities you recorded for Wild Water in January.

5 How are purchase orders closed out?

6 Explain the difference between the Expenses tab and the Items tab in the Write Checks window.

7 How should you account for advanced deposits received on customer orders?

8 Why are cash receipts initially recorded as undeposited funds?

9 Are time sheets required for QuickBooks Accountant to process payroll?

10 How does a business know when to create an invoice and when to create a sales receipt?

Chapter 7 Matching

Select the letter of the item below that best matches the definitions that follow.
Use the text or QuickBooks Accountant Help to complete this assignment.

a. Operating activity

b. Investing activity

c. Financing activity

d. Time sheet

e. Customer deposits

f. Accounts receivable

g. Undeposited Funds account

h. Sales receipt

i. Sales invoice

j. Purchase order

_____ A source document used to track cash sales, calculate sales tax, and totals.

_____ This document shows the time spent by one person doing any number of activities for any number of jobs within a seven-day period.

_____ A source document that has no effect on financial statements but helps in managing a company's ordering process.

_____ Cash received by a company for which a sale cannot be recorded because the product has not been delivered.

_____ An account used to record cash receipts not yet deposited to the bank.

_____ A source document that includes details about a sale to a customer who owes you money.

_____ An activity where cash or other resources are obtained from or paid to non-trade creditors, long-term creditors, and/or owners.

_____ An activity where cash or other resources are applied to nonoperating uses such as making long-term productive investments in equipment, buildings, land, etc.

_____ An activity where cash or other resources are used to purchase or produce goods and services for sale.

_____ Money that is owed to a business for sales that have already been made but for which payment has not yet been received.

Chapter 7 Exercises

Chapter 7 Exercise 1
CASH-ORIENTED FINANCING ACTIVITIES

Restore the file Boston Catering Ch 7 (Backup) that you downloaded from the text web site. Add the following transactions and then print a standard balance sheet as of 7/31/10.

a. On 7/6/10 the company sold 1,000 shares of common stock to a new private investor (Broad Investments) for $50,000. Funds were deposited directly into the company's checking account on the same date on their check 23413.

b. On 7/8/10 the company borrowed $25,000 from Bank of America at 8% due in 4 years. Bank of America's check 823908 was deposited directly into the company's checking account on the same date after the company signed the long-term note payable.

Chapter 7 Exercise 2
CASH-ORIENTED INVESTING ACTIVITIES

Restore the file Boston Catering Ch 7 (Backup) that you downloaded from the text web site. Do not use the file created in Exercise 1 above. Add the following transactions and then print a standard balance sheet as of 7/31/10.

a. On 7/13/10 the company purchased new equipment for $3,000 using check 1501 from Outlet Tool Supply, a vendor.

b. On 7/15/10 the company invested $5,000 on a short-term basis with an investment firm named North Eastern Investments using check 1502.

Chapter 7 Exercise 3
CASH-ORIENTED OPERATING ACTIVITIES – SALES

Restore the file Boston Catering Ch 7 (Backup) that you downloaded from the text web site. Do not use the file created in Exercise 1 or 2 above. Add the following transactions and then print a standard balance sheet as of 7/31/10 and a standard income statement for the month ended 7/31/10.

a. On 7/14/10 the company received check 25141 from MA General Hospital in the amount of $7,000 as payment on account. Amount was deposited to the bank the same day.

b. On 7/16/10 the company recorded sales receipt 930 for a new customer MIT, terms due on receipt, sales tax applicable, for 50 item A100 and 50 item A200, delivered. On the same date they received check 523420 from MIT in the amount of $1,575 as payment in full. Amount was deposited to the bank the same day. Hint: you can modify QuickBooks Accountant preferences to show the Create Sales Receipts icon on the home page to access a new sales receipt or you can select Enter Sales Receipts from the Customer menu.

Chapter 7 Exercise 4

CASH-ORIENTED OPERATING ACTIVITIES – PURCHASES

Restore the file Boston Catering Ch 7 (Backup) that you downloaded from the text web site. Do not use the file created in the exercises above. Add the following transactions and then print a standard balance sheet as of 7/31/10 and an item listing report showing just the item, description, type, cost, price, quantity on hand, and quantity on purchase order.

a.   On 7/5/10 the company ordered 24 bottles of item W100 from the Sanford Winery on purchase order 101.

b.   On 7/7/10 the company ordered 48 bottles of a new item W201 (Fiddlehead Syrah, Cost $25, Sales Price $40) on purchase order 102.

c.   On 7/28/10 the company ordered 12 bottles of a new item W300 (Foley Pinot Noir, Cost $50, Sales Price $70) from a new vendor Foley Estates (6121 Hwy. 246, Lompoc, CA 93436) on purchase order 103 with terms net 15.

d.   On 7/22/10 the company received the 24 bottles of item W100 from Sanford Winery; they had been ordered using purchase order 101 along with a bill due in 30 days.

e.   On 7/29/10 the company received the 48 bottles of item W201 from Fiddlehead Winery; they had been ordered using purchase order 102 along with a bill due in 30 days.

Chapter 7 Exercise 5

CASH-ORIENTED OPERATING ACTIVITIES – EXPENSES

Restore the file Boston Catering Ch 7 (Backup) that you downloaded from the text web site. Do not use the file created in the exercises above. Add the following transactions and then print a standard balance sheet as of 7/31/10 and a standard income statement for the month ended 7/31/10.

a.   On 7/15/10 the company paid rent to New England Property Management (a new vendor) on check 1503 for $3,000.

b.   On 7/29/10 the company paid a bill due Sanford Winery for $2,000 on check 1504.

c.   During the month of July, Nathan Chambers worked on salary. Kyle Hain worked 8 hours a day from the 19th through the 23rd, all of which was unbilled time. He also worked 6 hours of billable time on Saturday July 24th during the John Hancock summer supper catered event. Use a new service item (X100, Wait Staff, Rate $25, Account: Catering Sales, Tax Code: Non taxable). Amy Casey also worked 8 hours a day from the 19th through the 23rd, all of which was unbilled time. She also worked 8 hours of billable time on Saturday, July 24th during the John Hancock summer supper catered event. Payroll checks are issued starting with check #1505. Paycheck information is shown below:

Pay/Tax/Withholding	Chambers	Hain	Casey
Hours	n/a	46	48
Rate	$50,000	$ 16.00	$ 18.00
Gross pay	4,166.67	736.00	864.00
Federal withholding	570.83	100.83	118.37
Social Security employee	258.33	45.63	53.57
Medicare employee	60.42	10.67	12.53
MA withholding	283.99	23.26	32.99
MA Training Fund	0.42	0.07	0.09
Social Security employer	258.33	45.63	53.57
Medicare company	60.42	10.67	12.53
Federal unemployment	33.33	5.89	6.91
MA unemployment	125.00	22.08	25.92
Check amount	2,993.10	555.61	646.54

d. On 7/31/10 the company recorded sales receipt 931 for John Hancock, terms due on receipt, sales tax applicable, for 175 item S200 and 30 W200 delivered, and 14 hours of wait staff time. On the same date, they received check 12311 from the customer in the amount of $9,747.50 as payment in full. Amount was deposited to the bank the same day.

e. On 7/31/10 the company paid $2,000 to the US Food Service for food purchased and consumed for the various events in July using check 1508. (*Note:* this transaction is in addition to the existing liability to US Food Service.)

f. Change all wine items COGS Account from costs of goods sold to bar purchases.

Chapter 7 Assignments

Chapter 7 Assignment 1

ADDING MORE INFORMATION: WILD WATER SPORTS

Restore the file Wild Water Sports Ch 7A (Backup) that you downloaded from the text web site, and then add the following transactions.

corporation

merchandising

job costing

Event #	Date	Business Event
1	2/2/16	Wrote Check No. 1015 for $1,000 to Delco (new vendor) as payment for the purchase of five sets of tune-up parts.
2	2/2/16	Accepted a new job (50003) to tune up a boat owned by Orlando Water Sports.
3	2/2/16	Paid $24,000 to Coe Marketing (new vendor) for new advertising campaign, which will last one year, with Check No. 1016. (**Hint:** You'll need to create a new other current asset account type titled Prepaid Advertising.)
4	2/2/16	Deposited funds received 1/31 in the amount of $2,577.31 into the Bank of Florida account.
5	2/2/16	Created Purchase Order No. 4003 to MB Sports to order one MB B52 V23 (a new item) on behalf of our customer, Performance Rentals. Cost: $60,000; Sales Price: $75,000.

Event #	Date	Business Event
6	2/2/16	Collected $18,750 as an advance payment from Performance Rentals (their Check No. 2003), which was equal to the 25% down payment required on all boat orders. (*Hint:* Use the Receive Payments function to record receipt of this payment, and do not apply this payment to any existing balances owed.)
7	2/4/16	Pat Ng worked four hours on Job No. 50003, tuning up a boat owned by Orlando Water Sports. (*Hint:* Record on a time sheet now!)
8	2/4/16	Deposited $100,000 from a new investor, Sam Ski, in exchange for capital stock representing a 25% interest in the company. Payment received was in the form of his Check No. 987.
9	2/4/16	Recorded Sales Receipt No. 6005 to Orlando Water Sports under Job No. 50003, based on work performed by Pat Ng and one set of tune-up parts. Orlando Water Sports is subject to sales tax. $1,331.25 was collected via Check No. 9774.
10	2/5/16	Deposited the advance payment received from Performance Rentals and the check received from Orlando Water Sports.
11	2/5/16	Received Check No. 390 for $3,000 as payment on account from Buena Vista Water Sports.
12	2/5/16	Deposited a $50,000 check, No. 188774, from CitiBank (new vendor) as the proceeds from a three-year 6% loan negotiated by Sam Ski. The company plans to use these funds in the future to pay down some older, more expensive debt.
13	2/6/16	Wrote Check No. 1017 in the amount of $75,000 to ETrade as a short-term investment.
14	2/6/16	Deposited a $3,000 check received on 2/5.
15	2/6/16	Created Purchase Order No. 4004 to Malibu Boats to order one MS LSV and one MV on behalf of a new customer, Fantasy Sports, located at 345 Sunset Rd., Orlando, FL 31312.
16	2/6/16	Collected $28,250 as an advance payment from Fantasy Sports (its Check No. 1005), which was equal to the 25% down payment required on all boat orders.
17	2/8/16	Received Check No. 1988 for $43,000 as payment on account from Orlando Water Sports.
18	2/9/16	Sold an MW VLX from inventory to Walking on Water for $57,000 plus tax of $3,705, and recorded the sale with Sales Receipt No. 6006. Waling on Water is subject to sales tax. Received the customer's Check No. 232 as payment in full. Updated the customer's address as 874 Nightingale Dr., Kissimmee, FL 34743.
19	2/9/16	Accepted a new job (50004) to paint a boat owned by Alisa Hay.
20	2/9/16	Made a deposit of $131,955 from checks received from 2/6 to 2/9.
21	2/9/16	Ryder Zacovic worked five hours on Job No. 50004, painting a boat owned by Alisa Hay.
22	2/11/16	Recorded Sales Receipt No. 6007 from Alisa Hay under Job No. 50004, based on work performed by Ryder Zacovic. Check No. 741 collected for $426.
23	2/11/16	Deposited $426 from Sales Receipt No. 6007.
24	2/16/16	Wrote Check No. 1018 to Sunset Auto (vendor) for $45,000 to purchase a truck for the business. (Use Furniture and Equipment account.)
25	2/19/16	Wrote Check No. 1019 to MB Sports for $60,000 as payment for Purchase Order No. 4003 because the MB B52 V23 ordered on behalf of Performance Rentals was received.

Event #	Date	Business Event
26	2/20/16	Created Invoice No. 10003 to Performance Rentals for sale of MB B52 V23 received under Purchase Order No. 4003 on 2/19. Applied the deposit received upon order.
27	2/20/16	Record receipt of payment from Performance Rentals of $61,125 with their Check No. 23098 on Invoice No. 10003.
28	2/23/16	Deposited Performance Rentals check received 2/20.
29	2/26/16	Wrote Check No. 1020 to Bank of Florida to pay MasterCard liability of $1,000. (*Hint:* Record this payment to the MasterCard liability account.)
30	2/26/16	Wrote Check No. 1021 to Central Florida Gas & Electric for $930 for utilities expense.
31	2/26/16	Wrote Check No. 1022 to Verizon for $1,820 for telephone expense.
32	2/26/16	Wrote Check No. 1023 to Brian Ski (new vendor) for $2,700 for advertising and promotion expense.
33	2/26/16	Wrote Check No. 1024 to Staples for $4,500 for office supplies expense.
34	2/29/16	Record time sheet information provided in Table 7.1. *Note:* Some of these hours are in connection with jobs for which time had already been recorded and should already be on your time sheet. Those hours are designated in the table with an *. All other hours not designated by an * are for nonbillable activities.
35	2/29/16	Process payroll per the information provided in Table 7.2, starting with Check No. 1025.

Table 7.1

Time Sheet Information

Date	Ryder Zacovic	Date	Pat Ng
2/2/16	8 hrs.	2/4/16	4 hrs.*
2/5/16	5 hrs.	2/5/16	8 hrs.
2/6/16	5 hrs.	2/6/16	8 hrs.
2/9/16	5 hrs.*	2/9/16	8 hrs.
2/11/16	8 hrs.	2/11/16	8 hrs.
2/13/16	8 hrs.	2/13/16	8 hrs.
2/23/16	8 hrs.	2/23/16	8 hrs.
2/24/16	8 hrs.	2/24/16	8 hrs.
2/25/16	8 hrs.	2/25/16	8 hrs.
Total	63 hrs.		68 hrs.

Table 7.2

Payroll Information for Wild Water Sports

Item	Donna	Karen	Pat	Ryder
Earnings	4,166.67	4,166.67	1,224.00	945.00
Federal Withholding	−463.00	−710.00	−167.69	−129.47
Social Security Employee	−258.33	−258.33	−75.89	−58.59
Medicare Employee	−60.42	−60.42	−17.75	−13.70
Social Security Company	258.33	258.33	75.89	58.59
Medicare Company	60.42	60.42	17.75	13.70
Federal Unemployment	33.33	33.33	9.79	7.56
State Unemployment	112.50	112.50	33.05	25.52
Check Amount	3,384.92	3,137.92	962.67	743.24

Print and memorize the following for the month of February 2016.

a. Customer Balance Summary

b. Balance Sheet Standard

c. Profit & Loss Standard

d. Transaction List by Date

Chapter 7 Assignment 2

ADDING MORE INFORMATION: CENTRAL COAST CELLULAR

Restore the file Central Coast Cellular Ch 7 (Backup) that you downloaded from the text web site, and then add the following transactions. (**Hint:** You may want to disable the warning about transaction dates being greater than 90 days from the current system date; this is done in the Accounting Preferences section.)

sole proprietorship

merchandising

Event #	Date	Business Event
1	1/3/14	Mr. Van Morrison deposited $200,000 of his personal funds into the company checking account. (Remember, this is a sole proprietorship.) Use the Opening Balance Equity account to record this transaction.
2	1/3/14	Signed a lease with Central Coast Leasing (2830 McMillan Ave. #7, San Luis Obispo, CA 93401, 805-544-2875) to rent retail space at $3,000 a month for five years. Payment is due on the 13th of the month.
3	1/6/14	The company temporarily invested $75,000 by writing Check No. 3001 to Schwab Investments (a new vendor located at 1194 Pacific St., San Luis Obispo, CA 93401, 805-788-0502). (**Hint:** You will need to create an other bank type account named Short-Term Investments.)
4	1/7/14	The company borrowed and then deposited $125,000 from Wells Fargo Bank (a new vendor located at 665 Marsh St., San Luis Obispo, CA 93401, 805-541-0143), due in five years with annual interest of 8% and payments made monthly. (**Hint:** You will need to create a long-term liability account named Loan Payable.)
5	1/8/14	The company purchased furniture & equipment by writing Check No. 3002 for $20,000 to Russco (a new vendor located at 3046 S. Higuera St. #A, San Luis Obispo, CA 93401, 805-547-8440).
6	1/9/14	The company ordered inventory from the following vendors:

Purchase Order #	Vendor	Product	Quantity
101	Ericsson, Inc.	Ericsson LX588	40
		Ericsson T19LX	60
102	Nokia Mobile Phones	Nokia 3285	25
		Nokia 8290	50
		Nokia 8890	15

Event #	Date	Business Event
7	1/10/14	The company purchased supplies from Russco for $3,000 using Check No. 3003. These supplies are expected to last over the next year. (*Hint:* You will need to create a new other current asset type account named Supplies.)
8	1/13/14	The company wrote Check No. 3004 to Central Coast Leasing for $6,000 ($3,000 for January's rent and $3,000 as a security deposit). (*Hint:* You will need to create a new other asset type account named Security Deposit.)
9	1/14/14	The company received and deposited an advance payment of $10,000 from the City of San Luis Obispo (a customer) as part of a consulting contract to begin in February.
10	1/15/14	The company received a shipment of phones from Ericsson, Inc., on Purchase Order No. 101. Items were received and a bill was recorded that is due in 30 days.
11	1/16/14	The company created Sales Receipt No. 501 to record 50 hours of consulting services and the sale of 25 Ericsson LX588 phones to Sterling Hotels Corporation. A check was received and deposited for $7,425.
12	1/17/14	The company paid semi-monthly payroll starting with Check No. 3005 for the period January 1 to January 15, 2014. Jay Bruner and Alex Rodriguez worked the month on salary. Megan Paulson worked 80 hours during the period. Payroll tax information is shown in Table 7.3.

Table 7.3

Payroll Information for Central Coast Cellular

Item	Alex	Jay	Megan
Earnings	2,000.00	1,500.00	960.00
Federal Withholding	−300.00	−225.00	−144.00
Social Security Employee	−124.00	−93.00	−59.52
Medicare Employee	−29.00	−21.75	−13.92
CA Withholding	−100.00	−75.00	−48.00
CA Disability Employee	−10.00	−7.50	−4.80
CA Employee Training Tax	2.00	1.50	0.96
Social Security Company	124.00	93.00	59.52
Medicare Company	29.00	21.75	13.92
Federal Unemployment	6.40	4.80	3.07
CA Unemployment	24.00	18.00	11.52
Check Amount	1,437.00	1,077.75	689.76

Print the following as of 1/17/14.

a. Profit & Loss Standard

b. Balance Sheet Standard

c. Transaction List by Date

Chapter 7 Assignment 3

ADDING MORE INFORMATION: SANTA BARBARA SAILING

Restore the file Santa Barbara Sailing Ch 7 (Backup) that you downloaded from the text web site, and then add the following transactions.

corporation

service

Event #	Date	Business Event
1	7/2/15	Rob Dutton contributed an additional $100,000 to the company in exchange for capital stock; this amount was then immediately deposited into the company's checking account.
2	7/4/15	Rented the CAT 50 to Raytheon (RAY) for seven days using Sales Receipt No. 10001 and collected Check No. 983 for $4,233.60. Amounts are deposited later.
3	7/4/15	Rented the CAT 42 to a new customer, Deckers (Deckers Outdoor Corporation located at 495-A South Fairview Ave., Goleta, CA 93117, Terms: Due on receipt), for seven days using Sales Receipt No. 10002 and collected $3,515.40. Amounts are deposited later.
4	7/7/15	Purchased a new J-24 sailboat (to rent to customers) for $42,000 with Check No. 101 (be sure to uncheck the Print Later check box so you can enter this check number) from a new vendor (J-Boats, P.O. Box 90, Newport, RI 02840. Phone: 401-846-8410. Terms: Due on receipt).
5	7/7/15	Created a new service item J-24, to be rented out at a rate of $160 per day.
6	7/8/15	Deposited checks (two different deposits) from Raytheon and Deckers received on 7/4/15.
7	7/9/15	Paid existing bill from Catalina of $7,500 using Check No. 102.
8	7/9/15	Hired a new hourly employee, Nathan Snyder (SS# 390-09-2877, single male, earning $8 per hour and subject to all normal California and federal taxes).
9	7/10/15	Received full payment on account from Raytheon of $8,465 (their Check No. 39892).
10	7/11/15	Received advance payment of $1,000 (Check No. 974565) from a new customer, Montecito Bank (Montecito Bank and Trust, P.O. Box 2460, Santa Barbara, CA 93120. Phone: 805-963-7511. Terms: Due on receipt).
11	7/11/15	Deposited checks from Raytheon and Montecito Bank, a single deposit totaling $9,465.
12	7/14/15	Wrote Check No. 103 for $24,000 to Levy Property Management (new vendor) for rent of harbor facilities and docks for one year. (Classify all of this payment as Prepaid Rent, a new other current asset account that will be adjusted monthly.)
13	7/14/15	Rented the CAT 50 to Montecito Bank for 14 days using invoice 7001. Applied the advance deposit received 7/11/15 to this invoice and collected the balance owed of $7,467.20 via Check No. 974637.
14	7/14/15	Rented the CAT 42 to Santa Barbara Medical (SBMED) for 14 days using Sales Receipt No. 10003 and received a MasterCard payment for $7,030.80.
15	7/15/15	Rented the J-24 and CAT 28 to Deckers for 14 days using Sales Receipt No. 10004 and received a Visa payment for $5,745.60.
16	7/16/15	Paid employees for the period 7/1/15–7/15/15. Rob worked for salary during that period. Nathan and Jeanne worked 20 and 38 hours, respectively, during that period. Payroll tax information is shown in Table 7.4.

Table 7.4

Payroll and Earnings Information for Santa Barbara Sailing

Item	Rob	Jeanne	Nathan
Earnings	2,708.33	684.00	160.00
Federal Withholding	−514.58	−129.96	−30.40
Social Security Employee	−167.92	−42.41	−9.92
Medicare Employee	−39.27	−9.92	−2.32
CA Income tax	−216.67	−54.72	−12.80
CA Disability	−16.25	−4.10	−0.96
Check Amount	1,753.64	442.89	103.60
CA Employee Training Tax	2.71	0.68	0.16
Social Security Employer	167.92	42.41	9.92
Medicare Employer	39.27	9.92	2.32
Federal Unemployment	21.67	5.47	1.28
CA Unemployment	92.08	23.26	5.44
Check number	106	104	105

Print the following for the period 7/1/15 to 7/16/15.

a. Profit & Loss Standard

b. Balance Sheet Standard

c. Statement of Cash Flows

d. Transaction List by Date

Chapter 7 Assignment 4

ADDING MORE INFORMATION: DRONE CITY

Restore the file Drone City Ch 07 (Backup) that you downloaded from the text web site, and then add the following transactions.

Event #	Date	Business Event
1	1/2/17	You deposited $40,000 into your new checking account as an owner investment using your check #498 (Use your name as the "received from").
2	1/3/17	Paid first and last month's rent to Hay Leasing for a 36 month lease on a facility. Payment was for $3,000 ($1,500 per month) using company check #1001. Hint: record $1,500 rent expense and $1,500 prepaid rent (an other asset).
3	1/4/17	Purchased 4 Quad 1's from Quadcopters using check #1002 for $10,800.
4	1/4/17	Purchased 2 Hex Transports from Space Age Transport using check #1003 for $4,000.
5	1/5/17	Received and signed a long-term note payable for $25,000 from the Bank of Seattle for 3 years at 6%. Monthly payments of $761 begin next month. Borrowed amount was deposited into the checking account the same day.
6	1/6/17	Purchased 3 Max Transport drones as equipment from a new vendor (Ace Drones) to be used for consulting work or rentals in the future. Each cost $8,000 and were paid using check #1004. (Note: Be sure you account for this purchase as equipment and not inventory.)
7	1/6/17	Purchased promotional flyers and other advertising supplies from Jake Vordale a marketing consultant for $1,800 using check #1005. These are expected to be used over the next 12 months. Record them as Prepaid Advertising Supplies (a current asset).

sole proprietorship

1 2 3
easy step

Event #	Date	Business Event
8	1/6/17	Purchased one Super Drone from Drones International for $7,000 using check #1006.
9	1/9/17	Provided 15 hours of consulting services to US DOD recorded using sales receipt 100 then receiving payment of $3,195 via their check #98745 which was immediately deposited into the checking account.
10	1/9/17	Sold 2 Quad 1 and 1 Super Drone to Amazon, Inc. on sales receipt 101 then receiving payment of $16,401 via their check 12458 which was immediately deposited into the checking account.
11	1/10/17	Created purchase order 4000 to Ace Drones for the purchase of 5 Hex Transports for a new customer Rincon Flying.
12	1/11/17	Created job 500 for customer US DOD
13	1/12/13	Monica worked 5 billable hours and Emily worked 8 billable hours on job 500. Emily will use time sheet hours to have activities transferred to paychecks. Monica will not.
14	1/13/17	Billed US DOD for job 500 using sales receipt 102 and immediately deposited their check 9784 for $2,769.
15	1/13/17	Received inventory items ordered on purchase order 4000 from Ace Drones.
16	1/2/17 to 1/13/17	Emily worked 8 hours per day in the office (not billable) on 1/2/17, 1/3/17, 1/4/17, 1/5/17, 1/6/17, 1/9/17, 1/10/17, 1/11/17, and 1/13/17.
17	1/16/17	Paid employees for the period 1/2/17 – 1/13/17. Monica worked for salary and Emily worked 80 hours during that period. Payroll tax information is shown in Table 7.5.
18	1/16/17	Create a new income account called Consulting. Changed item Consulting to record business events to the newly created Consulting income account. Be sure to update existing transactions to reflect this change.

Item	Emily	Monica
Check number	1007	1008
Earnings	1,440.00	2,291.67
Medicare Employee Addl Tax	0	0
Federal Withholding	197.28	313.96
Social Security Employee	89.28	142.08
Medicare Employee	20.88	33.23
WA-Employment Admin. Fund	.43	.69
Social Security Company	89.28	142.08
Medicare Company	20.88	33.23
Federal Unemployment	49.10	78.15
WA-Unemployment	37.30	59.35

Table 7.5

Payroll and Earnings Information for Drone City Payroll as of 1/16/17

Place your name in the Extra Footer Line, remove subtitle, date and time prepared header information, and then print the following reports for the period 1/1/17 through 1/16/17.

a.   Profit & Loss Standard

b.   Balance Sheet Standard

c.   Statement of Cash Flows

d.   Transaction List by Date

sole proprietorship

service

Chapter 7 Cases

Chapter 7 Case 1

FOREVER YOUNG

In Chapter 6, you created a new QuickBooks Accountant file for Forever Young. Make a copy of that file, and use that copy to enter the following transactions:

Event #	Date	Business Event
1	1/2/15	Sebastian deposited $20,000 into his new company's checking account as his initial investment.
2	1/3/15	Paid Galas $6,000 in legal fees for setting up contracts with future customers (classify as Professional Fees Expense) using Check No. 1.
3	1/3/15	Signed a contract with Panasonic (new customer with terms due on receipt) to speak at its sales convention (half-day seminar) on 1/5/15. Collected a 50% deposit of $3,000 and immediately deposited this Check No. 9873 into the checking account.
4	1/4/15	Paid Office Depot (a new vendor) $4,000 for furniture using Check No. 2.
5	1/4/15	Paid Classic Leasing (a new vendor) $8,000 rent on office space using Check No. 3. (Half of payment represents January rent and half represents a security deposit.) (*Hint:* Create a new other asset account, named Security Deposit Asset.)
6	1/5/15	Spoke at the Panasonic sales convention, received remaining amount owed, provided invoice 501 to customer (billing them for services rendered), and applied previous credit.
7	1/7/15	Received and deposited Panasonic Check No. 9898 for $3,000 into checking account as final payment for services rendered.
8	1/9/15	Signed a contract with Gateway (new customer with terms due on receipt) to speak at its sales convention (full-day seminar) on 1/12/15. Collected a 50% deposit of $5,000 and immediately deposited this Check No. 15487 into the checking account.
9	1/10/15	Purchased supplies (new other current asset type of account) from Office Depot for $1,500 using Check No. 4; the supplies will be used over the next six months.
10	1/11/15	Signed a contract with Adobe (new customer with terms due on receipt) to speak at its officers' retreat (full-day seminar) on 1/19/15. Collected a 50% deposit of $5,000 and immediately deposited this Check No. 698747 into the checking account.
11	1/12/15	Spoke at the Gateway sales convention, received remaining amount owed, provided invoice 502 to customer (billing them for services rendered), and applied previous credit.
12	1/14/15	Received and deposited Gateway Check No. 15623 for $5,000 into checking account as final payment for services rendered.
13	1/15/15	Paid semi-monthly payroll starting with Check No. 5 for the period 1/1/15 to 1/15/15. Cory worked for salary during this period. Anne worked 23 hours during this period. Payroll tax information is shown in Table 7.6.

Item	Cory	Anne	Table 7.6
Earnings	3,333.33	460.00	Payroll and Earnings Information for Forever Young
Federal Withholding	−633.33	−87.40	
Social Security Employee	−206.67	−28.52	
Medicare Employee	−48.33	−6.67	
CA Income tax	−266.67	−36.80	
CA Disability	−20.00	−2.76	
Check Amount	2,158.33	297.85	
CA Employee Training Tax	3.33	0.46	
Social Security Employer	206.67	28.52	
Medicare Employer	48.33	6.67	
Federal Unemployment	26.67	3.68	
CA Unemployment	113.33	15.64	

Requirements:

Print the following as of 1/15/15.

1 Profit & Loss Standard

2 Balance Sheet Standard

3 Statement of Cash Flows

4 Transaction List by Date

Chapter 7 Case 2

OCEAN VIEW FLOWERS

In Chapter 6, you created a new QuickBooks Accountant file for Ocean View Flowers, a wholesale flower distributor. Make a copy of that file and use that copy to enter the following transactions:

corporation

merchandising

Event #	Date	Business Event
1	1/4/16	The company sold capital stock to investor Scott Cruz for $100,000 cash. The company deposited the check into the Union checking account.
2	1/4/16	The company borrowed $50,000 from Santa Barbara Bank & Trust. The long-term note payable (new account) is due in three years with interest due annually at 10%. The company deposited the check into the Union checking account.
3	1/4/16	The company temporarily invested $25,000 in a certificate of deposit, due in three months, that will earn 7% per annum. Check No. 101, drawn on the Union checking account, was made payable to Prudent Investments, 100 Main Street, San Francisco, CA 95154. (*Hint:* Create a new other current asset type account called Short-Term Investments to record this transaction.)
4	1/11/16	The company purchased office equipment from Stateside Office Supplies (324 G St., Lompoc, CA 93436) for $20,000 with Check No. 102.
5	1/12/16	The company purchased a used tractor from Gateway (100 Cowabunga Blvd., Sioux City, IA 23442) for $15,000 with Check No. 103.
6	1/14/16	The company created Purchase Order No. 5001 to order the following items from Brophy Bros. Farms, which specializes in daylilies.

Item	Quantity Ordered
Almond Puff	1,000
Calistoga Sun	2,000
Caribbean Pink Sands	500

7	1/15/16	The company paid payroll. All employees worked the entire period. Edward, Marie, and Stan worked for salary. Kelly Gusland worked 60 hours and Margie Cruz worked 75 hours. Checks were written using the Union Bank account starting with Check No. 104. (Do not print these checks.) Payroll taxes and withholding for employees during the period 1/1/16 through 1/15/16 are shown in Table 7.7.
8	1/18/16	The company received its order in full from Brophy Bros. Farms and paid the bill with Union Bank Check No. 109 in the amount of $34,500.
9	1/21/16	The company paid Stateside Office Supplies for supplies expected to last over the next six months using Union Bank Check No. 110 for $1,500. (*Hint:* Create a new other current asset account called Supplies.)

Table 7.7

Earnings Information 1/1/16 through 1/15/16

Item	Edward	Kelly	Margie	Marie	Stan
Earnings	2,916.67	900.00	900.00	2,500.00	2,083.33
Federal Withholding	−667.00	−118.00	−118.00	−402.00	−286.00
Social Security Employee	−180.83	−55.80	−55.80	−155.00	−129.17
Medicare Employee	−42.29	−13.05	−13.05	−36.25	−30.21
CA Withholding	−192.30	−19.32	−9.32	−153.55	−61.86
CA Disability employee	−14.58	−4.50	−4.50	−12.50	−10.42
Check Amount	1,819.67	689.33	699.33	1,740.70	1,565.67
CA Employee Training Tax	2.92	0.90	0.90	2.50	2.08
Social Security Company	180.83	55.80	55.80	155.00	129.17
Medicare Company	42.29	13.05	13.05	36.25	30.21
Federal Unemployment	23.33	7.20	7.20	20.00	16.67
CA Unemployment	1.46	0.45	0.45	1.25	1.04

Event #	Date	Business Event
10	1/22/16	The company recorded its first cash sale to Valley Florists, selling 100 Almond Puffs, 100 Calistoga Suns, and 100 Caribbean Pink Sands (Sales Receipt No. 701). The $6,600 sale was deposited directly to Union Bank.
11	1/25/16	The company recorded its second cash sale (Sales Receipt No. 702) to Eastern Scents, selling 600 Almond Puffs and 300 Caribbean Pink Sands. The $22,200 sale was deposited directly to Union Bank.
12	1/28/16	The company received a check as an advance payment on account from FTD in the amount of $5,000, which was deposited directly to the Union Bank account.
13	1/29/16	The company wrote the following three checks:

Check #	Payee	Amount	Category
111	Hawaiian Farms	$3,000	Rent Expense
112	Edison Inc.	$ 500	Utilities
113	GTE	$ 400	Telephone Expense

14	1/29/16		The company paid payroll for the period ended 1/31/16. All employees worked the entire period. Edward, Marie, and Stan worked for salary. Kelly Gusland worked 65 hours and Margie Cruz worked 70 hours. Checks were written using the Union Bank account starting with Check No. 114. (Do not print these checks.) Payroll taxes and withholding for employees during the period 1/16/16 through 1/31/16 are shown in Table 7.8.

Item	Edward	Kelly	Margie	Marie	Stan
Earnings	2,916.67	975.00	840.00	2,500.00	2,083.33
Federal Withholding	−667.00	−130.00	−109.00	−402.00	−286.00
Social Security Employee	−180.84	−60.45	−52.08	−155.00	−129.16
Medicare Employee	−42.29	−14.14	−12.18	−36.25	−30.21
CA Withholding	−192.30	−23.63	−8.12	−153.55	−61.86
CA Disability employee	−14.59	−4.88	−4.20	−12.50	−10.41
Check Amount	1,819.65	741.90	654.42	1,740.70	1,565.69
CA Employee Training Tax	2.91	0.98	0.84	2.50	2.09
Social Security Company	180.84	60.45	52.08	155.00	129.16
Medicare Company	42.29	14.14	12.18	36.25	30.21
Federal Unemployment	23.34	7.80	6.72	20.00	16.66
CA Unemployment	1.46	0.49	0.42	1.25	1.04

Table 7.8

Earnings Information 1/16/16 through 1/31/16

Requirements:

Record business transactions in chronological order (remember, dates are in the month of January 2016). After recording the transactions, create and print the following for January 2016. (Be sure to keep this QuickBooks Accountant file in a safe place since it will be used as a starting file for this case in Chapter 8.)

1 Balance Sheet Standard

2 Profit & Loss Standard

3 Statement of Cash Flows

4 Transaction List by Date

Chapter 7 Case 3

ALOHA PROPERTIES

In Chapter 6, you created a new QuickBooks Accountant file for Aloha Properties. Make a copy of that file, and use that copy to enter the following transactions:

corporation

service

Event #	Date	Business Event
1	1/3/14	Adventure Travel purchased capital stock from Aloha in exchange for $50,000 cash, which was deposited to the company's checking account.

Event #	Date	Business Event
2	1/4/14	Received payment on account from General Motors in the amount of $75,000 (their Check No. 6874).
3	1/4/14	Deposited the check from General Motors into the checking account.
4	1/7/14	Wrote Check No. 984 for $40,000 to World Investments (a new other name) as a short-term investment. (*Hint:* Create a new other current asset account called Short-Term Investments.)
5	1/8/14	Wrote Check No. 985 for $24,000 to GEICO Insurance (a new vendor) as payment for a one-year insurance policy with coverage provided from January 1, 2014, through December 31, 2014; recorded this transaction as Prepaid Insurance (a new account).
6	1/9/14	Received a $24,000 deposit from a new customer, Pixar Studios.
7	1/9/14	Deposited the check received from Pixar into the checking account.
8	1/11/14	Recorded Sales Receipt No. 5115 for rent of Villa Kailani Unit #1 for one week. Collected MasterCard payment in full of $3,120 from a new customer, Coast Union Bank.
9	1/11/14	Recorded Invoice No. 7508 for rental of Moana Unit #4 for one week to Sara Rice. Applied her previously received advance payment of $6,000 to this invoice, noted terms due on receipt, and recorded receipt of balance owed of $6,480 via Check No. 654.
10	1/11/14	Recorded Sales Receipt No. 5116 for rent of Villa Kailani Unit #2 for one week. Collected MasterCard payment in full of $4,680 from a new customer, Berkshire Hathaway.
11	1/14/14	Deposited checks and MasterCard payments of $14,280 to checking account.
12	1/14/14	Wrote Check No. 986 for $23,000 to Furniture King (a new vendor) as payment for new furniture.
13	1/15/14	Wrote Check No. 987 as payment on account to Reilly Custodial. (*Hint:* Use Pay Bills.)
14	1/18/14	Recorded Sales Receipt No. 5117 for rent of Moana Unit #3 and Villa Kailani Unit #3 for one week each. Collected American Express payment in full of $8,528 from a new customer, Bridgette Hacker.
15	1/18/14	Recorded Sales Receipt No. 5118 for rent of Moana Unit #4 for one week. Collected Check No. 909 as payment in full of $12,480 from a new customer, Lockheed Martin.
16	1/18/14	Recorded Invoice No. 7509 for rental of Villa Kailani Units #1 and #2 for one week to Boeing (Terms: net 30); net invoice $7,800.
17	1/21/14	Deposited $21,008 of undeposited funds to checking account.
18	1/23/14	Paid Reilly Custodial $3,000 via Check No. 988 for Cleaning (a new expense account).
19	1/24/14	Collected a $5,125 check from a new customer, ExxonMobil.
20	1/25/14	Recorded Invoice No. 7510 for rental of Villa Kailani Unit #4 for one week to Brice Montoya. Applied his advance payment to this invoice, noted terms due on receipt, and recorded receipt of balance owed of $3,240 via Check No. 1874.

Event #	Date	Business Event
21	1/28/14	Deposited $8,365 of undeposited funds to Bank of Hawaii.
22	1/30/14	Wrote Check No. 989 for $12,000 to Pacific Electric (a new vendor) for Utilities.
23	1/30/14	Wrote Check No. 990 for $3,700 to AT&T (a new vendor) for Telephone Expenses.
24	1/30/14	Wrote Check No. 991 for $15,000 to Sunset Media (a new vendor) for Advertising and Promotion.
25	1/31/14	Process payroll per the information provided in Table 7.9, starting with Check No. 992.

Item	Fran	Daniele
Hours	n/a	150
Rate		$ 20.00
Earnings	6,250.00	3,000.00
Federal Withholding	−856.25	−411.00
Social Security Employee	−387.50	−186.00
Medicare Employee	−90.63	−43.50
HI Withholding	−442.33	−195.33
HI Disability	−1.25	−0.60
HI E&T	0.63	0.30
Social Security Employer	387.50	186.00
Medicare Company	90.63	43.50
Federal Unemployment	50.00	24.00
HI Unemployment	187.50	90.00
Check Amount	4,472.04	2,163.57

Table 7.9

Earnings Information for Aloha Properties

Requirements:

Record business transactions in chronological order (remember, dates are in the month of January 2014). After recording the transactions, create and print the following for January 2014. (Be sure to keep this QuickBooks Accountant file in a safe place; it will be used as a starting file for this case in Chapter 8.)

1 Balance Sheet Standard (Be sure to show the Accumulated Depreciation account as the last fixed asset account.)

2 Profit & Loss Standard

3 Statement of Cash Flows

4 Transaction List by Date

Chapter 7 Comprehensive Problems

Comprehensive Problem 1: SARAH DUNCAN, CPA

service

Use the following information to create a new company in QuickBooks Accountant using the EasyStep Interview. Then create and print the reports as requested below.

Sarah Duncan, CPA, is starting her new sole proprietorship at One Constellation Road, Vandenberg Village, CA 93436. She'll start effective 9/1/14 and use a calendar year for fiscal and tax purposes. She'll be using QuickBooks

sole proprietorship

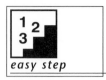

Accountant's manual payroll calculations feature to account for herself and her one employee, and her federal tax ID number, EIN, and California EDD number is 574-8541-2. Both employees were hired 9/1/14, payroll taxes are paid quarterly, and no wage code is necessary as they file manually. (Be sure to set payroll to monthly manual calculations and perform payroll setup before entering transactions below.) Sarah lives at 259 St. Andrews Way, Vandenberg Village, CA 93436. Her Social Security number is 574-85-4125. She's married (one income) and earns $72,000 per year. Bob Humphrey, her other employee, lives at 453 Sirius, Vandenberg Village, CA 93436. His Social Security number is 632-78-1245. He's single and earns $20 per hour. Sarah's California unemployment tax rate is 3.4%, the disability tax rate is 1.1%, and she pays all state taxes to the Employment Development Department. Her business, of course, is in the Accounting industry as a Certified Public Accountant. She does not collect sales tax for her services, nor does she use sales receipts because she invoices her clients for services provided and gives them 15-day credit terms. She does accept credit card payments and tracks time spent on each client's services for billing purposes. She will have two payroll items: salary and hourly wage. She will perform audit, tax, and accounting services for $150, $150, and $100 per hour, respectively. (***Hint:*** Create service items for each of these and assign the appropriate income accounts and descriptions to each.) Modify the Consulting Income account to be Auditing Services Income. Employees are paid monthly but file weekly time sheets on Friday of each week. Clients are also invoiced on Fridays of each week after time sheets have been processed. Add the following transactions. (***Note:*** Be sure to enter these transactions in the proper date period.)

Chronological List of Business Events

Event #	Date	Business Event
1	9/1/14	Opened a business checking account at Union Bank with a $50,000 deposit as her investment in the business (Bank account name: Checking).
2	9/1/14	Borrowed $15,000 from Union Bank to purchase a copier. Term was three years with monthly payments of $463.16 beginning 10/1/14.
3	9/1/14	Purchased a $15,000 copier from Xerox Corporation using Check No. 1001.
4	9/1/14	Signed an engagement letter to perform tax services for Valley Medical Group, a new client located at 234 Third St., Lompoc, CA 93436. Terms: net 15. Created a new job: 2014 Tax Services for Valley Medical.
5	9/4/14	Purchased furniture and fixtures from Sam Snead, a prior tenant in her rented office space, for $4,000 using Check No. 1002 from Union Bank.
6	9/4/14	Sarah worked four hours each day on 9/2, 9/3, and 9/4 on the Valley Medical job and four hours more on each of those days that were not billable. Bob worked six hours each day on 9/3 and 9/4 on the Valley Medical job and two more hours on each of those days that were not billable.
7	9/4/14	Created Invoice No. 5001 to Valley Medical based on time costs incurred (Terms: net 15). When you choose the hours worked for

Event #	Date	Business Event
		the week to be billed, be sure to click the Option button and then select the option "Combine activities with the same service items."
8	9/4/14	Wrote Check No. 1003 for $15,000 to Dean Witter for a short-term investment, another current asset.
9	9/7/14	Wrote Check No. 1004 to Wiser Realty as payment for the first and last months' rent and security deposit for $9,000 (one-third for rent, one-third for last month's rent recorded as prepaid rent, and one-third for the security deposit). (*Note:* Both the prepaid rent and security deposit are considered other assets.)
10	9/8/14	Signed an engagement letter to perform audit services for Pactuco, a new client located at 345 Central Ave., Lompoc, CA 93436. Created a new job: 2014 Audit Services for Pactuco.
11	9/9/14	Signed an engagement letter to perform compilation services for Celite Corporation, a new client located at 20 Central Ave., Lompoc, CA 93436. Created a new job: Second Quarter Accounting Services for Celite.
12	9/9/14	Received a payment in the amount of $5,000 from Celite Corporation as an advance on services to be rendered. Be sure to record this as a receipt from the job and not just the customer. Sarah anticipates completing services for this client by the end of the month. She then deposited the check into the Union checking account.
13	9/11/14	Sarah worked five hours each day on 9/7, 9/8, and 9/9 on the Valley Medical job, and three more hours on each of those days that were not billable. She also worked eight hours on 9/10 on the Pactuco job as well as eight hours on 9/11 on the Celite job. Bob worked three hours each day on 9/7, 9/8, and 9/9 on the Valley Medical job and four more hours on each of those days that were not billable. He also worked eight hours on 9/10 on the Pactuco job and eight hours on 9/11 on the Celite job.
14	9/11/14	Created Invoice Nos. 5002, 5003, and 5004 to Valley Medical, Pactuco, and Celite based on time costs incurred (Terms: net 15). Applied credits available for Celite.
15	9/14/14	Signed an engagement letter to perform compilation services for Lompoc Hospital, a new client located at 233 D St., Lompoc, CA 93436. Created a new job: Second Quarter Accounting Services for Lompoc Hospital.
16	9/16/14	Received check for $7,200 from Valley Medical as payment on account.
17	9/17/14	Deposited Valley Medical's check into the Union savings account.
18	9/18/14	Sarah worked four hours each day from 9/14 to 9/18 on the Pactuco job as well as two hours on 9/14 and 9/15 on the Celite job. She also worked five hours each on 9/17 and 9/18 on the Lompoc Hospital job. Bob worked eight hours on 9/14 on the Valley Medical job, eight hours on 9/15 on the Pactuco job, and eight hours each day on 9/16 and 9/17 on the Celite job. On 9/18, he attended eight hours of training at a local university.
19	9/18/14	Created Invoice Nos. 5005, 5006, 5007, and 5008 to Valley Medical, Pactuco, Celite, and Lompoc Hospital based on time costs incurred (Terms: net 15). Applied credits available for Celite.
20	9/25/14	Sarah worked six hours each day from 9/21 through 9/24 on the Pactuco audit and two hours each of those days as nonbillable hours. Bob worked six hours each day from 9/21 through 9/25 on the Lompoc Hospital job.

Event #	Date	Business Event
21	9/25/14	Created Invoice Nos. 5009 and 5010 to Pactuco and Lompoc Hospital based on time costs incurred (Terms: net 15).
22	9/29/14	Wrote Check No. 1005 to Pacific Gas & Electric for $400 in utilities expenses.
23	9/29/14	Wrote Check No. 1006 to Mark Jackson Insurance for $8,000 in professional liability insurance for the year 9/1/14 through 8/31/15. (Record to prepaid insurance!)
24	9/29/14	Wrote Check No. 1007 to Allan Hancock College for $300 in continuing education fees for Bob's training.
25	9/29/14	Received a bill from Verizon Wireless in the amount of $525 for telephone expenses for September. Terms are net 30.
26	9/29/14	Received a bill from Staples in the amount of $1,500 for supplies (a current asset). Terms are net 30.
27	9/30/14	Used Check Nos. 1008 and 1009 to pay herself her $6,000 monthly salary and her assistant Bob Humphrey for 123 hours of work at $20 per hour, as shown in Table 7.10.

Table 7.10

Earnings Information for Sarah Duncan, CPA

Item	Sarah	Bob
Hours	n/a	123
Annual Salary/Hourly Rate	$72,000.00	$ 20.00
Earnings	6,000.00	2,460.00
Federal Withholding	−770.50	−305.05
Social Security Employee	−372.00	−152.52
Medicare Employee	−87.00	−35.67
CA Withholding	−231.40	−77.98
CA Disability	−4.80	−1.97
CA Employee Training Tax	6.00	2.46
Social Security Employer	372.00	152.52
Medicare Company	87.00	35.67
Federal Unemployment	48.00	19.68
CA Unemployment	204.00	83.64
Check Amount	4,534.30	1,886.81

Requirements:

Create a QuickBooks Accountant file for Sarah Duncan, CPA, using the Easy-Step Interview. Add vendors, inventory items, customers, and employees first. Record business transactions in chronological order (remember, dates are in the month of September 2014). After recording the transactions, create and print the following for September 2014.

a. Customer Contact List (Customer, Bill to, and Balance Total only)

b. Vendor Contact List (Vendor, Address, and Balance Total only)

c. Employee Contact List (Employee, SS No., and Address only)

d. Profit & Loss Standard

e. Standard Balance Sheet

f. Statement of Cash Flows

g. Transaction List by Date (Type, Date, Number, Name, Account, and Amount Fields)

Comprehensive Problem 2: PACIFIC BREW

Pacific Brew was incorporated January 1, 2016, upon the issuance of 50,000 shares of $1 par value capital stock for $50,000. The business is located at 500 West Ocean, Arcata, California, 95521, and Michael Patrick oversees this wholesale distribution and sales operation. The company will have a calendar fiscal year, has a federal employer ID number of 77-1357465 and a state ID number of 387-1724-0, and plans to use QuickBooks Accountant's inventory, purchase orders, and payroll features. Payroll taxes are paid quarterly, and no wage code is necessary as they file manually. Listed below are the items the company intends to carry in its inventory, the suppliers it purchases from, and the customers (whose billing and shipping addresses are the same) it has lined up. No sales tax is collected because all of its customers are resellers.

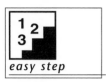

easy step

merchandising

corporation

In addition to distributing beer, Pacific Brew provides consulting services to customers on bar operations, menu plans, and beverage selection. These services are billed to customers at the rate of $85 per hour and are recorded in an income account called Consulting.

Pacific has two other employees, as shown below. The company's unemployment rate is 3%, its employee training tax rate is 0.1%, its disability tax rate is 1.1%, and it uses only two payroll items for wages: salary and hourly wage. All payroll taxes are paid quarterly. There is no need to track time for these employees because there are no jobs per se. Federal withholding, unemployment, Social Security, and Medicare are paid to the U.S. Treasury, while California withholding, unemployment, employee disability, and employee training tax are paid to the EDD. Payroll is paid semi-monthly and is handled manually. The company does not provide insurance or retirement benefits. Employees do not receive paid time off.

Vendors

	Mad River	Lost Coast	JD Salinger	Humboldt
Address	195 Taylor Way	123 West Third St.	101 Market St.	865 10th St.
City	Blue Lake	Eureka	San Francisco	Arcata
State	CA	CA	CA	CA
Zip	95525	95501	94102	95521

Items

#	Description	Cost	Price	Income Account
100	Consulting	—	$85.00	Consulting
302	Mad River Pale Ale	$ 5.00	$ 6.00	Sales
303	Mad River Stout	$ 6.00	$ 7.00	Sales
304	Mad River Amber Ale	$ 4.00	$ 5.00	Sales
305	Mad River Porter	$ 5.50	$ 6.50	Sales
402	Lost Coast Pale Ale	$ 5.25	$ 6.25	Sales
403	Lost Coast Stout	$ 6.25	$ 7.25	Sales
404	Lost Coast Amber Ale	$ 4.25	$ 5.25	Sales
502	Humboldt Pale Ale	$ 5.50	$ 6.50	Sales
506	Humboldt IPA	$ 6.50	$ 7.50	Sales
507	Humboldt Red Nectar	$ 7.00	$ 8.00	Sales

Customers

	Avalon Bistro	Hole in the Wall	Ocean Grove
Address	1080 3rd St.	590 G St.	570 Ewing St.
City	Arcata	Arcata	Trinidad
State	CA	CA	CA
Zip	95521	95521	95570

	River House	Michael's Brew House	Bon Jovi's
Address	222 Weller St.	2198 Union St.	4257 Petaluma Hill
City	Petaluma	San Francisco	Santa Rosa
State	CA	CA	CA
Zip	95404	94123	95404

Employees

	Michael Patrick	Shawn Lopez	Emilio Duarte
Address	333 Spring Rd.	234 University Dr.	23 Palm Dr. #23
City	Arcata	Arcata	Arcata
State	CA	CA	CA
Zip	95521	95521	95521
Hire Date	1/1/16	1/1/16	1/1/16
SS#	655-85-1253	702-54-8746	012-58-4654
Earnings	$50,000/year (salary)	$12/hour (wage)	$11/hour (wage)
Filing Status	Married (one income)	Single	Single

Chronological List of Business Events

Event #	Date	Business Event
1	1/2/16	Sold 50,000 shares of $1 par value common stock for $50,000 cash to various shareholders. Deposited these funds into a newly created Wells Fargo checking account (Name: Checking).
2	1/5/16	Using Purchase Order No. 1001, ordered 500 each of Items 302, 303, 304, and 305 for immediate delivery from Mad River (Terms: due on receipt). (*Hint:* Use QuickBooks Accountant Help to customize the purchase order so that the terms of the sale are specified on both the screen and print versions of the purchase order. Always save the terms for the vendor.)
3	1/5/16	Using Purchase Order No. 1002, ordered 400 each of Items 502, 506, and 507 for immediate delivery from Humboldt (Terms: due on receipt).
4	1/5/16	Using Purchase Order No. 1003, ordered 300 each of Items 402, 403, and 404 for immediate delivery from Lost Coast (Terms: 30 days).
5	1/5/16	Rented a warehouse from JD Salinger, landlord, for $2,500 per month by paying first month's rent and a security deposit with Wells Fargo Check No. 101 for $5,000. (*Hint:* Add a new other asset type account called Security Deposit.)
6	1/6/16	Purchased shelving, desks, and office equipment from JD Salinger for $8,000 via Wells Fargo Check No. 102.

Event #	Date	Business Event
7	1/7/16	Invested $30,000 in a short-term investment with Schwab Investments using Wells Fargo Check No. 103.
8	1/8/16	Borrowed $40,000 from Wells Fargo Bank as a long-term note due in three years. The money was deposited into the company's Wells Fargo account.
9	1/9/16	Purchased warehouse equipment for $10,200 from West Coast Supply using Wells Fargo Check No. 104.
10	1/12/16	Received and paid for items on Purchase Order No. 1001 to Mad River via Check No. 105 for $10,250.
11	1/12/16	Provided 50 hours of consulting services (Sales Receipt No. 5001) to Michael's Brew House. Payment of $4,250 in the form of a check was deposited into Wells Fargo Bank that same day.
12	1/12/16	Paid for items (Purchase Order No. 1002) received from Humboldt using Check No. 106 for $7,600.
13	1/13/16	Recorded Sales Receipt No. 5002 to Bon Jovi's for 25 units of Item 305, 30 units of Item 506, and 50 units of Item 507. Payment of $787.50 (in the form of a check) was deposited into Wells Fargo Bank that same day.
14	1/13/16	Provided 60 hours of consulting services (Sales Receipt No. 5003) to River House. Payment of $5,100 in the form of a check was deposited into Wells Fargo Bank that same day.
15	1/14/16	Recorded Sales Receipt No. 5004 to Ocean Grove for 30 units of Item 304, 40 units of Item 302, and 50 units of Item 502. Payment of $715 in the form of a check was deposited into Wells Fargo Bank that same day.
16	1/16/16	Paid employees. Duarte worked 80 hours and Lopez worked 75 hours during the period. Assign check numbers to handwritten checks starting with Check No. 107. See tax information in Table 7.11.
17	1/16/16	Recorded Sales Receipt No. 5005 to Avalon Bistro for 40 units of Item 302, 50 units of Item 507, and 35 units of Item 506. Payment of $902.50 in the form of a check was deposited into Wells Fargo Bank that same day.
18	1/16/16	Recorded Sales Receipt No. 5006 to Michael's Brew House for 100 each of Items 302, 305, and 506. Payment of $2,000 in the form of a check was deposited into Wells Fargo Bank that same day.

Requirements:

Create a QuickBooks Accountant file for Pacific Brew. Add vendors, inventory items, customers, and employees first. Record business transactions in chronological order (remember, dates are in the month of January 2016). After recording the transactions, create and print the following for January 2016. (Be sure to keep this QuickBooks Accountant file in a safe place since it will be used as a starting file for this case in Chapter 11.)

a. Customer Contact List (Customer, Bill to, and Balance Total only)

b. Vendor Contact List (Vendor, Address, and Balance Total only)

c. Employee Contact List (Employee, SS No., and Address only)

Table 7.11

Earnings Information for Pacific Brew

Item	Emilio	Shawn	Michael
Earnings	880.00	900.00	2,083.33
Federal Withholding	−120.56	−123.30	−285.42
Social Security Employee	−54.56	−55.80	−129.17
Medicare Employee	−12.76	−13.05	−30.21
CA Withholding	−48.40	−49.50	−114.58
CA Disability	−4.40	−4.50	−10.42
CA Employee Training Tax	0.88	0.90	2.08
Social Security Company	54.56	55.80	129.17
Medicare Company	12.76	13.05	30.21
Federal Unemployment	7.04	7.20	16.67
CA Unemployment Company	26.40	27.00	62.50
Check Amount	639.32	653.85	1,513.53

d. Item Listing (Item, Description, Type, Cost, Price, and Quantity On Hand only)

e. Balance Sheet Standard

f. Profit & Loss Standard

g. Statement of Cash Flows

h. Transaction List by Date

Comprehensive Problem 3: SUNSET SPAS

A family friend of your parents, Nancy Mandela, called and said she heard you were studying accounting and might be able to help her set up QuickBooks Accountant for a business she just purchased called Sunset Spas. She acquired the existing checking account, accounts receivable, inventory, fixed assets, and accounts payable as of 12/31/14. She chose to use QuickBooks Accountant starting January 1, 2015, and needed your help to set up and record the first two weeks of business transactions. You agreed and were anxious to get started.

The company's checking account at Bank of America (Name: Checking) had a reconciled balance on 12/31/14 of $23,558.75. Furniture and equipment were valued at $55,000.00, inventory at $23,000.00, accounts receivable at $33,941.25, accounts payable at $35,500.00, and capital stock at $100,000.00. Bryan Christopher oversees this retail operation, which is located at 300 West Street, Del Mar, California, 92014. The company will have a calendar fiscal year, a federal employer ID number of 77-9851247, and a California EDD number of 012-3435-8. It plans to use QuickBooks Accountant's inventory, purchase orders, and payroll features. The tables that follow list the suppliers Sunset purchases from, the items it intends to carry in inventory, and the customers it has lined up. The customers' billing and shipping addresses are the same. The company collects 7.75% sales tax on all spa sales and remits amounts collected to the State Board of Equalization quarterly. No sales tax is collected on installation or consulting services. The company records each sale individually.

In addition to selling spas, Sunset Spas also provides installation and consulting services to customers. These services are billed to customers at the rate of $75 and $80 per hour, respectively, and are recorded in an income account called Service Sales. Spa sales are recorded in an income account titled Merchandise Sales. All customers currently have credit terms of "due on receipt."

Sunset also employs two other people, as shown in the following tables. It does not provide insurance, retirement benefits, or paid time off. All employees were hired effective 1/1/15. All taxes are paid quarterly. The company's unemployment insurance rate is 3.4%. It uses only two payroll items for wages: salary and hourly wage. Federal withholding, unemployment, Social Security, and Medicare are paid to the U.S. Treasury, while California withholding, unemployment, employee disability, and employee training tax are paid to the EDD. Payroll is paid semi-monthly. The company would like to use time tracking in QuickBooks Accountant, but it plans to calculate payroll manually. Payroll taxes are paid quarterly, and no wage code is necessary as they file manually.

Vendors

	Sundance Spas	Cal Spas
Address	14525 Monte Vista Ave.	1462 East Ninth Street
City	Chino	Pomona
State	CA	CA
Zip	91710	91766
Phone	(909) 614-0679	(909) 623-8781
Beginning Balance	$18,000	$17,500
Terms	Due on receipt	Due on receipt

Inventory Service/Items

#	Description	Vendor	Cost	Price	Income Account	Beginning Balance
100	Installation	—	—	$ 75	Service Sales	—
101	Consulting	—	—	$ 85	Service Sales	—
201	Maxus	Sundance	$5,000	$7,000	Merchandise Sales	1
202	Optima	Sundance	$6,000	$8,000	Merchandise Sales	1
203	Cameo	Sundance	$7,000	$9,000	Merchandise Sales	0
301	Galaxy	Cal Spas	$4,500	$6,500	Merchandise Sales	1
302	Ultimate	Cal Spas	$5,500	$7,500	Merchandise Sales	0
303	Aqua	Cal Spas	$7,500	$9,500	Merchandise Sales	1

Customers

	J's Landscaping	Marriott Hotels	Pam's Designs
Address	12 Bones Way	97444 Miramar	5144 Union
City	San Diego	San Diego	San Diego
State	CA	CA	CA
Zip	92354	92145	92129
Phone	(858) 555-1348	(858) 555-7407	(707) 555-5748
Beginning Balance	$8,081.25	$18,317.50	$7,542.50
Terms	Due on receipt	Due on receipt	Due on receipt

Employees

	Bryan Christopher	Loriel Sanchez	Sharon Lee
Address	12 Mesa Way	2342 Court	323 Ridgefield Pl.
City	Del Mar	Del Mar	Del Mar
State	CA	CA	CA
Zip	92014	92014	92014
Phone	(858) 555-1264	(858) 555-3365	(858) 555-9874
SS#	556-95-4789	475-54-8746	125-58-8452
Earnings	$60,000/year (salary)	$13/hour (wage)	$12/hour (wage)
Filing Status	Married (one income)	Married (one income)	Single
Type	Regular	Regular	Regular

Chronological List of Business Events

Event #	Date	Business Event
1	1/4/15	Borrowed $200,000 from Hacienda Bank as a long-term note due in three years. The money was deposited into the company's bank account and a "Notes Payable" long-term liability type account was recorded.
2	1/4/15	Using Purchase Order No. 5001, ordered 10 each of Items 201, 202, and 203 for immediate delivery (Terms: due on receipt) from Sundance. (*Note:* Use QuickBooks Accountant Help to customize the purchase order so that the terms of the sale are specified on both the screen and print versions of the purchase order.) (*Hint:* Type **customize a purchase order** in the ask text box.)
3	1/4/15	Using Purchase Order No. 5002, ordered five each of Items 301, 302, and 303 for immediate delivery from Cal Spas (Terms: due on receipt).
4	1/4/15	Rented a retail store front from K Realty, landlord, for $3,000 per month by paying first and last month's rent with Check No. 101 for $6,000. This is a long-term lease for five years.
5	1/7/15	Time sheets were completed for the week ended 1/5/15. Sharon Lee worked eight hours of nonbillable time each day Wednesday (1/2/15) through Friday (1/4/15) and three hours on Saturday (1/5/15). Loriel Sanchez worked seven hours on 1/2/15, seven hours on 1/3/15, and six hours on 1/4/15, all of which was nonbillable time.
6	1/7/15	Received payment on account from Marriott of $18,317.50 and deposited their check immediately.
7	1/8/15	Purchased shelving, desks, and office equipment from Office Max for $8,000 using Check No. 102.
8	1/9/15	Invested $30,000 in a short-term investment (an "Other Current Asset" type of account) with Poole Investments via Check No. 103.
9	1/10/15	Purchased several computer systems and printers from Coast Computer Supply with Check No. 104 for $8,900.
10	1/11/15	Paid for items (Purchase Order No. 5001) received from Sundance using Check No. 105.
11	1/11/15	Created a new job (JL401) for J's Landscaping to consult on various clients.

Event #	Date	Business Event
12	1/11/15	Time sheets were completed for the week ended 1/11/15. Sharon Lee and Loriel Sanchez both worked eight hours of nonbillable time each day Monday (1/7/15) through Thursday (1/10/15). Sharon and Loriel worked five hours each on Job JL401 on Friday (1/11/15) and three hours each of nonbillable time.
13	1/11/15	Invoiced J's Landscaping for consulting (Job JL401) using invoice 6001. Payment was received and deposited that same day.
14	1/14/15	Paid for items (Purchase Order No. 5002) received from Cal Spas using Check No. 106.
15	1/14/15	Created a new job (PD402) for Pam's Design to install 3 Item 301, 1 Item 202, and 1 Item 303 spas in various locations.
16	1/15/15	Sharon Lee spent eight hours on 1/14/15 and eight hours on 1/15/15 installing spas on Job PD402. (Record on time sheet.)
17	1/15/15	Created a new job (JL403) for J's Landscaping to install 3 Item 201 and 2 Item 203 spas in various locations.
18	1/15/15	Created a new job (MH404) for Marriott to consult on future spa designs.
19	1/16/15	Loriel Sanchez spent seven hours on 1/15/15 and eight hours on 1/16/15 installing spas on Job JL403. (Record on time sheet.)
20	1/16/15	Bryan Christopher spent 10 hours on 1/15/15 consulting with Marriott on Job MH404. (Record on time sheet, but keep in mind that Bryan is paid a salary and not for hours worked.)
21	1/16/15	Invoiced Pam's Design for Job PD402 for both installation and spas sold (Invoice No. 6002). A check was received in payment but was not immediately deposited.
22	1/16/15	Invoiced J's Landscaping for Job JL403 for both installation and spas sold (Invoice No. 6003). A check was received in payment but was not immediately deposited.
23	1/16/15	Paid employees for work performed through 1/16/15. Sanchez worked 75 hours and Lee worked 83 hours during the period. Checks are to be handwritten starting with Check No. 107. See tax information in Table 7.12.
24	1/16/15	Received a check from Marriott Hotels for future consulting services of $5,000, which was deposited into the checking account that same day.
25	1/16/15	Deposited remaining balances in Undeposited Funds to checking account.
26	1/16/15	Paid a portion of bill owed to Sundance Spas for $5,000 with Check No. 110. (Be sure to use the Pay Bills feature; refer to QuickBooks Accountant Help if necessary.)

Requirements:

Create a QuickBooks Accountant file for Sunset Spas. Add vendors, inventory items, customers, and employees first. All quantities and balances on hand as of 12/31/14, including the Checking account and Furniture and Equipment account, should be recorded. Then record a journal entry to transfer the uncategorized income and expenses and opening balance equity as of 12/31/14 to capital stock. (**Hint:** The resulting capital stock balance should be $100,000.00.) Record business transactions in chronological order. (Remember, dates are in the month of January 2015.) After recording the transactions, create and print

Table 7.12

Earnings Information for Sunset Spas, Inc.

Item	Bryan	Loriel	Sharon
Hours	n/a	75	83
Rate	$60,000.00	$ 13.00	$ 12.00
Earnings	2,500.00	975.00	996.00
Federal Withholding	−342.50	−133.58	−136.45
Social Security Employee	−155.00	−60.45	−61.75
Medicare Employee	−36.25	−14.14	−14.44
CA Withholding	−137.50	−53.63	−54.78
CA Disability	−12.50	−4.88	−4.98
CA Employee Training Tax	2.50	0.98	1.00
Social Security Employer	155.00	60.45	61.75
Medicare Company	36.25	14.14	14.44
Federal Unemployment	20.00	7.80	7.97
CA Unemployment	6.25	2.44	2.49
Check Amount	1,816.25	708.32	723.60

the following for January 2015. (Be sure to keep this QuickBooks Accountant file in a safe place; it will be used as a starting file for this case in Chapter 11.)

a. Customer Contact List (Customer, Bill to, Phone, and Balance Total only)

b. Customer Balance Summary

c. Vendor Contact List (Vendor, Address, Phone, and Balance Total only)

d. Vendor Balance Summary

e. Employee Contact List (Employee, SS No., Phone, and Address only)

f. Item Listing (Item, Description, Type, Cost, Price, and Quantity On Hand only)

g. Trial Balance as of 1/1/15

h. Standard Balance Sheet as of 1/16/15

i. Profit & Loss Standard for 1/1/15 to 1/16/15

j. Statement of Cash Flows for 1/1/15 to 1/16/15

k. Transaction List by Date for 1/1/15 to 1/16/15

Comprehensive Problem 4: BRIDGETTE SWEET PHOTOGRAPHY

Bridgette Sweet has asked you to help her use QuickBooks Accountant for her photography business. She has been in business since January 2010 and has been using a spreadsheet to keep track of her business transactions. Now she wants to start using QuickBooks Accountant effective January 2013, the beginning of her fiscal year, because she is certain that QuickBooks Accountant will help her get organized. You begin your work creating her QuickBooks Accountant file.

Her corporation's name is Bridgette Sweet Photography, with a legal title of Bridgette Sweet Photography, Inc., with a federal employer ID of 77-6412488. Her studio is located at 828 S. Wabash Ave., Chicago, IL 60605. Her main focus is photographing weddings and corporate events and selling prints and frames resulting from her work. The company does keep an inventory of frames using the average cost method, so Bridgette wants to use QuickBooks Accountant inventory and purchase order features. She will also sell prints and albums at her cost but does not stock these items. She has a checking account that had a balance of $9,000 at 12/31/12.

As a general service-based company (photographer), she will use a chart of accounts appropriate to her business. She does not create estimates or use sales orders or statements. She does use invoices to bill her clients but does not use progress billing. She would like to use QuickBooks Accountant to manage her bills and keep track of her employees' time. (***Hint***: Be sure to set up preferences like you did in the previous chapter.) Her standard payment terms for customers are net 30 and credit limit is $15,000.

Bridgette does not plan to use QuickBooks Accountant payroll or payroll tax service and thus will be calculating payroll manually on a monthly basis. She employs two individuals as photography assistants and wants to track time using QuickBooks Accountant. Employees are all subject to Illinois taxes and are paid monthly. The company's unemployment rate is 5.4% and federal and state taxes are paid and filed quarterly. The company's Dept. of Employment Security Acct No. is 3383710-8 and their Dept. of Revenue FEIN and SEQ No. is 32-2930766 102. All taxes are paid quarterly. All employees use time tickets to record their time.

The state of Illinois imposes a 9.75% sales tax on all services and merchandise, which the company must collect and remit quarterly to the Illinois Dept. of Revenue. Use ST as the sales tax name. Use Sales Tax as the sales tax description. All customers located in Illinois must be charged this state sales tax.

As of 12/31/12, the company owned $10,000 in Furniture and $5,000 in Equipment, had $2,000 and $1,000 in Accumulated Depreciation related to each. (***Hint***: Remove the existing Furniture and Equipment and Accumulated Depreciation accounts and establish new accounts: Equipment, Acc. Dep. Equipment, Furniture, and Acc. Dep. Furniture, being sure to orient the accumulated depreciation accounts below the newly created Furniture and Equipment accounts.) The company also owed $12,000 on a note payable due in three years. Capital stock and retained earnings were $15,000 and $19,000 respectively as of 12/31/12. Details of accounts receivable ($26,000), inventory ($3,000)—and accounts payable ($4,000) balances are shown below. Once you have entered receivables, payables, and inventory items be sure to close the balance in Opening Balance Equity to Retained Earnings like you did in the previous chapter.

Vendors

Vendor Name	US	PF	GP	ILR
Company Name	US Photo	Peterson Framing	GP Leasing	Illinois Dept. of Revenue
Address	140 S. Dearborn St.	2420 W. Belmont	4045 North Rockwell St.	
City	Chicago	Chicago	Chicago	Springfield
State	Illinois	Illinois	Illinois	Illinois
Zip	60603	60618	60618	62726
Vendor Balance	$1,000	$500	$2,500	$0
Terms	Net 30	Net 30	Net 30	n/a
Credit Limit	$20,000	$25,000	$10,000	n/a

Customers

Customer Name	Hain	Foster	Yelp
Company Name	Hain Wedding	Foster Corporation	Yelp Corporation
Address	4011 W. 63rd	2139 S. Laramie Ave.	1640 W. Fulton St.
City	Chicago	Chicago	Chicago
State	Illinois	Illinois	Illinois
Zip	60629	60804	60605
Tax Code	ST	ST	ST
Customer Balance	$8,000	$3,000	$15,000
Terms	Net 30	Net 30	Net 30
Credit Limit	$15,000	$15,000	$15,000

Items

Item Name	On Hand	Type	Description	Cost	Rate/Sales Price	Account	COGS Account
1000	n/a	Service	Weddings		$200	Weddings*	n/a
1001	n/a	Service	Assistant 1		$ 75	Weddings*	n/a
1002	n/a	Service	Assistant 2		$ 60	Weddings *	n/a
1010	n/a	Service	Conferences		$250	Corporate Events *	n/a
1011	n/a	Service	Assistant 1		$ 75	Corporate Events *	n/a
1012	n/a	Service	Assistant 2		$ 60	Corporate Events *	n/a
2000	20	Inventory Part	Frames	$150	$350	Sales	Cost of Goods Sold
2010	n/a	Non-Inventory Part**	Prints	$20		Sales	n/a

*New income type accounts.

**Do not check the check box located under the button Enable.

Employees

Name	Bridgette Sweet	Kyle Garrett	Nick Pease
Address	323 Lakeshore Dr.	893 West 34th St.	100 Park Ave. #2
City	Chicago	Chicago	Chicago
State	Illinois	Illinois	Illinois
Zip	60000	60001	60602
Hire Date	1/1/10	3/1/10	7/1/10
Social Security #	215-85-9874	312-54-7125	556-84-7124
Earnings	$60,000/year	$25/hour	$20/hour
Filing Status	Married	Single	Single

Chronological List of Business Events

Event #	Date	Business Event
1	1/02/13	Created two new jobs: Job name 432 for Yelp Corporation and job name 433 for a new customer name Dutton with company name Dutton Wedding. Both are subject to sales tax.
2	1/03/13	Received $15,000 on check #4230980 from Yelp Corporation as payment on account and deposited it to the checking account.
3	1/04/13	Bridgette, Kyle, and Nick all worked six hours on job 432 for Yelp Corporation. Use item 1010 to bill Bridgette's time, 1011 to bill Kyle's time, and 1012 to bill Nick's time.
4	1/07/13	Created two new purchase orders: 6411 to Peterson Framing for 50 frames for inventory and 6412 to US Photo for 100 prints to be billed to Yelp Corporation on job 432.
5	1/10/13	Received all 50 frames ordered on purchase order 6411 with an invoice #8746 from Peterson Framing. Received all 100 prints ordered on purchase order 6412 with an invoice #10413 from US Photo.
6	1/11/13	Invoiced Yelp Corporation $14,333.35 on invoice 10207 for time and prints incurred on job 432 and for 25 frames with Net 30 terms. Be sure to click the **Options** button when choosing billable time and costs and select the **Transfer item descriptions** option.
7	1/14/13	Purchased $5,600 of additional equipment from new vendor name: CC, company name: Costco using check 9843.
8	1/19/13	Bridgette, Kyle, and Nick all worked seven, three, and two hours respectively on job 433, the Dutton Wedding. Use item 1000 to bill Bridgette's time, 1001 to bill Kyle's time, and 1002 to bill Nick's time.
9	1/21/13	Created purchase order 6413 to US Photo for 30 prints to be billed to Dutton Wedding job 433.
10	1/22/13	Paid rent to GP Leasing in the amount of $1,750 using check 9844.
11	1/24/13	Received all 30 prints ordered on purchase order 6413 with an invoice #10489 from US Photo.
12	1/25/13	Invoiced Dutton Wedding $14,097.39 on invoice 10208 for time and prints incurred on job 433 and for 30 frames with Net 30 terms.
13	1/28/13	Bridgette, Kyle, and Nick all worked four, three, and two hours respectively on a new job 434 for a new Customer name Benson, company name Benson Wedding. Use item 1000 to bill Bridgette's time, 1001 to bill Kyle's time, and 1002 to bill Nick's time. This customer is subject to sales tax.
14	1/29/13	Created purchase order 6414 to US Photo for 35 prints (new cost $24 each) and three albums (a new non-inventory part with Item name 2030, Description: Albums, price $75, account Sales, to be billed to Benson Wedding job 434).
15	1/30/13	Received and deposited check number 12533 for $8,000 as prepayment from a new customer name Krenwinkle, company name Krenwinkle Wedding, job 435, a photo shoot.
16	1/30/13	Received all 35 prints and all three albums ordered on purchase order 6414 with invoice #10599 from US Photo.
17	1/31/13	Invoiced Benson Wedding $4346.10 on invoice 10209 for time and costs incurred on job 434 and for five frames with Net 30 terms. Be sure to modify the print price to $24 per print.
18	Various	In addition to the billable hours described above, employees worked additional administrative hours. A listing of all hours worked is shown below.
19	1/31/13	Pay bills due by 1/31/13. Total payment $4,000 using checks 9845–9847.
20	1/31/13	Pay employees as per the schedule below using checks 9848–9850 from the regular checking account.

Pay/Tax/Withholding	Sweet	Garrett	Pease
Hours	n/a	46	44
Annual salary/hourly rate	$60,000.00	$ 25.00	$ 20.00
Gross pay	5,000.00	1,150.00	880.00
Federal withholding	−685.00	−157.55	−120.56
Social Security employee	−310.00	−71.30	−54.56
Medicare employee	−72.50	−16.68	−12.76
State withholding	−347.33	−54.73	−34.21
Social Security employer	310.00	71.30	54.56
Medicare company	72.50	16.68	12.76
Federal unemployment	40.00	9.20	7.04
State unemployment	150.00	34.50	26.40
Check amount	3,585.17	849.74	657.91

Date	Customer/Job ID	Activity	Billing Status	Sweet	Garrett	Pease
1/03			Non-Billable		2	2
1/04	Yelp/432	See above.	Billable	6	6	6
1/15			Non-Billable		8	8
1/17			Non-Billable		8	8
1/19	Dutton/433	See above.	Billable	7	3	2
1/22			Non-Billable		8	8
1/28	Benson/434	See above.	Billable	4	3	2
1/30			Non-Billable		8	8
Total				17	46	44

Requirements:

Create a QuickBooks Accountant file for Bridgette Sweet Photography. Modify the company name to include Ch 7 at the end so that the company name is Bridgette Sweet Photography Ch 7. Add vendors, inventory items, customers, and employees first and then record business transactions in chronological order (remember that dates are in the month of January 2013). Memorize and print the following reports for the month of January 2013 (unless otherwise indicated). Be sure to keep this QuickBooks Accountant file in a safe place; it will be used as a starting file for this case in Chapter 11.

a.   Trial Balance

b.   Profit & Loss Standard

c.   Balance Sheet Standard

d.   Statement of Cash Flows

e.   Collapsed A/R Aging Summary

f.   A/P Aging Summary

g.   Payroll Summary (located in the Employees & Payroll section of the Standard Report Center)

h.   Transactions List by Date (12/31/12–1/31/13)

Comprehensive Problem 5: CRYSTAL CLEAR POOL SERVICE

Sharon Calhoun, a college friend of yours, has been asked by her parents to help them computerize the accounting in their sole proprietorship. Her parents own Crystal Clear Pool Service. They have been in business for over a year and Sharon concurs with their desire to automate their accounting system. However, she's a marketing student and does not know the first thing about computerized accounting.

sole proprietorship

You have agreed to help them out. The plan is to start using the computerized accounting system October 1, 2012.

service

The company has a federal employer ID of 76-9421357. The business is located at 160 Portal Lane, Sedona, AZ 86336 and its phone number is 928-555-2900. The company will use a fiscal year (10/1 to 9/30) and will start entering business events as of 10/1/12 and beginning balances as of 9/30/12. It will use QuickBooks Accountant to manage payroll manually. The state unemployment tax rate for Crystal is 6%. The company does keep an inventory of pool supplies such as chlorine and muriatic acid and will be using the average cost method, so you decided to use QuickBooks Accountant inventory and purchase order features. You have chosen the General Service-based Business industry to establish a chart of accounts. (Be sure to modify the QuickBooks Accountant chart of accounts to match the table of accounts below.) Standard payment terms are net 30 and credit limit is $15,000. They do not plan to create estimates, track customer orders, use progress invoicing, or use statements in QuickBooks Accountant. The company plans to use invoices and manage bills with QuickBooks Accountant.

merchandising

The company employs two individuals as assistants but will not track time using QuickBooks Accountant but will process payroll manually. Employees are all subject to Arizona taxes and are paid monthly. All taxes are paid and filed quarterly to the Arizona Dept. of Revenue (DOR). The company's state employer ID is 1254871-8 and its state unemployment ID is 21-8741399111. (*Hint*: Set up payroll just like you did in the previous chapter.) All billing is done at the beginning of each month of service.

The state of Arizona imposes a 6% sales tax on all services and merchandise, which the company must collect and remit quarterly to the Arizona Dept. of Revenue (DOR). Use Tax as the tax code and Sales Tax as the sales tax name. All customers located in Arizona must be charged this state sales tax on all services and items.

Chart of Accounts

Account Name	Type	Balance at 9/30/12
Checking	Bank	8,000
Accounts Receivable	Accounts Receivable	15,000
Inventory Asset	Other Current Asset	5,000
Prepaid Expenses	Other Current Assets	3,000
Furniture and Equipment	Fixed Asset	22,000
Accumulated Depreciation	Fixed Asset	−2,000
Accounts Payable	Accounts Payable	6,500
Payroll Liabilities	Other Current Liability	0
Sales Tax Payable	Other Current Liability	0
Notes Payable	Long-Term Liability	20,000
Owners' Draw	Equity	
Owners' Equity	Equity	24,500
Pool Services Revenue	Income	
Pool Supplies Revenue	Income	
Cost of Goods Sold	Cost of Goods Sold	
Advertising and Promotion	Expense	
Bank Service Charges	Expense	
Depreciation Expense	Expense	
Insurance Expense	Expense	
Interest Expense	Expense	
Office Supplies	Expense	
Payroll Expenses	Expense	
Rent Expense	Expense	
Telephone Expense	Expense	
Utilities	Expense	

Vendors

Name	CPS	SS	DOR
Company Name	Cactus Pool Supply	Sun Systems	Arizona Dept. of Revenue
Address	1070 East Ray Road	2030 Pinnacle Peak	1600 West Monroe Street
City	Chandler	Phoenix	Phoenix
State	AZ	AZ	AZ
Zip	85225	85027	85007
Opening balance as of 9/30/12	$4,500	$2,000	$0

Customers

Name	WS	HR	PD	AG
Company Name	Wyndham Sedona	Hilton Resort	Poco Diablo	Adobe Grand
Address	1500 Kestrel Circle	90 Ridge Trail Drive	1752 Highway 179	35 Hozoni Drive
City	Sedona	Sedona	Sedona	Sedona
State	AZ	AZ	AZ	AZ
Zip	86336	86336	86336	86336
Opening balance at 9/30/12	$6,000	$4,000	$0	$5,000

Service Items and Inventory Parts

Type	Name/Description	Cost	Sales Price	Income Account	Expense Account	Sales Tax Code	On Hand
Service Item	Pool Service		$125	Pool Services Revenue	n/a	Tax	n/a
Service Item	Pool Repairs		$125	Pool Services Revenue	n/a	Tax	n/a
Inventory Part	Chlorine	$ 5	$ 8	Pool Supplies Revenue	Cost of Goods Sold	Tax	200
Inventory Part	Pool Shock	$12	$ 18	Pool Supplies Revenue	Cost of Goods Sold	Tax	125
Inventory Part	Pool Algaecide	$10	$ 14	Pool Supplies Revenue	Cost of Goods Sold	Tax	250

Employees

Name	Danielle Patrick	Jeev M Singh
Address	613 Desert Sage Lane	60 Cactus Drive
City	Sedona	Sedona
State	AZ	AZ
Zip	86336	86336
Social Security #	841-85-1478	351-78-9413
Hourly Rate	$18	$20
Filing Status	Single	Single

Event #	Date	Business Event
1	10/1/12	Invoiced customers AG, HR, PD, and WS 40 hours each for pool services to be rendered in October using invoice numbers 10130–10133 with sales tax.
2	10/5/12	Received following payments from customers on account and deposited amounts: check 8432 from customer WS for $6,000, check 23458 from customer HR for $2,000, VISA payment 6541384 from customer PD for $5,000.
3	10/8/12	Created purchase order 44 to Sun Systems (SS) for the purchase of $3,200 in non-inventory parts (parts) needed for repair work being completed for Poco Diablo (PD) on a new job name Pool repairs.
4	10/10/12	Received parts ordered on purchase order 44 from Sun Systems on its invoice 584922 terms net 15.
5	10/12/12	Completed job 261 for Poco Diablo and invoiced it on invoice number 10134, terms net 30, for 18 hours in pool repairs and for parts reimbursement and sales tax for a total of $5,777.
6	10/22/12	Purchased equipment from Cactus Pool Supply (CPS) using check 289 for $2,500.
7	10/25/12	Paid rent expense to Century 21 Leasing (a new vendor C21) using check 290 for $1,789.

Event #	Date	Business Event
8	10/30/12	Invoiced customers AG, HR, PD, and WS for pool supplies used in October using invoice numbers 10135–10138 with sales tax and terms of net 30. Customer AG – 25 units of chlorine, 10 units of pool shock, and 5 units of pool algaecide. Customer HR – 20 units of chlorine, 8 units of pool shock, and 4 units of pool algaecide. Customer PD – 15 units of chlorine, 5 units of pool shock, and 2 units of pool algaecide. Customer WS – 30 units of chlorine, 12 units of pool shock, and 7 units of pool algaecide.
9	10/31/12	Paid CPS bill of $4,500 and SS bill of $2,000 using checks 291 and 292.
10	10/31/12	Paid employees with checks 293 and 294 (see below for detail).

Pay/Tax/Withholding	Patrick	Singh
Hours	160	150
Rate	$ 18.00	$ 20.00
Gross pay	2,880.00	3,000.00
Federal withholding	−394.56	−411.00
Social security employee	−178.56	−186.00
Medicare employee	−41.76	−43.50
State withholding	−115.20	−120.00
Arizona job training tax	2.88	3.00
Social security employer	178.56	186.00
Medicare company	41.76	43.50
Federal unemployment	20.16	21.00
State unemployment	115.20	120.00
Check amount	2,149.92	2,239.50

Requirements:

Create a QuickBooks Accountant file for Crystal Clear Pool Service. Modify the company name to include Ch 7 at the end so that the company name is Crystal Clear Pool Service Ch 7. Add vendors, inventory items, customers, and employees first and then record business transactions in chronological order (remember that dates are in the month of October 2012). After you've created, memorized, and printed the following reports (for the month of October 2012 unless otherwise specified, with no page numbers, no date prepared, time prepared, or report basis header information, and no zero amounts), create a backup of this file and store it on some type of external medium (flash drive, Internet site, CD, disk, etc.). The backup file should be named Crystal Clear Pool Service Ch 7 for easy identification later. You'll be restoring this file in Chapter 11.

a. Trial Balance

b. Profit & Loss Standard

c. Balance Sheet Standard

d. Statement of Cash Flows

e. Collapsed A/R Aging Summary

f. A/P Aging Summary

g. Payroll Summary (located in the Employees & Payroll section of the Standard Report Center)

h. Transactions List by Date (9/30/12–10/31/12)

Additional Business Activities

Student Learning Outcomes

Upon completion of this chapter, the student will be able to:

- Record additional business transactions classified as financing activities, such as repayment of loans
- Record additional business transactions classified as investing activities, such as selling short-term investments for a gain or loss
- Record additional business transactions classified as operating activities, such as purchasing and selling inventory on account
- Record business transactions classified as noncash investing and financing activities, such as the purchase of equipment with long-term debt

Case: Wild Water Sports, Inc.

You and Karen have completed entering business events that took place during the months of January and February and are ready to begin recording transactions for March. Karen explains that, so far, the transactions entered have involved cash-related financing activities such as owner contributions; cash-related investing activities such as equipment purchases; and cash-related operating activities such as creating purchase orders, receipt of customer payments, cash sales, making deposits, receiving inventory, payment of purchases, invoicing time and costs, payment of expenses, accounting for employees' time, and payment of payroll.

In March and April, the company had similar business events to record in addition to some new ones. During these months, the company entered into some additional cash-related financing activities such as the payment of loans, additional cash-related investing activities such as the sale of short-term investments, and additional cash-related operating activities such as the purchase and sale of inventory on account and the related payment and receipt of those transactions. Further, the company entered into some non-cash investing and financing activities when it purchased some equipment with long-term debt.

Karen suggests that you work through these transactions for March, paying particular attention to those you haven't encountered yet.

Recording Additional Financing Activities

You recall that as of December 31, 2015, the company had a long-term liability of $383,800. Then, in January, the company borrowed an additional $250,000 from the Bank of Florida, which was due in five years and carried a 5% interest cost.

"When do we make payments on those loans?" you ask.

"Our agreement on the $250,000 loan with the Bank of Florida called for monthly payments of $4,717.81 beginning February 4th," Karen answers. "I was so busy with QuickBooks Accountant and the business that I completely forgot! I wrote two checks yesterday to cover our first two payments, and the bank has been kind enough to waive the late payment fee."

The company also borrowed an additional $50,000 from Citibank on January 1st. Payments on that loan are due annually. The loan payable of $383,800 has payments due July 1 of every year.

To record the checks written to make payment on the Bank of Florida loan:

1 Restore the Wild Water Sports Ch 8 (Backup) file that you downloaded from the text web site. See "Data Files" in Chapter 1 if you need more information.

2 Click the **Write Checks** icon from the Banking section of the home page. The Write Checks window appears with your current system date and with Check No. 1029 ready for entry. The bank provided the loan amortization schedule shown in Figure 8.1.

Month	Payment	Interest	Principal	Balance
				250,000.00
1	4,717.81	1,041.67	3,676.14	246,323.86
2	4,717.81	1,026.35	3,691.46	242,632.40
3	4,717.81	1,010.97	3,706.84	238,925.56
4	4,717.81	995.52	3,722.29	235,203.27
5	4,717.81	980.01	3,737.79	231,465.48
6	4,717.81	964.44	3,753.37	227,712.11
7	4,717.81	948.80	3,769.01	223,943.10
8	4,717.81	933.10	3,784.71	220,158.39
9	4,717.81	917.33	3,800.48	216,357.91
10	4,717.81	901.49	3,816.32	212,541.59
11	4,717.81	885.59	3,832.22	208,709.37
12	4,717.81	869.62	3,848.19	204,861.19

Figure 8.1

Loan Amortization Schedule

3 Enter the information for the check as shown in Figure 8.2. Be sure to enter the correct date.

Figure 8.2

Recording Payment on a
Bank Loan

Enter correct date

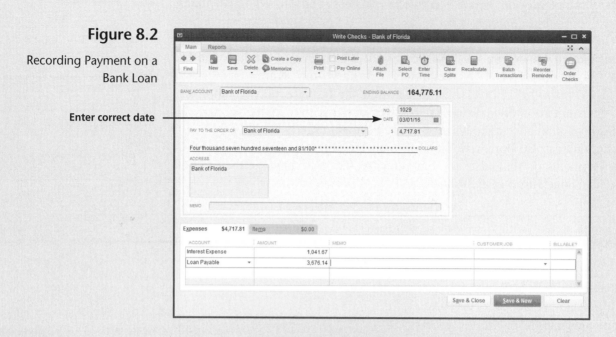

4   Click **Save & New** to record the check.

5   Using the amortization schedule, enter information for Check No. 1030, on the same date, to record the second payment using interest expense and principal information provided. Your screen should look like Figure 8.3.

Figure 8.3

Recording the Second
Payment on a Bank Loan

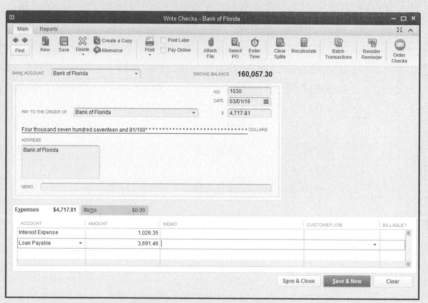

6   Click **Save & Close** to record the check.

With the addition of a new owner and the related funds received from their investment, the company decided to pay down the older, higher-interest (10%) debt with the Bank of Orlando. It made a payment of $387,690.58, which represented the interest at 10% for 37 days ($3,890.58) plus the principal balance due of $383,800. Before the company made this payment, it decided to electronically transfer $300,000 from its Short-Term Investments account with ETrade to its Bank of Florida checking account. Electronic transfers require no check and are recorded by using the account register. Karen suggests you try recording this transfer and loan payment that was made on 3/6 with Check No. 1031.

To record the electronic transfer of funds and record payment on a loan:

1 Click the **Chart of Accounts** icon in the Company section of the home page.

2 Double-click account **Short-Term Investments** to open the Short-Term Investments account register.

3 Type **3/6/16** in the Date section of the account register and leave the number field blank.

4 Type **Bank of Florida** in the Payee section of the account register.

5 Type **300000** in the Payment section of the account register.

6 Select **Bank of Florida** in the Account section of the account register.

7 Click **Record** to record this transaction. Your screen should look like Figure 8.4.

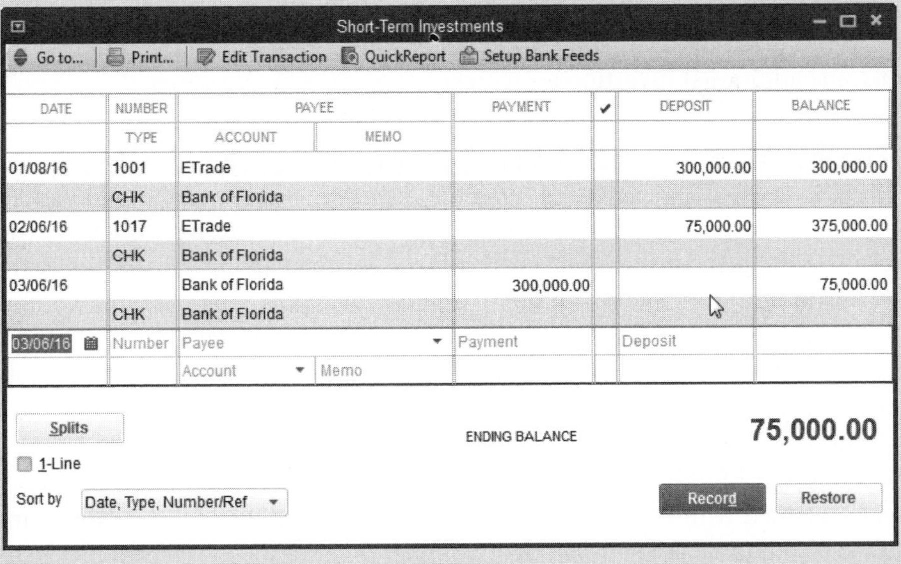

Figure 8.4

Transfer of Funds from ETrade to Bank of Florida

8 Close the Short Term Investments window.

9 Close the Chart of Accounts window.

10 Click the **Write Checks** icon from the Banking section of the home page. The Write Checks window appears with Check No. 1031 ready for entry.

11 Enter the information for the check as shown in Figure 8.5.

Figure 8.5

Recording a Check to Pay Off a Loan Payable

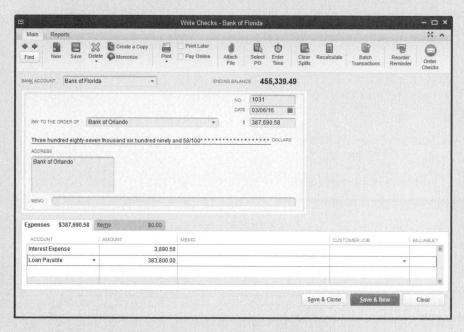

12 Click **Save & Close** to finish this transaction.

You have now recorded payments of long-term debt. Now it's time to look at some additional investing activities.

Recording Additional Investing Activities

You may recall from your accounting courses that investing activities generally result in the acquisition of noncurrent assets from buying or selling investment securities or productive equipment. Wild Water Sports engaged in several investing activities that you and Karen need to record in March. The company made some additional short-term investments, and it sold previously purchased investment securities for a profit.

In February, Wild Water Sports made an investment with ETrade for $75,000. On March 7, it sold that investment for a profit of $3,000. All funds were retained with ETrade. In addition, it used $35,000 of those money market funds to purchase stock in Apple Computer, again as a short-term investment.

To record short-term investment activity:

1 Click the **Chart of Accounts** icon in the Company section of the home page.

2 Double-click account **Short-Term Investments** to open the Short-Term Investments account register.

3 Type **3/9/16** in the Date section of the account register and leave the number field blank.

4   Type **ETrade** in the Payee section of the account register.

5   Type **3000** in the Deposit section of the account register.

6   Click <**Add New**> in the Account section of the account register. Create a new other income type of account with the name Other Income in the Account section of the account register. Click **Save & Close** after adding the new account.

7   Click **Record** to record this transaction. Your screen should look like Figure 8.6.

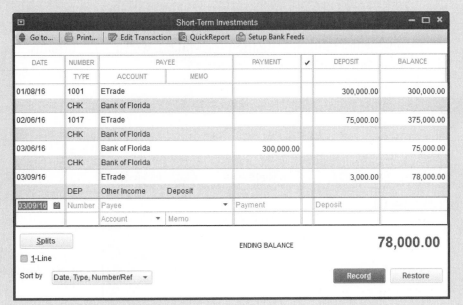

Figure 8.6

Recording Profit on a Short-Term Investment

8   Close the Short Term Investments window.

9   Close the Chart of Accounts window.

"Why didn't we record the Apple Computer stock purchase in our records?" you ask.

"Well, remember that the funds used to purchase this stock were already in our Short-Term Investments account," Karen answers. "Thus, this is just a reallocation of our short-term investment from a money market category to a stock category. We, as shareholders, consider both the money market funds and the stock investment to be short-term investments; thus, we don't differentiate them in the accounting records."

Recording Additional Operating Activities

Donna has been working hard to establish credit with the company's suppliers. Recently, she's convinced Malibu, MB Sports, and Tige to give Wild Water 30-day credit terms. Several purchase orders have been created to acquire more inventory for the company's showroom and to purchase inventory ordered by some new customers.

"Now that we have some credit with our suppliers, we'll be able to offer credit to some of our better customers," Donna points out. She suggests that you input the purchase orders created in March and the related bills received from suppliers.

To record purchase orders for the month of March:

1 Click the **Purchase Orders** icon from the Vendors section of the home page. Use QuickBooks Accountant Help to add a "terms" field to the customized purchase order form.

2 Enter purchase order information from Figure 8.7. Be sure to provide address and terms information for Malibu, which isn't currently a part of our information for this vendor.

Figure 8.7

Purchase Order No. 4005

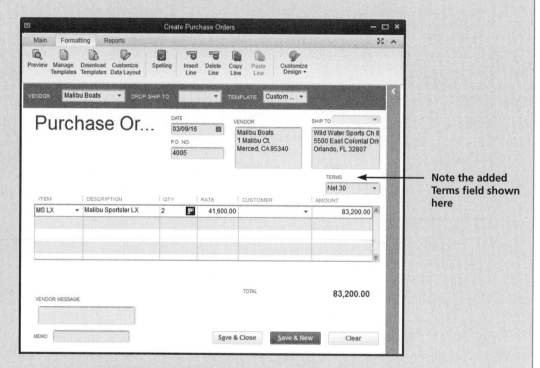

3 Click **Save & New**.

4 Click **Yes** to save the updated address and terms for Malibu Boats.

5 Create Purchase Order No. **4006** to Tige Boats on 3/12/16 ordering 1 T 22v and 1 T 24v (a new item with a description Tige 24v, cost of $70,000 and a sales price of $87,500 using the same cost of goods sold and income accounts as all other boats) with terms Net 30.

6 Create Purchase Order No. **4007** to MB Sports on 3/16/16 ordering 1 MB 220v (a new item with a description of MB 220v, cost of $52,000 and a sales price of $65,000 using the same cost of goods sold and income accounts as all other boats) for a new customer (Spirit

Adventures, 500 Butterfly Lake Rd., Fort Lauderdale, FL 33308) with terms Net 30. Be sure to place this customer's name in the Customer text box as shown in Figure 8.8.

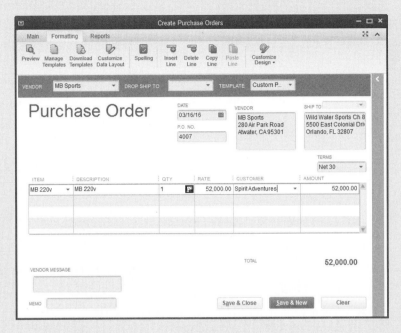

Figure 8.8

Purchase Order No. 4007 for Spirit Adventures

7 Click **Save & Close**. Click **Yes** when asked to update terms.

Some of the boats ordered via the purchase orders entered above were received in the month of March. Because these were all ordered on account, QuickBooks Accountant requires that you record the receipt of inventory at the same time you record the receipt of the bill invoicing the company for payment. In addition, boats ordered with Purchase Order No. 4004 issued in February were received in March.

To record receipt of inventory and bill:

1 Click the **Receive Inventory** icon from the Vendors section of the company's home page.

2 Select **Receive Inventory with Bill**.

3 Select **Malibu Boats** from the Vendor list.

4 Click **Yes** when asked if you want to receive against one or more of the open purchase orders for this vendor.

5 Select Purchase Order No. **4004** as shown in Figure 8.9.

Video Demonstration

DEMO 8B - Record receipt of inventory and bill

Figure 8.9

Selecting Purchase Orders
When Receiving Inventory

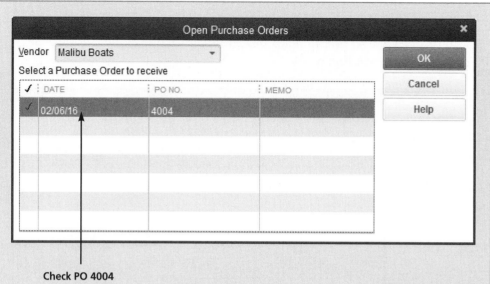

Check PO 4004

6   Click **OK**.

7   Type **3/6/16** as the bill date, click the **Hide History** arrow, and then press **[Tab]**.

8   Your screen should look like Figure 8.10.

Figure 8.10

Malibu Bill

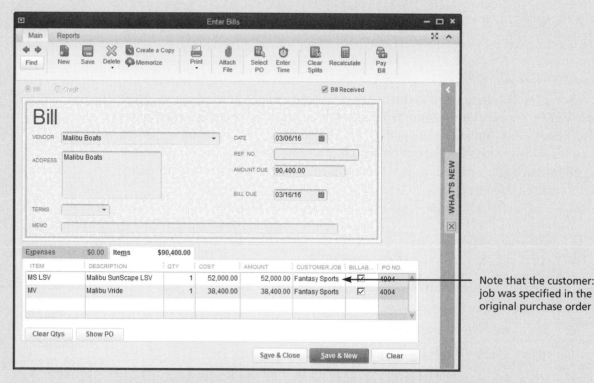

Note that the customer:
job was specified in the
original purchase order

9   Note the Bill Due date of 04/05/16 (30 days from the date of receipt). Click **Save & New**.

10   Select **Malibu Boats** from the Vendor list.

11   Click **Yes** when asked if you want to receive against one or more of the open purchase orders for this vendor.

12 Select Purchase Order No. **4005**.

13 Click **OK**.

14 Type **3/16/16** as the bill date and then press **[Tab]**.

15 Note the Bill Due date of 4/15/16 (30 days from the date of receipt). Click **Save & New**.

16 Select **Tige Boats** from the Vendor list.

17 Click **Yes** when asked if you want to receive against one or more of the open purchase orders for this vendor.

18 Select Purchase Order No. **4006**.

19 Click **OK**.

20 Type **3/30/16** as the bill date and then press **[Tab]**.

21 Note the Bill Due date of 4/29/16 (30 days from the date of receipt). Click **Save & Close**.

Two service-related jobs (50005 and 50006) were started and completed in the month of March. Both were for customers who were invoiced and given 15-day credit terms. Karen explains that, for both of these cases, jobs need to be created, time needs to be recorded, and invoices need to be recorded. Invoices are the source documents usually used to record sales on account.

job costing

To record service-related activity on account:

1 Click the **Customers** button from the Customers section of the home page.

2 Double-click **Buena Vista Water Sports**.

3 Click the **Payment Settings** tab.

4 Change the Payment Terms to **Net 15**, and then click **OK** to close the window.

5 Click **New Customer & Job** (while Buena Vista Water Sports is still selected).

6 Click **Add Job** from the drop-down menu presented.

7 Type **50005** as the Job Name and then click **OK**.

8 Double-click **Performance Rentals**.

9 Click the **Payment Settings** tab.

10 Change the Payment Terms to **Net 15**, and then click **OK** to close the window.

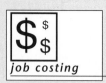

job costing

11   Click **New Customer & Job** (while Performance Rentals is still selected).

12   Click **Add Job** from the drop-down menu presented.

13   Type **50006** as the Job Name and then click **OK**.

14   Close the **Customer Center** window.

15   Click **Enter Time** and then click **Use Weekly Timesheet** from the Employees section of the home page.

16   Select **Ryder Zacovic** as the employee name.

17   Select the week of March 14 to March 20, 2016.

18   Enter the information shown in Figure 8.11.

Figure 8.11

Time Sheet for Ryder Zacovic for Week of 3/14

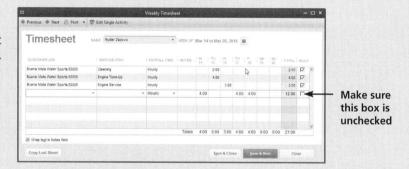

19   Click **Next**.

20   Enter the information shown in Figure 8.12.

Figure 8.12

Time Sheet for Ryder Zacovic for Week of 3/25

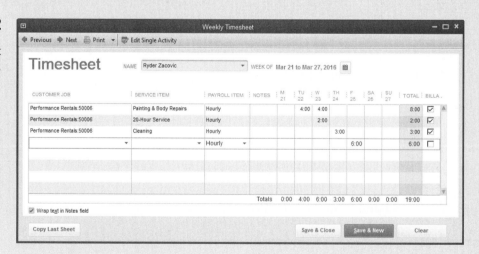

21   Click **Save & Close**.

22   Click **Create Invoices** from the Customers section of the home page.

23 Select **Buena Vista Water Sports 50005** from the Customer:Job list.

24 Click **Select All** to select all three employee charges and then click **OK**.

25 Type **3/18/16** as the invoice date.

26 Type **10005** as the invoice number.

27 Add the address and tax information provided in Figure 8.13.

28 Add the tune-up parts, engine oil, air filter, and oil filter to the invoice as shown in Figure 8.13.

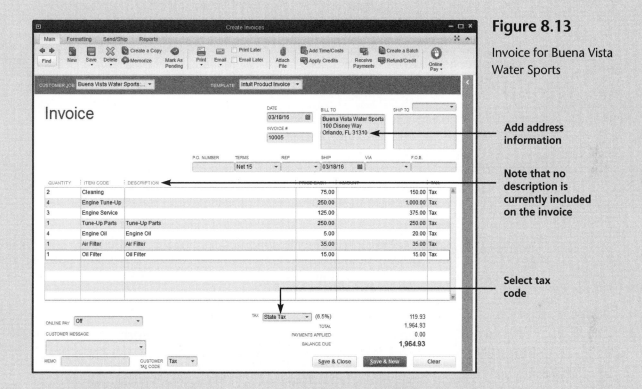

Figure 8.13

Invoice for Buena Vista Water Sports

29 Click **Save & New**.

30 Click **Yes** to save the new address and tax information for this customer.

31 Select **Performance Rentals 50006** from the Customer:Job list.

32 Click **Select All**. Click the **Options** button and select **Transfer item descriptions** and then click **OK** in the Options for Transferring Billable Time window. Now click **OK** in the Choose Billable Time and Costs window.

33 Type **3/26/16** as the invoice date.

34 Type **10006** as the invoice number. Your screen should look like Figure 8.14.

Figure 8.14

Invoice to
Performance
Rentals

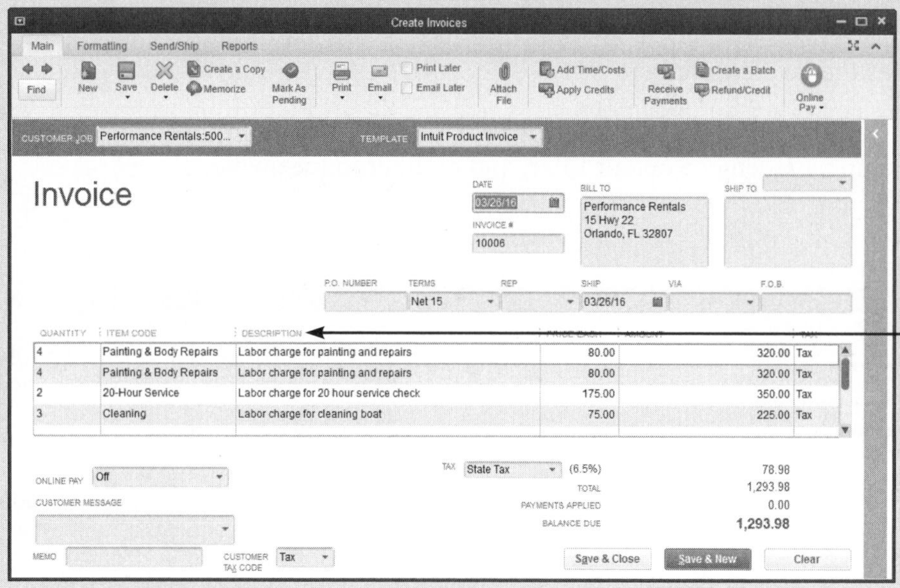

Note that now a description of each item is included in the invoice

35 Click **Save & Close**.

There was one cash boat purchase during the month to a new customer, Sonia Garcia. She purchased a Malibu Vride off the showroom floor on March 12 for $51,120 (including sales tax) using Check No. 8593.

To record a cash sale and deposit cash received:

1 Click **Create Sales Receipts** from the Customers section of the home page. (Click **No Thanks** if prompted to set up cash receipts.)

2 Click <**Add New**> in the Customer:Job text edit box.

3 Type **Sonia Garcia** as both the customer and company name and then click **OK**.

4 Type **3/12/16** as the date of sale and **6008** as the sale number.

5 Type **8593** as the check number, and select **Check** as the Payment Method.

6 Select **MV** as the Item.

7 Type **1** as the Qty.

8 Make sure **State Tax** is shown as the Tax item, click **Save & Close** to enter this sales receipt, and then click **Yes** when asked to confirm changes.

9 Click **Record Deposits** from the Banking section of the home page.

10 Select the deposit shown and click **OK**.

11 Type **3/12/16** as the deposit date.

12 Click **Save & Close** to record the deposit.

Three invoices were generated in the month of March for boat sales. One, to Fantasy Sports (Invoice No. 10004), represented an order received during the month for which Fantasy had already paid a deposit. Upon Fantasy's request, Donna approved net 15 credit terms on the balance owed. Credit terms specify the discount, if any, and amount of time that customers have to pay an invoice. The other two invoices were for sales from the showroom floor: sales on account using Invoice No. 10007 and No. 10008, respectively. Sales on account are sales to customers who are not required to pay the invoice immediately.

To record invoices from the sale of boats on account:

1 Click **Create Invoices** from the Customers section of the home page.

2 Select **Fantasy Sports** from the Customer:Job list.

3 Click the **Items** tab.

4 Click the **Select All** button to select both boats received from Malibu, and then click **OK** to close the window.

5 Type **3/6/16** as the invoice date.

6 Type **10004** as the invoice number.

7 Click the **Apply Credits** button, and then click **Yes** to save this invoice.

8 Click **Done** to apply the credit of $28,250.

9 Select terms of **Net 15** from the Terms list, select **State Tax** from the Tax field, and type **3/6/16** as the ship date. The completed invoice should look like Figure 8.15.

Video Demonstration

DEMO 8C - Record invoices and apply payments

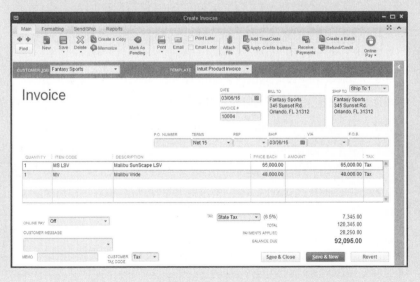

Figure 8.15

Invoice to Fantasy Sports

10   Click **Save & New**.

11   Click **Yes** to save changes, and then click **Yes** again to save the changed terms and tax for this customer.

12   Select **Freebirds** from the Customer:Job list.

13   Type **3/23/16** as the invoice date.

14   Type **10007** as the invoice number.

15   Select terms of **Net 15** from the Terms list and type **3/23/16** as the ship date. Type the Bill To, Quantity, and Item Code information as found in Figure 8.16.

Figure 8.16

Invoice to Freebirds

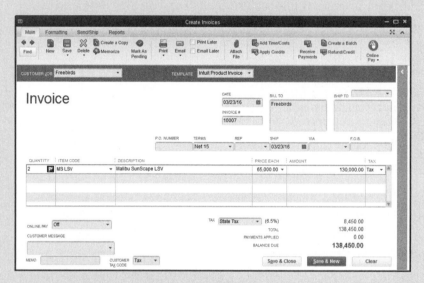

16   Click **Save & New**.

17   Click **Yes** to save the new terms.

18   Select **Florida Sports Camp** from the Customer:Job list.

19   Type **3/30/16** as the invoice date.

20   Type **10008** as the invoice number.

21   Select terms of **Net 15** from the Terms list and type **3/30/16** as the ship date.

22   Enter Quantity **1**, Item Code **T 22v**, and Tax **State Tax**.

23   Click **Save & Close**.

24   Click **Yes** to save the new terms.

At the end of the month, Wild Water Sports received a check from Performance Rentals for $10,000 as a deposit toward the purchase of a boat on its showroom floor.

To record receipt of deposit from Performance Rentals:

1 Click **Receive Payments** from the Customers section of the home page.

2 Select **Performance Rentals** from the Received from drop-down list.

3 Type **10000** as the amount.

4 Type **3/31/16** as the date, **Check** as the payment method, and **15687** as the Check #.

5 Click the **Un-Apply Payment** button, since this is a deposit on another transaction and not a payment on Invoice No. 10006 as suggested.

6 Click **Save & Close**.

7 Click **OK** in the Payment Credit window.

8 Click **Record Deposits**, select the **3/31/16** check box, and click **OK** to record the deposit of this $10,000.

9 Click **Save & Close**.

"When do we get around to paying the bills and collecting cash from these invoices?" you ask.

"It's important to pay bills on a timely basis, since this will keep our suppliers happy and keep our good credit," Karen answers. "First off, we can view what bills are outstanding and when they are due and then choose which to pay and when."

To choose which bills to pay and to pay those bills:

1 Click **Pay Bills** from the Vendors section of the home page.

2 Click the option button to **Show all bills**.

3 Click the check box next to the due date **04/05/16**.

4 Click the option button to **Assign check number**.

5 Type **3/31/16** as the payment date. Your screen should look like Figure 8.17.

Figure 8.17

Pay Bills Window

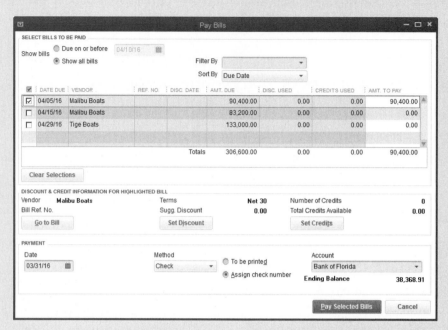

6   Click **Pay Selected Bills**.

7   Type **1032** as the check number in the Assign Check Numbers window, and then click **OK**.

8   Click **Done** in the Payment Summary window.

"We collected two payments from customers on account in March," Karen says. "Orlando Water Sports paid us $5,300 on 3/20, and Buena Vista paid us $1,964.93 on 3/27. Let's record those now."

To record cash collections on account and related deposit:

1   Click **Receive Payments** from the Customers section of the home page.

2   Select **Orlando Water Sports** as the customer received from.

3   Type **5300** as the Amount received.

4   Type **3/20/16** as the Date received.

5   Type **9152** as the Check # of the check received as payment. Your screen should look like Figure 8.18.

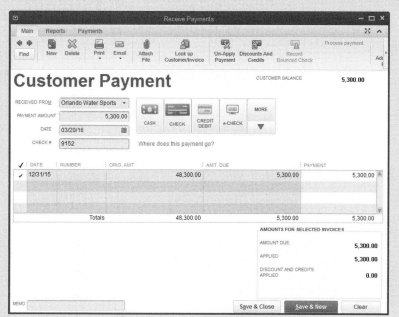

Figure 8.18

Receive Payments Window

6 Click **Save & New**.

7 Select **Buena Vista Water Sports** as the customer received from.

8 Type **1964.93** as the Amount received.

9 Type **3/27/16** as the Date received.

10 Type **741** as the Check # of the check received as payment.

11 Click **Save & Close**.

12 Click **Record Deposits** from the Banking section of the home page.

13 Select the two deposits shown and click **OK**.

14 Type **3/27/16** as the deposit date.

15 Click **Save & Close** to record the deposit.

"In addition to paying bills from vendors for merchandise purchased, the company also has to pay its sales tax and payroll tax liabilities," Karen reminds you. "Sales tax liabilities are created when we sell merchandise and collect sales tax from a customer. Payroll tax liabilities are created when we withhold payroll tax from employees' paychecks and recognize our obligation to pay employer payroll taxes. Before we can do that and pay the rest of our end-of-month bills and payroll, we'll need to transfer some funds from our Short-Term Investments account at ETrade to our checking account."

Donna offers to make the electronic transfer of $40,000 from ETrade to Bank of Florida, and you agree to record the accounting effect of that transfer and prepare checks to pay the sales tax and payroll tax obligations.

Video Demonstration

DEMO 8D - Pay sales and payroll taxes

To transfer funds and pay sales tax and payroll tax obligations:

1. Click the **Chart of Accounts** icon in the Company section of the home page.

2. Double-click the **Short-Term Investments** account.

3. Type **3/30/16** as the date.

4. Type **Bank of Florida** as the payee.

5. Type **40000** as the payment.

6. Select **Bank of Florida** as the Account.

7. Click **Record** and then close the Short-Term Investments and the Chart of Accounts windows.

8. Click the **Manage Sales Tax** icon from the Vendors section of the home page.

9. Click **Pay Sales Tax** and then type **3/30/16** as the check date.

10. Type **2/29/16** as the Show sales tax due through date.

11. Press the **[Tab]** key to refresh the screen.

12. Type **1033** as the Starting Check No.

13. Click in the **Pay** column next to State Tax. Your screen should look like Figure 8.19.

Figure 8.19

Pay Sales Tax Window

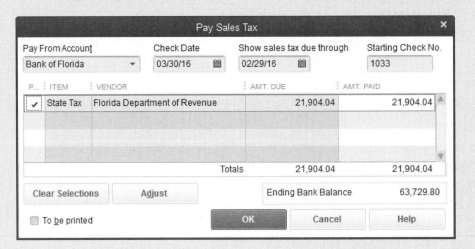

14. Click **OK** and then close the Manage Sales Tax window.

15. Click the **Pay Liabilities** icon from the Employees section of the home page.

16. Type **1/1/16** as the From date.

17　Type **2/29/16** as the Through date, and then click **OK**.

18　Uncheck the **To be printed** check box.

19　Select all of the Payroll Items.

20　Select the **Review liability check to enter expenses/penalties** option button.

21　Type **3/31/16** as the Check Date. Your screen should look like Figure 8.20.

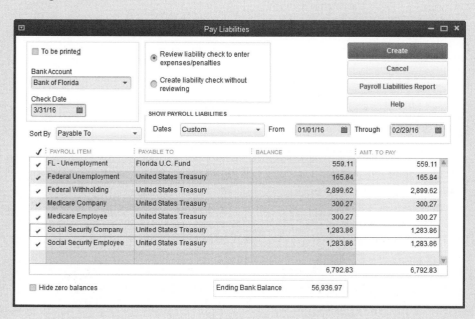

Figure 8.20

Pay Liabilities Window

22　Click **Create**. (If a Special Calculation Warning window pops up, click **Continue**.)

23　A Liability Check—Bank of Florida window should appear as in Figure 8.21.

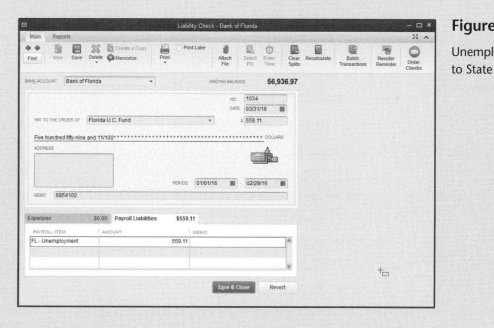

Figure 8.21

Unemployment Payment to State

24 Click the next arrow to view the United States Treasury check, which should look like Figure 8.22.

Figure 8.22

Check to U.S. Treasury

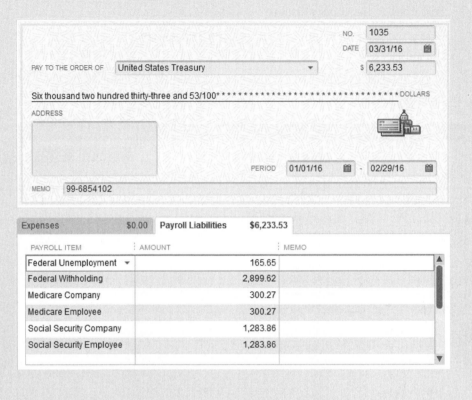

25 Close the check window.

"All that is left for March is for us to record checks written for expenses and to record payroll," Karen states. "Our expenses are about the same each month, so you shouldn't see too much variation in what you did the last two months. We didn't have much in the way of service this month, so Pat didn't work and Ryder just worked the hours we recorded earlier."

To record end-of-month expenses:

Video Demonstration

DEMO 8E - Pay bills

1 Click the **Write Checks** icon in the Banking section of the home page.

2 Type **1036** as the check number if it is not already there.

3 Type **3/31/16** as the Check Date.

4 Select **Central Florida Gas & Electric** from the Pay to the Order of section of the check.

5 Type **1050** as the amount and then press **[Tab]**.

6 Select **Utilities** from the Account drop-down list.

7 Click **Save & New**.

8 Type **1037** as the check number if it is not already there.

9   Type **3/31/16** as the Check Date if it is not already there.

10 Select **Verizon** in the Pay to the Order of section of the check.

11 Type **1500** as the amount and then press **[Tab]**.

12 Select **Telephone Expense** from the Account drop-down list.

13 Click **Save & Close**.

To record end-of-month payroll:

1   Click the **Pay Employees** icon in the Employees section of the home page.

2   Type **3/31/16** as the Check Date and **3/31/16** as the Pay Period Ends date. Click **Yes** when asked if you want to update the hours worked from the new pay period. Then place a check next to Donna, Karen, and Ryder's names. Your screen should look like Figure 8.23.

Figure 8.23

Select Employees to Pay

3 Use the information below to create payroll for Donna, Karen, and Ryder. Click each employee's name to provide tax information. (*Note:* Pat Ng did not work any hours this month.)

4 Click **Continue**.

Trouble? Depending on your monitor size, the Continue and Cancel buttons may not be visible. To view them, just maximize the window.

Item	Donna	Karen	Ryder
Earnings	4,166.67	4,166.67	600.00
Federal Withholding	−463.00	−710.00	−82.20
Social Security Employee	−258.33	−258.33	−37.20
Medicare Employee	−60.42	−60.42	−8.70
Social Security Company	258.33	258.33	37.20
Medicare Company	60.42	60.42	8.70
Federal Unemployment	33.33	33.33	4.80
FL Unemployment Company	112.50	112.50	16.20
Check Amount	3,384.92	3,137.92	471.90

5 Now review the paycheck data. Assign Check No. 1038 as the first check number for these paychecks. Then click **Create Paychecks**.

6 Click **Close**.

Recording Noncash Investing and Financing Activities

Although noncash investing and financing activities do not affect the cash position of a company, they do have an impact on a firm's financial position. One example of such an activity was Wild Water Sports's purchase of computer equipment in March, which was completely financed with long-term debt (a loan payable to Staples with no interest and no payment due until 10/1/16). Karen explains the nature of this transaction to you and demonstrates how it should be recorded.

To record the purchase of equipment with long-term debt:

1 Click the **Chart of Accounts** icon from the Company section of the home page.

2 Double-click the **Furniture and Equipment** account.

3 Type **3/31/16** as the Date.

4 Type **Staples** as the Payee.

5 Type **5000** as the amount in the Increase column.

6 Select **Loan Payable** as the Account.

7 Click **Record**. Your screen should look like Figure 8.24.

Figure 8.24

Entering an Equipment Purchase in Exchange for a Loan

8 Close the Furniture and Equipment window and the Chart of Accounts window.

Evaluate a Firm's Performance and Financial Position

Once again, the best way to evaluate a firm's performance and financial position at this point is to generate an income statement and balance sheet. Karen suggests that you do this for the entire three months ended March 31, 2016 (the first quarter of 2016) and then prepare a Transaction List by Date report like you did last month.

To prepare a comparative income statement, balance sheet, and transaction by date report for the first quarter of 2016:

1 Click the **Report Center** icon from the icon toolbar. Select the **Standard** Tab and then click the **Company & Financial** section.

2 Double-click the **Profit & Loss Standard** view under the Profit & Loss section.

3 Change the From date to **1/1/16**.

4 Change the To date to **3/31/16**, and then click **Refresh**.

5 Select **Month** from the Columns list.

6 Modify the report header to remove the date prepared, time prepared, and report basis fields.

7 Click the **Print** button from the toolbar, then click **Report**, and then click **Print** in the Print Reports window. Your report should look like Figure 8.25.

Figure 8.25

Income Statement for the Three Months Ending March 31, 2016

Wild Water Sports Ch 8
Profit & Loss
January through March 2016

	Jan 16	Feb 16	Mar 16	TOTAL
Ordinary Income/Expense				
Income				
Boat Sales	200,750.00	132,000.00	369,750.00	702,500.00
Part Sales	40.00	250.00	320.00	610.00
Service	2,545.00	1,400.00	2,740.00	6,685.00
Total Income	203,335.00	133,650.00	372,810.00	709,795.00
Cost of Goods Sold				
Cost of Goods Sold	160,632.00	105,800.00	296,056.00	562,488.00
Total COGS	160,632.00	105,800.00	296,056.00	562,488.00
Gross Profit	42,703.00	27,850.00	76,754.00	147,307.00
Expense				
Advertising and Promotion	0.00	2,700.00	0.00	2,700.00
Interest Expense	0.00	0.00	5,958.60	5,958.60
Office Supplies	0.00	4,500.00	0.00	4,500.00
Payroll Expenses	11,343.22	11,673.35	9,929.40	32,945.97
Telephone Expense	1,700.00	1,820.00	1,500.00	5,020.00
Uncategorized Expenses	0.00	0.00	0.00	0.00
Utilities	890.00	930.00	1,050.00	2,870.00
Total Expense	13,933.22	21,623.35	18,438.00	53,994.57
Net Ordinary Income	28,769.78	6,226.65	58,316.00	93,312.43
Other Income/Expense				
Other Income				
Other Income	0.00	0.00	3,000.00	3,000.00
Total Other Income	0.00	0.00	3,000.00	3,000.00
Net Other Income	0.00	0.00	3,000.00	3,000.00
Net Income	28,769.78	6,226.65	61,316.00	96,312.43

8 Memorize and then close the **Profit & Loss** report window as you have done in the past.

9   Click **Chart of Accounts** from the Home page and then click and drag **Accumulated Depreciation** to move it below Furniture and Equipment as shown in Figure 8.26.

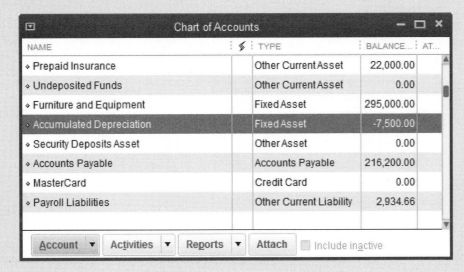

Figure 8.26

Moving the Accumulated Depreciation Account

10   Close the **Chart of Accounts** window, returning to the Reports Center, and then double-click the **Balance Sheet Standard** view under the Balance Sheet and Net Worth section. Now change the As of date to **3/31/16**, and then click **Refresh**.

11   Modify the report header to remove the subtitle, date prepared, time prepared, and report basis fields. Change the From date in the Display tab to **1/1/16** and change the Display columns by text box to **Month**. Then click **OK**.

12   Click the **Print** button from the toolbar, then click **Report**, and then click **Print** in the Print Reports window. Your report should look like Figure 8.27.

13   Memorize this report as you have done in the previous exercises and then close the Balance Sheet report window.

14   Click the **Accountant & Taxes** section and then double-click the **Transaction List by Date** view from the Account Activity section.

15   Type **3/1/16** in the From text box.

Figure 8.27

First Quarter Balance
Sheet by Month

Wild Water Sports Ch 8
Balance Sheet

	Jan 31, 16	Feb 29, 16	Mar 31, 16
ASSETS			
Current Assets			
Checking/Savings			
Bank of Florida	19,789.30	164,775.11	47,392.42
Short-Term Investments	300,000.00	375,000.00	38,000.00
Total Checking/Savings	319,789.30	539,775.11	85,392.42
Accounts Receivable			
Accounts Receivable	66,300.00	-7,950.00	320,707.73
Total Accounts Receivable	66,300.00	-7,950.00	320,707.73
Other Current Assets			
Inventory Boats	330,400.00	284,800.00	295,600.00
Inventory Parts	1,568.00	2,368.00	2,112.00
Prepaid Advertising	0.00	24,000.00	24,000.00
Prepaid Insurance	22,000.00	22,000.00	22,000.00
Undeposited Funds	2,577.31	0.00	0.00
Total Other Current Assets	356,545.31	333,168.00	343,712.00
Total Current Assets	742,634.61	864,993.11	749,812.15
Fixed Assets			
Furniture and Equipment	245,000.00	290,000.00	295,000.00
Accumulated Depreciation	-7,500.00	-7,500.00	-7,500.00
Total Fixed Assets	237,500.00	282,500.00	287,500.00
TOTAL ASSETS	980,134.61	1,147,493.11	1,037,312.15
LIABILITIES & EQUITY			
Liabilities			
Current Liabilities			
Accounts Payable			
Accounts Payable	0.00	0.00	216,200.00
Total Accounts Payable	0.00	0.00	216,200.00
Credit Cards			
MasterCard	1,000.00	0.00	0.00
Total Credit Cards	1,000.00	0.00	0.00
Other Current Liabilities			
Payroll Liabilities	3,348.04	6,792.64	2,934.66
Sales Tax Payable	13,216.79	21,904.04	24,232.66
Total Other Current Liabilities	16,564.83	28,696.68	27,167.32
Total Current Liabilities	17,564.83	28,696.68	243,367.32
Long Term Liabilities			
Loan Payable	633,800.00	683,800.00	297,632.40
Total Long Term Liabilities	633,800.00	683,800.00	297,632.40
Total Liabilities	651,364.83	712,496.68	540,999.72
Equity			
Capital Stock	300,000.00	400,000.00	400,000.00
Net Income	28,769.78	34,996.43	96,312.43
Total Equity	328,769.78	434,996.43	496,312.43
TOTAL LIABILITIES & EQUITY	980,134.61	1,147,493.11	1,037,312.15

16 Type **3/31/16** in the To text box, and then click **Refresh**.

17 Click the **Print** button from the toolbar, then click **Report**, and then click **Print** in the Print Reports window. Modify the report header to remove the date prepared and time prepared fields. The report as shown in Figure 8.28 should appear.

Wild Water Sports Ch 8
Transaction List by Date
March 2016

Type	Date	Num	Adj	Name	Memo	Account	Clr	Split	Debit	Credit
Mar 16										
Check	03/01/16	1029		Bank of Florida		Bank of Florida		-SPLIT-		4,717.81
Check	03/01/16	1030		Bank of Florida		Bank of Florida		-SPLIT-		4,717.81
Check	03/06/16			Bank of Florida		Short-Term Investm...		Bank of Florida		300,000.00
Check	03/06/16	1031		Bank of Orlando		Bank of Florida		-SPLIT-		387,690.58
Bill	03/06/16			Malibu Boats		Accounts Payable		-SPLIT-		90,400.00
Invoice	03/06/16	10004		Fantasy Sports		Accounts Receivable		-SPLIT-	120,345.00	
Deposit	03/09/16			ETrade	Deposit	Short-Term Investm...		Other Income	3,000.00	
Sales Receipt	03/12/16	6008		Sonia Garcia		Undeposited Funds	X	-SPLIT-	51,120.00	
Deposit	03/12/16				Deposit	Bank of Florida		Undeposited F...	51,120.00	
Bill	03/16/16			Malibu Boats		Accounts Payable		-SPLIT-		83,200.00
Invoice	03/18/16	10005		Buena Vista Water ...		Accounts Receivable		-SPLIT-	1,964.93	
Payment	03/20/16	9152		Orlando Water Sports		Undeposited Funds	X	Accounts Rec...	5,300.00	
Invoice	03/23/16	10007		Freebirds		Accounts Receivable		-SPLIT-	138,450.00	
Invoice	03/26/16	10006		Performance Rental...		Accounts Receivable		-SPLIT-	1,293.98	
Payment	03/27/16	741		Buena Vista Water ...		Undeposited Funds	X	Accounts Rec...	1,964.93	
Deposit	03/27/16				Deposit	Bank of Florida		-SPLIT-	7,264.93	
Bill	03/30/16			Tige Boats		Accounts Payable		-SPLIT-		133,000.00
Invoice	03/30/16	10008		Florida Sports Camp		Accounts Receivable		-SPLIT-	83,868.75	
Check	03/30/16			Bank of Florida		Short-Term Investm...		Bank of Florida		40,000.00
Sales Tax Payment	03/30/16	1033		Florida Department ...		Bank of Florida		Sales Tax Pay...		21,904.04
Payment	03/31/16	15687		Performance Rentals		Undeposited Funds	X	Accounts Rec...	10,000.00	
Deposit	03/31/16				Deposit	Bank of Florida		Undeposited F...	10,000.00	
Bill Pmt -Check	03/31/16	1032		Malibu Boats		Bank of Florida		Accounts Pay...		90,400.00
Liability Check	03/31/16	1034		Florida U.C. Fund	6854102	Bank of Florida		Payroll Liabiliti...		559.11
Liability Check	03/31/16	1035		United States Treas...	99-6854102	Bank of Florida		-SPLIT-		6,233.53
Check	03/31/16	1036		Central Florida Gas ...		Bank of Florida		Utilities		1,050.00
Check	03/31/16	1037		Verizon		Bank of Florida		Telephone Ex...		1,500.00
Paycheck	03/31/16	1038		Donna Chandler		Bank of Florida		-SPLIT-		3,384.92
Paycheck	03/31/16	1039		Karen Wilson		Bank of Florida		-SPLIT-		3,137.92
Paycheck	03/31/16	1040		Ryder Zacovic		Bank of Florida		-SPLIT-		471.90
General Journal	03/31/16	6		Staples		Furniture and Equip...		Loan Payable	5,000.00	
Mar 16										

Figure 8.28

Transaction List by Date for March 2016

18 Close all report windows.

"Not bad for our first three months," Karen comments. "But we still need to accrue some revenues and expenses, adjust some prepaid assets and unearned revenue, and record depreciation."

End Note

You've now helped Karen understand even more of QuickBooks Accountant's features, including how to record the repayment of loans, sale of investments, receipt of inventory items and related bills, credit sales, and receipt of payments on account.

Business Events Summary

Business Event	Process Steps	Page
Financing Activities:		
Pay loan	Write checks from Banking section	225
Transfer funds	Open account registers from chart of accounts	227
Investing Activities:		
Record short-term investment activity	Open account register from chart of accounts	228
Operating Activities:		
Order inventory; create purchase orders	Purchase orders from Vendors section	230
Receive inventory and enter bill	Receive inventory from Vendors section	231
Create new jobs	Add job from Customers section	233
Enter employee hours	Enter time from the Employees section	234
Invoice customers for billable hours	Create invoices from Customers section	234
Sell inventory for cash	Create sales receipts from Customers section	236
Invoice customers for sales on account	Create invoices from Customers section	237
Record deposits from customers	Receive payments from Customers section	239
Pay bills	Pay bills from Vendors section	239
Collect cash from customers	Receive payments from Customers section	240
Pay sales taxes	Manage sales tax from Company section	242
Pay payroll taxes	Pay liabilities from Employees section	242
Process payroll and pay employees	Pay employees from the Employees section	245
Other:		
Purchase assets with long-term debt	Open account register from chart of accounts	246
Evaluate a firm's financial performance		247

Chapter 8 Questions

1 Of the information contained in a loan amortization schedule, what part is recorded in QuickBooks Accountant?

2 How does a firm account for a transfer of funds from one bank to another bank in QuickBooks Accountant?

3 How do you update vendor records for changes in terms from the home page?

4 What payment terms are available in QuickBooks Accountant for vendors?

5 Consider this statement: "QuickBooks Accountant records revenue when an invoice is generated even though cash has not been received." Is this practice acceptable? Why or why not?

6 What icon is clicked in the Vendors section to record the receipt of inventory and the related bill?

7 What steps are necessary to record services performed on account for Wild Water Sports?

8 How does the QuickBooks Accountant software respond if a bill is entered with a vendor name that is not included on the vendor list?

9 What are the steps for paying sales tax?

10 What are noncash investing and financing activities, and how are they recorded in QuickBooks Accountant?

Chapter 8 Matching

Select the letter of the item below that best matches the definitions that follow. Use the text or QuickBooks Accountant Help to complete this assignment.

a. Loan amortization table

b. Electronic transfers

c. Credit terms for customers

d. Credit terms from suppliers

e. Purchases on account

f. Sales on account

g. Sales invoices

h. Apply credits

i. Sales tax liabilities

j. Payroll tax liabilities

_____ Sales to a customer for which the company allows some time for the invoice to be paid.

_____ Used on invoices to specify how previous payments made by customers should be applied to an invoice.

_____ A source document used to record sales on account.

_____ A schedule of the payments, including interest and principal, that are required to pay down a loan.

_____ Purchases from a supplier who allows the purchaser some time to pay the bill.

_____ Liabilities created when a company sells merchandise and collects sales taxes from a customer.

_____ Specify the discount, if any, and amount of time that customers have to pay an invoice.

_____ Used to move amounts from one bank account to another.

_____ Liabilities created when payroll taxes are withheld from an employee's paycheck.

_____ Specify the discount, if any, and amount of time that companies have to pay a bill.

Chapter 8 Exercises

Chapter 8 Exercise 1
FINANCING ACTIVITIES

Restore the file Boston Catering Ch 8 (Backup) that you downloaded from the text web site. Add the following transactions and then print a standard balance sheet as of 8/31/10:

a. On 8/2/10 the company wrote check #1509 to Citibank for $926.29 as an installment on notes payable ($416.67 of which was for interest expense).

b. On 8/2/10 the company wrote check #1510 to Bank of America for $610.32 as an installment on notes payable ($166.67 of which was for interest expense).

c. On 8/3/10 the company electronically transferred $20,000 from the Bank of America checking account to the short-term investments account.

Chapter 8 Exercise 2
INVESTING ACTIVITIES

Restore the file Boston Catering Ch 8 (Backup) that you downloaded from the text web site. Do *not* use the file created in Exercise 1 above. Add the following transactions and then print a standard balance sheet as of 8/31/10:

a. On 8/6/10 the company purchased some additional equipment from a restaurant that closed the previous month. The equipment was valued at $10,000 for which the company signed a two-year 6% note payable to Evian Sprinter with no payment due until maturity.

b. On 8/9/10 the company purchased furniture from Outlet Tool Supply for $1,000 using check 1511.

Chapter 8 Exercise 3
OPERATING ACTIVITIES – PURCHASES AND PAYMENTS FROM/TO VENDORS

Restore the file Boston Catering Ch 8 (Backup) that you downloaded from the text web site. Do *not* use the file created in the exercises above. Add the following transactions and then print a vendor contact list showing only the vendor, address, and balance totals columns:

a. On 8/5/10 the company ordered 48 bottles of a new item W400 Vintage Brut from Domain Chandon, 1 California Drive, Yountville, CA 94599 terms net 30, on purchase order 104. This champagne cost $36 per bottle and sells for $48 per bottle.

b. On 8/6/10 the company paid bills due Fiddlehead Cellars and US Food Service as of 7/30/10 assigning check numbers 1512 and 1513.

c. On 8/26/10 the company received the 48 bottles of item W400 from Domain Chandon along with a bill due in 30 days.

Chapter 8 Exercise 4

OPERATING ACTIVITIES – EXPENSES & SALES

Restore the file Boston Catering Ch 8 (Backup) that you downloaded from the text web site. Do *not* use the file created in the previous exercises. Add the following transactions and then print a standard balance sheet as of 8/31/10 and a standard income statement for the month ended 8/31/10:

a. On 8/6/10 the company contracted with a new customer, Boston College, terms net 15, that is subject to sales tax. The company anticipates many future engagements with this customer and thus created a new job (Event 1).

b. On 8/15/10 the company paid rent to New England Property Management (a new vendor) on check 1513 for $3,000.

c. On 8/16/10 the company contracted with MIT. The company anticipates many future engagements with this customer and thus created a new job (Dean Bumble).

d. On 8/21/10 the company paid all bills outstanding using checks 1514–1516.

e. During the month of August Kyle Hain worked 10 hours and Amy Casey worked 9 hours on 8/15 during the Boston College Event 1 party as wait staff. Kyle worked 12 hours and Amy worked 10 hours on 8/29 during the MIT Dean Bumble party as wait staff. Otherwise they did not work. Payroll checks are issued on 8/31/10 starting with check 1517. Paycheck information is shown below. (*Note:* No premium is paid for overtime.)

Pay/Tax/Withholding	Chambers	Hain	Casey
Hours	n/a	22	19
Rate	$50,000	$ 16.00	$ 18.00
Gross pay	4,166.67	352.00	342.00
Federal withholding	−570.83	−48.22	−46.85
Social Security employee	−258.33	−21.82	−21.20
Medicare employee	−60.42	−5.10	−4.96
MA withholding	−283.99	−5.92	−6.68
MA Training Fund	0.42	0.04	0.03
Social Security employer	258.33	21.82	21.20
Medicare company	60.42	5.10	4.96
Federal unemployment	33.33	2.82	2.74
MA unemployment	125.00	10.56	10.26
Check amount	2,993.10	270.94	262.31

f. On 8/15/10 the company catered the Boston College Event 1 party. On 8/16/10 the company invoiced Boston College using invoice number 1123. They used 30 bottles of W100 and served 150 heavy appetizers (A100).

g. On 8/29/10 the company catered the MIT Dean Bumble party. On 8/30/10 the company invoiced MIT using invoice number 1124. They used 45 bottles of W201 and served 200 light appetizers (A200).

h. On 8/31/10 the company received a bill from US Food Service for $800 in food purchases for the Boston College event. A bill for the MIT party food purchases was expected next month.

i. On 8/31/10 the company paid sales tax due as of 8/31/10 using check 1520.

j. On 8/31/10 the company paid payroll liabilities due as of 7/31/10 using checks 1521 and 1522. (**Hint:** be sure to modify payroll items and set vendor for federal withholding to the IRS.)

Chapter 8 Assignments

Chapter 8 Assignment 1

ADDING MORE INFORMATION: WILD WATER SPORTS

Restore the file Wild Water Sports Ch 8A (Backup) that you downloaded from the text web site, and then add the following transactions in chronological order:

Event #	Date	Business Event
1	4/2/16	Wrote Check No. 1041 for $4,717.81 as payment no. 3 on loan to Bank of Florida. See loan amortization schedule in Figure 8.1 for interest and principal breakdown.
2	4/3/16	Received $92,095 as payment on account from Fantasy Sports (their Check No. 234).
3	4/3/16	Deposited payment received from Fantasy Sports.
4	4/3/16	Paid Malibu Boats bill by writing Check No. 1042 for $83,200.
5	4/6/16	Created Purchase Order No. 4008 to Tige Boats for the purchase of one T 22v and one T 24v for showroom floor inventory.
6	4/6/16	Received items ordered and bill on Purchase Order No. 4007 from MB Sports.
7	4/9/16	Received $1,293.98 as payment on account from Performance Rentals (their Check No. 987).
8	4/9/16	Accepted a new job (50007) to service a boat owned by Seth Backman.
9	4/11/16	Pat Ng worked two hours performing an engine service and three hours cleaning on job 50007.
10	4/11/16	Sold the investment in Apple Computer stock, originally purchased for $35,000, for a loss of $2,000. (**Hint:** the loss should be recorded to the Other Income account.)
11	4/10/16	Deposited payment received from Performance Rentals.
12	4/10/16	Created Invoice No. 10009 to Spirit Adventures to record the sale of an MB 220v (Terms: net 30), with a balance due of $69,225.00.
13	4/10/16	Created Invoice No. 10010 to Seth Blackman for service under job 50007 and five quarts of oil, one air filter, and one oil filter. Terms: net 15, with a balance due of $585.75.
14	4/13/16	Created Purchase Order No. 4009 to MB Sports for the purchase of one MB 220v and one MB B52 V23 for showroom floor inventory.

Event #	Date	Business Event
15	4/13/16	Received $83,868.75 as payment on account from Florida Sports Camp (their Check No. 8741).
16	4/13/16	Deposited payment received from Florida Sports Camp.
17	4/13/16	Transferred $20,000 from short-term investments to checking.
18	4/13/16	Paid Tige Boats bill by writing Check No. 1043 for $133,000.
19	4/16/16	Accepted a new job (50008) to paint a boat owned by Fantasy Sports.
20	4/16/16	Ryder Zacovic worked eight hours painting and repairing on job 50008.
21	4/17/16	Created Invoice No. 10011 to High Flying Fun (a new customer, subject to state sales tax) to record sale of one T 24v and one MW XTI (Terms: net 15).
22	4/17/16	Created Sales Receipt No. 6009 to Orlando Water Sports to record the sale of one MS LXi in exchange for their Check No. 10005.
23	4/17/16	Deposited payment received from Orlando Water Sports.
24	4/20/16	Created invoice 10012 to Fantasy Sports for service under job 50008.
25	4/23/16	Created Purchase Order No. 4010 to Malibu Boats for the purchase of one MS LX for Freebirds, one MS LSV for Buena Vista Water Sports, and one MV for showroom floor inventory.
26	4/24/16	Received items ordered and bill on Purchase Order No. 4009 from MB Sports.
27	4/24/16	Received items ordered and bill on Purchase Order No. 4008 from Tige Boats.
28	4/24/16	Created invoice 10013 to Half Moon Sports (a new customer, subject to sales tax) to record sale of one MB 220v (Terms: net 15).
29	4/26/16	Purchased a computer, printer, and other electronic equipment from Staples for $12,000—again completely financed with a no-interest loan and with no payment due until 11/1/16.
30	4/26/16	Paid payroll tax liabilities (accrued during March) of $2,934.66 using Check No. 1044 to the Florida U.C. Fund and Check No. 1045 to the United States Treasury.
31	4/26/16	Paid sales tax liability (accrued during March) of $24,232.66 to the Florida Dept. of Revenue using Check No. 1046.
32	4/29/16	Wrote Check No. 1047 to Central Florida Gas & Electric in the amount of $1,250 for utilities expense.
33	4/29/16	Wrote Check No. 1048 to Verizon in the amount of $1,800 for telephone expense.
34	4/29/16	Wrote Check No. 1049 to Brian Ski in the amount of $3,000 for advertising and promotion expense.
35	4/30/16	Pat Ng worked 8 hours per day on 4/1, 4/2, and 4/3. He worked 4 hours per day on 4/6, 4/7, 4/8, 4/9, 4/13, 4/14, 4/15, 4/16, 4/20, 4/21, 4/22, 4/23, and 4/24. All of these hours were unbillable. Pat also worked 5 (billable) hours on 4/10, which were already recorded, for a total of 81 hours during the month of April. Ryder Zacovic worked 8 hours per day on 4/1, 4/2, and 4/3. He worked 4 hours per day on 4/6, 4/7, 4/8, 4/9, 4/13, 4/14, 4/15, 4/17, 4/20, 4/21, 4/22,

Event #	Date	Business Event
		4/23, and 4/24 as well as 8 hours on 4/27. All of these hours were unbillable. Ryder also worked 8 (billable) hours on 4/16, which were already recorded, for a total of 92 hours during the month of April.
36	4/30/16	Received $681.60 as payment on account from Fantasy Sports (their Check No. 1874).
37	4/30/16	Received $585.75 as payment on account from Seth Blackman (his Check No. 1547).
38	4/30/16	Received $13,000 as a deposit from Freebirds (their Check No. 2514) toward the purchase of a Malibu Sportster LX ordered 4/23. (*Note:* Do not apply this amount to their existing balance.)
39	4/30/16	Received $16,250 as a deposit from Buena Vista Water Sports (their Check No. 8742) toward the purchase of a Malibu Sunscape LSV ordered 4/23.
40	4/30/16	Deposited $30,517.35 worth of checks received 4/30 into checking account.
41	4/30/16	Process payroll per the information provided in Table 8.1, starting with Check No. 1050.

Table 8.1

Earnings Information for Wild Water Sports

Item	Donna	Karen	Pat	Ryder
Earnings	4,166.67	4,166.67	1,458.00	1,380.00
Federal Withholding	−463.00	−710.00	−199.75	−189.06
Social Security Employee	−258.33	−258.33	−90.40	−85.56
Medicare Employee	−60.42	−60.42	−21.14	−20.01
Social Security Company	258.33	258.33	90.40	85.56
Medicare Company	60.42	60.42	21.14	20.01
Federal Unemployment	0	0	11.66	11.04
State Unemployment	0	0	39.37	37.26
Check Amount	3,384.92	3,137.92	1,146.71	1,085.37

Memorize and print the following as of 4/30/16:

a. Customer Balance Summary

b. Vendor Balance Summary

c. Item Listing (list only Item, Description, Type, Price, Quantity On Hand, and Cost)

d. Balance Sheet Standard

e. Profit & Loss Standard by month for January through April

f. Transaction List by Date for the month of April

Chapter 8 Assignment 2

ADDING MORE INFORMATION: CENTRAL COAST CELLULAR

Restore the file Central Coast Cellular Ch 8 (Backup) that you downloaded from the text web site, and then add the following transactions:

Event #	Date	Business Event
1	1/20/14	The company received a shipment of phones from Nokia on Purchase Order No. 102. Items were received and a bill recorded (due in 30 days).
2	1/21/14	The company invoiced the City of San Luis Obispo, using Invoice No. 10001 for 20 Nokia 8290 phones, 15 Nokia 8890 phones, 30 hours of consulting time, and 35 commissions earned. (You'll need to add a new service item called Commissions, with a description of Commissions earned on cell phone contracts ($50 per contract) and recorded to a new income account titled Commissions.) Applied available credits to this invoice.
3	1/22/14	The company purchased equipment in the amount of $95,000 cash from Kyle Equipment, Inc., using Check No. 3008.
4	1/23/14	The company paid the Ericsson bill of $6,500 with Check No. 3009.
5	1/31/14	The company paid semi-monthly payroll starting with Check No. 3010 for the period of January 16 to January 31, 2014. Megan Paulson worked 85 hours during the period. Payroll tax information is shown in Table 8.2.

Item	Alex	Jay	Megan	
Earnings	2,000.00	1,500.00	1,020.00	**Table 8.2**
Federal Withholding	−300.00	−225.00	−153.00	Payroll Information for Central
Social Security Employee	−124.00	−93.00	−63.24	Coast Cellular
Medicare Employee	−29.00	−21.75	−14.79	
CA Withholding	−100.00	−75.00	−51.00	
CA Disability Employee	−10.00	−7.50	−5.10	
CA Employee Training Tax	2.00	1.50	1.02	
Social Security Company	124.00	93.00	63.24	
Medicare Company	29.00	21.75	14.79	
Federal Unemployment	6.40	4.80	3.26	
CA Unemployment	24.00	18.00	12.24	
Check Amount	1,437.00	1,077.75	732.87	

Print the following:

a. Profit & Loss Standard report for the month of January 2014

b. Balance Sheet Standard as of January 31, 2014

c. Transaction List by Date for the period January 1 through January 31, 2014

Chapter 8 Assignment 3

ADDING MORE INFORMATION: SANTA BARBARA SAILING

Restore the file Santa Barbara Sailing Ch 8 (Backup) that you downloaded from the text web site, and then add the following transactions:

Event #	Date	Business Event
1	7/17/15	Deposited three checks, which had been collected earlier in the week, into the checking account for a total of $20,243.60.
2	7/17/15	Hired a new employee, Jack Sparrow, to serve as a charter boat captain. Jack is single and earns $25 per hour but is billed out to customers at $50 per hour (a new service item called Charter Boat Captain with a new income type account called Charter Income). His Social Security number is 999-23-8722, and his address is 1 Black Pearl Road, Montecito, CA 93109. He is paid semi-monthly like other employees, but all of his hours are billable to customers. Maximum billing is eight hours per day.
3	7/18/15	Borrowed an additional $50,000 from the Bank of the Caribbean at 7% interest due in monthly installments over the next three years. Deposited these funds directly into the company's checking account.
4	7/18/15	Collected $5,000 from Raytheon via their MasterCard as a deposit on charter with Captain Jack Sparrow using the CAT 50 for 10 days. The company's policy for credit customers is to collect a deposit in advance and then bill customers when they return. Raytheon is given terms of net 15. Deposited this advance later in the week.
5	7/21/15	Rented the CAT 42 to a new customer, SBNEWS (Santa Barbara News-Press, located at 715 Anacapa Street, Santa Barbara, CA 93101) for one week in the future, on terms of net 15. Collected a deposit of $2,500 (Check No. 0932), which was deposited into the bank the same day.
6	7/21/15	Rented the CAT 28 to Deckers for seven days using Sales Receipt No. 10005 and collected Visa payment for $1,663.20.
7	7/22/15	Deposited Raytheon and Deckers credit card payments.
8	7/25/15	Rented the CAT 32 to a new customer, Barry Cohen (located at 398 Alameda Padre Serra, Santa Barbara, CA 93105, Terms: Due on receipt) for 14 days using Sales Receipt No. 10006 and collected MasterCard payment for $4,158.00.
9	7/27/15	Captain Jack returns in the evening with the Raytheon charter and records his 10 days of work at eight hours per day from 7/18/15 to 7/27/15.
10	7/28/15	Paid utilities expenses of $1,500 to Edison (new vendor) using Check No. 107.
11	7/28/15	Paid computer and Internet expenses of $1,200 to Verizon (new vendor) using Check No. 108.
12	7/28/15	Paid repairs and maintenance expenses of $3,000 to Harbor Marineworks (located at 122 Harbor Way, Santa Barbara, CA 93109) using Check No. 109.
13	7/29/15	The company bills Raytheon for 10 days of Charter Boat Captain and 10 days of CAT 50 (Terms: net 15) using Invoice

Event #	Date	Business Event
		No. 7002. Applied the deposit already received to this invoice. (*Note:* Be sure to combine hours into one line item on the invoice.)
14	7/30/15	Made a payment of $2,940.93 to Bank of the Caribbean, using Check No. 110, as an installment on the long-term note. ($1,324.50 of this amount is interest expense.)
15	7/31/15	Received a $3,400 bill from Creative Resource Group (a new vendor) for advertising services provided in July. Terms: net 30. (*Hint:* Use QuickBooks Accountant Enter Bills to record this transaction. Payment is not made until the following month.)
16	7/31/15	Paid employees for the period 7/16/15–7/31/15. Rob worked for salary during that period. Nathan and Jeanne worked 33 and 42 hours, respectively, during that period. Jack Sparrow has already recorded his time sheet. Start with Check No. 111. Payroll withholding information is shown in Table 8.3.

Item	Rob	Jeanne	Nathan	Jack	Table 8.3
Earnings	2,708.33	756.00	264.00	2,000.00	Payroll and Withholding Information for Santa Barbara Sailing
Federal Withholding	−514.58	−143.64	−50.16	−380.00	
Social Security Employee	−167.92	−46.87	−16.37	−124.00	
Medicare Employee	−39.27	−10.96	−3.83	−29.00	
CA Income Tax	−216.67	−60.48	−21.12	−160.00	
CA Disability	−16.25	−4.54	−1.58	−12.00	
CA Employee Training Tax	2.71	0.76	0.26	2.00	
Social Security Employer	167.92	46.87	16.37	124.00	
Medicare Employer	39.27	10.96	3.83	29.00	
Federal Unemployment	21.67	6.05	2.11	16.00	
CA Unemployment	92.08	25.70	8.98	68.00	
Check Amount	1,753.64	489.51	170.94	1,295.00	

Print the following for the month of July 2015:

a.   Profit & Loss Standard

b.   Balance Sheet Standard

c.   Statement of Cash Flows

d.   Transaction List by Date

Chapter 8 Assignment 4
ADDING MORE INFORMATION: DRONE CITY

Restore the file Drone City Ch 08 (Backup) that you downloaded from the text web site, and then add the following transactions.

sole proprietorship

easy step

Event #	Date	Business Event
1	1/17/17	Created purchase order 4001 to Ace Drones for the purchase of 4 Hex Transports for a new customer Folly Free with payment terms net 30.

Event #	Date	Business Event
2	1/18/17	Created job 501 for customer Amazon, Inc.
3	1/18/17	Hired a new hourly ($17/hr.) employee Sneed Snow, a single male with social security number 841-97-1478 subject to all WA taxes and who resides at 302 W. Prince Lane, Seattle, WA, 98445. Recall that all employees are paid semi-monthly.
4	1/20/17	Created purchase order 4002 to Zip Drones (a new vendor) for the purchase of 3 Video Gems (new item with a cost of $1,800 and a sales price of $2,300) for inventory.
5	1/23/17 to 1/25/17	Monica worked 4 billable hours and Sneed worked 3 billable hours each day (on 1/23, 1/24, and 1/25) on job 501. Sneed will use time sheet hours to have activities transferred to paychecks. Monica will not.
6	1/26/17	Received inventory items ordered on purchase order 4001 from Ace Drones.
7	1/27/17	Received and deposited $2,000 as a deposit on an order from Folly Free.
8	1/27/17	Paid bill from Ace Drones of $10,000 using check #1009.
9	1/30/17	Created invoice #7000 for consulting services rendered to Amazon on job 501.
10	1/30/17	Delivered items ordered and received for Folly Free and created invoice 7001 applying any credits available.
11	1/30/17	Paid $760.55 to Bank of Seattle on note payable ($125 represented interest the balance principal) using check #1010
12	1/30/17	Paid $1,200 to Sprint (a new vendor) for telephone expense using check #1011.
13	1/30/17	Paid $2,400 to Office Depot (a new vendor) for supplies (a new other current asset account) using check #1012.
14	1/30/17	Received inventory items ordered on purchase order 4002 from Zip Drones.
15	1/16/17 to 1/31/17	Emily worked 8 hours per day in the office (not billable) on 1/17/17, 1/18/17, 1/19/17, 1/20/17, 1/23/17, 1/24/17, 1/25/17, 1/26/17, 1/27/17, and 1/30/17. Sneed worked 9 billable hours (already recorded above) and then 8 hours per day in the office (not billable) on 1/17/17, 1/18/17, 1/19/17, 4 hours per day 1/23/17, 1/24/17, 1/25/17, and 5 hours per day on 1/26/17, 1/27/17 and 1/30/17. Record this time in time sheets.
16	1/31/17	Paid employees for the period 1/16/17 – 1/31/17. Monica worked for salary and Emily worked 80 hours (already recorded on the timesheet above) and Sneed worked 60 hours (also already recorded on the timesheet above) during that period. Payroll tax information is shown in Table 8.4.
17	1/31/17	Changed the existing Sales Income account to be titled Sales and then change the Prepaid Advertising Supplies account to be titled Prepaid Advertising.
18	1/31/17	Created sales receipt #103 for the sale of 1 Hex Transport to ICE T (a new customer) and received check 30 for $2,982.00 which was held for deposit.

Place your name in the Extra Footer Line, remove subtitle, date and time prepared header information, and then memorize (in a report group with your name) and print the following reports as of 1/31/17.

a. Profit & Loss Standard (Change the name on the report to Income Statement).

b. Balance Sheet Standard

c. Statement of Cash Flows

d. Transaction List by Date (for the period 1/17/17 through 1/31/17).

Item	Emily	Monica	Sneed
Check number	1013	1014	1015
Earnings	1,440.00	2,291.67	1,020.00
Federal Withholding	197.28	313.96	139.74
Social Security Employee	89.28	142.08	63.24
Medicare Employee	20.88	33.23	14.79
WA-Employment Admin. Fund	.43	.69	.31
Social Security Company	89.28	142.08	63.24
Medicare Company	20.88	33.23	14.79
Federal Unemployment	49.10	78.15	34.78
WA-Unemployment	37.30	59.35	26.42

Table 8.4

Payroll and Earnings Information for Drone City Payroll on 1/31/17

Chapter 8 Cases

Chapter 8 Case 1

FOREVER YOUNG

In Chapter 7, you added some transactions to your QuickBooks Accountant file for Forever Young. Make a copy of that file, and use that copy to enter the following transactions:

service

sole proprietorship

Event #	Date	Business Event
1	1/16/15	Sebastian ran into an old friend, Larry Rice, at one of his speaking engagements and decided to hire Larry to speak with him at selected events. Larry agreed to work on an hourly basis at $500 per hour, and Sebastian planned to bill Larry's time to customers at $750 per hour to cover overhead costs. Larry's Social Security number is 133-20-7357; he's married with one income and is subject to all California taxes. He'll constitute a new payroll item called Professional Hourly and will be paid semi-monthly like other employees. Be sure to set up a new service item named 004, description: Professional Services, rate: $750, to account Consulting Income.
2	1/17/15	Signed a contract with Microsoft (Terms: net 30) to provide a full-day seminar on 1/25/15 at their sales convention with Mr. Rice speaking for two hours. Received a $2,000 deposit via Microsoft's Check No. 09380991, which was deposited that day.
3	1/19/15	Spoke at the Adobe officer's retreat (a full-day seminar), prepared Invoice No. 503, applied the previous credit, and received the remaining $5,000 due via Adobe's Check No. 698903, which was immediately deposited into the company's checking account.

Event #	Date	Business Event
4	1/21/15	Borrowed $50,000 on a three-year 7% note payable from Wells Fargo Bank. The funds were deposited into the company's checking account that day.
5	1/22/15	Wrote Check No. 7 in the amount of $6,000 to Westwood Design and Production for the purchase of brochures to promote future speaking engagements. Sebastian expects these brochures to last throughout for two years and treated them as Prepaid Advertising.
6	1/25/15	Provided a full-day seminar at Microsoft's sales convention, where Mr. Rice spoke for two hours. (*Hint:* Record his time on a time sheet.)
7	1/28/15	Prepared Invoice No. 504 to Microsoft (billing it for the full-day seminar and Mr. Rice's time), applied the previous credit, and mailed the invoice to Microsoft's accounting department.
8	1/30/15	Wrote Check No. 8 to Global Travel for $5,600 in travel expenses.
9	1/30/15	Wrote Check No. 9 to Hertz for $800 in automobile expenses.
10	1/30/15	Wrote Check No. 10 to Cingular Wireless for $500 of telephone expenses.
11	1/31/15	Paid semi-monthly payroll starting with Check No. 11 for the period 1/16/15 to 1/31/15. Payroll tax information is shown in Table 8.5. Anne worked 45 hours during this period.
12	1/31/15	Signed a contract with ITP Thomson (Terms: net 30) to provide a full-day seminar on 2/12/15 at their sales convention with Mr. Rice speaking for three hours. Received a $3,000 deposit via ITP's Check No. 15474, which was deposited the next day.
13	1/31/15	Wrote Check No. 14 to Sebastian Young for $5,000 as an owner's draw.

Table 8.5

Payroll and Withholding Information for Forever Young

Item	Cory	Anne	Larry
Earnings	3,333.33	900.00	1,000.00
Federal Withholding	−633.33	−171.00	−190.00
Social Security Employee	−206.67	−55.80	−62.00
Medicare Employee	−48.33	−13.05	−14.50
CA Income Tax	−266.67	−72.00	−80.00
CA Disability	−20.00	−5.40	−6.00
CA Employee Training Tax	3.33	0.90	1.00
Social Security Employer	206.67	55.80	62.00
Medicare Employer	48.33	13.05	14.50
Federal Unemployment	26.67	7.20	8.00
CA Unemployment	113.33	30.60	34.00
Check Amount	2,158.33	582.75	647.50

Requirements:

Print the following as of 1/31/15:

1   Profit & Loss Standard

2   Balance Sheet Standard

3   Statement of Cash Flows

4 Transaction List by Date (from 1/16/15 to 1/31/15)

5 Customer Balance Summary

6 Item Listing

Chapter 8 Case 2

OCEAN VIEW FLOWERS

In Chapter 7, you created a new QuickBooks Accountant file for Ocean View Flowers, a wholesale flower distributor. Make a copy of that file and use that copy to enter the following transactions:

corporation

merchandising

Event #	Date	Business Event
1	2/1/16	The company repaid a portion of the long-term debt it borrowed from Santa Barbara Bank & Trust with Union Bank Check No. 119 in the amount of $1,000. (All of this payment was principal and none was interest.)
2	2/4/16	The company prepaid a one-year liability insurance policy to State Farm Insurance with Union Bank Check No. 120 in the amount of $2,500. (The transaction was recorded to Prepaid Insurance, an other current asset account.)
3	2/5/16	The company created Purchase Order No. 5002 to Vordale Farms for the following items to be purchased on terms of net 30. (*Hint:* Use QuickBooks Accountant Help to add terms to the purchase order form.) All anthuriums are recorded as Sales.

Flower	Quantity Ordered	Cost	Sales Price
Bright Red Anthuriums	700	$20.00	$35.00
Peach Anthuriums	800	$22.00	$40.00
White Anthuriums	600	$27.00	$50.00

Event #	Date	Business Event
4	2/8/16	The company cashed in $5,000 of its $25,000 short-term investment early and received $5,200, which was deposited into the Union Bank account. The $200 difference represents Interest Income, a new other income account.
5	2/12/16	The company received the following bills. (Accept any changes in terms and add new vendors as necessary.)

Vendor	Amount	Terms	Expense
GTE	$250	Net 15	Telephone
Edison	$300	Net 15	Utilities
FlowerMart	$60	Net 30	Subscriptions

Event #	Date	Business Event
6	2/15/16	The company paid payroll. All employees worked the entire period; Kelly Gusland worked 62 hours and Margie Cruz worked 72 hours. Checks were written using the Union Bank account starting with Check No. 121. Payroll taxes and withholding for employees are shown in Table 8.6.

Table 8.6

Payroll Taxes and Withholding for Employees from February 1, 2016, through February 15, 2016

Item	Edward	Kelly	Margie	Marie	Stan
Federal Withholding	−667.00	−123.00	−113.00	−402.00	−286.00
Social Security Employee	−180.83	−57.66	−53.57	−155.00	−129.17
Medicare Employee	−42.30	−13.48	−12.53	−36.25	−30.20
CA Withholding	−192.30	−20.93	−8.60	−153.55	−61.86
CA Disability Employee	−14.58	−4.65	−4.32	−12.50	−10.42
CA Employee Training Tax	1.17	0.93	0.86	2.00	2.08
Social Security Company	180.83	57.66	53.57	155.00	129.17
Medicare Company	42.30	13.48	12.53	36.25	30.20
Federal Unemployment	9.33	7.44	6.91	16.00	16.67
CA Unemployment	0.58	0.46	0.43	1.00	1.05
Check Amount	1,819.66	710.28	671.98	1,740.70	1,565.68

7	2/18/16	The company received items and entered the bill from Purchase Order No. 5002 to Vordale Farms on terms of net 30.
8	2/22/16	The company created invoices to customers as follows: (If terms change, accept them as permanent; also, apply any available credits to these invoices.)

Customer	Invoice #	Item Sold	Quantity	Terms	Invoice
Latin Ladies	10001	Calistoga Sun	400	Net 15	$ 9,000
		Caribbean Pink Sands	100		
California Beauties	10002	White Anthuriums	500	2/10 Net 30	$25,000
FTD	10003	Bright Red Anthuriums	300	Net 30	$10,500

9	2/25/16	The company paid its GTE and Edison bills using Union Bank Checks Nos. 126 and 127, respectively.
10	2/25/16	The company received $9,000 as payment on account from Latin Ladies. The amount was held for deposit at a later time.

Event #	Date	Business Event
11	2/26/16	The company purchased a warehouse and land for $300,000 ($50,000 of the purchase price is attributable to the land). A cash payment using Check No. 128 for $30,000 was made to Hawaiian Farms. The remaining balance of $270,000 was satisfied by signing a long-term note payable to the Bank of California. (*Hint:* Use the check to record this entire transaction.) (Be sure to create two new accounts: a land account and a building fixed asset account. Also make sure the land account appears in the chart of accounts before all other fixed assets and that the accumulated depreciation account is the last fixed asset account.)
12	2/29/16	The company paid payroll for the period ending February 29, 2016. All employees worked the entire period; Kelly Gusland worked 50 hours and Margie Cruz worked 45 hours. Checks were written using the Union Bank account starting with Check No. 129. Payroll taxes and withholding for employees are shown in Table 8.7.

Item	Edward	Kelly	Margie	Marie	Stan
Federal Withholding	−667.00	−96.00	−64.00	−402.00	−286.00
Social Security Employee	−180.83	−46.50	−33.48	−155.00	−129.17
Medicare Employee	−42.29	−10.88	−7.83	−36.25	−30.21
CA Withholding	−192.30	−13.32	0.00	−153.55	−61.86
CA Disability Employee	−14.58	−3.75	−2.70	−12.50	−10.42
CA Employee Training Tax	0.00	0.75	0.54	0.00	0.75
Social Security Company	180.83	46.50	33.48	155.00	129.17
Medicare Company	42.29	10.88	7.83	36.25	30.21
Federal Unemployment	0.00	6.00	4.32	0.00	6.00
CA Unemployment	0.00	0.38	0.27	0.00	0.37
Check Amount	1,819.67	579.55	431.99	1,740.70	1,565.67

Table 8.7

Payroll Taxes and Withholding for Employees from February 16, 2016, through February 29, 2016

Requirements:

Record business transactions in chronological order (remember, dates are in the month of February 2016). After recording the transactions, create and print the following for February 2016:

1 Standard Balance Sheet

2 Profit & Loss Standard

3 Statement of Cash Flows

4 Transaction List by Date

Chapter 8 Case 3

ALOHA PROPERTIES

In Chapter 7, you created a new QuickBooks Accountant file for Aloha Properties. Make a copy of that file and use that copy to enter the following transactions:

corporation

service

Event #	Date	Business Event
1	2/1/14	Wrote Check No. 994 for $31,000 to GMAC Mortgage (a new vendor) as an installment payment on a 7% note payable. (Interest expense, $22,604; note payable, $8,396.)
2	2/1/14	Recorded Invoice No. 7511 for rental of Moana Units #1, #3, and #4 and Villa Kailiana Units #1 and #4 for one week to Pixar. Applied $14,000 of their advance payment to this invoice, noted terms due on receipt, and recorded receipt of balance owed of $14,080 in the form of Check No. 87275. (When you apply credits, type 14000 in the column Amt. To Use and then click **Done**.)
3	2/1/14	Deposited Pixar check for $14,080 into checking account.
4	2/4/14	Received payment on account from Apple Computer of $25,000 (their Check No. 987426).
5	2/4/14	Received a bill from Reilly Custodial for cleaning expenses of $3,500.
6	2/5/14	Collected a $15,000 deposit from a new customer, American Airlines.
7	2/6/14	Deposited $40,000 from Apple Computer and American Airlines into the Bank of Hawaii checking account.
8	2/7/14	Received a bill from Blue Sky Pools for maintenance expenses of $1,800.

Event #	Date	Business Event
9	2/8/14	Recorded Invoice No. 7512 for rental of Moana Unit #4 and Villa Kailiana Units #1 and #4 for one week to Pixar. Applied $10,000 of their advance payment to this invoice, noted terms due on receipt, and recorded receipt of balance owed of $11,840 in the form of Check No. 87351.
10	2/8/14	Deposited Pixar check for $11,840 into checking account.
11	2/8/14	Recorded Sales Receipt No. 5119 for rent of Moana Units #1, #2, and #3 for one week each. Collected American Express payment in full of $8,840 from new customer Accenture.
12	2/8/14	Deposited Accenture's American Express credit card payment of $8,840 into the checking account.
13	2/11/14	Received a bill from Pacific Electric for utilities expenses of $2,600 with terms of net 15.
14	2/15/14	Recorded Invoice No. 7513 for rental of Moana Unit #3 and Villa Kailiana Unit #4 for one week to ExxonMobil. Applied their advance payment to this invoice, noted terms due on receipt, and recorded receipt of balance owed of $5,275 from ExxonMobil's Check No. 943098.
15	2/15/14	Deposited ExxonMobil's check for $5,275 into checking account.
16	2/18/14	Received a bill from Service Connection (a new vendor) for repairs of $5,200. Terms are net 15.
17	2/20/14	Received a bill from Sunset Media for advertising of $1,450. Terms are net 30.
18	2/22/14	Recorded Invoice No. 7514 for rental of all units for one week to Boeing. Terms are net 30; invoice total is $39,728.
19	2/25/14	Collected a $3,250 deposit from new customer UCLA with their Check No. 1025575.
20	2/26/14	Collected a $7,500 deposit from new customer UCB with their Check No. 7031223.
21	2/26/14	Deposited both checks (items 19 and 20) into checking account.
22	2/27/14	Paid all bills due on or before 2/28/14 for a total of $9,700 using Check Nos. 995–997. Note that even though there are four bills requiring payment, two are to the same vendor (Blue Sky Pools) and thus only three checks are required.
23	2/28/14	Paid sales tax of $2,128 due on 1/31/14 with Check No. 998.
24	2/28/14	Paid payroll tax liabilities due on 1/31/14. Federal taxes are paid to the U.S. Treasury (Check Nos. 999 and 1000). State taxes are all paid to the State of Hawaii Department of Taxation using ID 84325184.
25	2/28/14	Process payroll per the information provided in Table 8.8, starting with Check No. 1001.

Requirements:

Record business transactions in chronological order (remember that dates are in the month of February 2014). After recording the transactions, create and print the following for February 2014:

1 Standard Balance Sheet

2 Profit & Loss Standard

3 Statement of Cash Flows

4 Transaction List by Date

Item	Fran	Daniele
Hours	n/a	160
Rate	75,000	20.00
Earnings	6,250.00	3,200.00
Federal Withholding	−856.25	−438.40
Social Security Employee	−387.50	−198.40
Medicare Employee	−90.63	−46.40
HI Withholding	−442.33	−210.53
HI Disability	−1.25	−0.64
HI E&T	0.63	0.32
Social Security Employer	387.50	198.40
Medicare Company	90.63	46.40
Federal Unemployment	50.00	25.60
HI Unemployment	187.50	96.00
Check Amount	4,472.04	2,305.63

Table 8.8

Earnings Information

Adjusting Entries

Case: **Wild Water Sports, Inc.**

Karen has recorded the majority of Wild Water's financing, investing, and operating activities for January through April 2016. To help her prepare financial statements for the first quarter, she asks you to prepare any necessary adjusting entries for the period January 1 through March 31, 2016.

"Some people have trouble with adjusting entries," you remark, "but I'm not one of them. I was always helping my classmates understand these types of journal entries. Why don't I give them a try?"

"Okay with me," Karen responds. "Traditional journal entries are available in QuickBooks Accountant, but you don't have to use them." Karen explains that in QuickBooks Accountant the most common adjusting entries—accruing expenses, accruing revenue, recording asset expirations, and recording liability reductions—can be made by using the Make Journal Entry menu item in the Company menu or by using account registers. You decide to use the traditional journal entry process.

Accruing Expenses

Video Demonstration

DEMO 9A - Accruing expenses

Wild Water Sports had a long-term liability of $383,800 when Karen and Donna made their initial investment. That loan was paid off along with accrued interest on March 6, 2016. The remaining balance in the Loan Payable account represents three different loans. The first—a $250,000, five-year, 5% loan from the Bank of Florida—was made on January 4, 2016. The second was a $50,000, three-year, 6% loan from Citibank made on January 1, 2016. The third was just recently acquired when the company purchased a computer from Staples for $5,000. Since then the company has made two payments on the Bank of Florida loan.

According to the loan amortization schedule (see Figure 8.1), a payment of $4,717.81 is due to be made at the beginning of April on the $250,000 loan; $1,010.97 of this payment represents interest owed. As of March 31, 2016, that interest should be included in interest expense for March. Payments are due annually on the $50,000 loan. Thus, as of March 31, 2016, the company owes $750 of interest ($50,000 × 6% × 3/12). The Staples loan bears no interest.

"QuickBooks Accountant automatically assigns journal entry numbers for reference," Karen points out. "Thus, the journal numbers we'll use for March 31 adjustments may follow journal entries used for April business events. What's important is the date specified in the journal." QuickBooks Accountant also gives us the option to identify these as adjusting entries. QuickBooks Accountant places a check in the Adjusting Entry check box located in the Make General Journal Entries window. By identifying these entries as adjusting, we can get a summary of adjusted entries by account in the Adjusted Trial Balance report and view a list of all adjusting journal entries in the Adjusting Journal Entries report.

"Okay," you respond. "I'll take the information you've provided and create the adjustment necessary for interest expense as of March 31."

To accrue interest expense:

1 Restore the Wild Water Sports Ch 9 (Backup) file from your Data Files CD or download it from the Internet.

2 Click **Company** (from the menu bar), and then click **Make General Journal Entries**. If a message pops up about assigning numbers to journal entries, check the **Do not display this message in the future** check box and then click **OK**.

3 Type **3/31/16** as the journal entry date.

4 Type **8** as the Entry No and then place a check in the Adjusting Entry check box.

5 Select **Interest Expense** as the first account.

6 Type **1010.97** as the amount in the Debit column. This will increase Interest Expense (an expense account).

7 Type **Accrued Liabilities** as the second account and then press **[Tab]**.

8 Click **Setup** in the Account Not Found window and create a new account called Accrued Liabilities, an other current liability account.

9 **1,010.97** should now appear as the amount in the Credit column. This will increase Accrued Liabilities. Click the **Hide List** button in the ribbon shown at the top of the Make Journal Entries window. The resulting journal entry should look like Figure 9.1.

Figure 9.1

Accruing Interest Expense

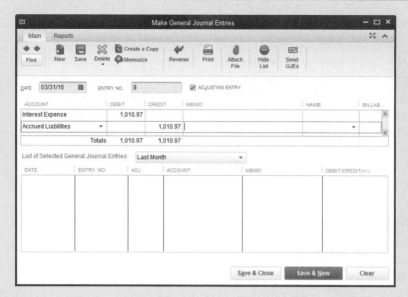

10   Click **Save & New**.

11   **3/31/16** should appear as the journal entry date.

12   **9** should appear as the Entry No and the Adjusting Entry check box should be checked already.

13   Select **Interest Expense** as the first account.

14   Type **750** as the amount in the Debit column.

15   Select **Accrued Liabilities** as the second account, and then press **[Tab]**.

16   **750** should appear as the amount in the Credit column.

17   Click **Save & New**.

Karen explains that this process reflects interest expenses in the correct accounting period (first quarter of 2016) and establishes the liability as of March 31, 2016. However, when the company pays the next installment on the $250,000 loan in April, it will have to remember that the interest has already been accrued.

"Either that, or we can reverse the adjustment as of April 1 and then just record the next payment as we've done in the past, with a portion of the payment going to interest expense and a portion going to reduce the loan principal," you suggest.

"I like that idea," Karen answers. "Do we do the same for the $50,000 loan?"

"Not necessarily," you respond. "The $50,000 loan is on an annual payment plan, so if we reverse the journal entry as of April 1 then we'll have to reestablish it again as of March 31 and accrue more interest for the second quarter. Even so, I suggest we reverse all accrual entries to be consistent using the QuickBooks Reverse button."

To reverse all accrued expense entries:

1 Click the **previous arrow** on the journal entry until you view Entry No. 8 recently entered. (Unhide the iconbar if it is not visible.)

2 Click the **Reverse** button. Your entry should look like Figure 9.2.

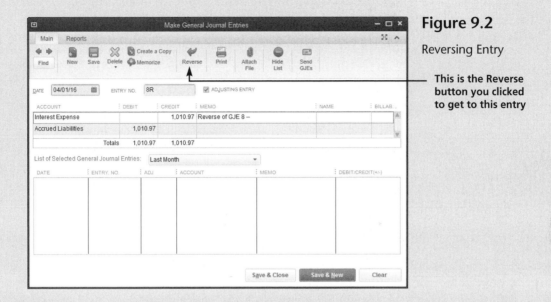

Figure 9.2

Reversing Entry

This is the Reverse button you clicked to get to this entry

3 Click **Save & New**.

4 Repeat the same process to reverse the $750 accrual with a new journal entry 9R.

5 Click **Save & Close**.

"After these entries were recorded on April 1, the Accrued Liability balance was 0 and interest expense for April has a credit balance of $1,760.97. Now," you explain, "when we record the next payment on this loan, we can use the amortization schedule to record the interest paid and reduction of principal. The payment will reduce cash and increase interest expense by $1,010.97, creating a credit balance of 750 in interest expense for April related to the Citibank loan. If we need to provide GAAP-based financial statements in April, we'll need to accrue interest owed at April 30 for both loans. The Citibank accrual at the end of April will accrue 4 months of interest ($50,000 \times 6\% \times 4/12 = $1,000$) thus recording a net $250 of interest expense in April."

Accruing Revenue

Karen tells you that she can also use journal entries to record revenue earned on investments. She points out that, during the quarter, the company had some short-term investments with ETrade that earned money market interest, which is paid quarterly. Since no interest was paid during the quarter, no interest income has been recorded. After checking with their investment advisor, Karen learns that $1,890.41 of interest income was earned but unpaid as of March 31, 2016.

To accrue interest income:

1   Click **Company** (from the menu bar), and then click **Make General Journal Entries**.

2   Type **3/31/16** as the journal entry date.

3   10 should appear as the Entry No and the Adjusting Entry check box should be checked already.

4   Select **Short-Term Investments** as the first account.

5   Type **1890.41** as the amount in the Debit column.

6   Type **Interest Income** as the second account.

7   Click **Setup** in the Account Not Found window and create a new account called Interest Income, an other income account.

8   Accept **1890.41** as the amount in the Credit column.

9   Click **Save & New**.

"Aren't we going to record more interest income?" you ask. "Why did we choose to record this as interest income?"

"QuickBooks Accountant doesn't follow the accounting convention of recording interest revenue," you point out. "QuickBooks Accountant was originally created as a tool for businesses preparing tax returns, and the Internal Revenue Service uses the income reference for interest instead of revenue. Rather than changing the account title, we'll just use Interest Income."

Karen reminds you that you should reverse the interest income accrual, as you did with interest expense, on the first day of the following month. That way, when the interest income is actually received, it can be recorded and will be offset by the previous accrual.

To reverse the interest income accrual:

1   Click the **previous arrow** on the journal entry until you view Entry No. 10 recently entered.

2   Click the **Reverse** button.

3   Click **Save & New**.

"Another issue we have to address is whether any products were delivered to customers but not recorded as sales at the end of the month," Karen comments. "For example, our records show that we delivered a boat to Spirit Adventures on March 31 but didn't invoice them until April 2. Thus, as of March 31, 2016, we need to accrue that additional revenue, sales tax, and cost of goods sold."

"Don't you also have to reduce inventory, since our records show that boat in inventory March 31?" you ask.

To adjust for sales occurring in March but not invoiced until April:

1   Type **3/31/16** as the journal entry date.

2   11 should appear as the Entry No and the Adjusting Entry check box should be checked already.

3   Select **Accounts Receivable** as the first account.

4   Type **69225** as the amount in the Debit column.

5   Select **Spirit Adventures** as the Name in this row.

6   Select **Boat Sales** as the second account.

7   Type **65000** as the amount in the Credit column.

8   Select **Spirit Adventures** as the Name in this row.

9   Select **Sales Tax Payable** as the third account (a new account).

10 Accept **4225** as the amount in the Credit column.

11 Select **Florida Department of Revenue** as the Name in this row.

12 Select **Cost of Goods Sold** as the fourth account.

13 Type **52000** as the amount in the Debit column.

14 Select **Spirit Adventures** as the Name in this row.

15 Select **Inventory Boats** as the fifth account.

16 Accept **52000** as the amount in the Credit column.

17 Select **Spirit Adventures** as the Name in this row.

18 Mark Cost of Goods Sold and Inventory Boats as unbillable by clicking the **Billable?** icon so the check box is unchecked. Your journal entry should look like Figure 9.3.

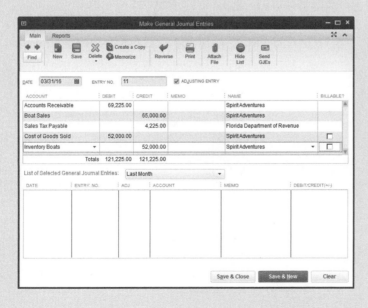

Figure 9.3

Accruing Sales Revenue

19 Click **Save & New**.

"Exactly," Karen answers, "plus, since this transaction is recorded as an invoice in April, we'll need to reverse this accrual entry on April 1."

"Where did you get the Cost of Goods Sold and Inventory Boat information?" you ask.

"I got it from our list of items, which provides the sales price, income account, and cost," Karen answers. "When we accrue the sales revenue, we must also accrue the related cost of goods sold."

Karen explains that this is another case where it is best to reverse this accrual the first of the next month so that, when the actual invoice is recorded in April, it will be offset by the previous accrual.

"This accrual accounting process is a lot of work!" you comment.

"Yes," Karen agrees. "But at least we get a picture of our performance and financial position based on when events occur, not just when we get around to recording them."

To reverse the sales accrual:

1 Click the **previous arrow** on the journal entry until you view Entry No. 11 recently entered.

2 Click the **Reverse** button. Your entry should look like Figure 9.4.

Figure 9.4

Reversing the Sales Accrual April 1

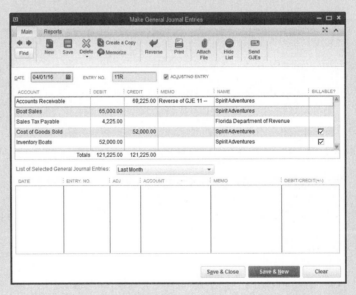

3 Click **Save & Close**.

Recording Expenses Incurred but Previously Deferred

The adjustments that you and Karen have recorded account for previously unrecorded transactions. Now Karen wants to demonstrate how to record adjustments that affect previously recorded business activity, such as the prepayment of expenses and the purchase of fixed assets.

On February 7, 2016, Wild Water Sports paid $24,000 to Coe Marketing for a one-year advertising campaign. Since this payment represented an expenditure that benefited more than the one accounting period, it was correctly recorded to Prepaid Advertising, an asset account.

On March 31, 2016, two months of the time period covered by the ad campaign had expired. Thus, two-twelfths of the cost ($4,000) should be recorded as Advertising and Promotion Expense with the Prepaid Advertising account reduced accordingly. Each month thereafter, one-twelfth of the cost ($2,000) should be recorded as Advertising and Promotion Expense with the Prepaid Advertising account reduced accordingly.

Video Demonstration

DEMO 9C - Recording expenses previously deferred

To adjust prepaid advertising:

1 Click **Company** (from the menu bar), and then click **Make General Journal Entries**.

2 Type **3/31/16** as the journal entry date.

3 12 should appear as the Entry No and the Adjusting Entry check box should be checked already.

4 Select **Advertising and Promotion** as the first account.

5 Type **4000** as the amount in the Debit column.

6 Select **Prepaid Advertising** as the second account.

7 Accept **4000** as the amount in the Credit column.

8 Click **Save & New**.

On January 31, 2016, Wild Water Sports paid $22,000 to Manchester Insurance for a one-year liability insurance policy covering it for the calendar year 2016. Once again, since this payment represented an expenditure that benefited more than one accounting period, it was correctly recorded to Prepaid Insurance, an asset account.

On March 31, 2016, three months of the time period covered by the insurance policy had expired. Thus, three-twelfths of the cost ($5,500) should be recorded as insurance expense and the Prepaid Insurance account reduced accordingly. Each month thereafter, one-twelfth of the cost ($1,833.33) should be recorded as insurance expense and the Prepaid Insurance account reduced accordingly.

To adjust prepaid insurance:

1   Accept **3/31/16** as the journal entry date.

2   13 should appear as the Entry No and the Adjusting Entry check box should be checked already.

3   Select **Insurance Expense** as the first account.

4   Type **5500** as the amount in the Debit column.

5   Select **Prepaid Insurance** as the second account.

6   Accept **5500** as the amount in the Credit column.

7   Click **Save & New**.

A similar adjustment called *depreciation* is needed to allocate the cost of previously recorded depreciable fixed assets. Depreciation on fixed assets is usually accumulated in a contra-asset account on the balance sheet for control purposes.

Although QuickBooks Accountant does have a separate Fixed Asset Manager available to track fixed assets and calculate depreciation, Karen has chosen not to use it at this time (see Chapter 12). Instead, she maintains a separate spreadsheet to track when fixed assets were purchased, how much depreciation should be recorded, and when fixed assets are sold. Her analysis indicates that $10,333 of depreciation should be recorded as of March 31, 2016, to reflect depreciation for the first quarter of 2016.

To record depreciation expense:

1   Accept **3/31/16** as the journal entry date.

2   14 should appear as the Entry No and the Adjusting Entry check box should be checked already.

3   Select **Depreciation Expense** as the first account.

4   Type **10333** as the amount in the Debit column.

5   Select **Accumulated Depreciation** as the second account.

6 Accept **10333** as the amount in the Credit column. Your journal entry should look like Figure 9.5.

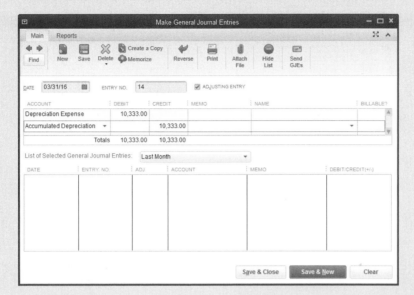

Figure 9.5

Depreciation Adjustment

7 Click **Save & Close**.

8 If the Tracking Fixed Assets on Journal Entries window appears, check the box **Do not display this message in the future** and then click **OK**.

You ask Karen about reversing the prepaid advertising, insurance, and depreciation adjusting entries. She explains that accruals of income and expense need reversal entries but that adjustments of deferrals like prepaids and depreciation do not.

"They won't have subsequent events that we need to offset," she explains. "These adjustments are permanent."

You find these procedures to be very straightforward but are curious about the financial statement impact of these adjusting entries so far. You wonder if QuickBooks Accountant provides a way to view financial statements so you can see what effect these adjustments have had. Karen tells you that QuickBooks Accountant does have such a feature—you can view financial statements at any time without having to post entries. She suggests that you look at the balance sheet as of March 31, 2016, to see the effect of this adjustment on the balance sheet.

To view the fixed assets portion of the balance sheet as of March 31, 2016:

1 From the Reports Center create a Standard Balance Sheet.

2 Enter **3/31/16** in the As of text box, remove the Date Prepared, Time Prepared, and Report Basis fields as you've done in the past, and then click **Refresh**.

3 Follow Karen's analysis (next paragraph) while referring to Figure 9.6.

Figure 9.6

Balance Sheet after Adjusting Entries So Far

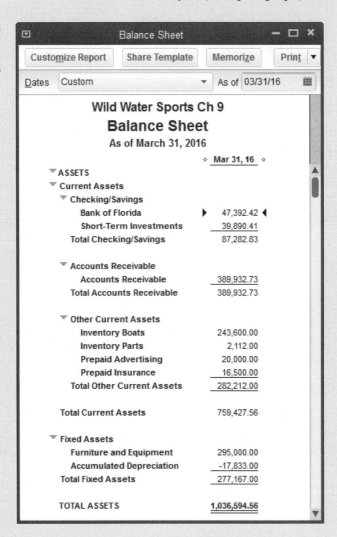

4 Close all windows and do not memorize this report.

Karen remarks that the ending balance in Prepaid Advertising as of March 31, 2016, makes sense given that Wild Water has 10 months left of the ad campaign (10 months × $2,000 per month = $20,000). She also says that the ending balance in Prepaid Insurance as of March 31, 2016, also makes sense because Wild Water has 9 months left of insurance coverage (9 months × $1,833.33 per month = $16,500). Finally, she notes the new balances in the Accumulated Depreciation accounts.

Having tackled the adjustments for prepaid and for depreciable assets, you and Karen are now ready to move on to the last category—adjusting unearned revenue.

Adjusting for Unearned Revenues

On March 31, 2016, Wild Water Sports received $10,000 from its customer Performance Rentals as a deposit on a boat in stock. On this date, Performance Rentals had an existing balance outstanding, but you and Karen chose to account for this as a separate transaction and not to apply this payment to the amount due. As described in Chapter 8, Karen recorded this transaction by increasing the checking account and decreasing Performance Rental's Accounts Receivable. Karen has decided to reclassify it as Unearned Revenue, a liability, on March 31, 2016. Here's why. Cash has been received, but the boat has not been delivered. Thus, on March 31, you need to reclassify the $10,000 to an unearned revenue account (a liability). When the company actually sells the boat to Performance Rentals in a future period, Wild Water will create an invoice, record the sale, and apply the credit remaining.

The effect of this adjusting journal entry is to increase accounts receivable and increase unearned revenue, reflecting the fact that Wild Water still has a balance owed by Performance Rentals of $1,293.98 and owes Performance Rentals $10,000 if it doesn't deliver the boat on which Performance placed the deposit. This entry is then reversed on 4/1/16 so that, when the sale takes place later, the credit can be applied.

Video Demonstration

DEMO 9D - Recording revenues previously deferred

To reclassify the $10,000 as unearned revenue at 3/31/16 and then reverse the reclassification on 4/1/16:

1 Click **Company** (from the menu bar), and then click **Make General Journal Entries**.

2 Type **3/31/16** as the journal entry date.

3 15 should appear as the Entry No and the Adjusting Entry check box should be checked already.

4 Select **Accounts Receivable** as the first account.

5 Type **10000** as the amount in the Debit column.

6 Select **Performance Rentals** as the Name of the customer to which this journal entry applies.

7 Type **Unearned Revenue** as the second account, and then press **[Tab]**.

8 Click **Setup** to create a new account.

9 Select **Other Current Liability** from the drop-down list of other account types.

10 Verify **Unearned Revenue** as the Name.

11 Click **Save & Close** to create this new account.

12 Accept **10000** as the amount in the Credit column.

13 Select **Performance Rentals** as the Name of the customer to which this journal entry applies. Your screen should look like Figure 9.7.

Figure 9.7

Adjusting for Unearned Revenue

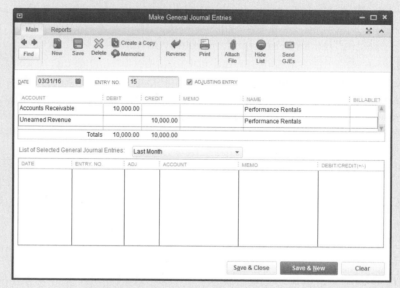

14 Click **Save & New**.

15 Click the **previous arrow** on the journal entry until you view Entry No. 15 recently entered.

16 Click the **Reverse** button.

17 Click **Save & Close**.

"I always like to print out a copy of my adjustments to make sure every-thing was recorded correctly," Karen comments. "QuickBooks Accountant has a journal feature that we can use to print just those transactions occurring on March 31 and April 1 so we can see the effects of our adjustments."

To print the journal for March 31 and April 1:

1 Click **Reports** from the menu bar, click **Accountant & Taxes**, and then click **Adjusting Journal Entries**. (Click **OK** if a warning window appears about expanding and collapsing transactions.)

2 Click the **Customize Report** button.

3 Click the **Display** tab.

4 Type **3/31/16** as the From date and the To date.

5 Click the **Header/Footer** tab and then uncheck the **Date Prepared, Time Prepared**, and **Report Basis** check boxes.

6 Click **OK**.

7 Click **Print** and then click **Report** in the report toolbar, choose **Landscape** orientation, and then **Print** in the Print Reports window. Your report should look like Figure 9.8.

Wild Water Sports Ch 9
Adjusting Journal Entries
March 31, 2016

Date	Num	Name	Memo	Account	Debit	Credit
03/31/16	8			Interest Expense	1,010.97	
				Accrued Liabilities		1,010.97
					1,010.97	1,010.97
03/31/16	9			Interest Expense	750.00	
				Accrued Liabilities		750.00
					750.00	750.00
03/31/16	10			Short-Term Investments	1,890.41	
				interest Income		1,890.41
					1,890.41	1,890.41
03/31/16	11	Spirit Adventures		Accounts Receivable	69,225.00	
		Spirit Adventures		Boat Sales		65,000.00
		Florida Department ...		Sales Tax Payable		4,225.00
		Spirit Adventures		Cost of Goods Sold	52,000.00	
		Spirit Adventures		Inventory Boats		52,000.00
					121,225.00	121,225.00
03/31/16	12			Advertising and Prom...	4,000.00	
				Prepaid Advertising		4,000.00
					4,000.00	4,000.00
03/31/16	13			Insurance Expense	5,500.00	
				Prepaid Insurance		5,500.00
					5,500.00	5,500.00
03/31/16	14			Depreciation Expense	10,333.00	
				Accumulated Depreci...		10,333.00
					10,333.00	10,333.00
03/31/16	15	Performance Rentals		Accounts Receivable	10,000.00	
		Performance Rentals		Unearned Revenue		10,000.00
					10,000.00	10,000.00
TOTAL					**154,709.38**	**154,709.38**

Figure 9.8

Journal Entries on 3/31/16

8 Type **4/1/16** in both the From and To text boxes and then click **Refresh**.

9 Click **Print** and then click **Report** in the report toolbar, choose **Landscape** orientation, and then **Print** in the Print Reports window. Your report should look like Figure 9.9.

Figure 9.9

Journal Entries on 4/1/16

Wild Water Sports Ch 9
Adjusting Journal Entries
April 1, 2016

Date	Num	Name	Memo	Account	Debit	Credit
04/01/16	8R		Reverse of GJE 8 –	Interest Expense		1,010.97
			Reverse of GJE 8 –	Accrued Liabilities	1,010.97	
					1,010.97	1,010.97
04/01/16	9R		Reverse of GJE 9 –	Interest Expense		750.00
			Reverse of GJE 9 –	Accrued Liabilities	750.00	
					750.00	750.00
04/01/16	10R		Reverse of GJE 10 –	Short-Term Investments		1,890.41
			Reverse of GJE 10 –	Interest Income	1,890.41	
					1,890.41	1,890.41
04/01/16	11R	Spirit Adventures	Reverse of GJE 11 –	Accounts Receivable		69,225.00
		Spirit Adventures	Reverse of GJE 11 –	Boat Sales	65,000.00	
		Florida Department ...	Reverse of GJE 11 –	Sales Tax Payable	4,225.00	
		Spirit Adventures	Reverse of GJE 11 –	Cost of Goods Sold		52,000.00
		Spirit Adventures	Reverse of GJE 11 –	Inventory Boats	52,000.00	
					121,225.00	121,225.00
04/01/16	15R	Performance Rentals	Reverse of GJE 15 –	Accounts Receivable		10,000.00
		Performance Rentals	Reverse of GJE 15 –	Unearned Revenue	10,000.00	
					10,000.00	10,000.00
TOTAL					134,876.38	134,876.38

10 Close all windows without memorizing the report and return to the home page.

Karen explains that most of these journals reflect the adjustments you just made and seem to be in order. She points out that each transaction has a transaction number, a type, a date, and a journal number (if applicable) as well as names, accounts, debits, and credits.

Preparing a Bank Reconciliation and Recording Related Adjustments

Video Demonstration

DEMO 9E - Preparing a bank reconciliation

Every month, the Bank of Florida sends Wild Water Sports a bank account statement that lists all deposits received by the bank and all checks and payments that have cleared the bank as of the date of the statement. You and Karen examine the bank statements for the months of January, February, and

March; the latter shows an ending balance of $47,172.23 as of March 31, 2016. You would normally reconcile your statement each month, but you've been a little busy these last couple of months. You now turn your attention toward reconciling that balance with the balance reported by QuickBooks Accountant. You note that QuickBooks Accountant indicates an ending checking account balance of $47,392.42 at that same date. You believe that most of the difference between these two amounts is probably attributable to "outstanding checks" that Wild Water Sports has written but that the bank hasn't yet paid, deposits it has recorded but have not been received by the bank, bank service charges, and interest income.

A review of all three statements shows that all checks recorded by Wild Water Sports have been paid by the bank except payroll checks written on 3/31/16, totaling $6,994.74. All deposits recorded by the company have been received by the bank except one dated 3/29/16 for $7,264.93. Bank charges per the bank statement total $75, which has not yet been recorded by the company. Interest income credited to the company's bank account in the amount of $125 also has not yet been recorded by the company.

To reconcile the bank statement as of 3/31/16:

1 Click **Reconcile** in the Banking section of the home page.

2 Select **Bank of Florida** as the account to be reconciled.

3 Type **3/31/16** as the Statement Date.

4 Type **47,172.23** as the Ending Balance.

5 Type **75** as the Service Charge, **3/31/16** as the Date, and **Bank Service Charges** as the Account.

6 Type **125** as the Interest Earned, **3/31/16** as the Date, and **Interest Income** as the Account. Your screen should look like Figure 9.10.

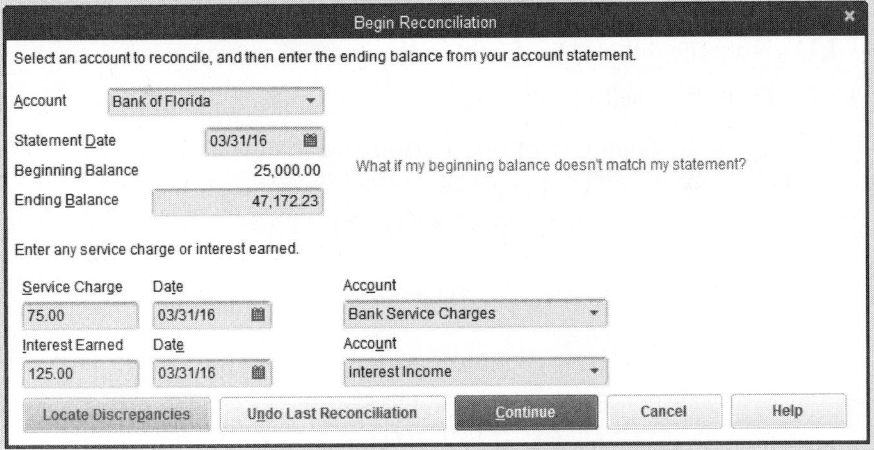

Figure 9.10

Beginning a Bank Reconciliation

7   Click **Continue**.

8   When the Reconcile – Bank of Florida window appears, click in the check box at the top of the page that says **Hide transactions after the statement's end date**.

9   Place a check mark next to all of the checks and payments in January, February, and March of 2016 except Check Nos. 1038, 1039, and 1040. (These are the payroll checks issued 3/31/16 that have not yet cleared the bank.)

10 Place a check mark next to all of the deposits and other credits in January, February, and March of 2016 except the deposit of $7,264.93 dated 3/27/16. Your screen should look like Figure 9.11.

Figure 9.11

Bank Reconciliation Process

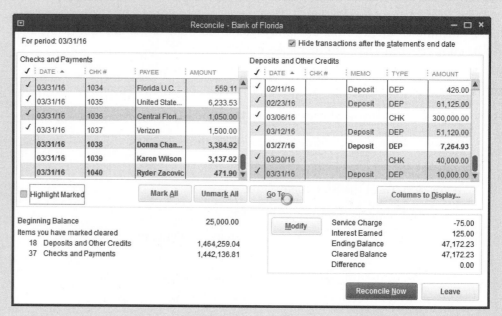

11 Note the difference of 0.00 in the lower right corner of the window.

12 Click **Reconcile Now**.

13 Click the **Summary** option button and then click **Display**.

14 Click **OK** and then click the **Print** button, click **Report**, and then click **Print** again to print this report. Your printout should look like Figure 9.12.

Wild Water Sports Ch 9
Reconciliation Summary
Bank of Florida, Period Ending 03/31/16

	Mar 31, 16
Beginning Balance	25,000.00
Cleared Transactions	
Checks and Payments - 38 items	-1,442,211.81
Deposits and Credits - 19 items	1,464,384.04
Total Cleared Transactions	22,172.23
Cleared Balance	47,172.23
Uncleared Transactions	
Checks and Payments - 3 items	-6,994.74
Deposits and Credits - 1 item	7,264.93
Total Uncleared Transactions	270.19
Register Balance as of 03/31/16	47,442.42
New Transactions	
Checks and Payments - 13 items	-262,890.05
Deposits and Credits - 6 items	291,675.08
Total New Transactions	28,785.03
Ending Balance	76,227.45

Figure 9.12

Summary Bank Reconciliation Report

15 Close the Reconciliation Summary window.

The only adjustments created in this bank reconciliation were the recognition of bank service fees and interest income. QuickBooks Accountant automatically records these in the checking account. Once reconciled, QuickBooks Accountant also inserts a check mark next to each transaction that has cleared the bank in the check register.

End Note

You've now helped Karen record various adjustments including accrued expenses, accrued revenues, expiration of prepaid and depreciable assets, creation of unearned revenue, and one reflecting the completion of bank reconciliation. You're now almost ready to create Wild Water Sports's financial statements.

Business Events Summary

Business Event	Process Steps	Page
Accruing expenses	Use make journal entries from Company menu	271
Reversing accrued expenses	Use make journal entries from Company menu	273
Accruing revenues	Use make journal entries from Company menu	274
Reversing accrued revenues	Use make journal entries from Company menu	274
Adjusting prepaid expenses	Use make journal entries from Company menu	277
Recording depreciation	Use make journal entries from Company menu	278
Adjusting unearned revenue	Use make journal entries from Company menu	281
Reconciling bank accounts	Use reconcile from Banking section of home page	285

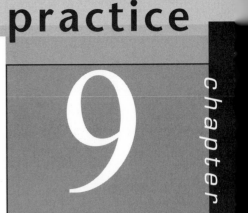

Chapter 9 Questions

1 Explain the journal entry method of recording end-of-period adjustments.

2 Give an example of accrued revenue other than the examples given in this chapter. Explain how your example of accrued revenue would be adjusted using journal entries.

3 Give an example of an accrued expense other than the example given in this chapter. Explain how your example of accrued expense would be adjusted using journal entries.

4 Give an example of asset expiration other than the example given in this chapter. Explain how your example would be adjusted using journal entries.

5 Give an example of unearned revenue, and explain the process for end-of-period adjustments involving unearned revenue.

6 Explain how to access general journal entries.

7 What menu item do you use to start bank reconciliations?

8 What account is typically used to record service charges?

9 When you've finished reconciling a bank account, what should be the difference between the ending balance and the cleared balance?

10 What information is included in the Reconciliation Summary report?

Chapter 9 Matching

Select the letter of the item below that best matches the definitions that follow.
Use the text or QuickBooks Accountant Help to complete this assignment.

a. Adjusting entries   _____ A liability for expenses created with adjusting journal entries.

b. Accrued expenses   _____ An asset for expenses paid but not yet incurred.

c. Prepaid expenses   _____ Entries made on the first of the following month that offset adjusting entries recorded in the previous period.

d. Accumulated depreciation   _____ Deposits/checks that the bank has received/paid and have been recorded in the accounting records.

e. General journal entries   _____ A liability for amounts received from customers before a company delivers a product or service.

f. Unearned revenues   _____ Deposits/checks that the bank has not received/paid but have been recorded in the accounting records.

g. Reversing entries   _____ Entries made to record the correct amount of revenue earned or expenses incurred that are not correctly recorded in the accounting records.

h. Reconciliation   _____ Used to record business events made without the use of a source document like an invoice, bill, or check.

i. Cleared transactions   _____ A contra-asset account used to amass the effects of a fixed asset's depreciation.

j. Uncleared transactions   _____ A comparison made between the bank's records and a business's accounting records.

Chapter 9 Exercises

Chapter 9 Exercise 1

ACCRUING EXPENSES

Restore the file Boston Catering Ch 9 (Backup) that you downloaded from the text web site. Make the following adjustments and then print an income statement and balance sheet for the period 7/1/10 through 9/30/10 setting the columns to Month so that you view an income statement for July, August, and September 2010 and a balance sheet as of 7/31/10, 8/31/10, and 9/30/10.

a. Accrue interest expense (a new other expense type account) and the related accrued expense liability as of 7/31/10 and 8/31/10 based on the following schedules (note that on 8/2/10 the company made the July payments of 926.29 and 610.32):

Month	Payment	Interest	Principal	Balance
				$50,000.00
Jul 2010	$926.29	$416.67	$509.63	$49,490.37
Aug 2010	$926.29	$412.42	$513.87	$48,976.50
Sep 2010	$926.29	$408.14	$518.15	$48,458.35

Month	Payment	Interest	Principal	Balance
				$25,000.00
Jul 2010	$610.32	$166.67	$443.66	$24,556.34
Aug 2010	$610.32	$163.71	$446.61	$24,109.73
Sep 2010	$610.32	$160.73	$449.59	$23,660.14

Month	Payment	Interest	Principal	Balance
				$10,000.00
Jul 2010	$0	$50.00	$0	$10,000.00
Aug 2010	$0	$50.00	$0	$10,000.00
Sep 2010	$0	$50.00	$0	$10,000.00

b. Reverse accrued interest expense for the first two loans on 8/1/10 and 9/1/10 as appropriate. Do not reverse accrued interest expense on the $10,000 loan.

Chapter 9 Exercise 2

ACCRUING REVENUE

Restore the file Boston Catering Ch 9 (Backup) that you downloaded from the text web site. Do not use the file created in Exercise 1 above. Make the following adjustments and then print an income statement and balance sheet for the period 7/1/10 through 9/30/10 setting the columns to Month so that you view an income statement for July, August, and September 2010 and a balance sheet as of 7/31/10, 8/31/10, and 9/30/10.

a. Accrue interest income (a new other income type account) as of 7/31/10 of $11 to the short-term investments account. Interest is paid at the end of every calendar quarter.

b. On 8/1/10 reverse the interest income accrual you made above.

c. Accrue interest income as of 8/31/10 of $115 to the short-term investments account.

d. On 9/1/10 reverse the interest income accrual you made above.

e. On 9/1/10 the company billed Fidelity Investments on invoice 1125 for a catering engagement held on 8/31/10 for 200 Fall Suppers (Item Code S300) resulting in $13,000 in catering sales and $650 in sales tax, which were billed on account (total $13,650). Sales tax is paid to Mass. Dept. of Revenue. The food purchases of $4,000 were set up as accounts payable to US Food Service. Accrue this revenue and expense as of 8/31/10.

f. On 9/1/10 reverse the revenue and expense accrual made above.

g. On 9/1/10 record the invoice described in (e) above.

h. On 9/1/10 record check 1512 to US Food Service for $4,000 in food purchases.

Chapter 9 Exercise 3

RECORDING EXPENSES INCURRED BUT PREVIOUSLY DEFERRED

Restore the file Boston Catering Ch 9 (Backup) that you downloaded from the text web site. Do not use the file created in the exercises above. Make the following adjustments and then print an income statement and balance sheet for the period 7/1/10 through 9/30/10 setting the columns to Month so that you view an income statement for July, August, and September 2010 and a balance sheet as of 7/31/10, 8/31/10, and 9/30/10.

a. The $3,000 prepaid insurance balance recorded as of 6/30/10 represented three months of insurance premiums, which expire equally in July, August, and September.

b. Depreciation expense was $1,000, $1,075, and $1,350 for the months of July, August, and September.

Chapter 9 Exercise 4

PREPARING BANK RECONCILIATION

Restore the file Boston Catering Ch 9 (Backup) that you downloaded from the text web site. Do not use the file created in the exercises above. Reconcile the Bank of America checking account and then print a summary bank reconciliation for each month.

a. The 7/31/10 Bank of America bank statement shows an ending balance of $78,881 with service charges of $39. All deposits made in July were received by the bank except that made on 7/31/10, which was received by the bank on 8/1/10. All checks written in July were cashed by the bank except check numbers 1505 through 1508, which cleared the bank in August.

b. The 8/31/10 Bank of America bank statement shows an ending balance of $54,036.64 with service charges of $45. All deposits made in August were received by the bank. All checks written in August were cashed by the bank except check numbers 1517 through 1522.

Chapter 9 Assignments

Chapter 9 Assignment 1

ADDING MORE INFORMATION: WILD WATER SPORTS

corporation

merchandising

Restore the file Wild Water Sports Ch 9A (Backup) that you downloaded from the text web site. Then add the following adjustments and perform bank reconciliation on the checking account as of April 30, 2016.

Event #	Date	Business Event
1	5/1/16	Invoice No. 10014 was recorded on this date for the sale of an MS LX to Alisa Hay for $52,000 plus tax. (Even though this isn't an adjusting entry, record this invoice on 5/1/16 in QuickBooks Accountant to illustrate how the accrual and reversal works.)
2	4/30/16	Accrue interest expense of $995.52 on the $250,000 loan as per the amortization schedule in Figure 8.1 with journal entry no. 16.
3	5/1/16	Prepare reversing entry of the preceding interest accrual.
4	4/30/16	Accrue interest expense of $1,000 on the $50,000 loan and record related reversing entry on 5/1/16.
5	4/30/16	Accrue interest income of $3,600 on short-term investments and record related reversing entry on 5/1/16.
6	4/30/16	Records show that the company delivered an MS LX to Alisa Hay on April 30 but did not invoice her until May 1. The boat was sold for $52,000 and cost $41,600. Sales tax in the amount of $3,380 was collected on May 1 from the sale. Sales tax is paid to the Florida Dept. of Revenue. Prepare the appropriate adjusting entry.
7	5/1/16	Reverse the preceding sales revenue accrual.
8	4/30/16	Adjust prepaid advertising $2,000 for April.
9	4/30/16	Adjust prepaid insurance $1,833 for April.
10	4/30/16	Record depreciation expense of $3,870 for the month of April.
11	4/30/16	Reclassify the deposit of $16,250 received from Buena Vista Water Sports on 4/30/16 to unearned revenue and record the related reversing entry on 5/1/16.
12	4/30/16	The Bank of Florida bank statement as of 4/30 has an ending balance of $54,475.02. All checks cleared the bank account except Check Nos. 1050 through 1053. All deposits cleared the bank account except the $30,517.35 deposit made 4/30. The bank statement shows interest income of $35 and bank charges of $25.

a. Perform a reconciliation on the checking account and then memorize and print a summary bank reconciliation as of April 30, 2016 like you did in the chapter.

b. Memorize and print a Profit & Loss Standard report for the month of April 2016 like you did in the chapter.

c. Memorize and print a Balance Sheet Standard report as of April 30, 2016 like you did in the chapter.

d. Memorize and print an adjusting journal entries report showing all journal entries recorded on April 30, 2016 like you did in the chapter (no memo field).

e. Memorize and print an adjusting journal entries report showing all journal entries recorded on May 1, 2016 like you did in the chapter (no memo field).

f. Memorize and print a Profit & Loss Standard report for the month of May 2016 like you did in the chapter.

Chapter 9 Assignment 2

ADDING MORE INFORMATION: CENTRAL COAST CELLULAR

Restore the file Central Coast Cellular Ch 9 (Backup) that you downloaded from the text web site. Then add the following adjustments and perform bank reconciliation on the checking account as of January 31, 2014.

sole proprietorship

Event #	Date	Business Event
1	1/31/14	Record depreciation expense of $1,500 for equipment and office furniture.
2	1/31/14	Accrue interest expense of $950.
3	1/31/14	Reclassify the credit balance of $10,000 in the City of San Luis Obispo account to unearned revenue.
4	1/31/14	The bank statement dated January 31, 2013, indicated a bank balance of $133,640.49, with all checks clearing except numbers 3010, 3011, and 3012. All deposits cleared. A bank service charge of $80 was reported.
5	2/1/14	Make all appropriate reversing entries.

merchandising

a. Perform a reconciliation on the checking account and then print a summary bank reconciliation as of January 31, 2014.

b. Print a Profit & Loss Standard report for the month of January 2014.

c. Print a Balance Sheet Standard report as of January 31, 2014.

d. Print journal entries recorded from January 31, 2014, to February 1, 2014 (no memo field, and make sure that you filter the transaction type for journal items only).

corporation

Chapter 9 Assignment 3

ADDING MORE INFORMATION: SANTA BARBARA SAILING

Restore the file Santa Barbara Sailing Ch 9 (Backup) that you downloaded from the text web site, and then record the following events.

service

Event #	Date	Business Event
1	7/31/15	Adjust prepaid rent for $2,000 to rent expense (a new account) with journal entry no. 5.
2	7/31/15	Accrue interest expense on the $50,000 Bank of Caribbean loan for $134.25 with journal entry no. 6.
3	7/31/15	Record depreciation for the month of $5,750 with journal entry no. 7.
4	7/31/15	The boat rented to Barry Cohen for 14 days was paid in advance and recorded in full. Of this amount, $2,079 was unearned as of 7/31/15. Reduce rental income accordingly and create unearned revenue with journal entry no. 8.
5	8/1/15	Create reversing journal entries for events 2 and 4 only.
6	7/31/15	The bank statement dated 7/31/15 indicated a bank balance of $122,206.74, with all checks clearing except numbers 111–114. The bank charged a fee of $43 and provided interest income (an other income account) of $70. All deposits were accounted for.

a. Perform a reconciliation on the checking account, and then print a summary bank reconciliation as of July 31, 2015.

b. Print a Profit & Loss Standard report for the month of July 2015.

c. Print a Balance Sheet Standard report as of July 31, 2015.

d. Print an Adjusting Journal Entries report from July 31, 2015, to August 1, 2015 (no memo field).

Chapter 9 Assignment 4

ADDING MORE INFORMATION: DRONE CITY

sole proprietorship

easy step

Restore the file Drone City Ch 09 (Backup) that you downloaded from the text web site, and then add the following adjustments and perform a bank reconciliation on the checking account as of 1/31/17.

Event #	Date	Business Event
1	1/31/17	Record depreciation expense of $200.
2	1/31/17	On 1/27/17 Folly Free paid $2,000 as a deposit on a future order. That payment was not related invoice #7001. Thus the amount needs to re-classified to a new unearned revenue account and then reversed the first of next month.
3	1/31/17	Prepaid advertising of $300 was consumed during the month.
4	1/31/17	Supplies of $2,000 remain at the end of the month.
5	1/31/17	On 1/31/17 the company delivered 5 Hex Transports ordered by Rincon Flying but an invoice wasn't created until 2/1/17. Prepare the adjusting and reversing journal entries based on information obtained by creating the 2/1/17 invoice below.
6	2/1/17	The company created invoice #7002 to Rincon Flying for 5 Hex Transports on terms net 30. (Exclude any outstanding billable time and cost from this invoice.)
7	1/31/17	The company received a bill from Comcast for Computer and Internet expenses for $2,700 on 2/1/17 for services rendered in January. Accrue this expense and create the reversal entry as well.
8	1/31/17	Prepare a bank reconciliation. The bank statement dated 1/31/17 indicated a bank balance of $23,861.49 with all checks clearing except 1012 − 1015. The bank charged a fee of $30 and paid interest income of $22. The deposit made on 1/31/17 did not appear on the bank statement.

Place your name in the Extra Footer Line, remove subtitle, date and time prepared header information, and then memorize (in a report group with your name) and print the following reports as of 1/31/17.

a. Profit & Loss Standard (Change the name on the report to Income Statement).

b. Balance Sheet Standard

c. Statement of Cash Flows

d. Reconciliation Summary

e. Transaction List by Date (for the period 1/01/17 through 2/1/17).

Chapter 9 Cases

Chapter 9 Case 1

FOREVER YOUNG

In Chapter 8, you added some transactions to your QuickBooks Accountant file for Forever Young. Make a copy of that file, and use that copy to record the following transactions:

sole proprietorship

service

Event #	Date	Business Event
1	1/31/15	Record the use of office supplies for January with journal entry no. 1 (assume that supplies are used evenly throughout the period for which they were purchased).
2	1/31/15	Accrue interest expense on Wells Fargo note payable of $96 with journal entry no. 2.
3	1/31/15	Record the use of brochures for January with journal entry no. 3 (assume that brochures are used equally each month).
4	1/31/15	Reclassify ITP's deposit to unearned revenue with journal entry no. 4.
5	1/31/15	Record depreciation of $67 for the month with journal entry no. 5.
6	2/1/15	Make all appropriate reversing journal entries.
7	1/31/15	The bank statement dated 1/31/15 indicated a bank balance of $63,233.82, with all checks clearing except numbers 11–14. The bank charged a fee of $25 and provided interest income (other income account) of $115. All deposits were accounted for.

Requirements:

1 Perform reconciliation on the checking account and then print a summary bank reconciliation as of January 31, 2015.

2 Print a Profit & Loss Standard report for the month of January 2015.

3 Print a Balance Sheet Standard report as of January 31, 2015.

4 Print journal entries recorded from January 31, 2015, to February 1, 2015 (no memo field, and make sure that you filter the transaction type for journal items only).

Chapter 9 Case 2

OCEAN VIEW FLOWERS

corporation

merchandising

In Chapter 8, you modified your QuickBooks Accountant file for Ocean View Flowers. Make a copy of that file, and use that copy to record the following transactions:

Event #	Date	Business Event
1	1/31/16	The January bank statement reported an ending balance of $76,340.30, bank service charges of $45, and interest revenue of $100 as of January 31, 2016. Deposits for $100,000, $50,000, $6,600, and $22,200 were received by the bank. Checks 101–110 were paid by the bank.
2	2/29/16	Accrue interest expense of $3,190 on the $319,000 loan with journal entry no. 1.
3	3/1/16	Prepare reversing entry of the preceding interest expense accrual with journal entry no. 2.
4	2/29/16	Accrue interest income of $800 on short-term investments with journal entry no. 3.
5	3/1/16	Prepare reversing entry for the preceding interest income accrual with journal entry no. 4.
6	2/29/16	Record expired prepaid insurance of $100 for the months of January and February 2016 with journal entry no. 5.
7	2/29/16	Record depreciation expense of $3,100 with journal entry no. 6.
8	2/29/16	Reclassify the deposit of $5,000 received from FTD on 1/28/16 to unearned revenue with journal entry no. 7.
9	3/1/16	Prepare reversing entry for the preceding unearned revenue reclassification with journal entry no. 8.
10	2/29/16	A review of the shipping records indicates that a shipment of 2/28 was not invoiced until 3/3. Invoice No. 10004, recorded in the next accounting period, billed California Beauties $16,000 for 800 Calistoga Sun Daylilies, $7,200 for 300 Almond Puff Daylilies, and $20,000 for 500 Peach Anthuriums (cost: $22,600). Accrue this event with journal entry no. 9.
11	3/1/16	Prepare reversing entry for Invoice No. 10004 with journal entry no. 10.
12	2/29/16	The February bank statement reported an ending balance of $65,579.64, bank service charges of $55, and interest income of $75 as of February 29, 2016. Deposits for $5,000 and $5,200 were received by the bank. Checks 111–127 were paid by the bank.

Requirements:

1 Perform a reconciliation on the checking account, and then print a summary bank reconciliation as of January 31, 2016.

2 Perform a reconciliation on the checking account and then print a summary bank reconciliation as of February 29, 2016.

3 Print a Profit & Loss Standard report for the two months ended February 29, 2016.

4 Print a Balance Sheet Standard report as of February 29, 2016.

5 Print journal entries recorded from February 29 to March 1, 2016 (no memo field, and make sure that you filter the transaction type for journal items only).

Chapter 9 Case 3

ALOHA PROPERTIES

In Chapter 8, you modified your QuickBooks Accountant file for Aloha Properties. Make a copy of that file and use that copy to record the following transactions:

Event #	Date	Business Event
1	2/29/14	Accrue interest expense of $22,555 on the $3,875,000 loan to a new account: Accrued Expenses.
2	3/1/14	Prepare reversing entry of the preceding interest accrual.
3	2/29/14	Accrue interest income of $210 on short-term investments.
4	2/29/14	Adjust prepaid insurance for January and February 2014 to insurance expense.
5	2/29/14	Record depreciation expense of $34,612 for the months of January and February 2014.
6	2/29/14	Reclassify the deposits received from American Airlines, UCLA, and UCB on 2/5/14, 2/25/14, and 2/26/14, respectively, to unearned revenue (a new other current liability account).
7	2/29/14	Prepare a reversing entry for the unearned reclassification.
8	2/29/14	The Bank of Hawaii bank statement as of 2/29 shows an ending balance of $115,292.39. All checks cleared the bank account except Checks 998–1002. All deposits cleared the bank account except for the 2/26 deposit of $10,750. The bank statement reports interest income of $175 and bank charges of $35.

Requirements:

1 Perform a reconciliation on the checking account, and then print a summary bank reconciliation as of February 29, 2014.

2 Print a Profit & Loss Standard report for the month of February 2014.

3 Print a Balance Sheet Standard report as of February 29, 2014.

4 Print journal entries recorded February 29 through March 1, 2014 (no memo field, and make sure that you filter the transaction type for journal items only).

Budgeting

Upon completion of this chapter, the student will be able to:

- Create budgets for revenues
- Create budgets for expenses
- Create a budget for assets, liabilities, and equities
- Create a budgeted income statement
- Create a budgeted balance sheet

Case: Wild Water Sports, Inc.

Today Donna asks you and Karen to prepare financial statements for the first quarter of the year. She reminds you that you have already recorded all of the transactions for January through April, so you're ready to prepare the statements as of the end of the first quarter, March 31.

"But preparing the statements is only half the job," Karen points out. "We must be able to interpret these statements. How will we know if the company is doing well?"

Donna is quick to respond, "At the beginning of the year, I used a spreadsheet program to establish budgets for the year. I can compare the actual results shown in the statements you prepare with these budgets."

"Doesn't QuickBooks Accountant have a budgeting feature?" you ask.

"You're right!" exclaims Donna, "I didn't use that feature, but now that you mention it, I should have. Would the two of you mind entering my budget estimates into QuickBooks Accountant as well?"

"Not at all," you respond.

After Donna leaves, Karen explains to you that QuickBooks Accountant allows you to set up a budget for an account or for a customer within an account. To do this, you enter budget amounts for the income statement accounts or balance sheet accounts that you wish to track.

"Are you able to track actual versus budgeted amounts?" you ask.

"Yes," Karen replies. "I'll show you how to use QuickBooks Accountant's budget reports to examine the budget by itself as well as how to compare Wild Water Sports's actual results to its budgeted amounts."

You have another question. "Can we create different budgets based on different assumptions in QuickBooks Accountant?"

"No," Karen answers. "QuickBooks Accountant allows you to have a different budget for different fiscal years, but you may have only one budget per fiscal year."

Karen explains that QuickBooks Accountant allows you to set up budgets for specific accounts within financial statements or for all specific financial statements. It is easier to budget for specific accounts, but it might be more useful to prepare a budgeted income statement or budgeted balance sheet.

To begin, Karen suggests that you print Donna's spreadsheet budget. Then the two of you can establish the monthly budget for revenues.

Budgeting Revenues

QuickBooks Accountant provides a setup window to enter budget information. In this window you specify fiscal year, account, customer and/or class, and the corresponding amounts for each month. As you fill in this information, you are setting up a budget for a single account, such as a balance sheet or an income statement account. If you also choose a customer:job or a class, you can set up a budget for that account and for that customer:job or class.

"I remember entering customer:job information in QuickBooks Accountant, but what are classes?" you ask.

"Classes are categories QuickBooks Accountant provides to help you group data into departments, product lines, locations, and the like," Karen responds.

"Do we need to set up budgets for customers or classes?" you ask.

"Donna's budget isn't that detailed," Karen responds. "We'll enter information for accounts only."

You also ask about QuickBooks Accountant's use of the term "income" instead of "revenues" for products and services. Karen reminds you that although "revenues" is the traditional accounting term for these items, QuickBooks Accountant has chosen to classify them as "income" in the type section of the chart of accounts.

Donna's budget predicts boat sales of $200,000 in January 2016 and increasing by $50,000 each month throughout the year. Service and parts revenue is expected to remain constant, at $3,000 and $500 per month throughout the year.

Video Demonstration

DEMO 10A - Budgeting revenues and expenses

To create a budget for specific revenues:

1 Restore the Wild Water Sports Ch 10 (Backup) file that you downloaded from the text web site. See "Data Files CD" in Chapter 1 if you need more information.

2 Click **Company** from the menu bar, click **Planning & Budgeting**, and then click **Set Up Budgets**.

3 Select **2016** as the budget year and **Profit and Loss** as the budget type in the Create New Budgets window, and then click **Next** twice.

4 Select the **Create budget from scratch** option, and click **Finish**.

5 The resulting Set Up Budgets window is shown in Figure 10.1.

Figure 10.1

Setting Up Budgets

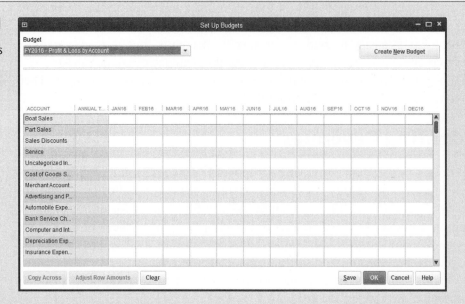

Trouble? Your screen may show the budget split into two 6-month periods based on your screen size. If that occurs, then you will need to press the **Show Next 6 Months** or **Show Prev 6 Months** button in order to enter information in the other 6-month period. Screen shots displayed in this chapter presume that your screen size will accommodate all 12 months.

6   Click in the cell at the intersection of the Jan16 column and the Boat Sales row. Type **200000**.

7   Click the **Adjust Row Amounts** button.

8   Select **Currently selected month** from the Start at drop-down list.

9   Select the first option button and type **50000** as the amount you want to increase each remaining month.

10 Select the **Enable compounding** check box. Your screen should look like Figure 10.2.

Figure 10.2

Adjusting Row Amounts

Adjust Row Amounts

Start at | Currently selected month |

⦿ Increase each remaining monthly amount in this row by this dollar amount or percentage   50,000.00

○ Decrease each remaining monthly amount in this row by this dollar amount or percentage   0.0%

☑ Enable compounding

OK   Cancel   Help

11 Click **OK**.

12 Click in between the Annual Total column title and the Jan16 title. Hold the mouse button down and increase the column width so that the amounts are completely visible.

13 Use the same method to increase the column width of the Jan16, Feb16, Mar16, and Apr16 columns as well as the Account column.

14 Click on the **Part Sales** title of the next row so you can see the Boat Sales row amounts more clearly. Your screen should look like Figure 10.3.

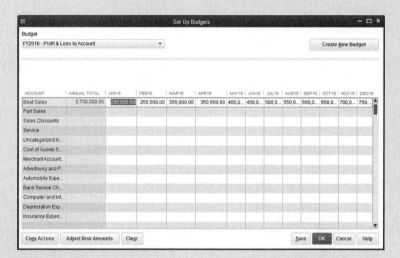

Figure 10.3

Increased Column Widths

15 Click in the cell at the intersection of the Jan16 column and the Part Sales row. Type **500**.

16 Click the **Copy Across** button.

17 Click in the cell at the intersection of the Jan16 column and the Service row. Type **3000**.

18 Click the **Copy Across** button. The income portion of your budget for January through April 2016 should look like Figure 10.4.

ACCOUNT	ANNUAL TOTAL	JAN16	FEB16	MAR16	APR16	
Boat Sales	5,700,000.00	200,000.00	250,000.00	300,000.00	350,000.00	
Part Sales	6,000.00	500.00	500.00	500.00	500.00	
Sales Discounts						
Service	36,000.00	3,000.00	3,000.00	3,000.00	3,000.00	

Figure 10.4

Budgeted Revenue

Now you're ready to set up budget amounts for expenses.

Budgeting Expenses

The budget for Wild Water Sports cost of goods sold depends on product sales. Donna estimated that product cost should amount to approximately 80% of sales, since they mark up the boats 25% above their cost. Thus, as budgeted sales increase, so should budgeted cost of sales. Karen recalls that in January you set up the budget to include merchandise sales of $200,000. Thus, expected cost of sales should be 80% of the total January sales of $200,000, or $160,000. Each month thereafter, Donna expects sales of merchandise to increase by $50,000. Accordingly, the related costs of goods sold should increase monthly by 80% of $50,000, or $40,000.

Karen expects payroll expenses, the largest budgeted expense item for Wild Water Sports, to remain constant at $12,000 per month throughout the year. Depreciation expenses are expected to be $3,500 per month, insurance expenses $2,000 per month, office supplies $1,000 per month, advertising and promotion $2,500 per month, interest expense $2,800 per month, telephone expenses $2,100 per month, and utilities $900 per month.

To create a budget for specific expenses:

1   Increase the column width of the Account column so that account descriptions are all visible and then click in the cell at the intersection of the Jan16 column and the Cost of Goods Sold row. Type **200000*.80** and then press the [**Enter**] key. This illustrates how to use the calculator function of the Budget process. The result should be 160,000.00.

2   Click the **Adjust Row Amounts** button.

3   Select **Currently selected month** from the Start at drop-down list.

4   Select the first option button, and type **40000** as the amount you want to increase each remaining month.

5   Select the **Enable compounding** check box.

6   Click **OK**. Once again increase the width of the Jan16 through Apr16 columns if necessary.

7   Click in the cell at the intersection of the Jan16 column and the Advertising and Promotion row. Type **2500**.

8   Click the **Copy Across** button.

9   Click in the cell at the intersection of the Jan16 column and the Depreciation Expense row. Type **3500**.

10   Click the **Copy Across** button.

11   Click in the cell at the intersection of the Jan16 column and the Insurance Expense row. Type **2000**.

12   Click the **Copy Across** button.

13   Click in the cell at the intersection of the Jan16 column and the Interest Expense row. Type **2800**.

14   Click the **Copy Across** button.

15 Click in the cell at the intersection of the Jan16 column and the Office Supplies row. Type **1000**.

16 Click the **Copy Across** button.

17 Click in the cell at the intersection of the Jan16 column and the Payroll Expenses row. Type **12000**.

18 Click the **Copy Across** button.

19 Click in the cell at the intersection of the Jan16 column and the Telephone Expense row. Type **2100**.

20 Click the **Copy Across** button.

21 Click in the cell at the intersection of the Jan16 column and the Utilities row. Type **900**.

22 Click the **Copy Across** button.

23 Click **Save** to save your newly created budget, and then click **OK** to close the window.

Now that all of the detailed income and expense amounts have been created for our budget, you can create a budgeted income statement.

Budgeted Income Statement

Karen has entered budgetary information for several specific Profit & Loss report accounts, and she is curious to see a complete budget. To do this, she will create and print a budgeted Profit & Loss report for the first quarter of 2016.

To create, memorize, and print a budget overview report:

1 From the **Report Center**, select **Budgets & Forecasts** and then double-click **Budget Overview**.

2 Select **FY2016—Profit & Loss by Account**, and then click **Next**.

3 Select **Account by Month**, and then click **Next**.

4 Click **Finish**.

5 Enter **1/1/16** and **3/31/16** as the From date and To date, respectively, in the Profit & Loss Budget Overview window. (Alternatively, you could use the calendar icons and choose specific dates.)

6 Click the **Refresh** button, and then modify the report to exclude the date prepared, time prepared, and report basis fields. Your window should look like Figure 10.5.

Figure 10.5

Budget Overview Report

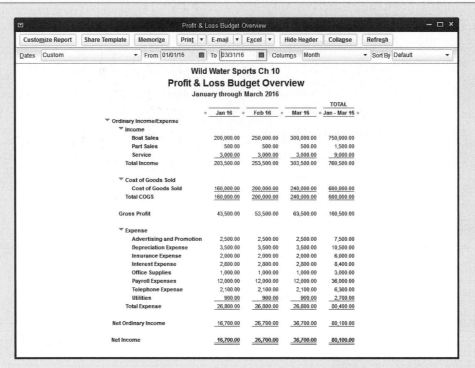

7 Create a new group with your name in memorized reports and then memorize this report in your group. Click the **Print** button and then click **Report** in the Report window.

8 Click **Portrait**, click the **Fit Report to 1 Page Wide** check box, and then click **Print** to print the report.

9 Review the revised report, and then close its window.

Karen explains that this report simply describes the current budget but does not compare that budget with actual results from the quarter ended March 31, 2016. She suggests that you create a Budget vs. Actual report for the quarter ended March 31, 2016, showing only quarterly amounts.

"Why not monthly?" you ask.

"Remember, we made our adjusting entries only at the end of March," Karen reminds you. "We didn't make adjusting entries at the end of January and February. As a result, a monthly analysis of budget versus actual would reveal all sorts of discrepancies. Take insurance, for example. We budgeted insurance expense of $2,000 per month for January, February, and March. Our actual insurance expense will not be recorded until March, when we made an adjusting entry for prepaid insurance. Thus, we'll be under budget in January and February and over budget in March just because of when we recorded our adjustments."

"Then why don't we make adjusting entries every month?" you ask.

"Good question," Karen answers. "We could, but it would take lots of time. Instead, we'll just produce financial statements every quarter, since that's when the bank wants to see how we're doing."

To create, memorize, and print a Budget vs. Actual report for the first quarter of 2016:

1 From the **Report Center**, select **Budgets & Forecasts** and then double-click **Budget vs. Actual**.

2 Select **FY2016—Profit & Loss by Account** then click **Next**.

3 Select **Account by Month**, and then click **Next**.

4 Click **Finish**.

5 Enter **1/1/16** and **3/31/16** as the From date and To date, respectively, in the Profit & Loss Budget vs. Actual window.

6 Select **Quarter** from the drop-down list of Columns.

7 Click the **Refresh** button, and then modify the report to exclude the date prepared, time prepared, and report basis fields. Your window should look like Figure 10.6.

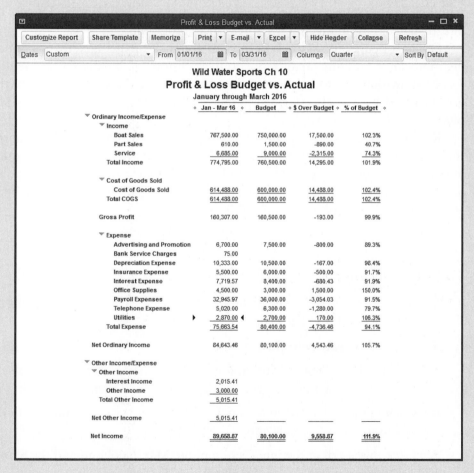

Figure 10.6

Budget vs. Actual Report

8 Memorize this report in your group and then click the **Print** button and then click **Report** in the report window.

9 Click **Portrait**, click the **Fit Report to 1 Page Wide** check box, and then click **Print** to print the report.

Karen points out that, based on the Budget vs. Actual report, the company is doing pretty well. She'll ask Donna about budgeting for bank service charges and other income, since neither was included in the budget. She also wants to investigate the actual office supplies, which the report indicates were 50% over budget.

Budgeting Assets, Liabilities, and Equities

Video Demonstration

DEMO 10B - Budgeting assets, liabilities, and equities

Karen explains why creating specific budgets for assets, liabilities, and stockholders' equity accounts is not a simple task. First, you cannot complete this task until the budget for revenues and expenses has been established. This is due to the relationship that exists between net income and retained earnings. Budgeted retained earnings are dependent on net income/net loss. That is, budgeted retained earnings must be increased by monthly net income and decreased by monthly net losses, if any.

Second, budgets for accounts receivable are dependent on sales, whereas budgets for inventory and accounts payable are dependent on cost of sales and projected sales. Budgeted accumulated depreciation accounts are increased by monthly depreciation expenses. Fortunately for you and Karen, Donna has already created this budget in her spreadsheet program.

Donna's budget for assets had forecast the cash financing activities of issuing more stock, offering credit terms to their customers, buying more inventory for the showroom, temporarily investing some cash, and then eventually paying down some debt. She also planned to increase accounts payable by getting suppliers to offer credit terms.

Karen suggests that you complete this task one step at a time—first entering the budget for assets, then the budget for liabilities and for stockholders' equity. You agree and remind her that the budget amounts for these accounts are the ending balance expected for each quarter. For now, you'll just be creating budgeted balances for assets at the end of March 2016.

To create a budget for assets:

1 Click **Company** from the menu bar, then click **Planning & Budgeting**, and then click **Set Up Budgets**.

2 Click the **Create New Budget** button.

3 Select **2016** as the budget year and **Balance Sheet** as the budget type in the Create New Budgets window, click **Next**, and then click **Finish**.

4 Click in the cell at the intersection of the Mar16 column and the Bank of Florida row. Type **34250**.

5 Click in the cell at the intersection of the Mar16 column and the Short-Term Investments row. Type **50000**.

6 Click in the cell at the intersection of the Mar16 column and the Accounts Receivable row. Type **400000**.

7 Click in the cell at the intersection of the Mar16 column and the Inventory Boats row. Type **200000**.

8 Click in the cell at the intersection of the Mar16 column and the Inventory Parts row. Type **2000**.

9 Click in the cell at the intersection of the Mar16 column and the Prepaid Advertising row. Type **20000**.

10 Click in the cell at the intersection of the Mar16 column and the Prepaid Insurance row. Type **16500**.

11 Click in the cell at the intersection of the Mar16 column and the Furniture and Equipment row. Type **295000**.

12 Click in the cell at the intersection of the Mar16 column and the Accumulated Depreciation row. Type **–17750**.

13 Click **Save**. Your screen should look like Figure 10.7.

ACCOUNT	ANNUAL TOTAL	JAN16	FEB16	MAR16
Bank of Florida	34,250.00			34,250.00
Short-Term Investments	50,000.00			50,000.00
Accounts Receivable	400,000.00			400,000.00
Inventory Boats	200,000.00			200,000.00
Inventory Parts	2,000.00			2,000.00
Prepaid Advertising	20,000.00			20,000.00
Prepaid Insurance	16,500.00			16,500.00
Undeposited Funds				
Furniture and Equipment	295,000.00			295,000.00
Accumulated Depreciation	-17,750.00			-17,750.00

Figure 10.7

Entering Asset Information into the Budget

The liabilities and stockholders' equity items are less numerous, but they include (among others) accounts payable, loan payable, capital stock, and retained earnings. Loan payable was relatively easy to predict because the owners planned to borrow funds when they first opened up and then to pay down some of that debt when they took on another investor and sold some inventory. Capital stock was also easy, since Donna and Karen knew what they were going to invest and had already planned on a fourth investor. Retained earnings were linked to Donna's estimate for net income; because the company started the year with no retained earnings, ending retained earnings as of March 31 had to equal their budgeted net income, given that they hadn't planned to distribute any earnings via dividends.

To create a budget for liabilities and stockholders' equity:

1 Click in the cell at the intersection of the Mar16 column and the Accounts Payable row. Type **200000**.

2 Click in the cell at the intersection of the Mar16 column and the Accrued Liabilities row. Type **1500**.

3 Click in the cell at the intersection of the Mar16 column and the Payroll Liabilities row. Type **3000**.

4 Click in the cell at the intersection of the Mar16 column and the Sales Tax Payable row. Type **15400**.

5 Click in the cell at the intersection of the Mar16 column and the Loan Payable row. Type **300000**.

6 Click in the cell at the intersection of the Mar16 column and the Capital Stock row. Type **400000**.

7 Click in the cell at the intersection of the Mar16 column and the Retained Earnings row. Type **80100**.

8 Click **Save**. The lower portion of your screen should look like Figure 10.8.

Figure 10.8

Entering Liability and Equity Information into the Budget

Accounts Payable	200,000.00		200,000.00
MasterCard			
Unearned Revenue			
Accrued Liabilities	1,500.00		1,500.00
Payroll Liabilities	3,000.00		3,000.00
Sales Tax Payable	15,400.00		15,400.00
Loan Payable	300,000.00		300,000.00
Capital Stock	400,000.00		400,000.00
Dividends Paid			
Opening Balance Equity			
Retained Earnings	80,100.00		80,100.00

9 Click **OK** to close the budget window.

"You've explained how to enter one period's ending balances of assets, liabilities, and equities," Karen states. "What if we wanted to project our balances of assets, liabilities, and equities for future periods?"

You explain that after entering a month's balance, future months are entered into the budget as ending balances. "For example," you state, "you previously entered 34,350 as your expected ending balance in the Bank of Florida checking account at the end of March 2016. If you predicted your balance at the end of the next month would be 40,000 you would then type 40,000 in the April 2016 column of the Bank of Florida row in the Balance Sheet by Account budget worksheet. If instead you predicted your balance at the end of next month would be 30,000 you would type 30,000 in the April 2016 column of the Bank of Florida row in the Balance Sheet by Account budget worksheet. If there is no expected change then you type 34,350 in the cell at the intersection of the April 2016 column and the Bank of Florida row."

Now that all of the detail asset, liability, and stockholders' equity amounts have been created for our budget, you can create a budgeted balance sheet.

Budgeted Balance Sheet

Karen has entered budgetary information for several specific balance sheet accounts, and she'd now like to see a complete budget. Thus, she will create and print a budgeted balance sheet for the quarter ended March 31, 2016.

To create, memorize, and print a budget overview report:

1 From the **Report Center**, select **Budgets & Forecasts** and then double-click **Budget Overview**.

2 Select **FY2016—Balance Sheet by Account**, and then click **Next**.

3 Click **Finish**.

4 Enter **1/1/16** and **3/31/16** as the From date and To date, respectively, in the Balance Sheet Budget Overview window. Select **Total only** from the Columns drop-down list box and then click the **Refresh** button. Your report should look like Figure 10.9.

Wild Water Sports Ch 10
Balance Sheet Budget Overview
As of March 31, 2016

	Mar 31, 16			Mar 31, 16
ASSETS		**LIABILITIES & EQUITY**		
Current Assets		**Liabilities**		
Checking/Savings		**Current Liabilities**		
Bank of Florida	34,250.00	**Accounts Payable**		
Short-Term Investments	50,000.00	Accounts Payable	200,000.00	
Total Checking/Savings	84,250.00	Total Accounts Payable	200,000.00	
Accounts Receivable		**Other Current Liabilities**		
Accounts Receivable	400,000.00	Accrued Liabilities	1,500.00	
Total Accounts Receivable	400,000.00	Payroll Liabilities	3,000.00	
		Sales Tax Payable	15,400.00	
Other Current Assets		Total Other Current Liabilities	19,900.00	
Inventory Boats	200,000.00			
Inventory Parts	2,000.00	Total Current Liabilities	219,900.00	
Prepaid Advertising	20,000.00			
Prepaid Insurance	16,500.00	**Long Term Liabilities**		
Total Other Current Assets	238,500.00	Loan Payable	300,000.00	
		Total Long Term Liabilities	300,000.00	
Total Current Assets	722,750.00			
		Total Liabilities	519,900.00	
Fixed Assets				
Furniture and Equipment	295,000.00	**Equity**		
Accumulated Depreciation	-17,750.00	Capital Stock	400,000.00	
Total Fixed Assets	277,250.00	Retained Earnings	80,100.00	
		Total Equity	480,100.00	
TOTAL ASSETS	1,000,000.00			
		TOTAL LIABILITIES & EQUITY	1,000,000.00	

Figure 10.9

Balance Sheet Budget Overview

5   Modify the report to exclude the date prepared, time prepared, and report basis fields.

6   Memorize this report in your group and then click the **Print** button and then click **Report** in the Report window.

7   Click **Portrait**, click the **Fit Report to 1 Page Wide** check box, and then click **Print** to print the report. Close the report.

Karen explains that, once again, the report describes only the current budget and does not compare that budget with actual results. She suggests that you create a Budget vs. Actual report for the quarter ended March 31, 2016.

To create and print a Budget vs. Actual report for the first quarter of 2016:

1   From the Report Center, select **Budgets & Forecasts**, and then double-click **Budget vs. Actual**.

2   Select **FY2016—Balance Sheet by Account**, and then click **Next**.

3   Click **Finish**.

4   Enter **1/1/16** and **3/31/16** as the From date and To date, respectively, in the Balance Sheet Budget vs. Actual window.

5   Select **Quarter** from the drop-down list of Columns.

6   Click the **Refresh** button, and then modify the report to exclude the date prepared, time prepared, and report basis fields.

7   Memorize this report in your group and then click the **Print** button in the Report window.

8   Click **Portrait**, click the **Fit Report to 1 Page Wide** check box, and then click **Print** to print the report. Your report should look like Figure 10.10.

9   Close the Balance Sheet Budget vs. Actual window.

Wild Water Sports Ch 10
Balance Sheet Budget vs. Actual
As of March 31, 2016

	Mar 31, 16	Budget	$ Over Budget	% of Budget
ASSETS				
Current Assets				
Checking/Savings				
Bank of Florida	47,442.42	34,250.00	13,192.42	138.5%
Short-Term Investments	39,890.41	50,000.00	-10,109.59	79.8%
Total Checking/Savings	87,332.83	84,250.00	3,082.83	103.7%
Accounts Receivable				
Accounts Receivable	399,932.73	400,000.00	-67.27	100%
Total Accounts Receivable	399,932.73	400,000.00	-67.27	100%
Other Current Assets				
Inventory Boats	243,600.00	200,000.00	43,600.00	121.8%
Inventory Parts	2,112.00	2,000.00	112.00	105.6%
Prepaid Advertising	20,000.00	20,000.00	0.00	100.0%
Prepaid Insurance	16,500.00	16,500.00	0.00	100.0%
Undeposited Funds	0.00			
Total Other Current Assets	282,212.00	238,500.00	43,712.00	118.3%
Total Current Assets	769,477.56	722,750.00	46,727.56	106.5%
Fixed Assets				
Furniture and Equipment	295,000.00	295,000.00	0.00	100.0%
Accumulated Depreciation	-17,833.00	-17,750.00	-83.00	100.5%
Total Fixed Assets	277,167.00	277,250.00	-83.00	100%
TOTAL ASSETS	**1,046,644.56**	**1,000,000.00**	**46,644.56**	**104.7%**
LIABILITIES & EQUITY				
Liabilities				
Current Liabilities				
Accounts Payable				
Accounts Payable	216,200.00	200,000.00	16,200.00	108.1%
Total Accounts Payable	216,200.00	200,000.00	16,200.00	108.1%
Credit Cards				
MasterCard	0.00			
Total Credit Cards	0.00			
Other Current Liabilities				
Unearned Revenue	10,000.00			
Accrued Liabilities	1,760.97	1,500.00	260.97	117.4%
Payroll Liabilities	2,934.66	3,000.00	-65.34	97.8%
Sales Tax Payable	28,457.66	15,400.00	13,057.66	184.8%
Total Other Current Liabilities	43,153.29	19,900.00	23,253.29	216.9%
Total Current Liabilities	259,353.29	219,900.00	39,453.29	117.9%
Long Term Liabilities				
Loan Payable	297,632.40	300,000.00	-2,367.60	99.2%
Total Long Term Liabilities	297,632.40	300,000.00	-2,367.60	99.2%
Total Liabilities	556,985.69	519,900.00	37,085.69	107.1%
Equity				
Capital Stock	400,000.00	400,000.00	0.00	100.0%
Opening Balance Equity	0.00			
Retained Earnings	0.00	80,100.00	-80,100.00	0.0%
Net Income	89,658.87	0.00	89,658.87	100.0%
Total Equity	489,658.87	480,100.00	9,558.87	102%
TOTAL LIABILITIES & EQUITY	**1,046,644.56**	**1,000,000.00**	**46,644.56**	**104.7%**

Figure 10.10

Balance Sheet Budget vs. Actual Report

Karen points out that, based on the Budget vs. Actual report, the company is right on target. She'll ask Donna about budgeting for the MasterCard and Unearned Revenue accounts, since neither was included in the budget. She does want to investigate the Inventory Boats account, which was 21% over budget, and Sales Tax Payable, which exceed the budgeted sales tax payable ($15,400) by 84%.

End Note

You and Karen have now entered all budgetary information for the first quarter of 2016. Donna can make changes to the budget at any time if additional information becomes available, and QuickBooks Accountant will automatically update any related budget report.

Business Events Summary

Business Event	Process Steps	Page
Create budgets for revenues and expenses	Planning and budgeting from Company menu	299
Create budgets for assets, liabilities, and equities	Planning and budgeting from Company menu	306
Create budgeted income statement	Budgets from Reports Center	313
Create budgeted balance sheet	Budgets from Reports Center	309

Chapter 10 Questions

1 Explain how the budgeting process is accomplished in QuickBooks Accountant.

2 Can multiple budgets be created in QuickBooks Accountant? Explain.

3 Explain how the Copy Across feature helps in creating QuickBooks Accountant budgets.

4 Explain how the Adjust Row Amounts feature helps in creating QuickBooks Accountant budgets.

5 Explain the typical relationship between sales and cost of goods sold, and describe how this information is included in the QuickBooks Accountant budgeting process.

6 Compare the process of budgeting revenues and expenses with the process of budgeting assets, liabilities, and owners' equity, and explain how this information is included in the QuickBooks Accountant budgeting process.

7 Describe the typical relationship between accumulated depreciation and depreciation expense and how this information is included in the QuickBooks Accountant budgeting process.

8 Which menus are used to create budget reports in QuickBooks Accountant?

9 Describe how you use the calculator feature that is built into QuickBooks Accountant.

10 Explain the typical relationship between retained earnings and net income/loss, and describe how this information is included in the QuickBooks Accountant budgeting process.

Chapter 10 Matching

Select the letter of the item below that best matches the definitions that follow. Use the text or QuickBooks Accountant Help to complete this assignment.

a. Copy Across button

b. Adjust Row Amounts button

c. Enable compounding

d. Budget types

e. Fit Report to 1 Page Wide

f. Balance Sheet Budget Overview

g. Profit & Loss Budget Overview

_____ Budgeted revenues are compared with actual revenues.

_____ Allow amounts that are copied across different months in a budget to compound.

_____ Copies amounts from one month to many months in a budget without modification.

_____ Budgeted accounts receivable are compared with actual accounts receivable.

_____ Must be account based.

_____ A budget can be in a profit & loss format or balance sheet format.

_____ Provides information about budgeted assets, liabilities, and equities only.

h. Balance Sheet Budget vs. Actual

_____ Copies amounts from one month to many months in a budget that has been increased or decreased by an amount or a percentage.

i. Profit & Loss Budget vs. Actual

_____ Provides information about budgeted revenue and expenses only.

j. Budgets

_____ Forces a report to print in a defined amount of space.

Chapter 10 Exercises

Chapter 10 Exercise 1
BUDGETING REVENUES AND EXPENSES

Restore the file Boston Catering Ch 10 (Backup) that you downloaded from the text web site. Enter budgeted revenues and expenses described below and then print the profit & loss budget overview and profit & loss budget vs. actual reports for the month ended July 2010.

a. Budgeted revenues for July include bar sales of $2,000 and catering sales of $20,000.

b. Budgeted expenses for July include bar purchases of $1,400, food purchases of $2,500, interest expense of $600, depreciation expense of $1,000, insurance expense of $1,000, payroll expenses of $6,000, and rent expense of $3,000.

Chapter 10 Exercise 2
BUDGETING ASSETS, LIABILITIES, AND EQUITIES

Restore the file Boston Catering Ch 10 (Backup) that you downloaded from the text web site. Do not use the file created in the exercises above. Enter budgeted assets, liabilities, and equities described below and then print the balance sheet budget overview and balance sheet budget vs. actual reports.

a. Budgeted assets as of July 31, 2010 include cash in bank (Bank of America) $80,000, short-term investments $5,000, accounts receivable $20,000, food inventory $5,000, furniture and equipment $76,500, and accumulated depreciation $3,000.

b. Budgeted liabilities as of July 31, 2010 include accounts payable $10,000, payroll liabilities $2,000, notes payable (Bank of America) $25,000, and notes payable (Citibank) $50,000,

c. Budgeted equities as of July 31, 2010 include capital stock $90,000 and retained earnings $6,500.

Chapter 10 Assignments

Chapter 10 Assignment 1

ADDING MORE INFORMATION: WILD WATER SPORTS

Restore the file Wild Water Sports Ch 10A (Backup) file that you downloaded from the text web site, and then modify the existing budget for 2016 as follows:

Boat sales for April are expected to be 10% higher than in March.

Cost of goods sold for April is still estimated at 80% of boat sales.

Payroll expenses for April are expected to be $15,000.

Assets, liabilities, and equities are as follows.

corporation

merchandising

Bank of Florida	60,000	Accounts Payable	345,200
Short-Term Investments	30,000	Accrued Liabilities	2,000
Accounts Receivable	500,000	Payroll Liabilities	3,000
Prepaid Advertising	18,000	Sales Tax Payable	30,000
Inventory Boats	290,000	Loan Payable	300,000
Inventory Parts	2,000	Capital Stock	400,000
Prepaid Insurance	14,250	Retained Earnings	?
Furniture and Equipment	307,000		
Accumulated Depreciation	−21,250		

You'll need to compute ending retained earnings based on the previous month's budget and your budget of April net income.

a. Memorize and print a Profit & Loss Budget Overview report for the month of April 2016.

b. Memorize and print a Profit & Loss Budget vs. Actual report for the month of April 2016.

c. Memorize and print a Balance Sheet Budget Overview report for the month of April 2016.

d. Memorize and print a Balance Sheet Budget vs. Actual report for the month of April 2016.

Chapter 10 Assignment 2

ADDING MORE INFORMATION: CENTRAL COAST CELLULAR

Restore the file Central Coast Cellular Ch 10 (Backup) that you downloaded from the text web site, and use that copy to record the following events in 2014.

Commissions of $2,000 are expected each month. Consulting income of $8,000 is expected in January, increasing 10% each month thereafter. Product sales of $10,000 are expected in January, increasing by $5,000 each month thereafter. Cost of goods sold is estimated at 50% of product sales. Bank service charges of $80 and depreciation of $1,500 are expected each month. Interest expense of $1,000 and rent of $3,000 are expected each month. Payroll expenses of $10,000 are expected in January, increasing by $2,000 each month thereafter.

sole proprietorship

merchandising

Telephone expenses of $500 are expected in January, increasing $100 each month thereafter. Utilities of $300 are expected in January, increasing 5% each month thereafter. Assets, liabilities, and equities as of January 31, 2014, are as follows.

Checking	130,000	Accounts Payable	24,380
Short-Term Investments	68,500	Accrued Expenses	1,000
Accounts Receivable	14,000	Payroll Liabilities	4,000
Inventory Asset	18,000	Sales Tax Payable	2,000
Supplies	3,000	Loan Payable	120,000
Furniture and Equipment	115,000	Owners Equity	198,620
Accumulated Depreciation	−1,500		
Security Deposit	3,000		

a. Print a Profit & Loss Budget Overview report by month for the quarter ending March 2014.

b. Print a Profit & Loss Budget vs. Actual report for the month of January 2014.

c. Print a Balance Sheet Budget Overview report as of January 31; 2014.

d. Print a Balance Sheet Budget vs. Actual report as of January 31, 2014.

Chapter 10 Assignment 3

ADDING MORE INFORMATION: SANTA BARBARA SAILING

corporation

service

Restore the file Santa Barbara Sailing Ch 10 (Backup) that you downloaded from the text web site, and use that copy to record the following budget information for 2015–16.

Charter income is expected to be $5,000 in July, increasing $1,000 per month thereafter. Rental income is expected to be $30,000 in July, increasing 10% each month throughout the year. Expenses are budgeted as follows and are expected to remain constant for the year. (Move the Rent Expense account down in the chart of accounts so that all expenses are listed in alphabetical order.)

Advertising and Promotion	3,500
Computer and Internet Expenses	1,300
Depreciation Expense	5,750
Interest Expense	1,000
Payroll Expenses	10,000
Rent Expense	2,000
Repairs and Maintenance	2,500
Utilities	1,200

Budgeted assets, liabilities, and equities as of July 31, 2015, are as follows.

Checking	115,000
Accounts Receivable	4,000
Prepaid Rent	22,000
Boats	350,000
Furniture and Equipment	2,500
Accumulated Depreciation	−5,750
Accounts Payable	4,000
Payroll Liabilities	4,500
Sales Tax Payable	4,000
Loan Payable	317,500
Capital Stock	150,000
Retained Earnings	7,750

a. Print and memorize a Profit & Loss Budget Overview report for the quarter ended September 30, 2015.

b. Print and memorize a Profit & Loss Budget vs. Actual report for the month ended July 31, 2015.

c. Print and memorize a Balance Sheet Budget Overview report as of July 31, 2015.

d. Print and memorize a Balance Sheet Budget vs. Actual report as of July 31, 2015.

Chapter 10 Assignment 4

ADDING MORE INFORMATION: DRONE CITY

Restore the file Drone City Ch 10 (Backup) that you downloaded from the text web site, and then add the following budget information for 2017. For balance sheet input, be sure to read through the explanation on page 301.

sole proprietorship

easy step

Account	January	Remaining Months of the Year
Consulting	$10,000	Increasing $500 per month thereafter
Sales	50,000	Increasing 10% per month thereafter
Cost of Goods Sold	42,500	Increasing 10% per month thereafter
Advertising and Promotion	500	Constant for the year
Bank Service Charges	50	Constant for the year
Computer and Internet Expenses	250	Constant for the year
Depreciation Expense	250	Same each month until July when it increases to 500
Interest Expense	200	Constant for the year
Office Supplies	450	Constant for the year
Payroll Expenses	10,000	Increasing 5% per month thereafter
Rent Expense	1,500	Constant for the year
Telephone Expense	1,200	Constant for the year

Account	January	February	March
Checking	$23,150	$25,700	$25,750
Accounts Receivable	27,000	28,600	32,000
Inventory Asset	13,000	14,000	15,000
Prepaid Advertising	1,500	1,500	1,500
Supplies	2,000	2,000	2,000
Furniture and Equipment	24,000	24,000	24,000
Accumulated Depreciation	−250	−500	−750

Account	January	February	March
Accounts Payable	13,400	14,150	13,400
Accrued Liabilities	3,100	3,100	3,100
Payroll Liabilities	3,000	3,300	3,600
Sales Tax Payable	3,500	3,500	3,500
Notes Payable	24,300	24,300	24,300
Owners' Equity	43,100	46,950	51,600

Place your name in the Extra Footer Line; remove subtitle, date, and time prepared header information; and then memorize (in a report group with your name) and print the following reports.

a.   Profit & Loss Budget Overview report for January through March 2017.

b.   Balance Sheet Budget Overview report for January through March 2017.

c.   Profit & Loss Budget vs. Actual report for the month of January 2017.

d.   Balance Sheet Budget vs. Actual report for the month of January 2017.

Chapter 10 Cases

Chapter 10 Case 1
FOREVER YOUNG

sole proprietorship

service

In Chapter 9, you added some transactions to your QuickBooks Accountant file for Forever Young. Make a copy of that file, and use that copy to record the following budget information.

Consulting income is expected to be $40,000 in January, increasing $5,000 per month thereafter. Expenses are budgeted as follows and are expected to remain constant for the next three months.

Advertising and Promotion	500
Automobile Expense	1,000
Depreciation Expense	100
Interest Expense	100
Payroll Expenses	10,000
Professional Fees	4,000
Rent Expense	3,800
Telephone Expense	500
Travel Expense	7,000

Budgeted assets, liabilities, and equities as of January 31, 2015, are as follows.

Checking	50,000
Accounts Receivable	15,000
Prepaid Advertising	5,000
Supplies	2,100
Furniture and Equipment	4,000
Accumulated Depreciation	−100
Security Deposits Asset	4,000
Payroll Liabilities	5,000
Notes Payable	50,000
Owners Equity	25,000

Requirements:

1   Print a Profit & Loss Budget Overview report for the quarter ended March 31, 2015.

2   Print a Profit & Loss Budget vs. Actual report for the month ended January 31, 2015.

3   Print a Balance Sheet Budget Overview report as of January 31, 2015.

4   Print a Balance Sheet Budget vs. Actual report as of January 31, 2015.

Chapter 10 Case 2

OCEAN VIEW FLOWERS

In Chapter 9, you modified your QuickBooks Accountant file for Ocean View Flowers, a wholesale flower distributor. Make a copy of that file, and use that copy to enter the following transactions for 2016. Budgeted revenues and expenses are as follows.

corporation

merchandising

Account	January	February
Sales	$35,000	$80,000
Cost of Goods Sold	16,000	42,000
Depreciation Expense	1,500	1,500
Insurance Expense	100	100
Interest Expense	1,600	1,600
Payroll Expenses	20,000	20,000
Professional Fees	500	500
Rent Expense	1,400	1,400
Telephone Expense	400	400
Utilities	300	300
Interest Income	500	1,000

Budgeted balances as of February 29, 2016, for assets, liabilities, and equity accounts follow.

Union Checking	46,300	Accounts Payable	52,800
Accounts Receivable	62,200	Payroll Liabilities	14,000
Inventory Asset	30,000	Long-Term Note Payable	320,000
Prepaid Insurance	1,000	Capital Stock	100,000
Short-Term Investments	25,000	Retained Earnings	13,200
Supplies	1,500		
Land	50,000		
Building	250,000		
Furniture and Equipment	37,000		
Accumulated Depreciation	−3,000		

Requirements:

1   Print a Profit & Loss Budget Overview report by month for the two months ended February 2016.

2   Print a Profit & Loss Budget vs. Actual report in total for the two months ended February 2016.

3 Print a Balance Sheet Budget Overview report as of February 29, 2016.

4 Print a Balance Sheet Budget vs. Actual report as of February 29, 2016.

Chapter 10 Case 3

ALOHA PROPERTIES

In Chapter 9, you modified your QuickBooks Accountant file for Aloha Properties. Make a copy of that file, and use that copy to enter the following budget information for 2014.

Rental income is expected to be $60,000 in January and $100,000 in February, and it is expected to increase 18% per month thereafter through 2014. Advertising and promotion is expected to be $12,500 in January (for an initial advertising campaign) and then $1,500 per month thereafter. Cleaning costs vary with the number of units rented (these costs should average about 5% of rental income). Depreciation should be about $17,000 per month. Insurance, interest, repairs and maintenance, telephone, utilities, and payroll expenses are expected to be $2,000, $23,000, $3,400, $4,000, $3,000, and $10,000, respectively each month throughout the year. Expected assets, liabilities, and equities as of February 29, 2014, are as follows.

Checking	101,000	Accounts Payable	10,000
Accounts Receivable	50,000	Accrued Expenses	23,000
Prepaid Insurance	20,000	Payroll Liabilities	4,000
Short-Term Investments	40,000	Sales Tax Payable	5,000
Buildings	5,000,000	Notes Payable	3,859,600
Furniture and Equipment	23,000	Capital Stock	60,000
Accumulated Depreciation	−1,234,000	Retained Earnings	38,400

Requirements:

1 Print a Profit & Loss Budget Overview report for the two-month period ending February 2014.

2 Print a Profit & Loss Budget vs. Actual report for the two-month period ending February 2014.

3 Print a Balance Sheet Budget Overview report as of February 29, 2014.

4 Print a Balance Sheet Budget vs. Actual report as of February 29, 2014.

Reporting Business Activities

Case: Wild Water Sports, Inc.

Now that you have entered the budget information for Wild Water Sports's first year and have entered the first four months of operating, investing, and financing transactions as well as adjustments, you are finally ready to prepare financial statements to send to the bank for Wild Water Sports's first three months. Donna has asked you and Karen to prepare these statements and to provide any additional information that will help her better understand Wild Water's financial performance. You and Karen would like to create more customized financial statements than you've printed so far and to give Donna the related supporting schedules and graphs that QuickBooks Accountant can so easily create.

You decide to prepare a customized income statement, a customized balance sheet, an accounts receivable and accounts payable schedule, and some sales reports. To further enhance Donna's financial analysis of the business, you also decide to prepare one graph showing income and expenses and another graph showing the aging of accounts receivable and payable.

"The report and graph features of QuickBooks Accountant are quite extensive," Karen explains. "You can customize each report by adding percentages, hiding cents, changing report titles, and modifying the page layout."

"Can we graphically compare the current quarter's results with the budget we just created?" you ask.

"Absolutely!" Karen confirms. "Now that we have created the budget in QuickBooks Accountant, we can use the report information we created when comparing our budgeted activity with our actual results and produce a graphic illustration. This will help Donna or other users of this information to visually evaluate the financial results."

"Sounds like QuickBooks Accountant saves hours of work," you remark. "Let's get started."

Creating and Memorizing a Customized Income Statement

Karen decides to create one customized income statement for the three-month period ended March 31 without examining each month separately because adjustments were made only as of March 31.

Karen explains that QuickBooks Accountant enables you to create reports for any period you desire. It also lets you create separate columns for a time segment—such as a day, a week, four weeks, a month, a quarter, and so on—within each period. At the end of the fiscal year, Karen will create an income statement report for the year with separate columns for each quarter.

Karen decides to print two customized versions of the income statement. One will be a "left page" layout alignment without cents and will include a % of Income column; it will be titled Income Statement for the three months ended March 31, 2016, and will be in an expanded format. The other will be a collapsed version of the same report but sorted by total from largest to smallest amounts.

"Do we have to go through this customization effort every time?" Karen asks.

"No," you reply. "QuickBooks Accountant has a Memorize feature that can 'memorize' or retain the customization—what columns we want, what period, what layout, and so on. That way, the next time we want a similar report, it will be available from a memorized report list."

To create and memorize a customized Income Statement:

1 Restore the Wild Water Sports Ch 11 (Backup) file that you downloaded from the text web site.

2 From the Report Center, click **Company & Financial** and then double-click **Profit & Loss Standard**.

3 Click the **Customize Report** button, and then click the **Display** tab.

4 Change the report dates to read from **1/1/16** to **3/31/16** in the Modify Report window, and then click the **% of Income** check box.

5 Click the **Fonts & Numbers** tab, and then click the **Without Cents** check box.

6 Click the **Header/Footer** tab. Change the Report Title to **Income Statement**. Select **Left** from the Page Layout alignment drop-down edit box, and alter the Subtitle to read **for the three months ended March 31, 2016**.

7 Uncheck the **Date Prepared, Time Prepared**, and **Report Basis** check boxes and then click **OK**.

8 Click the **Print** button and then click **Report**.

9 Click **Portrait** in the Orientation box. (If the Print Features window appears, click **OK**.) Then click **Print** in the Print Reports window to print the report shown in Figure 11.1.

Wild Water Sports Ch 11
Income Statement
for the three months ended March 31, 2016

	Jan - Mar 16	% of Income
Ordinary Income/Expense		
Income		
Boat Sales	767,500	99%
Part Sales	610	0%
Service	6,685	1%
Total Income	774,795	100%
Cost of Goods Sold		
Cost of Goods Sold	614,488	79%
Total COGS	614,488	79%
Gross Profit	160,307	21%
Expense		
Advertising and Promotion	6,700	1%
Bank Service Charges	75	0%
Depreciation Expense	10,333	1%
Insurance Expense	5,500	1%
Interest Expense	7,720	1%
Office Supplies	4,500	1%
Payroll Expenses	32,946	4%
Telephone Expense	5,020	1%
Utilities	2,870	0%
Total Expense	75,664	10%
Net Ordinary Income	84,643	11%
Other Income/Expense		
Other Income		
Interest Income	2,015	0%
Other Income	3,000	0%
Total Other Income	5,015	1%
Net Other Income	5,015	1%
Net Income	**89,659**	**12%**

Figure 11.1

Customized Income Statement

10 Change the sorting by selecting **Total** from the Sort By drop-down list and clicking the **Sort** button next to the Sort By drop-down list so that it reads Z to A (meaning largest to smallest).

11 Click the **Print** button and then click **Report**.

12 Click **Portrait** in the Orientation box. (If the Print Features window appears, click **OK**.) Then click **Print** in the Print Reports window to print the report shown in Figure 11.2.

Figure 11.2

Variation on the Customized Income Statement

Wild Water Sports Ch 11
Income Statement
for the three months ended March 31, 2016

	Jan - Mar 16	% of Income
Ordinary Income/Expense		
Income		
Boat Sales	767,500	99%
Service	6,685	1%
Part Sales	610	0%
Total Income	774,795	100%
Cost of Goods Sold		
Cost of Goods Sold	614,488	79%
Total COGS	614,488	79%
Gross Profit	160,307	21%
Expense		
Payroll Expenses	32,946	4%
Depreciation Expense	10,333	1%
Interest Expense	7,720	1%
Advertising and Promotion	6,700	1%
Insurance Expense	5,500	1%
Telephone Expense	5,020	1%
Office Supplies	4,500	1%
Utilities	2,870	0%
Bank Service Charges	75	0%
Total Expense	75,664	10%
Net Ordinary Income	84,643	11%
Other Income/Expense		
Other Income		
Other Income	3,000	0%
Interest Income	2,015	0%
Total Other Income	5,015	1%
Net Other Income	5,015	1%
Net Income	**89,659**	**12%**

13 From the Report Center (not the report you just created), click the **Memorized** tab located at the top of the window.

14 Click the **Edit Memorized List** button at the top of the window and then click the **Memorized Report** button at the bottom of the Memorized Report List and then click **New Group** from the menu shown.

15 Type **your name** in the Name text box and then click **OK**.

16 Close the Memorized Report List window.

17 Activate the Profit & Loss report window you created earlier.

18 Click the **Memorize** button.

19 Type **Customized Income Statement** in the Name text box, click in the **Save in Memorized Report Group** check box and select **your name** from the drop-down list as shown in Figure 11.3. Student Name is shown in the figure as the memorized group. On your screen, your name should show as the memorized group.

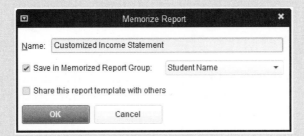

Figure 11.3

Memorizing Reports

20 Click **OK** to retain this customized report as Customized Income Statement.

21 Close the Customized Income Statement window.

22 From the Report Center, click the **Memorized** tab and then click **your name** from the list of Groups shown in the left hand column as shown in Figure 11.4.

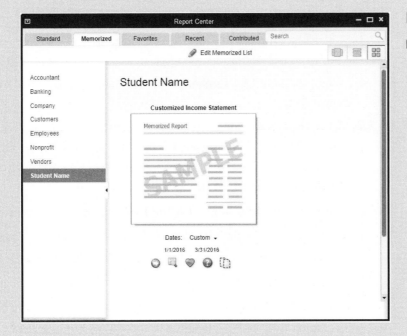

Figure 11.4

Retrieving a Memorized Report

23 Close all windows.

Karen suggests that you take note of the % of Income column. She explains how this column reports each item's percentage of total revenue (what Quick-Books Accountant calls total income). Cost of goods sold at 79% and payroll expenses at 4% are the company's largest costs as a percentage of total revenue. Notice also that Wild Water's profit margin ratio (net income divided by total revenue) is 12%. You suggest a cup of coffee before you come back to customize a balance sheet.

Creating and Memorizing a Customized Balance Sheet

Video Demonstration

DEMO 11B - Create and memorize a customized balance sheet

You return to your office to create the balance sheet Donna needs as of 3/31/16. Karen explains to you that QuickBooks Accountant can prepare balance sheets for any accounting period you specify. Since Donna needs balance results as of 3/31/16, the two of you start by preparing a standard balance sheet. You want to keep the report simple—you'll include the main accounts from the chart of accounts and collapse the subaccounts into their main accounts. You decide to customize the balance sheet to include a percentage column.

To create and memorize a customized balance sheet:

1 From the Report Center, click the **Standard** tab and then **Company & Financial**. Scroll down the list of reports and then double-click **Balance Sheet Standard** under Balance Sheet & Net Worth.

2 Click the **Customize Report** button.

3 Click the Display tab and then change the report dates to read from **1/1/16** to **3/31/16** and then click in the **% of Column** check.

4 Click the **Fonts & Numbers** tab, and then click the **Without Cents** check box.

5 Click the **Header/Footer** tab. Select **Left** from the Page Layout alignment drop-down edit box and then change the subtitle to March 31, 2016.

6 Uncheck the **Date Prepared, Time Prepared**, and **Report Basis** check boxes and then click **OK**.

7 Click **Refresh** and then click the **Print** button and then click **Report**.

8 Click **Portrait** in the Orientation box, and then click **Print** in the Print Reports window to print the report shown in Figure 11.5.

Figure 11.5

Customized Balance Sheet

Wild Water Sports Ch 11
Customized Balance Sheet
As of March 31, 2016

	Mar 31, 16	% of Column
ASSETS		
Current Assets		
Checking/Savings		
Bank of Florida	47,442	5%
Short-Term Investments	39,890	4%
Total Checking/Savings	87,333	8%
Accounts Receivable		
Accounts Receivable	399,933	38%
Total Accounts Receivable	399,933	38%
Other Current Assets		
Inventory Boats	243,600	23%
Inventory Parts	2,112	0%
Prepaid Advertising	20,000	2%
Prepaid Insurance	16,500	2%
Total Other Current Assets	282,212	27%
Total Current Assets	769,478	74%
Fixed Assets		
Furniture and Equipment	295,000	28%
Accumulated Depreciation	-17,833	-2%
Total Fixed Assets	277,167	26%
TOTAL ASSETS	1,046,645	100%
LIABILITIES & EQUITY		
Liabilities		
Current Liabilities		
Accounts Payable		
Accounts Payable	216,200	21%
Total Accounts Payable	216,200	21%
Other Current Liabilities		
Unearned Revenue	10,000	1%
Accrued Liabilities	1,761	0%
Payroll Liabilities	2,935	0%
Sales Tax Payable	28,458	3%
Total Other Current Liabilities	43,153	4%
Total Current Liabilities	259,353	25%
Long Term Liabilities		
Loan Payable	297,632	28%
Total Long Term Liabilities	297,632	28%
Total Liabilities	556,986	53%
Equity		
Capital Stock	400,000	38%
Net Income	89,659	9%
Total Equity	489,659	47%
TOTAL LIABILITIES & EQUITY	1,046,645	100%

9 Click the **Memorize** button.

10 Type **Customized Balance Sheet** in the Name text box and save this new report in your report group like you did before.

11 Click **OK** to memorize this customized report.

12 Close all windows.

Trouble? Notice that QuickBooks Accountant includes a line item called "Net Income" in the (Owners') Equity section. Standard accounting practice does not allow inclusion of such an income statement category in a balance sheet. Usually, this net income is included in the Retained Earnings account.

Karen comments that at first she thought the percentage column was the same as the one shown in the income statement: each item's percentage of the total revenue (what QuickBooks Accountant calls "income"). But now she sees that this column actually shows the percentage of total assets. For example, total cash (i.e., the total amount in checking and savings) is 8% of Wild Water Sports's total assets, and accounts receivable is 38% of total assets. She comments that it looks like a large portion of those assets came from accounts payable (21%) and loans payable (28%) and that most of the balance is from equity (47%).

Creating Graphs to Illustrate Financial Information

"This is very helpful information," Donna comments as she quickly skims the customized income statement, balance sheet, and budget versus actual reports you previously created. "I can see Wild Water's financial position and how we stand in relation to where I thought we'd be. Can I see this information expressed in graphical form?" she asks. "I'm afraid I might miss something when I look at this detailed report. A graph would help me see things I might miss when I look at just numbers."

Both you and Karen agree that some graphs would be helpful. In particular, Donna is anxious to know more about product sales and expenses. It is clear that graphic representations of sales, revenue, and expenses will be helpful.

To create a Sales Graph:

1 From the Report Center, click **Sales** and then double-click **Sales Graph** located under Sales by Customer.

2 Click the **Dates** button and change the dates to read from **1/1/16** to **3/31/16** in the Change Graph Dates window. Then click **OK**.

3 Click the **By Item** button in the QuickInsight: Sales Graph window, if it is not already selected. Selecting this button causes QuickBooks Accountant to display sales in the graph by item, in this case by the boats and the services that Wild Water sells.

4 QuickBooks Accountant generates two graphs—a bar chart and a pie chart.

5 Click **Print** from the button bar, and then click **Print** from the Print Graphs window. Your printed graph should look like Figure 11.6.

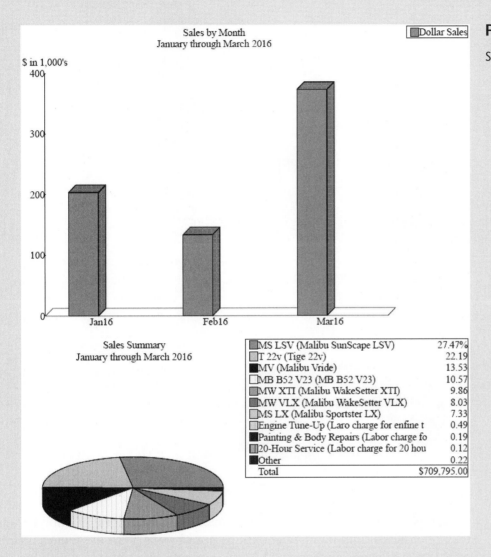

Figure 11.6

Sales Graph by Item

6 Click the **By Customer** button in the QuickInsight: Sales Graph window to create a graph that illustrates sales for the quarter by customer.

7 Click **Print** from the button bar, and then click **Print** from the Print Graphs window. Your printed graph should look like Figure 11.7.

8 Close the Sales Graph window.

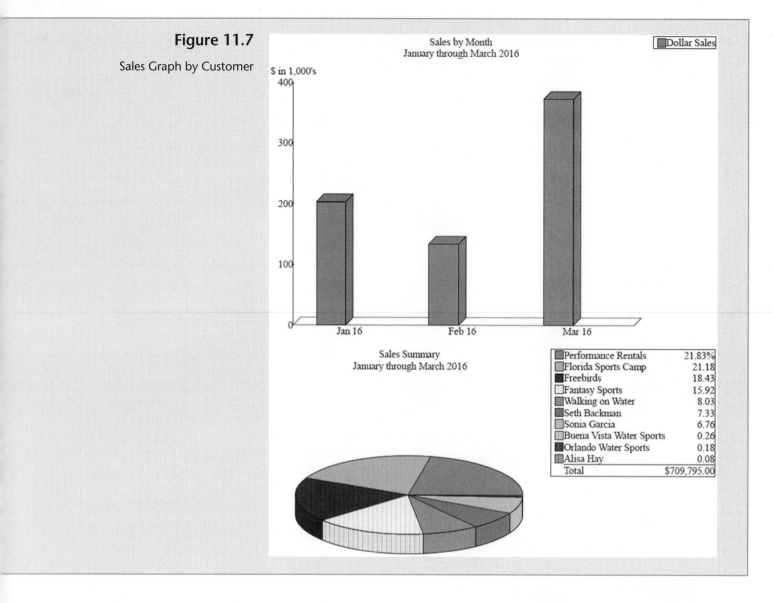

Figure 11.7

Sales Graph by Customer

Graphs such as these help managers interpret financial information because they often reveal important relationships not obvious from the financial statements. For example, in Figure 11.7, sales growth by month is illustrated and the source of sales by customer is revealed. In this case, customer Performance Rentals represents almost 22% of sales for the three months.

Next, you decide to produce a graph that illustrates Wild Water Sports's revenues (or "income," as QuickBooks Accountant calls it) and expenses.

To create an Income and Expense Graph:

1   From the Report Center, click **Company & Financial** and then double-click **Income & Expense Graph** located under Income & Expenses.

2   Click the **Dates** button and change the dates to read from **1/1/16** to **3/31/16** in the Change Graph Dates window. Then click **OK**.

3 Click the **By Account** button at the top of the screen and the **Expense** button at the bottom of the QuickInsight: Income and Expense Graph window, if they are not already selected.

4 Click **Print** from the button bar, and then click **Print** from the Print Graphs window. Your printed graph should look like Figure 11.8. *Trouble?* Your vertical axis scale might be different, depending on the size of the figure you choose to view.

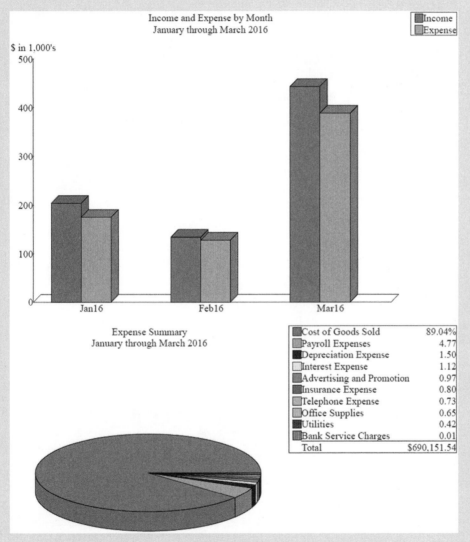

Figure 11.8

Income and Expense by Account Graph

5 Close all windows.

These two graphs help to explain revenues and expenses, but they do not provide insight into the financial position of the company as of March 31.

"Does QuickBooks Accountant have similar graphing capabilities for items such as accounts receivable and accounts payable?" you ask.

"Yes," Karen responds. "In fact, we should probably create a graph for both accounts to demonstrate how current or noncurrent our receivables and payables are. QuickBooks Accountant can create a bar chart that illustrates aging for accounts receivable and then another for accounts payable, and it can simultaneously identify who owes us (and whom we owe) at any given time, such as March 31, 2016."

To create an Accounts Receivable Graph and an Accounts Payable Graph:

1   From the Report Center, click **Customers & Receivables**, and then double-click **Accounts Receivable Graph**.

2   Click the **Dates** button, and change the date to **3/31/16** in the Change Graph Dates window. Then click **OK**.

3   Click **Print** from the button bar, and then click **Print** from the Print Graphs window. Your printed graph should look like Figure 11.9.

Figure 11.9

Accounts Receivable Graph

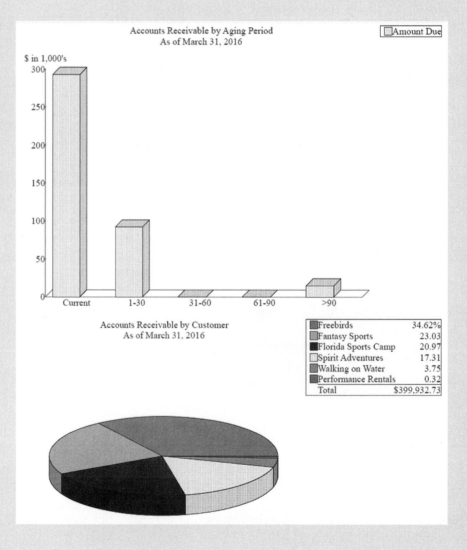

4   From the Report Center, click **Vendors & Payables**, and then double-click **Accounts Payable Graph**.

5 Click the **Dates** button, and change the date to **3/31/16** in the Change Graph Dates window. Then click **OK**.

6 Click **Print** from the button bar, and then click **Print** from the Print Graphs window. Your printed graph should look like Figure 11.10.

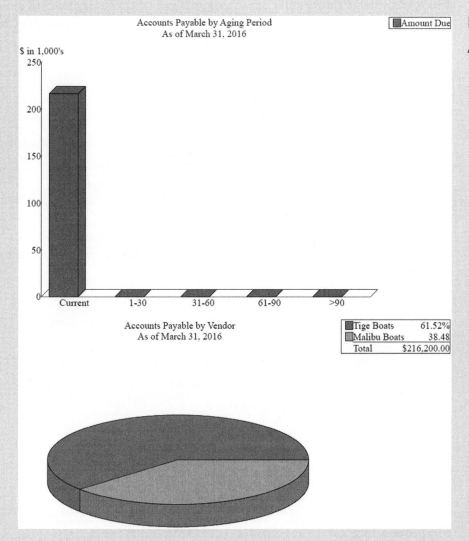

Figure 11.10

Accounts Payable Graph

7 Close all windows.

When you show Donna these graphs, she comments that they will be very helpful. But she wants to see even more information derived from the financial statements—specifically, she wants to see detailed reports on sales, purchases, accounts receivable, and accounts payable.

Create Additional Detail Reports

With QuickBooks Accountant, you can generate many supporting reports for the financial statements—what accountants consider traditional support in the form of schedules. Karen reads through QuickBooks Accountant Help and discovers two reports that QuickBooks Accountant generates that will help Donna: the Sales by Customer Summary and the Summary Sales by Item. Together, you decide that the Sales by Customer Summary should identify sales for each month of the quarter so you can identify the customer to which you sold products or services. The Summary Sales by Item reports on the number of items sold, the average price of each item sold, and each item's related average cost. This report also identifies the gross margin (sales revenue minus cost of goods sold) for each item and summarizes the gross margin for all items sold during the period. Karen suggests that you produce this report on a monthly basis.

To create the Sales by Customer Summary and the Summary Sales by Item reports:

1 From the Report Center, click **Sales**, and then double-click **Sales by Customer Summary** located under Sales by Customer.

2 Change the report dates to read from **1/1/16** to **3/31/16**.

3 Click **Refresh** and then click the **Collapse** button.

4 Select **Total** in the Sort By drop-down list, and then click the sort button to read Z – A so that the report lists sales to customers from largest to smallest.

5 Select **Month** from the Columns drop-down edit box and then click **OK**.

6 Remove the date prepared, time prepared, and report basis from the report.

7 Click **Print** from the button bar, then click **Report**, and then click **Print** from the Print Reports window. Your printed report should look like Figure 11.11.

Figure 11.11

Sales by Customer Summary

Wild Water Sports Ch 11A
Sales by Customer Summary
January through March 2016

	Jan 16	Feb 16	Mar 16	TOTAL
Performance Rentals	78,750.00	75,000.00	1,215.00	154,965.00
Florida Sports Camp	71,575.00	0.00	78,750.00	150,325.00
Freebirds	845.00	0.00	130,000.00	130,845.00
Fantasy Sports	0.00	0.00	113,000.00	113,000.00
Walking on Water	0.00	57,000.00	0.00	57,000.00
Seth Backman	52,000.00	0.00	0.00	52,000.00
Sonia Garcia	0.00	0.00	48,000.00	48,000.00
Buena Vista Water Sports	0.00	0.00	1,845.00	1,845.00
Orlando Water Sports	0.00	1,250.00	0.00	1,250.00
Alisa Hay	165.00	400.00	0.00	565.00
TOTAL	203,335.00	133,650.00	372,810.00	709,795.00

8 Click **Memorize**.

9 Type **Customized Sales by Customer Summary** in the Name text box and save it in your memorized report group; then click **OK**.

10 Close the Sales by Customer Summary window.

11 From the Report Center, double-click **Sales by Item Summary** located under Sales by Item.

12 Change the report dates to read from **1/1/16** to **3/31/16**.

13 Click **Refresh** and then select **Total Only** from the Columns drop-down edit box.

14 Adjust the column width to view more of the report on your screen. You may need to scroll down the report to view items sold and total sales.

15 Remove the date prepared, time prepared, and report basis from the report.

16 Click **Print** from the button bar, then click **Report**, and then click **Print** from the Print Reports window. Your printed report should look like Figure 11.12.

Wild Water Sports Ch 11
Sales by Item Summary
January through March 2016

	Qty	Amount	% of Sales	Avg Price	COGS	Avg COGS	Gross Margin	Gross Margin %
				Jan - Mar 16				
Inventory								
Air Filter (Air Filter)	1	35.00	0.0%	35.00	28.00	28.00	7.00	20.0%
Engine Oil (Engine Oil)	9	45.00	0.0%	5.00	36.00	4.00	9.00	20.0%
MB B52 V23 (MB B52 V23)	1	75,000.00	10.6%	75,000.00	60,000.00	60,000.00	15,000.00	20.0%
MS LSV (Malibu SunScape LSV)	3	195,000.00	27.5%	65,000.00	156,000.00	52,000.00	39,000.00	20.0%
MS LX (Malibu Sportster LX)	1	52,000.00	7.3%	52,000.00	41,600.00	41,600.00	10,400.00	20.0%
MV (Malibu Vride)	2	96,000.00	13.5%	48,000.00	76,800.00	38,400.00	19,200.00	20.0%
MW VLX (Malibu WakeSetter VLX)	1	57,000.00	8.0%	57,000.00	45,600.00	45,600.00	11,400.00	20.0%
MW XTI (Malibu WakeSetter XTI)	1	70,000.00	9.9%	70,000.00	56,000.00	56,000.00	14,000.00	20.0%
Oil Filter (Oil Filter)	2	30.00	0.0%	15.00	24.00	12.00	6.00	20.0%
T 22v (Tige 22v)	2	157,500.00	22.2%	78,750.00	126,000.00	63,000.00	31,500.00	20.0%
Tune-Up Parts (Tune-Up Parts)	2	500.00	0.1%	250.00	400.00	200.00	100.00	20.0%
Total Inventory	25.00	703,110.00	99.1%	28,124.40	562,488.00	22,499.52	140,622.00	20.0%
Service								
20-Hour Service (Labor charge for 20 hour service check)	5	875.00	0.1%	175.00				
Cleaning (Labor charge for cleaning boat)	6	450.00	0.1%	75.00				
Engine Service (Labor charge for changing engine oil and filter)	4	500.00	0.1%	125.00				
Engine Tune-Up (Laro charge for enfine tune-up)	14	3,500.00	0.5%	250.00				
Painting & Body Repairs (Labor charge for painting and repairs)	17	1,360.00	0.2%	80.00				
Total Service	46.00	6,885.00	0.9%	145.33				
TOTAL	71	709,795.00	100.0%	9,997.11		7,922.37		

Figure 11.12

Sales by Item Summary

17 Click **Memorize**.

18 Type **Customized Sales by Item Summary** in the Name text box, save it in your memorized report group, and then click **OK**.

19 Close the Sales by Item Summary window.

Karen tells you that two additional reports are commonly prepared to support the balance sheet: Accounts Receivable Aging and Accounts Payable Aging. QuickBooks Accountant can easily generate these reports.

To create Accounts Receivable and Accounts Payable Aging reports:

1 From the Report Center, click **Customers & Receivables** and then double-click **A/R Aging Summary** located under A/R Aging.

2   Change the report date to read **3/31/16** and then click **Refresh**.

3   Click the **Collapse** button.

4   Remove the date prepared and time prepared fields.

5   Click the **Print** button in the button bar, then click **Report**, and then click **Print** in the Print Reports window.

6   Choose a **Portrait** orientation.

7   The report shown in Figure 11.13 appears. Examine this report.

Figure 11.13

A/R Aging Summary

Wild Water Sports Ch 11
A/R Aging Summary
As of March 31, 2016

	Current	1 - 30	31 - 60	61 - 90	> 90	TOTAL
Fantasy Sports	0.00	92,095.00	0.00	0.00	0.00	92,095.00
Florida Sports Camp	83,868.75	0.00	0.00	0.00	0.00	83,868.75
Freebirds	138,450.00	0.00	0.00	0.00	0.00	138,450.00
Performance Rentals	1,293.98	0.00	0.00	0.00	0.00	1,293.98
Spirit Adventures	69,225.00	0.00	0.00	0.00	0.00	69,225.00
Walking on Water	0.00	0.00	0.00	0.00	15,000.00	15,000.00
TOTAL	292,837.73	92,095.00	0.00	0.00	15,000.00	399,932.73

8   Click **Memorize**.

9   Type **Customized A/R Aging Summary** in the Name text box and save it in your memorized report group; then click **OK**. (Click **Replace** to create a new report.)

10   Close the A/R Aging Summary window.

11   From the Report Center, click **Vendors & Payables** and then double-click **A/P Aging Summary** located under A/P Aging Summary.

12   Remove date and time prepared from the report, change the report date to read **3/31/16**, and then click **Refresh**.

13   Click the **Print** button in the button bar, then click **Report**, and then click **Print** in the Print Reports window.

14   Choose a **Portrait** orientation.

15   The report shown in Figure 11.14 appears. Examine this report.

Figure 11.14

A/P Aging Summary

Wild Water Sports Ch 11
A/P Aging Summary
As of March 31, 2016

	Current	1 - 30	31 - 60	61 - 90	> 90	TOTAL
Malibu Boats	83,200.00	0.00	0.00	0.00	0.00	83,200.00
Tige Boats	133,000.00	0.00	0.00	0.00	0.00	133,000.00
TOTAL	216,200.00	0.00	0.00	0.00	0.00	216,200.00

16   Click **Memorize**.

17 Type **Customized A/P Aging Summary** in the Name text box, save it in your memorized report group, and then click **OK**.

18 Close the A/P Aging Summary window.

Karen forwards these detail reports to Donna, who can now follow up on the Walking on Water outstanding accounts receivable of $15,000 that she believes is left over from when they bought the company January 1. She also plans to follow up on the Fantasy Sports receivable and to pay the Malibu Boats accounts payable soon.

Exporting Reports to Excel

Karen explains that in QuickBooks Accountant you can export any reports you create to Microsoft's Excel spreadsheet program.

"Why export to Microsoft Excel when QuickBooks Accountant gives us so many report options?" you ask.

Karen explains that she may occasionally need to change a report's appearance or contents in ways that are not available within QuickBooks Accountant. Since the changes you make in Excel do not affect your QuickBooks Accountant data, you can freely customize a report as needed or even change report data in order to run "what if" scenarios.

Karen reads through QuickBooks Accountant Help and discovers that exporting a report to Excel is as simple as clicking a new button on the report's button bar. She suggests that the two of you experiment with this feature by exporting an income statement you have already memorized.

Video Demonstration

DEMO 11C - Exporting reports to Excel

To export a previously memorized report:

1 Open the Customized Income Statement that you previously memorized.

2 Click the **Excel** button on the report button bar.

3 Select **Create New Worksheet** from the submenu to display the Send Report to Excel window as shown in Figure 11.15.

4 Click the **Advanced** button in the Send Report to Excel window to view advanced options such as formatting and printing, as shown in Figure 11.16.

5 Make sure the options checked in the Advanced Excel Options window are the same as those shown in Figure 11.16. Click **OK**.

Figure 11.15

Exporting a Report

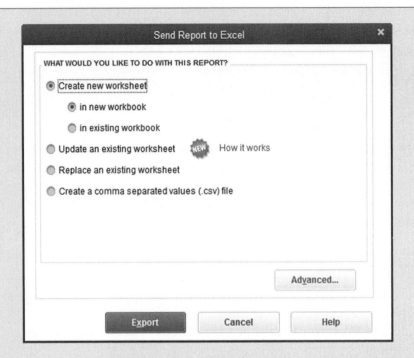

Figure 11.16

Advanced Options for Exporting a Report to Excel

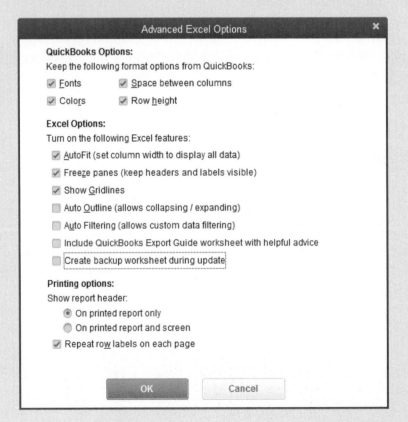

6   Now click **Export** in the Export Report window. Your Excel program
     will now be opened and the report exported into Excel.
     Trouble? To export reports to Excel, you must have Microsoft
     Excel 97 or higher installed on your computer. The figure shown below
     was created in Excel 2013. Your window may be different.

7   Select cell **F12** in the report just exported. Note that the export process
     has created a spreadsheet that has both numerical values and formulas,
     as shown in Figure 11.17.

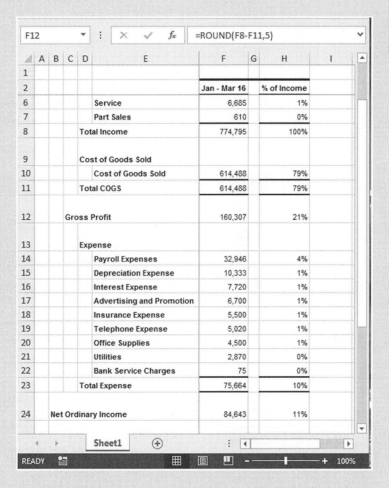

Figure 11.17

Exported Excel Report

8   Click **File** and then click **Print** in Excel. Note the header information
     reflects your previous modifications in QuickBooks Accountant.

9   Click **Page Setup** and then click the **Sheet** tab in the Page Setup
     window. Place a check mark in the **Gridlines** and **Row and column
     headings** check boxes. (This will enable the printing of gridlines and
     row and column headings.)

10 Click the **Page** tab then click the **Fit to:** option button to scale printing
     to one page wide and one page tall. Click the **Margins** tab and change
     the Top: margin to 1 and then click **OK**.

11 Click **Print** to print the Excel document you just created. Your spread-
     sheet should look like Figure 11.18.

Figure 11.18

Printed Excel Report

Wild Water Sports Ch 11
Income Statement
for the three months ended March 31, 2016

	A	B	C	D	E	F	G	H
1								
2						Jan - Mar 16		% of Income
3		Ordinary Income/Expense						
4				Income				
5					Boat Sales	767,500		99%
6					Service	6,685		1%
7					Part Sales	610		0%
8				Total Income		774,795		100%
9				Cost of Goods Sold				
10					Cost of Goods Sold	614,488		79%
11				Total COGS		614,488		79%
12			Gross Profit			160,307		21%
13				Expense				
14					Payroll Expenses	32,946		4%
15					Depreciation Expense	10,333		1%
16					Interest Expense	7,720		1%
17					Advertising and Promotion	6,700		1%
18					Insurance Expense	5,500		1%
19					Telephone Expense	5,020		1%
20					Office Supplies	4,500		1%
21					Utilities	2,870		0%
22					Bank Service Charges	75		0%
23				Total Expense		75,664		10%
24			Net Ordinary Income			84,643		11%
25			Other Income/Expense					
26				Other Income				
27					Other Income	3,000		0%
28					Interest Income	2,015		0%
29				Total Other Income		5,015		1%
30			Net Other Income			5,015		1%
31	Net Income					89,658		12%

12 Click **File** in Excel and then **Exit** to quit the Excel program.

13 Click **Yes** to save the spreadsheet in a safe location.

14 Close all windows in QuickBooks Accountant.

End Note

You've completed the reports for Donna and decide to deliver them to her office. After quickly skimming each report, she compliments both you and Karen on your fine work. Walking back to your office, you comment, "That's the first time I've ever created financial statements without using debits and credits. How is that possible?"

"All the debits and credits are done for you," Karen explains. "Tomorrow I'll show you that QuickBooks Accountant, in fact, still keeps data in a debit and credit format and can provide the traditional general ledger, journal entries, and trial balance procedures you are more familiar with."

Business Events Summary

Business Event	Process Steps	Page
Create and memorize a report	Company and financial from Reports Center	322
Create graphs	Various sections from the Reports Center	328
Create additional detail reports	Various sections from the Reports Center	333
Exporting reports to Excel	Export from individual reports	337

practice

Chapter 11 Questions

1. Explain how you can use QuickBooks Accountant to modify any report.
2. What are the optional columns available in the Modify Report window when you create a balance sheet?
3. What time periods are available for the columns of a balance sheet?
4. What options are available in the Fonts & Numbers tab for a balance sheet?
5. How do you resize a report that would normally print on two pages so that it will fit on one page?
6. When you create a balance sheet, what is the result of clicking the Collapse button?
7. What different graphs are available in QuickBooks Accountant?
8. Discuss why percentage changes identified in the budgeted vs. actual reports need to be interpreted carefully.
9. Describe the information available in the accounts receivable and accounts payable aging reports.
10. Describe the information available in the sales by item report.

Chapter 11 Matching

Select the letter of the item below that best matches the definitions that follow. Use the text or QuickBooks Accountant Help to complete this assignment.

a. Memorized reports

b. Sales Graph by Item

c. Sales Graph by Customer

d. Income and Expense Graph

e. Accounts Receivable Graph

f. Accounts Payable Graph

g. Sales by Customer Summary

h. Sales by Item Report

i. A/R Aging Summary

j. A/P Aging Summary

_____ A report listing amounts owed by customers and organized by date due.

_____ A report illustrating income and expense by month.

_____ A report listing amounts owed to vendors and organized by date due.

_____ A process to keep customized versions of various reports.

_____ A report illustrating amounts owed to vendors by aging period.

_____ A report illustrating sales by month and by item.

_____ A report listing sales by item for a period.

_____ A report illustrating sales by month and by customer.

_____ A report listing sales by customer for a period.

_____ A report illustrating amounts owed by customers by aging period.

Chapter 11 Exercises

Chapter 11 Exercise 1
GRAPHS

Restore the file Boston Catering Ch 11 (Backup) that you downloaded from the text web site and create the following graphs for the period 7/1/10 through 8/31/10 unless otherwise specified.

a. Income and expense graph by month by account.

b. Income and expense graph by month by customer.

c. Sales graph by item.

d. Sales graph by customer.

e. Accounts receivable graph as of 8/31/10.

f. Accounts payable graph as of 8/31/10.

Chapter 11 Exercise 2
ADDITIONAL REPORTS

Restore the file Boston Catering Ch 11 (Backup) that you downloaded from the text web site and create the following reports for the period 7/1/10 through 8/31/10 (unless otherwise specified) in a manner similar to that used in the chapter.

a. Sales by customer summary.

b. Sales by item summary.

c. Accounts receivable aging summary as of 8/31/10.

d. Accounts payable aging summary as of 8/31/10.

Chapter 11 Exercise 3
EXPORT TO EXCEL

Restore the file Boston Catering Ch 11 (Backup) that you downloaded from the text web site.

a. Create a standard profit and loss report for the month of August 2010 removing the date prepared, time prepared, and report basis from the header.

b. Export the report created in (a) above to Excel in a manner similar to that used in the chapter.

c. Print the resulting Excel worksheet with gridlines and row and column headlines.

Chapter 11 Assignments

Chapter 11 Assignment 1

ADDING MORE INFORMATION: WILD WATER SPORTS

Open the file you completed in this chapter, change the name in the company information section (My Company from the Company menu) to Wild Water Sports Ch 11A, and then create, memorize, and print the following reports, graphs, or spreadsheets. (*Hint:* Be sure to use the memorized reports you created before, where applicable, and just change the dates as appropriate. When memorizing do not replace the existing report if one existed. Instead memorize it as a new report adding Ch 11A to the name of the memorized report. For example, in (a) below you should memorize this report as Customized Income Statement Ch 11A.) As with all reports, remove the date prepared, time prepared, and report basis.

a. Income Statement for the four months ended 4/30/16 that includes a % of Income column, prepared with a left page layout and without cents, titled "Income Statement" and subtitled "for the four months ended April 30, 2016," and sorted by total from largest to smallest amount.

b. Balance Sheet as of 4/30/16 with a % of Column, without cents, and with a left page layout.

c. Sales Graph by Item for the four-month period ended 4/30/16.

d. Sales Graph by Customer for the four-month period ended 4/30/16.

e. Income and Expense by Account graph for the four-month period ended 4/30/16.

f. Accounts Receivable graph as of 4/30/16.

g. Accounts Payable graph as of 4/30/16.

h. Collapsed Sales by Customer Summary Report for the four-month period ended 4/30/16, sorted by total from largest to smallest amount with month columns.

i. Sales by Item Summary Report for the four-month period ended 4/30/16, where columns display total only.

j. Collapsed Accounts Receivable Aging Summary Report as of 4/30/16.

k. Collapsed Accounts Payable Aging Summary Report as of 4/30/16.

l. Export item (a) to Excel, and then print the Excel worksheet with gridlines and row and column headers.

Chapter 11 Assignment 2

ADDING MORE INFORMATION: CENTRAL COAST CELLULAR

Restore the file Central Coast Cellular Ch 11 (Backup) that you downloaded from the text web site, and use that copy to create and print the following. Be sure to remove the date prepared, time prepared, and report basis fields where appropriate, and memorize where possible in a report group called Solutions. When memorizing you can choose to replace the existing report if one existed or add the chapter number to the title. (i.e. Balance Sheet Ch 11)

a. Income Statement for the month ended 1/31/14 with a left page layout and without cents, including a % of Income column. Use the title "Income Statement" and the subtitle "January 2014," and sort by total from largest to smallest amount.

b. Balance Sheet as of 1/31/14 with a % of Column, without cents, and with a left page layout.

c. Sales Graph by Item for the month ended 1/31/14.

d. Sales Graph by Customer for the month ended 1/31/14.

e. Income and Expense by Account graph for the month ended 1/31/14.

f. Accounts Receivable graph as of 1/31/14.

g. Accounts Payable graph as of 1/31/14.

h. Sales by Customer Summary Report for the month ended 1/31/14, sorted by total from largest to smallest amount with month columns.

i. Sales by Item Summary Report for the month ended 1/31/14, where columns display total only.

j. Accounts Receivable Aging Summary Report as of 1/31/14.

k. Accounts Payable Aging Summary Report as of 1/31/14.

l. Export item (a) to Excel, and then print the Excel worksheet with gridlines and row and column headers.

Chapter 11 Assignment 3
ADDING MORE INFORMATION: SANTA BARBARA SAILING

Restore the file Santa Barbara Sailing Ch 11 (Backup) that you downloaded from the text web site, and use that copy to create and print the following. As before, be sure to remove the date prepared, time prepared, and report basis fields where appropriate, and memorize where possible in a report group called Solutions. When memorizing you can choose to replace the existing report if one existed or add the chapter number to the title. (i.e. Balance Sheet Ch 11)

corporation

service

a. Income Statement for the month ended 7/31/15 with a left page layout and without cents, including a % of Income column, titled "Income Statement," and sorted by total from largest to smallest amount.

b. Balance Sheet as of 7/31/15, with a % of Column, without cents, and with a left page layout.

c. Sales Graph by Item for the month ended 7/31/15.

d. Income and Expense Graph by Account for the month ended 7/31/15.

e. Sales by Customer Summary Report for the month ended 7/31/15.

f. A/R Aging Summary Report as of 7/31/15.

g. A/P Aging Summary Report as of 7/31/15.

h. Export item (a) to Excel, and then print the Excel worksheet with gridlines and row and column headers.

Chapter 11 Assignment 4

ADDING MORE INFORMATION: DRONE CITY

Restore the file Drone City Ch 11 (Backup) that you downloaded from the text web site. Use that copy to create and print the following. As before, be sure to remove the date prepared, time prepared, and report basis fields where appropriate, and memorize where possible in a report group called Solutions. When memorizing you can choose to replace the existing report if one existed or add the chapter number to the title. (i.e. Balance Sheet Ch 11)

a. Income Statement for the month ended 1/31/17 with a left page layout and without cents, including a % of Income column, titled "Income Statement," and sorted by total from largest to smallest amount.

b. Balance Sheet as of 1/31/17, with a % of Column, without cents, and with a left page layout.

c. Sales Graph by Item for the month ended 1/31/17.

d. Income and Expense Graph by Account for the month ended 1/31/17.

e. Sales by Customer Summary Report for the month ended 1/31/17.

f. A/R Aging Summary Report as of 1/31/17.

g. A/P Aging Summary Report as of 1/31/17.

h. Export item (a) to Excel, and then print the Excel worksheet with gridlines and row and column headers.

Chapter 11 Cases

Chapter 11 Case 1

FOREVER YOUNG

In Chapter 10, you added some transactions to your QuickBooks Accountant file for Forever Young. Make a copy of that file, and use that copy to create and print the following. Be sure to remove the date prepared, time prepared, and report basis fields where appropriate, and memorize where possible in a report group called Solutions. When memorizing you can choose to replace the existing report if one existed or add the chapter number to the title. (i.e. Balance Sheet Ch 11)

Requirements:

1 Income Statement for the month ended 1/31/15 with a left page layout without cents, including a % of Income column, titled "Income Statement," and sorted by total from largest to smallest amount.

2 Balance Sheet as of 1/31/15, with a % of Column, without cents, and with a left page layout.

3 Sales Graph by Item for the month ended 1/31/15.

4 Income and Expense Graph by Account for the month ended 1/31/15.

5 Sales by Customer Summary Report for the month ended 1/31/15.

6 A/R Aging Summary Report as of 1/31/15.

7 A/P Aging Summary Report as of 1/31/15.

8 Export item (1) to Excel, and then print the Excel worksheet with grid-lines and row and column headers.

Chapter 11 Case 2

OCEAN VIEW FLOWERS

In Chapter 10, you added some transactions to your QuickBooks Accountant file for Ocean View Flowers. Make a copy of that file, and use that copy to create and print the following. Be sure to remove the date prepared, time prepared, and report basis fields where appropriate, and memorize where possible in a report group called Solutions. When memorizing you can choose to replace the existing report if one existed or add the chapter number to the title. (i.e. Balance Sheet Ch 11)

Requirements:

1 Income Statement for the two months ended 2/29/16 with a left page layout and without cents, including a % of Income column, titled "Income Statement" and subtitled "for the two months ended February 29, 2016," and sorted by total from largest to smallest amount.

2 Balance Sheet as of 2/29/16 with a % of Column, without cents, and with a left page layout.

3 Sales Graph by Item for the two-month period ended 2/29/16.

4 Sales Graph by Customer for the two-month period ended 2/29/16.

5 Income and Expense by Account graph for the two-month period ended 2/29/16.

6 Accounts Receivable graph as of 2/29/16.

7 Accounts Payable graph as of 2/29/16.

8 Sales by Customer Summary Report for the two-month period ended 2/29/16, sorted by total from largest to smallest amount with month columns.

9 Sales by Item Summary Report for the two-month period ended 2/29/16, where columns display total only.

10 Accounts Receivable Aging Summary Report as of 2/29/16.

11 Accounts Payable Aging Summary Report as of 2/29/16.

12 Export item (1) to Excel, and then print the Excel worksheet with grid-lines and row and column headers.

Chapter 11 Case 3

ALOHA PROPERTIES

In Chapter 10, you added some transactions to your QuickBooks Accountant file for Aloha Properties. Make a copy of that file, and use that copy to create and print the following. Be sure to remove the date prepared, time prepared, and report basis fields where appropriate, and memorize where possible in a report group

called Solutions. When memorizing you can choose to replace the existing report if one existed or add the chapter number to the title. (i.e. Balance Sheet Ch 11)

Requirements:

1 Income Statement for the two months ended 2/29/14 with a left page layout and without cents, including a % of Income column, titled "Income Statement" and subtitled "for the two months ended February 29, 2014," and sorted by total from largest to smallest amount.

2 Balance Sheet as of 2/29/14 with a % of Column, without cents, and with a left page layout.

3 Sales Graph by Item for the two-month period ended 2/29/14.

4 Sales Graph by Customer for the two-month period ended 2/29/14.

5 Income and Expense by Account graph for the two-month period ended 2/29/14.

6 Accounts Receivable graph as of 2/29/14.

7 Accounts Payable graph as of 2/29/14.

8 Sales by Customer Summary Report for the two-month period ended 2/29/14, sorted by total from largest to smallest amount with month columns.

9 Sales by Item Summary Report for the two-month period ended 2/29/14, where columns display total only.

10 Accounts Receivable Aging Summary Report as of 2/29/14.

11 Accounts Payable Aging Summary Report as of 2/29/14.

12 Export item (1) to Excel, and then print the Excel worksheet with grid-lines and row and column headers.

Chapter 11 Comprehensive Problems

Comprehensive Problem 1: SPORTS CITY

Restore the Sports City (Backup) file that you downloaded from the text web site. Record the following business events in chronological order (remember, dates are in the month of April 2015).

Chronological List of Business Events

Event #	Date	Business Event
1	4/16/15	Received a bill for $250 from Office Max for supplies purchased on account (record as Supplies, an expense; terms: due on receipt).
2	4/17/15	Received items and entered a bill from Nike for previously recorded Purchase Order No. 1 (terms: due on receipt).
3	4/20/15	Received items and entered a bill from Wilson Sporting Goods for previously recorded Purchase Order No. 2 (terms: due on receipt).

Event #	Date	Business Event
4	4/20/15	Hired a new employee, Anne Franks (112 East Fir #3, Lompoc, CA 93436), a single woman with Social Security number 233-89-4232. She will earn an hourly wage of $8.00, will be paid semi-monthly like all employees, and is subject to all payroll taxes including the training tax.
5	4/20/15	Received on account from Cabrillo High School a $400 payment, which is grouped with other undeposited funds.
6	4/21/15	Invoiced Buena Vista Elementary (a new customer) for 100 shirts and 5 footballs.
7	4/22/15	Received on account from Lompoc High School a $600 payment, which is also grouped with other undeposited funds.
8	4/24/15	Borrowed $10,000 from Mid-State Bank with a short-term note payable.
9	4/24/15	Paid all bills due by 4/30/15 starting with Check No. 6.
10	4/27/15	Invoiced Cabrillo High School for 75 basketball shoes, 75 shirts, 75 shorts, 50 running shoes, 150 soccer balls, and 20 sports bags (terms: net 15).
11	4/29/15	Deposited by mail all previously received but undeposited payments, totaling $1,000, to Mid-State Bank.
12	4/30/15	Paid all employees for the pay period 4/16–4/30. Ms. Franks worked 75 hours during this period. Start with Check No. 12. (See tax information in Table 11.1.)
13	4/30/15	Recorded depreciation of $2,000 on furniture & fixtures.
14	4/30/15	Recorded the expiration of $3,000 in prepaid rent.
15	4/30/15	Reclassified the advance payment of $1,000 made by Arroyo Grande High School to Unearned Revenue (a new account).
16	4/30/15	Reconciled the bank account. The ending bank balance shown on the statement was $5,333.52. The bank charged a $40 service charge. Checks for the April 30 payroll do not appear on the statement, nor does the $1,000 deposited by mail on April 29. (Print a reconciliation summary report.)
17	4/30/15	Budget information for April through June 2015 is given in Table 11.2.

Item	Anne	Kelly	Sam	
Earnings	600.00	1,250.00	1,458.33	**Table 11.1**
Federal Withholding	−73.00	−147.00	−244.00	Earnings Information for
Social Security Employee	−37.20	−77.50	−90.41	Sports City
Medicare Employee	−8.70	−18.12	−21.14	
CA Withholding	−7.66	−40.72	−57.39	
CA Disability Employee	−3.00	−6.25	−7.29	
CA Employee Training Tax	0.60	1.25	1.46	
Social Security Employer	37.20	77.50	90.41	
Medicare Employer	8.70	18.12	21.14	
Federal Unemployment	4.80	10.00	11.66	
CA Unemployment	0.30	0.62	0.73	
Check Amount	470.44	960.41	1,038.10	

Account	April 09	Following
Sales	$30,000	15% increase each month thereafter
Cost of Sales	18,000	60% of sales
Depreciation Expense	2,000	Constant each month thereafter
Payroll Expenses	6,500	$500 increase each month thereafter
Rent	3,000	Constant each month thereafter
Telephone	100	5% increase each month thereafter
Utilities	200	5% increase each month thereafter

Table 11.2

Budget Information for Sports City

Create, memorize, and print the following reports with no date prepared, time prepared, or report basis fields.

a.   Transaction List by Date for April 2015 in landscape orientation.

b.   Profit & Loss Standard for April 2015 with a % of Income column.

c.   Balance Sheet Standard as of 4/30/15 with a % of Column.

d.   Statement of Cash Flows for April 2015.

e.   Profit & Loss Budget vs. Actual for April 2015.

f.   Profit & Loss Budget Overview for April 2015 through June 2015.

g.   Sales by Customer Summary Report for the month ended 4/30/15, sorted by total from largest to smallest amount with month columns.

h.   Sales by Item Summary Report for the month ended 4/30/15, sorted by total from largest to smallest amount with total only columns in landscape orientation.

i.   Accounts Receivable Aging Summary Report as of 4/30/15.

j.   Income and Expense by Account graph for the month ended 4/30/15.

k.   Export the Balance Sheet created in (c) to Excel, and then print the Excel worksheet with gridlines and row and column headers.

l.   Reconciliation Summary as of 4/30/15.

Comprehensive Problem 2: PACIFIC BREW

This is a continuation of the Pacific Brew comprehensive problem from Chapter 7. Make a copy of the QuickBooks Accountant file you created for Pacific Brew in that chapter. Record the following business events in chronological order (remember, dates are in the month of January 2016).

Chronological List of Business Events

Event #	Date	Business Event
1	1/17/16	Received items and entered a bill from Purchase Order No. 1003 to Lost Coast.
2	1/17/16	Received a bill for $2,500 from Staples (a new vendor) for supplies purchased on account (terms: net 15). These supplies will be used over the next six months; thus, you will need to create a Supplies (other current asset) account.

corporation

merchandising

Event #	Date	Business Event
3	1/17/16	Using Purchase Order No. 1004, ordered from Lost Coast 1,000 of item #402, 1,500 of item #403, and 2,000 of item #404 for immediate delivery (terms: net 15).
4	1/17/16	Using Purchase Order No. 1005, ordered from Mad River 750 each of items #302, #303, #304, and #305 for immediate delivery (terms: net 30).
5	1/18/16	The manager believes that the company charges too little for its products and therefore increases all product prices 50%. (Search QuickBooks Accountant Help on prices to find out how to increase sales prices of items by a percentage. Be sure your new prices are 50% higher and not $50 higher!)
6	1/19/16	Using Purchase Order No. 1006, ordered from Humboldt 500 each of items #502, #506, and #507 for immediate delivery (terms: net 15).
7	1/20/16	Received and shipped an order to Bon Jovi's for 200 units of item #302, 150 units of item #303, and 100 units of item #507. Invoice No. 7001 was generated to bill the customer on terms of net 15.
8	1/20/16	Received and shipped an order to Ocean Grove for 100 units each of items #302, #304, and #305. Invoice No. 7002 was generated to bill the customer (terms: net 15).
9	1/23/16	Received and shipped an order to Avalon Bistro for 150 units each of items #502, #506, and #507. Invoice No. 7003 was generated to bill the customer (terms: net 30).
10	1/24/16	Received items and entered a bill from Purchase Order No. 1004 to Lost Coast.
11	1/24/16	Received a bill for $500 from Verizon (a new vendor) for January telephone expenses (terms: due on receipt).
12	1/24/16	Received a bill for $1,500 from the City of Arcata (a new vendor) for January utilities (terms: due on receipt).
13	1/26/16	Received a $4,575 check from Bon Jovi's on account (Invoice No. 7001), which will be deposited later in the week.
14	1/26/16	Received an advance on future orders from River House in the amount of $1,200, a check that will be deposited later in the week.
15	1/27/16	Deposit checks received earlier in the week to checking account.
16	1/30/16	Received items and entered a bill from Purchase Order No. 1005 to Mad River.
17	1/30/16	Paid bills from Verizon, City of Arcata, and Staples for a total of $4,500, using Check Nos. 110, 111, and 112, respectively.
18	1/30/16	Received and shipped an order (5007) to Hole in the Wall for 250 units each of items #303, #305, and #404. Payment of $7,032.50 was deposited and mailed to the checking account that same day.
19	1/31/16	Paid employees starting with Check No. 113. During the period, Duarte worked 83 hours and Lopez worked 79 hours. See tax information in Table 11.3.

Table 11.3

Earnings Information for Pacific

Item	Emilio Duarte	Michael Patrick	Shawn Lopez
Earnings	913.00	2,083.33	948.00
Federal Withholding	−125.08	−285.42	−129.88
Social Security Employee	−56.61	−129.17	−58.78
Medicare Employee	−13.24	−30.21	−13.75
CA Withholding	−50.22	−114.58	−52.14
CA Disability	−4.57	−10.42	−4.74
CA Employee Training Tax	0.91	2.08	0.95
Social Security Employer	56.61	129.17	58.78
Medicare Company	13.24	30.21	13.75
Federal Unemployment	7.30	16.67	7.58
CA Company Unemployment	27.39	62.50	28.44
Check Amount	663.28	1,513.53	688.71

Event #	Date	Business Event
20	1/31/16	Recorded depreciation of $800 for the month with journal entry no. 1.
21	1/31/16	Recorded supplies expense (a new expense account) of $400 with journal entry no. 2.
22	1/31/16	Reclassified payment of $1,000 from River House to Unearned Revenue (a new other current liability account) with journal entry no. 3.
23	1/31/16	Accrued interest income (a new other income account) on Short-Term Investments of $2,000 with journal entry no. 4.
24	1/31/16	Accrued interest expense of $2,600 to Accrued Expenses (a new other current liability account) with journal entry no. 5.
25	1/31/16	Reconciled the Wells Fargo bank account. No bank service charges were noted on the bank statement. The ending bank balance was $31,173.30. All deposits were recorded by the bank except the $7,032.50 deposit of 1/30/16. All checks cleared the bank except those issued for payroll on 1/31/16.
26	1/31/16	Budget information for January through March is as follows. Consulting revenue is expected to remain constant at $15,000 per month. Sales of $20,000 are expected in January, increasing $5,000 each month thereafter. Cost of goods sold of $15,000 is expected in January, increasing $2,500 each month thereafter. Depreciation, interest, rent, and office supplies expenses are expected to remain constant at $1,000, $2,000, $2,500, and $500, respectively. Telephone expenses of $450 are budgeted for January and are expected to increase $50 each month thereafter. Payroll expenses are budgeted at $8,500 for January and February and then at $10,000 for March. Utilities expenses are budgeted at $1,200 for January and are expected to increase by 5% each month thereafter. Interest income of $1,500 is expected each month.

Create, memorize, and print the following reports with no date prepared, time prepared, or report basis fields. When memorizing you can choose to replace the existing report if one existed or add the chapter number to the title. (i.e. Balance Sheet Ch 11)

a. Transaction List by Date for January 2016 in landscape orientation.

b. Profit & Loss Statement for January 2016 with a % of Income column using a right layout and without cents. Sort by total, largest to smallest.

c. Balance Sheet as of 1/31/16 with a % of Column with a right layout and without cents.

d. Statement of Cash Flows for January 2016 with a right layout and without cents.

e. Profit & Loss Budget vs. Actual for January 2016, without cents, sorted by total (largest to smallest).

f. Profit & Loss Budget Overview for January 2016 through March 2016, without cents, sorted by total (largest to smallest).

g. Sales by Customer Summary Report for the month ended 1/31/16, sorted by total (from largest to smallest amount) with month columns.

h. Sales by Item Summary Report for the month ended 1/31/16, without cents, sorted by total (from largest to smallest amount) with total only columns and in landscape orientation.

i. Income and Expense by Account graph for the month of January 2016.

j. Inventory Stock Status by Item report for January 2016.

k. Export the Profit & Loss Statement created in (b) to Excel, and then print the Excel worksheet with gridlines and row and column headers.

l. Reconciliation Summary as of 1/31/16.

Comprehensive Problem 3: SUNSET SPAS

This is a continuation of the Sunset Spas comprehensive problem from Chapter 7. Make a copy of the QuickBooks Accountant file you created for Sunset in that chapter. Record the following business events in chronological order (remember, dates are in the month of January 2015).

corporation

Chronological List of Business Events

merchandising

Event #	Date	Business Event
1	1/17/15	Paid $18,000 in liability insurance for the year to Hartford Insurance (a new vendor) using Check No. 111. (**Hint:** Record this in a new other current asset account called Prepaid Insurance.)
2	1/17/15	Received a bill for $500 from Staples (a new vendor) for office supplies purchased on account. Terms are net 30. (All supplies are expected to be consumed this month.)
3	1/17/15	Using Purchase Order No. 5003, ordered from Cal Spas one each of items #301, #302, and #303 for immediate delivery (terms: net 30).
4	1/18/15	Sold two of item #302 to Landmark Landscaping (a new customer, located at 8500 Ridgefield Place, San Diego, CA 92129) with six hours of installation (item #100) on sales Invoice No. 6004 (terms: net 15).
5	1/18/15	Sold two of item #202 and one of item #302 to Marriott Hotels with 15 hours of installation on sales Invoice No. 6005 (terms: net 15). Marriott Hotels had paid an advance toward future sales on 1/16/15; apply any remaining credit to this invoice when prompted.

Event #	Date	Business Event
6	1/20/15	Hired a new employee, Walton Perez (530 Miramar Rd., Apt. 230, San Diego, CA 92145), who is a single man with Social Security number 323-99-2394. He will earn an hourly wage of $9.00, will be paid semi-monthly, and is subject to all payroll taxes. He will start work 2/1/15.
7	1/21/15	Received a bill for $25,000 from Outlet Tool Supply for tools and equipment used for installation and support of spa services; terms of net 30. (Record as furniture and equipment.)
8	1/22/15	Deposited a $3,500 check from a new customer, Kristen's Spa Resort, for work to be performed next month. (Record this as a customer payment.)
9	1/23/15	Received a $23,000 bill from the City of San Diego for licenses and permits (a new expense account), payable with terms of net 15.
10	1/24/15	Sold three of item #203 to Pam's Designs with 18 hours of installation on sales Invoice No. 6006 (terms: net 15).
11	1/25/15	Received a $1,400 bill from Verizon for telephone installation and services; terms of net 15. (Record as telephone expense.)
12	1/28/15	Took delivery of a shipment from Cal Spas (our Purchase Order No. 5003). All items were received (terms: net 30).
13	1/28/15	Received $5,000 payment on account from Landmark Landscaping; this payment was deposited into the checking account.
14	1/30/15	Paid in full two bills (from City of San Diego and from Verizon) with Check Nos. 112 and 113, respectively.
15	1/31/15	Paid employees. During the period, Sanchez worked 84 hours and Lee worked 67 hours. Checks are to be handwritten starting with Check No. 114. See tax information in Table 11.4.
16	1/31/15	Sold four of item #201, three of item #202, two of item #301, and two of item #303 to a new customer, Hilton Hotels (Invoice No. 6007). Collected payment of $90,510, which was deposited the same day.
17	1/31/15	Recorded the expiration of $1,500 in prepaid insurance costs to the Insurance Expense account with journal entry no. 3.
18	1/31/15	Recorded depreciation expense of $1,750 with journal entry no. 4.

Table 11.4

Earnings Information for Sunset

Item	Bryan Christopher	Loriel Sanchez	Sharon Lee
Hours	n/a	84	67
Rate	$60,000.00	$ 13.00	$ 12.00
Earnings	2,500.00	1,092.00	804.00
Federal Withholding	−342.50	−149.60	−110.15
Social Security Employee	−155.00	−67.70	−49.85
Medicare Employee	−36.25	−15.83	−11.66
CA Withholding	−137.50	−60.06	−44.22
CA Disability	−12.50	−5.46	−4.02
CA Employee Training Tax	2.50	1.09	0.80
Social Security Employer	155.00	67.70	49.85
Medicare Company	36.25	15.83	11.66
Federal Unemployment	20.00	8.74	6.43
CA Unemployment	6.25	2.73	2.01
Check Amount	1,816.25	793.35	584.10

Event #	Date	Business Event
19	1/31/15	Accrued interest expense on note payable for $1,000 with journal entry no. 5. (*Hint:* Create a new other current liability account titled "Accrued Expenses.")
20	1/31/15	Accrued interest income on Short-Term Investments (a new account) for $75 with journal entry no. 6.
21	1/31/15	Reconciled the bank account. There were no bank service charges. The bank statement balance was $63,803.08 at 1/31/15, and Check Nos. 104, 114, 115, and 116 had not yet been paid. One deposit, made on 1/28/15 for $5,000, was not reflected on the bank statement.
22	1/31/15	Budget information for January through March is as follows. Merchandise sales of $170,000 are expected in January, increasing $10,000 per month thereafter. Service sales of $10,000 are expected in January, increasing $1,000 per month thereafter. Cost of goods sold are expected to be 75% of merchandise sales. Depreciation, insurance, interest, office supplies, rent, and telephone are expected to remain constant at $1,800, $1,500, $1,000, $500, $3,000, and $1,500, respectively. A one-time license and permit fee of $20,000 was expected for January. Payroll expenses are estimated at $10,000 per month.

Create, memorize, and print the following reports with no date prepared, time prepared, or report basis fields. When memorizing you can choose to replace the existing report if one existed or add the chapter number to the title. (i.e. Balance Sheet Ch 11)

a. Transaction List by Date for the period 1/17/15–1/31/15 in landscape orientation.

b. Profit & Loss Statement for January 2015 with a % of Income column, without cents, and centered.

c. Balance Sheet as of 1/31/15 with a % of Column, without cents, and centered.

d. Statement of Cash Flows for January 2015 without cents and centered.

e. Reconciliation Summary for January 2015 without cents and centered.

f. Profit & Loss Budget vs. Actual for January 2015 without cents and centered.

g. Profit & Loss Budget Overview for January 2015 through March 2015 without cents and centered.

h. Collapsed Sales by Customer Summary Report for the month ended 1/31/15, sorted by total (from largest to smallest amount) with total only columns, centered and without cents.

i. Sales by Item Summary Report for the month ended 1/31/15, sorted by total (from largest to smallest amount) with total only columns, centered, without cents, and in landscape orientation.

j. Accounts Receivable Aging Summary Report as of 1/31/15.

k. Accounts Payable Aging Summary Report as of 1/31/15.

l. Export the Profit & Loss Statement created in (b) to Excel, and then print the Excel worksheet with gridlines and row and column headers.

Comprehensive Problem 4: BRIDGETTE SWEET PHOTOGRAPHY

corporation

service

merchandising

Restore the backup you made for Bridgette Sweet Photography in Chapter 7. Change the company name to include Ch 11 at the end so that the new company name is Bridgette Sweet Photography Ch 11. Add the following business events:

Chronological List of Business Events

Event #	Date	Business Event
1	2/1/13	Transferred funds from checking into a new short-term investments account (type other current assets) with ETrade in the amount of $7,000 using journal entry 18.
2	2/4/13	Wrote check 9851 for $1,800 to GEICO (new vendor) to prepay auto insurance for one year beginning 2/1/13. Create a new other current asset account.
3	2/5/13	Created two new jobs: 436 for IPAD and 437 for Boss Design both new customers. Both new jobs are for photo shoots. Received and deposited check 2309 from an IPAD in the amount of $12,000 related to job 436.
4	2/6/13	Received and deposited check 9432 as payment on account from Foster Corporation in the amount of $3,000.
5	2/7/13	Received an invoice from Chicago Electric (new vendor) for utilities consumed in January 2013. Paid $234 with check 9852 charging it to utilities expense.
6	2/8/13	Wrote check 9853 for $370.53 to Bank of Chicago (new vendor) as payment of note payable. This was the payment due on 1/31/13 of which $70 was applied to interest expense.
7	Various	Created new time sheets for all employees based on the table below. Remember, Bridgette bills her time using service items 1000 or 1010 depending on the event. Depending on the event, Garrett bills his time using service items 1001 or 1011 and Pease bills his time using service items 1002 or 1012 or both.
8	2/15/13	Created purchase order 6415 to US Photo (US) for 100 prints for job 435 and 200 prints and five albums for job 436. Prints cost was reduced to $21 and albums cost $75 each. (Be sure to update item costs accordingly.) Items are for customer pickup. All items ordered on this purchase order were picked up on 2/19 and billed with US Photo invoice 10622. Created purchase order 6416 to Peterson Framing (PF) for 20 frames at a cost of $150 each for inventory to be shipped via Airborne. Frames were received on 2/16 with invoice 8926.
9	2/20/13	Invoiced Krenwinkle for job 435 for photo shoot time, prints, and 10 frames on invoice 10210 for $9,021.45. Applied payment received on 1/30 against this invoice. Invoiced customer IPAD for photo shoot time and expenses and 12 frames on invoice 10211 for $13,010.86. Applied payment received on 2/5 against this invoice. Both customers are charged sales tax.
10	2/22/13	Received and deposited check 974123 as payment on account from Benson job 434 in the amount of $4,346.10 and check 23908 for $10,000 as advance payment on future services from Foster.
11	2/27/13	Paid sales tax owed as of 1/31/13 to the Illinois Department of Revenue using check 9854.

Event #	Date	Business Event
12	2/28/13	Paid employees with checks 9855–9857 based on the table shown after all events. Paid bills due as of 2/28/13 for a total amount of $10,100 using checks 9858–9859.
13	2/28/13	Reconciled the regular checking account as of 2/28/13. Checks 9854–9859 have not yet cleared the bank. Bank charges amount to $60. The statement ending balance is $35,438.75.
14	2/28/13	On 3/4/13 the company created invoice 10212 to Customer ID: BD for job 437. No prints or albums were ordered but 5 frames were delivered on 2/28. Time sheets indicate hours had been incurred and sales tax was collected. Record this invoice on 3/4/13 and accrue sales (Corporate Events and Sales) and the cost of goods sold as of 2/28/13 using journal entry reference 19.
15	1/31/13 and 2/28/13	Accrued utility expense as of 1/31/13 related to January but paid on 2/7 with check 9852 using journal entry reference 20. Accrue interest expense related to 1/31/13 but paid on 2/8 with check 9853 using journal entry reference 21. (*Hint:* Accrue in January and set up for reversal in February using a new other current liability account called "Accrued Liabilities.") Also accrue utility expense of $250 and interest expense of $68.25 on 2/28/13 using journal entry references 22 and 23, respectively.
16	2/28/13	Adjusted prepaid expenses for one month of insurance expense based on the previously deferred cost incurred on 2/4 using journal entry reference 24.
17	2/28/13	Adjusted accounts receivable for the $10,000 received from Foster Corporation on 2/22/13 to unearned revenue (a new other current liability account) using journal entry reference 25.
18	1/31/13 and 2/28/13	Recorded depreciation expense of $450 each for January and February ($250 for furniture and $200 for equipment) using journal entry references 26 and 27.
19	2/28/13	Recorded loss on sale of short-term investments as other income (a new account) of $300 using journal entry reference 28.
20	2/28/13	Budget data is shown in a table below.
21	2/1/13 and 3/1/13	Reverse accrual entries on the first day of the month following the accrual. For example, all accruals as of 1/31/13 should be reversed 2/1/13 and so on. Start with journal entry reference 29. Reverse journal entry references 19, 20, 21, 22, 23, and 25.

Employee Timesheet Information

Date	Customer/Job ID	Service Item	Billing Status	Sweet	Garrett	Pease
2/01/13			Non-Billable		6	6
2/02/13	Krenwinkle/435	1000	Billable	8		
2/02/13	Krenwinkle/435	1001	Billable		8	
2/02/13	Krenwinkle/435	1002	Billable			7
2/11/13			Non-Billable		8	8
2/12/13			Non-Billable		8	8
2/15/13	IPAD/436	1010	Billable	8		
2/15/13	IPAD/436	1011	Billable		8	
2/15/13	IPAD/436	1012	Billable			8
2/22/13			Non-Billable		6	8
2/23/13	Boss Design/437	1010	Billable	12		
2/23/13	Boss Design/437	1011	Billable		7	
2/23/13	Boss Design/437	1012	Billable			5
Total				28	51	50

Employee Payroll Information

Pay/Tax/Withholding	Sweet	Garrett	Pease
Hours	n/a	51	50
Salary/Hourly Rate	$60,000.00	$ 25.00	$ 20.00
Gross Pay	5,000.00	1,275.00	1,000.00
Federal Withholding	−685.00	−174.68	−137.00
Social Security Employee	−310.00	−79.05	−62.00
Medicare Employee	−72.50	−18.49	−14.50
State Withholding	−347.33	−64.23	−43.33
Social Security Employer	310.00	79.05	62.00
Medicare Company	72.50	18.49	14.50
Federal Unemployment	40.00	10.20	8.00
State Unemployment	150.00	38.25	30.00
Check Amount	3,585.17	938.55	743.17

Budget Data

Income Statement Budget Data	January	February
Weddings	3,000	3,000
Corporate Events	4,000	4,000
Sales	15,000	18,000
Other Income	0	0
Cost of Goods Sold	7,500	9,000
Bank Service Charges	0	0
Depreciation Expense	450	450
Insurance Expense	150	150
Interest Expense	80	80
Payroll Expense	7,350	7,850
Rent Expense	1,750	1,750
Utilities	200	225

Balance Sheet Budget Data	1/31/13	2/28/13
Checking Account	10,970	12,000
Short-Term Investment	0	7,000
Accounts Receivable	36,000	44,000
Inventory Asset	1,000	900
Furniture	10,000	10,000
Equipment	10,000	10,000
Accumulated Depreciation Furniture	−2,250	−2,500
Accumulated Depreciation Equipment	−1,200	−1,400
Accounts Payable	10,000	15,985
Sales Tax Payable	1,500	3,000
Payroll Liabilities	2,500	5,000
Notes Payable	12,000	12,000
Capital Stock	15,000	15,000
Retained Earnings	23,520	29,015

Create, memorize, and print the following reports with no date prepared, time prepared, or report basis fields. When memorizing you can choose to replace the existing report if one existed or add the chapter number to the title. (i.e. Balance Sheet Ch 11)

a.   Transaction List by Date for the period 2/1/13–3/31/13 in landscape orientation.

b.   Balance Sheet Budget Overview report from 1/1/13 to 2/28/13.

c.   Profit & Loss Budget Overview report from 1/1/13 to 2/28/13.

d.   Balance Sheet Budget vs. Actual report from 2/1/13 to 2/28/13.

e.   Profit & Loss Budget vs. Actual report from 2/1/13 to 2/28/13.

f.   Statement of Cash Flows for February 2013 without cents and centered.

g.   Reconciliation Summary for February 2013.

h.   Collapsed Sales by Customer Summary Report for the month ended 2/28/13, sorted by total (from largest to smallest amount) with total only columns, centered, and without cents.

i.   Sales by Item Summary Report for the month ended 2/28/13, sorted by total (from largest to smallest amount) with total only columns, centered, without cents, and in landscape orientation.

j.   Accounts Receivable Aging Summary Report as of 2/28/13.

k.   Accounts Payable Aging Summary Report as of 2/28/13.

l.   Export the Profit & Loss Budget vs. Actual created in (e) to Excel, and then print the Excel worksheet with gridlines and row and column headers.

Comprehensive Problem 5: CRYSTAL CLEAR POOL

Restore the backup you made for Crystal Clear Pool Service in Chapter 7. Change the company name to include Ch 11 at the end so that the new company name is Crystal Clear Pool Service Ch 11. Add the following business events:

sole proprietorship

service

merchandising

Chronological List of Business Events

Event #	Date	Business Event
1	11/1/2012	Invoiced customers AG, HR, PD, and WS 40 hours each for pool services to be rendered in November using invoice numbers 10139–10142 with sales tax.
2	11/5/2012	Received the following payments from customers on account and deposited amounts the same day: check 8852 from customer PD for $5,777, check 124891 from customer HR for $7,300, VISA payment 6579514 from customer WS for $5,300.
3	11/6/2012	Created purchase order 45 to Cactus Pool Supply for the purchase of $1,850 in parts needed for repair work being completed for Adobe Grand (AG) on a new job Pool Repairs. Also created purchase order 46 to Sun Systems for the purchase of $1,200 in parts needed for repair work to be done for Hilton Resorts (HR) on a new job Pool Repairs.
4	11/9/2012	Received parts ordered on purchase order 45 from Cactus Pool Supply on its invoice 585421 and purchase order 46 from Sun Systems on its invoice 2323.
5	11/12/2012	Completed job HR Pool Repairs and invoiced the customer on invoice number 10143 for 10 hours in pool repairs and for parts reimbursement for a total of $2,597.

Event #	Date	Business Event
6	11/13/2012	Purchased cleaning supplies from Cactus Pool Supply in the amount of $1,200 using check 295 and charged the purchase to a new other current asset account Supplies.
7	11/14/2012	Paid rent expense to Century 21 Leasing using check 296 for $1,789.
8	11/15/2012	Wrote check 297 to Goldman Sachs (a new vendor with vendor name GS) for $5,000 as a short-term investment (a new other current asset account).
9	11/26/2012	Invoiced customers AG, HR, PD and WS for pool supplies consumed in November using invoice numbers 10144–10147 with sales tax. Customer AG—20 units of chlorine, 9 units of pool shock, and 4 units of pool algaecide. Customer HR—22 units of chlorine, 9 units of pool shock, and 3 units of pool algaecide. Customer PD—16 units of chlorine, 7 units of pool shock, and 3 units of pool algaecide. Customer WS—28 units of chlorine, 15 units of pool shock, and 8 units of pool algaecide.
10	11/29/2012	Paid bill from SS for $3,200 using check 298. Received following payments from customers on account and deposited amounts immediately: check 8944 from customer WS for $5,300 for invoice 10142, check 125600 from customer HR for $5,300 for invoice 10140, VISA payment 6558411 from customer AG for $5,777 for invoices 10130 and 10135, and $4,000 from new customer Sheraton of Sedona (SOS) on check 301000 as an advance payment for work to be done in December.
11	11/29/12	Paid sales tax owed as of 10/31/12 to the Arizona Dept. of Revenue using check 299 for $1,623.12.
12	11/30/12	Paid employees with checks 300–301 based on the table below.
13	11/30/12	Reconciled the regular checking account as of 11/30/12. Checks 298, 300, and 301 have not yet cleared and the deposit made on 11/29/12 does not appear on the bank statement. Bank service charges amount to $23. The statement ending balance is $14,563.46.
14	11/30/12, 12/1/12, and 12/3/12	On 12/3/12 the company created invoice 10148 to customer AG pool repairs, which was completed on 11/30/12 after incurring five hours in pool repairs and for parts reimbursement for a total of $2,623.50 including sales tax. Record this invoice on 12/3/12 and accrue the effects of this invoice as of 11/30/12 using journal entry reference 123. Record a reversing entry 135 on 12/1/12.
15	10/31/12 and 11/30/12	Accrued utility expense of $500 and $550 for 10/31/12 and 11/30/12, respectively, but paid in December using journal entry references 124 and 125. Accrue interest expense of $117 and $115 for 10/31/12 and 11/30/12, respectively, but paid in December using journal entry references 126 and 127. (**Hint:** Don't set either of these up for reversal since they were not paid until December. Do set up a new current liability type account called "Accrued Liabilities.")
16	10/31/12 and 11/30/12	Adjusted prepaid expenses to insurance expense $500 for both October and November using journal entry references 128 and 129. Adjust supplies to office supplies expense for $350 of supplies used in November using journal entry reference 130. No supplies were used in October.
17	11/30/12	Adjusted accounts receivable for the $4,000 received from Sheraton of Sedona to unearned revenue (a new other current liability account) using journal entry reference 131.

Event #	Date	Business Event
18	10/31/12 and 11/30/12	Recorded depreciation expense of $200 each for October and November using journal entry references 132 and 133.
19	11/30/12	Recorded decline in market value of short-term investments (record in new account type other income with description Unrealized Loss) of $600 using journal entry reference 134
20	11/30/12	Input budget data shown in a table below.

Employee Payroll Information

Pay/Tax/Withholding	Patrick	Singh
Hours	155	162
Rate	$ 18.00	$ 20.00
Gross Pay	2,790.00	3,240.00
Federal Withholding	−382.23	−443.88
Social Security Employee	−172.98	−200.88
Medicare Employee	−40.46	−46.98
State Withholding	−111.60	−129.60
Arizona Job Training	2.79	3.24
Social Security Employer	172.98	200.88
Medicare Company	40.46	46.98
Federal Unemployment	19.53	22.68
State Unemployment	111.60	129.60
Check Amount	2,082.73	2,418.66

Budget Data

Income Statement Budget Data	October	November
Pool Service Revenue	20,000	20,000
Pool Supplies Revenue	2,000	2,000
Cost of Goods Sold	2,000	2,000
Depreciation Expense	200	200
Insurance Expense	500	500
Interest Expense	100	100
Office Supplies Expense	200	200
Payroll Expense	6,250	6,250
Rent Expense	1,800	1,800
Utilities Expense	500	500

Balance Sheet Budget Data	October	November
Checking	3,700	26,400
Accounts Receivable	30,000	25,000
Short-Term Investments	0	5,000
Supplies	0	0
Inventory Asset	4,000	2,000
Prepaid Expenses	2,500	2,000
Furniture and Equipment	22,000	22,000
Accumulated Depreciation	−2,200	−2,400
Accounts Payable	1,050	8,600
Unearned Revenue	0	0
Accrued Liabilities	500	500
Payroll Liabilities	2,000	4,000

Balance Sheet Budget Data	October	November
Sales Tax Payable	1,500	1,500
Notes Payable	20,000	20,000
Owners Draw	0	0
Owners Equity	34,950	45,400

Create, memorize, and print the following reports with no date prepared, time prepared, or report basis fields. When memorizing you can choose to replace the existing report if one existed or add the chapter number to the title. (i.e. Balance Sheet Ch 11)

a. Transaction List by Date for the period 10/31/12–12/3/12 in landscape orientation.

b. Balance Sheet Budget Overview report from 10/1/12 to 11/30/12.

c. Profit & Loss Budget Overview report from 10/1/12 to 11/30/12.

d. Balance Sheet Budget vs. Actual report from 10/1/12 to 11/30/12.

e. Profit & Loss Budget vs. Actual report from 10/1/12 to 11/30/12.

f. Statement of Cash Flows for November 2012 centered.

g. Reconciliation Summary for November 2012.

h. Collapsed Sales by Customer Summary Report for the month ended 11/30/12, sorted by total (from largest to smallest amount) with total only columns, centered and without cents.

i. Sales by Item Summary Report for the month ended 11/30/12, sorted by total (from largest to smallest amount) with total only columns, centered, without cents, and in landscape orientation.

j. Collapsed Accounts Receivable Aging Summary Report as of 11/30/12.

k. Collapsed Accounts Payable Aging Summary Report as of 11/30/12.

l. Export the Collapsed Accounts Receivable Aging Summary Report created in (i) to Excel, and then print the Excel worksheet with gridlines and row and column headers.

Managing Fixed Assets

Upon completion of this chapter, the student will be able to:

• Create a new client in the fixed asset management application
• Create and modify the fixed asset item list
• Synchronize the fixed asset item list with the fixed asset manager application
• Change fixed assets details
• Create a report of depreciation for a specific period
• Generate and post a depreciation adjusting journal entry
• Generate projections of future depreciation
• Account for the disposal of a fixed asset

Case: **Wild Water Sports, Inc.**

You have now prepared financial statements to send to the bank for Wild Water Sports' first three months. In doing so, Karen recalls that she deferred utilizing the Fixed Asset Manager application and just recorded the purchase and depreciation of furniture and equipment in the general ledger accounts. She explains that fixed assets (defined as long-term tangible property that a firm owns and uses in the production of its income and is not expected to be consumed or converted into cash any sooner than at least one year's time) are an important part of the company's business. QuickBooks Fixed Asset Manager calculates depreciation for fixed assets and lets you post QuickBooks Accountant journal entries using these calculated depreciation amounts.

"Do you recall that in the last several months we recorded the purchase of furniture and equipment from various vendors for $307,000 by simply recording a check or journal entry to the Furniture and Equipment general ledger account?" Karen asks.

"I do," you respond. "However, I don't remember specifying what assets we purchased or using any fixed asset manager."

"You are correct," Karen says. "I suggest we go back and modify those transactions to identify the specific assets that were acquired so that we can use the Fixed Asset Manager to track them and help us manage depreciation adjustments."

Karen explains that when the Fixed Asset Manager is started from within QuickBooks Accountant it pulls in information about fixed assets from an open company file. Then the accountant can determine depreciation for the assets and post a journal entry back to the company file. The accountant can also enter assets in the Fixed Asset Manager and send that information back to QuickBooks Accountant.

Fixed Asset Manager provides tight integration with QuickBooks Accountant data, a detailed, customizable asset entry screen, six depreciation bases (Book, State, Federal, Other, AMT, ACE), projected depreciation calculations, and disposition tracking.

Starting the Fixed Asset Manager Application

To begin, Karen offers to illustrate how to access the Fixed Asset Manager and how to create a new client.

Video Demonstration

DEMO 12A - Using the Fixed Asset Manager and modifying the Fixed Asset Item list

To start Fixed Asset Manager and create a new client:

1   Start QuickBooks Accountant.

2   Restore the Wild Water Sports Ch 12 (Backup) file that you downloaded from the text web site.

3   The newly restored Wild Water Sports Ch 12.qbw file should now be open.

4   From the Accountant menu click **Manage Fixed Assets** as shown in Figure 12.1.

Figure 12.1

Starting the Fixed Asset Manager

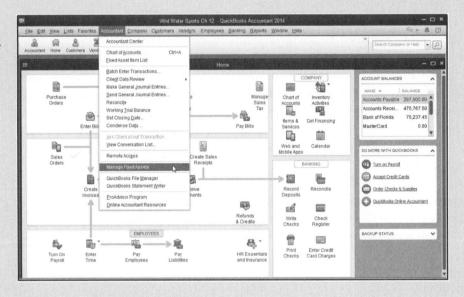

5   With the Create a new Fixed Assets Manager client options selected, click **OK** in the QuickBooks Fixed Asset Manager window.

6   Click **Next** in the New Client – Introduction window. Your window should look like Figure 12.2.

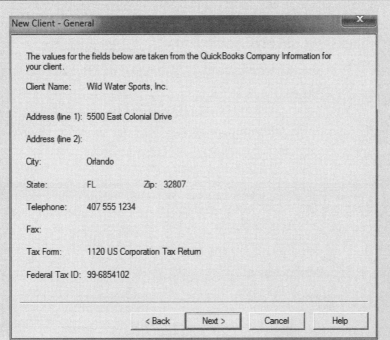

Figure 12.2

New Client Wizard

7   Click **Next** and then type **1/1/2016** in the Beginning of Year text box and then press [**Tab**]. 12/31/2016 should appear in the End of Year text box.

8   Click **Next** and then uncheck the **ACE**, **State**, **AMT**, and **Other** check boxes (leaving only the Federal and Book checkboxes checked) and then click **Next**.

9   Change the Book default depreciation method to **Straight line** and then click **Next**.

10   Accept the default selection to automatically bring into the Fixed Asset Manager both new and modified fixed asset items and then click **Next**.

11   Accept the default selection to automatically save into QuickBooks Accountant both new and modified fixed assets and then click **Next**.

12   Click **Finish** to complete the wizard. If a release notes window appears, close the window.

13   Close the Fixed Asset Manager for now.

"Now that the Fixed Asset Manager is set up, we need to populate the Fixed Asset Item List," says Karen.

Fixed Asset Item List

Karen explains that previously the two of you recorded the purchase of fixed assets using journal entries and checks. In both cases a debit was recorded to the Furniture and Equipment account, and no specific fixed asset was identified. If she had planned on using the Fixed Asset Manager, she would have recorded those transactions by creating a fixed asset item that would affect the Fixed Asset List. For now she decides to go back to those fixed assets recorded by a check and change them so that a fixed asset item is created. She explains that this process works for checks but not journal entries.

To modify the way previous fixed assets purchases (paid for using checks) were recorded:

1. Click **Chart of Accounts** from the QuickBooks Accountant Home page.

2. Double-click the **Furniture and Equipment** account to view the Furniture and Equipment account register shown in Figure 12.3.

Figure 12.3

Furniture and Equipment
Account Register

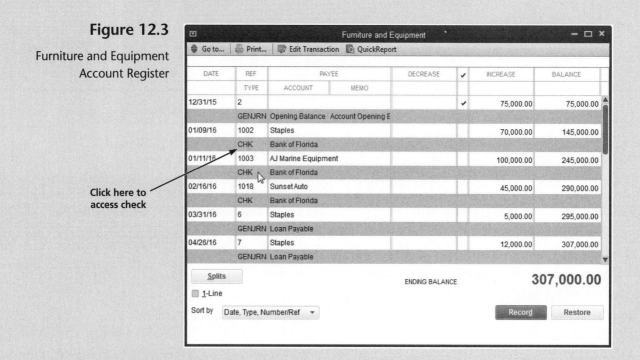

3. Double-click the **CHK** (representing the word check), located under the check number 1002, to view the underlying check used to pay for $70,000 worth of equipment as shown in Figure 12.4.

Figure 12.4

Check 1002

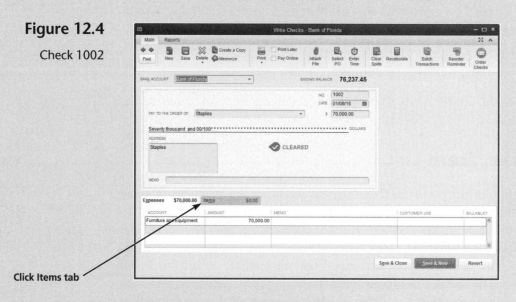

4 Click the **Expenses** tab and then delete the Account and Amount previously recorded.

5 Click the **Items** tab.

6 Select <**Add New**> from the top of the Item column drop-down list as shown in Figure 12.5.

Figure 12.5

Creating a New Fixed Asset Item

7 Select **Fixed Asset** from the Type drop-down list.

8 Type information about this fixed asset purchase as shown in Figure 12.6.

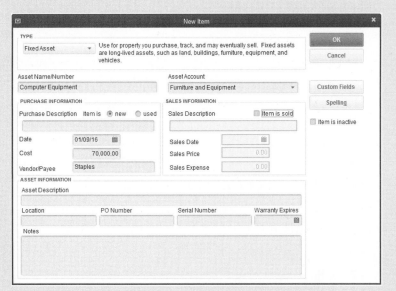

Figure 12.6

Entering a New Fixed Asset Item

9 Click **OK**.

10 Note that an error window appeared indicating that all fixed asset purchases must have a purchase description. Click **OK**.

11 Type **Computers, printers, and network** in the Purchase Description text box and then click **OK**.

12 Check 1002 has now been changed to reflect the purchase of specifically defined fixed assets. See Figure 12.7. Note that the Qty column is not available for use in this case.

Figure 12.7

Revised Check 1002

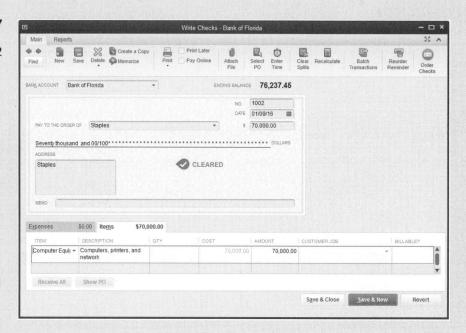

13 Click **Save & Close** and then click **Yes** to record changes.

14 Double-click **CHK** under check 1003.

15 Click the **Expenses** tab and then delete Account and Amount previously recorded.

16 Click the **Items** tab.

17 Click <**Add New**> in the Item column.

18 Click **Fixed Asset** from the Type drop-down list.

19 Type **Marine Equipment** as the Asset Name and as the Purchase Description, **1/11/16** as the date, and **100000** as the cost.

20 Select **Furniture and Equipment** as the Asset Account and then click **OK**. Your window should look like Figure 12.8.

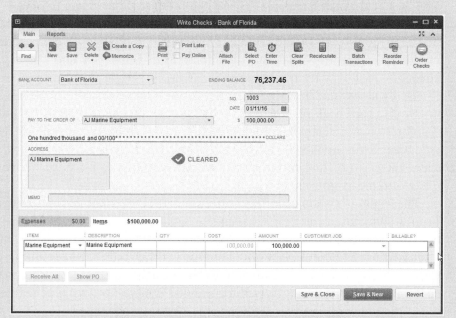

Figure 12.8

Revised Check 1003

21 Click **Save & Close** and then click **Yes** to record changes.

22 Double-click **CHK** under check 1018.

23 Click the **Expenses** tab and then delete Account and Amount previously recorded.

24 Click the **Items** tab.

25 Click <**Add New**> in the Item column.

26 Click **Fixed Asset** from the Type drop-down list.

27 Type **Truck** as the Asset Name and as the Purchase Description, **2/16/16** as the date, and **45000** as the cost.

28 Select **Furniture and Equipment** as the Asset Account and then click **OK**.

29 Click **Save & Close** and then click **Yes** to record changes.

30 Click **Fixed Asset Item List** from the Lists menu; modify the column widths to match Figure 12.9 by clicking and dragging the line between each column title.

Figure 12.9

Fixed Asset Item List

Click and drag
between each
column title
to resize the
column width

31 Do not close this list.

The Fixed Asset Item List reflects the modifications made to checks previously recorded. This list will be used later to update the Fixed Asset Manager.

"That takes care of the checks," Karen states. "Now we have to account for the journal entries that recorded fixed asset purchases and the beginning balance."

She explains that the fixed asset list is not integrated with the journal entry process like the check process is. In other words, if a check records the purchase of a fixed asset, and it is recorded using the Item tab like we just illustrated, the fixed asset list is updated. However, if a journal entry is used to record a purchase, there is no Item tab option. Thus the fixed asset list must be manually updated to record journal entry purchases.

The beginning balance in the Furniture and Equipment account represented furniture purchased on 1/1/15 that had an estimated useful life of 10 years with no expected salvage value. The journal entry on 3/31/16 represented a computer purchased for $5,000 using a note payable with an estimated useful life of five years with no expected salvage value. The journal entry on 4/27/16 represented a computer and printer purchased for $12,000 using a note payable with an estimated useful life of five years with no expected salvage value.

To manually update the Fixed Asset Item List:

1 In the Fixed Asset Item List (left open above), click **Item** and then click **New**.

2 Type **Furniture** as the Asset Name and as the Purchase Description, **1/1/15** as the date, and **75000** as the cost.

3 Select **Furniture and Equipment** as the Asset Account and then click **OK**.

4 Click **Item** and then click **New**.

5 Type **Computer** as the Asset Name and as the Purchase Description, **3/31/16** as the date, and **5000** as the cost.

6 Select **Furniture and Equipment** as the Asset Account and then click **OK**.

7 Click **Item** and then click **New**.

8 Type **Computer/Printer** as the Asset Name and as the Purchase Description, **4/27/16** as the date, and **12000** as the cost.

9 Select **Furniture and Equipment** as the Asset Account and then click **OK**. Your Fixed Asset Item List should now look like Figure 12.10.

Figure 12.10

Updated Fixed Asset Item List

10 Close the Fixed Asset Item List window, the Furniture and Equipment account window, and the Chart of Accounts window.

"The Fixed Asset Item List now lists assets with an aggregate cost of $307,000, which matches the furniture and equipment account on the general ledger," comments Karen. "Our next step is to start the Fixed Asset Manager application and use the newly modified Fixed Asset Item List as input."

Synchronizing the Fixed Asset Manager

Karen explains that now you'll reopen the Fixed Asset Manager and synchronize the newly created Fixed Asset Item List with the Fixed Asset Manager application.

To synchronize the Fixed Asset Item List with the Fixed Asset Manager:

1 From the Accountant menu, click **Manage Fixed Assets**. The Asset Synchronization Log shown in Figure 12.11 should appear.

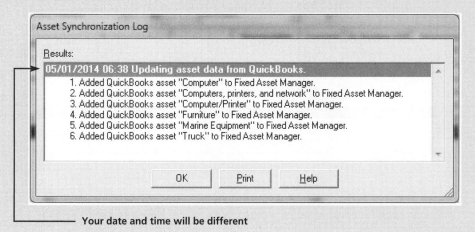

Figure 12.11

Asset Synchronization Log

2 Click **OK**. A portion of the updated Fixed Asset Manager is shown in Figure 12.12.

Figure 12.12

Updated Fixed Asset Manager (Partial Federal Tax View)

Click Book to view book depreciation

3 Click the **Book** tab at the bottom to switch from the Federal tax view to the Book view. Your window should now look like Figure 12.13.

Figure 12.13

Updated Fixed Asset Manager (Partial Book View)

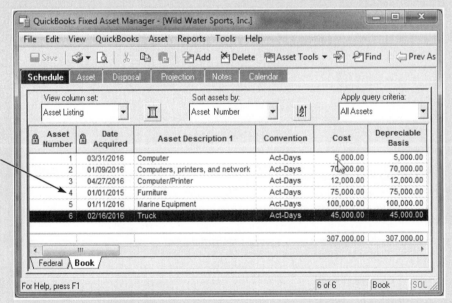

Double-click this fixed asset number

4 Double-click Asset Number **4**.

5 Resize the window so it looks like Figure 12.14.

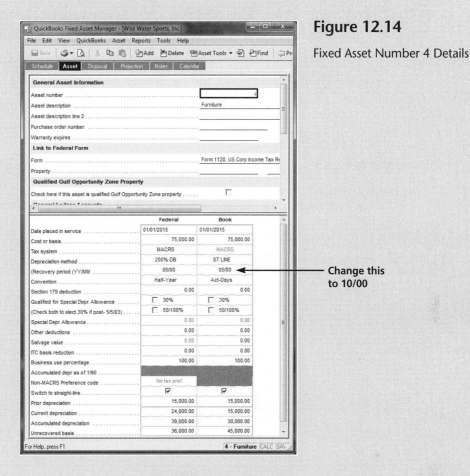

Figure 12.14

Fixed Asset Number 4 Details

Change this to 10/00

6 Click in the Recovery period row under the Book column and type **10/00** replacing the old recovery period of 05/00. (*Note:* The first two digits are years, the second two digits are months. The system defaults to a 5-year, 0-month recovery period otherwise known as useful life.) Once you change the recovery period, the depreciation amounts will change.

7 Click **Save** to save your changes. Note that in the Book column, prior depreciation under the 5-year recovery period was 15,000. Under the new 10-year recovery plan, prior depreciation is 7,500. (Do not close the Fixed Asset Manager.)

Depreciation Report

Now that you have synchronized the Fixed Asset List from within QuickBooks Accountant to the Fixed Asset Manager and have modified the recovery period for Asset Number 4, you can create a report to calculate depreciation for a specific period. Karen asks you to try it out by creating a book depreciation report for the three months ended 3/31/16. You are up to the task.

Video Demonstration

DEMO 12B - Depreciation using the Fixed Asset Manager

To create a depreciation report as of 3/31/16:

1 With the Fixed Asset Manager window still open, click the **Reports** menu in the Fixed Asset Manager and then click **Display Report. . . .**

2 Select the **Depreciation Schedule by G/L Account Number** report.

3 Choose the **Book** Use Basis option.

4 Type **3/31/16** as the Print depreciation through date. Your Print Preview window should look like Figure 12.15. (*Note:* Your printer will be different.)

Figure 12.15

Depreciation Report

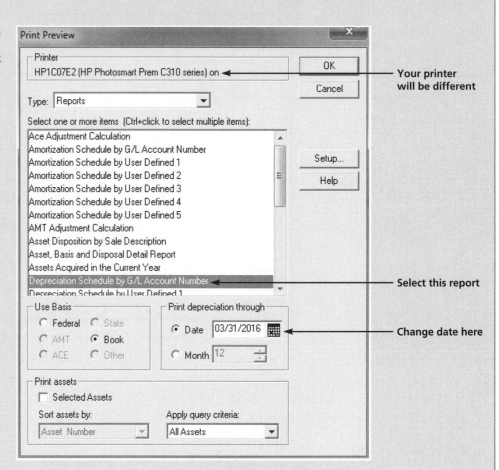

5 Click **OK** to view the report shown in Figure 12.16.

Figure 12.16

Depreciation Schedule

Book Basis

Wild Water Sports, Inc.
Depreciation Schedule by G/L Account Number
For the 3 Months Ended 03/31/16

Asset No.	Asset Description	Date Acquired	Method	Life	Sold?	Cost	AccumDepr 01/01/16	Current Depreciation	AccumDepr 03/31/16
15000 Furniture and Equipment									
4	Furniture	01/01/15	ST LINE	10/00	N	75,000.00	7,500.00	1,864.75	9,364.75
2	Computers, printers, and networ	01/09/16	ST LINE	05/00	N	70,000.00	0.00	3,174.86	3,174.86
5	Marine Equipment	01/11/16	ST LINE	05/00	N	100,000.00	0.00	4,426.23	4,426.23
6	Truck	02/16/16	ST LINE	05/00	N	45,000.00	0.00	1,106.56	1,106.56
1	Computer	03/31/16	ST LINE	05/00	N	5,000.00	0.00	2.73	2.73
	Total for (Furniture and Equipment)					295,000.00	7,500.00	10,575.13	18,075.13
	Client Subtotal Before Sales					295,000.00	7,500.00	10,575.13	18,075.13
	Less Assets Sold					0.00			0.00
	Total					295,000.00	7,500.00	10,575.13	18,075.13

6 Click **Print** to print and then click **Close** to close this report.

Depreciation Journal Entry

The report generated above identified depreciation expense of $10,575.13 for the period ended 3/31/16. Karen had already estimated depreciation for the period and recorded a journal entry recording depreciation expense of $10,333.00 for the same period. Now that she's using Fixed Asset Manager, she can create the correcting journal entry for the period and post it to QuickBooks Accountant. Note that the Fixed Asset Manager will compare the depreciation it calculates to the depreciation already recorded and create an entry to correct QuickBooks Accountant to match itself. First Karen needs to assign general ledger accounts to all assets.

To assign general ledger accounts and prepare and post the depreciation entry:

1 Click the **Schedule** tab on the Fixed Asset Manager if not already selected.

2 Click Asset Number **1**; then with the Shift Key held down, click Asset Number **6** such that all assets are selected.

3 Click the **Asset** menu item (not the Asset tab) in the Fixed Asset Manager, and then click **Assign G/L Accounts to Assets. . . .**

4 Select **Accumulated Depreciation** and **Depreciation Expense** as the appropriate accounts as shown in Figure 12.17.

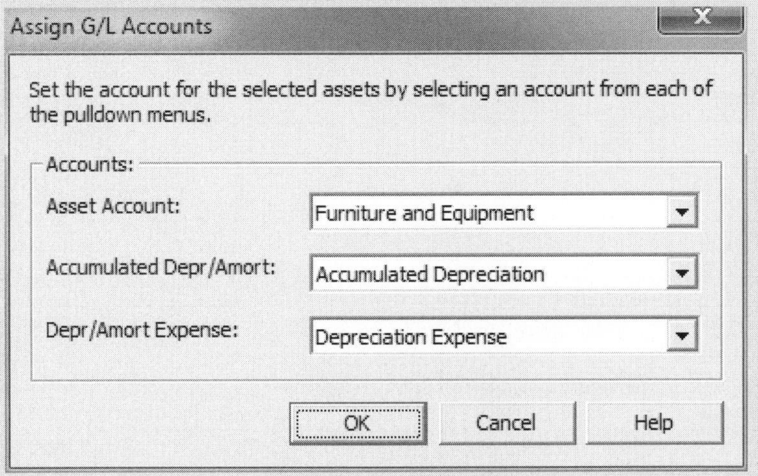

Figure 12.17

Assign G/L Accounts

5 Click **OK**.

6 Click the **QuickBooks** menu and then click **Post Journal Entry to QuickBooks. . . .**

7 Type **3/31/16** as the Depreciation through date.

8 Select **Book** as the Basis to post.

9 Be sure the Show Balances check box is checked. Your window should look like Figure 12.18. If your screen does not look like Figure 12.18 be sure you've selected "Book" as the Basis to post.

Figure 12.18

Post to QuickBooks General Journal

Change date to 3/31/2016

Balances per the Fixed Asset Manager

Change to Book

Make sure Show Balances is checked

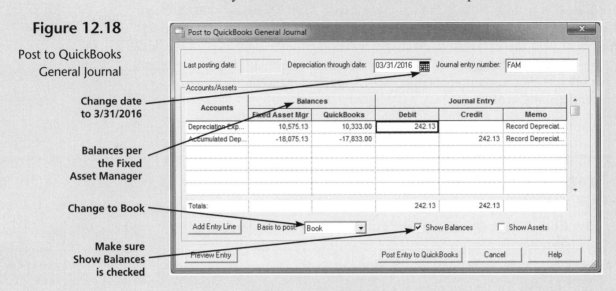

10 Click **Post Entry to QuickBooks**.

11 Check **Do not show again** if an alert window appears and then click **OK**.

12 Close the Fixed Asset Manager application.

13 Click **Chart of Accounts** from the Company section of the Home page.

14 Double-click **Accumulated Depreciation** to view the account register in Figure 12.19.

Figure 12.19

Accumulated Depreciation Register

Double-click here to view general journal

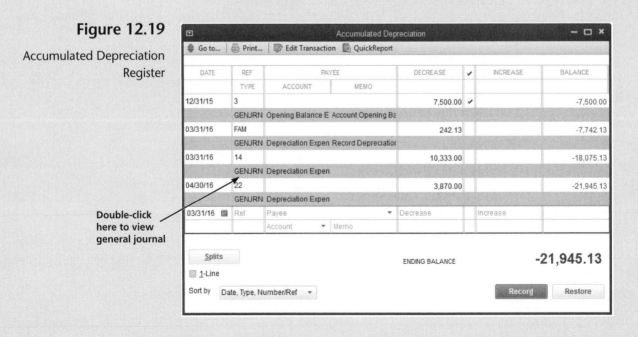

15 Double-click **GENJRNL** located underneath your recently posted adjustment from the Fixed Asset Manager to view the journal entry in full as shown in Figure 12.20.

Figure 12.20

Journal Entry to Adjust Depreciation

Click Print to print a General Journal Transaction report

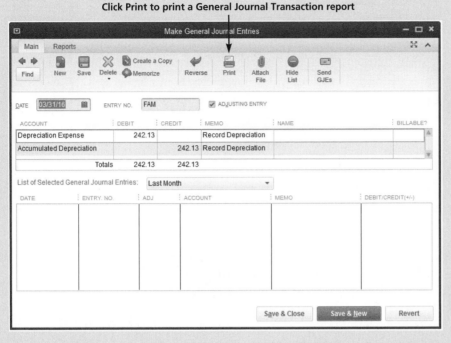

16 Click **Print** to print a General Journal Transaction report.

17 Close all windows and return to the Home page.

Projections of Future Depreciation

You are curious as to what depreciation will be in future years for any particular asset. Karen offers to demonstrate the Fixed Asset Manager's ability to produce a depreciation schedule.

To view a depreciation schedule for an asset:

1 Click **Manage Fixed Assets** from the Accountant menu to start the Fixed Asset Manager again.

2 Click the **Schedule** tab on the Fixed Asset Manager if not already selected.

3 Double-click Asset Number **4** (Furniture purchased 1/1/15).

4 Click the **Projection** tab to view the Federal tax depreciation schedule shown in Figure 12.21.

Figure 12.21

Tax Depreciation Schedule for
Asset Number 4

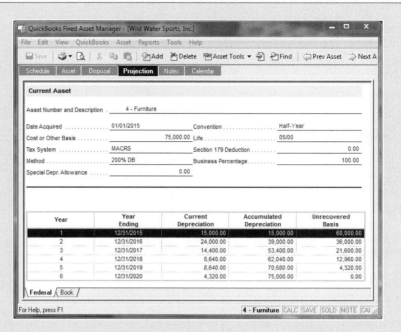

5   Click the **Book** tab at the bottom to view the Book depreciation
schedule for Asset Number 4 as shown in Figure 12.22.

Figure 12.22

Book Depreciation Schedule for
Asset Number 4

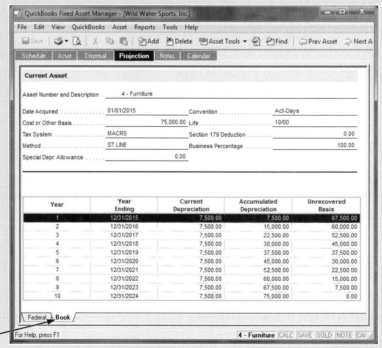

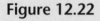

Be sure to click
the Book tab

6   Leave Asset Number 4 open.

Disposal of an Asset

If an asset is sold or otherwise disposed of, it must be accounted for in both QuickBooks Accountant and the Fixed Asset Management application. In other words, there is no integration between the two when it comes to asset disposition like there is with depreciation.

"I recall that when you sell or dispose of a fixed asset, financial accounting requires you to remove both the asset's cost and accumulated depreciation, record the proceeds from the sale, and record a gain or loss," you comment. "Is that the case here as well?"

"Yes," responds Karen. "Let me demonstrate assuming we sold part of Asset Number 4 on 4/1/16."

Karen explains that when this asset was recorded, it represented many different pieces of furniture. If part of an asset is sold, like an office desk, it must first be split off from the original asset. This must be done first, by defining what percentage of the old asset is being disposed of, before accounting for the disposal in both QuickBooks Accountant and Fixed Asset Manager.

To split an asset and then record the disposal of that asset:

1 Click the **Schedule** tab in the Fixed Asset Manager.

2 Select Asset Number **4**.

3 Select **Split Asset** from the Asset menu.

4 Type **5** in the Percent column of the (1) Furniture row on the Split asset: Furniture window and then press [**Tab**].

5 Type **95** in the Percent column of the (2) Furniture row on the Split asset: Furniture window and then press [**Tab**]. Your window should look like Figure 12.23.

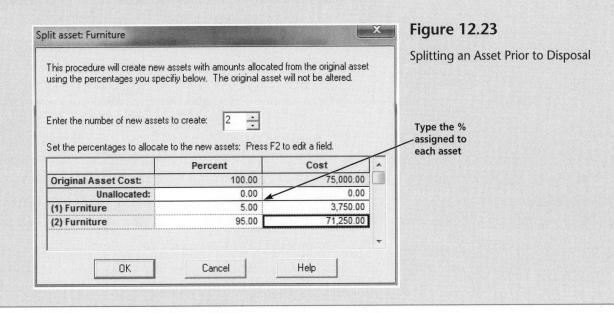

Figure 12.23

Splitting an Asset Prior to Disposal

6 Click **OK** and then click **Yes** to confirm.

7 Double-click Asset Number **7** (created when you split the asset above).

8 Type **Office Desk** as the Asset Description replacing (1) Furniture.

9 Click **Save** and then click the **Schedule** tab.

10 Double-click Asset Number **8** (created when you split the asset above).

11 Type **Office Furniture** as the Asset Description replacing (2) Furniture.

12 Click **Save** and then click the **Schedule** tab.

13 Select Asset Number **4** (the original asset just split), then click **Delete Asset** from the Asset menu, and then click **Yes** to confirm.

14 Click **Save Assets to QuickBooks** from the QuickBooks menu and then click **OK** with the **Both new and modified assets** option button selected.

15 Click **OK** when the Asset Synchronization Log appears. Your Schedule folder should look like Figure 12.24.

Figure 12.24

Revised Schedule Folder after Asset Split

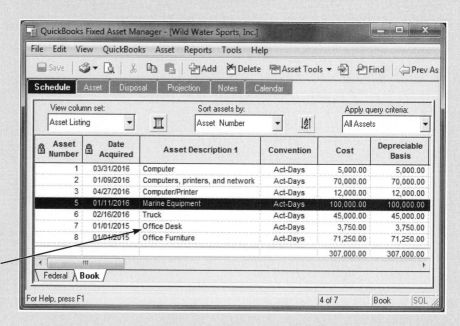

Note the two new assets with new asset descriptions and the removal of asset number 4

16 Select Asset Number **7**.

17 Click the **Disposal** tab.

18 Click in the **Yes** check box to indicate the asset has been sold

19 Type **Sale of Office Desk** as the description of the sale.

20 Type **4/1/16** as the date of disposal in the Federal column and then press [**Tab**] (it should then appear in the Book column as well).

21 Type **2000** as the Sales price in the Federal column and then press [**Tab**].

22 Type **100** as the Expense of sale in the Federal column and then press [**Tab**]. Your window should look like Figure 12.25.

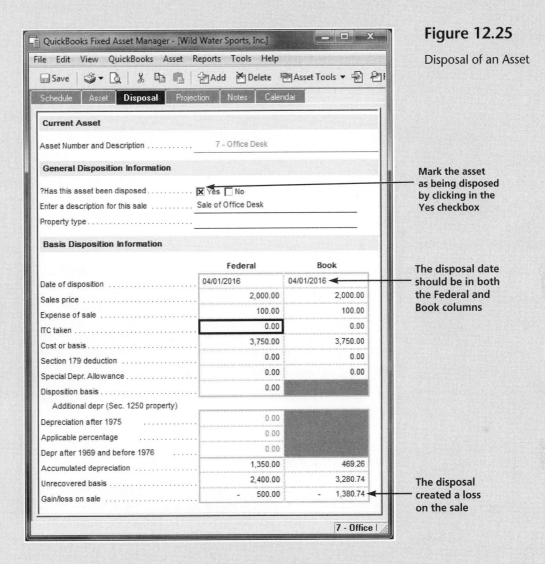

Figure 12.25

Disposal of an Asset

Mark the asset as being disposed by clicking in the Yes checkbox

The disposal date should be in both the Federal and Book columns

The disposal created a loss on the sale

23 Click **Save** to save your work.

24 Close the Fixed Asset Manager and then click **OK** in the Asset Synchronization Log. (If a message that Asset #8 changed appears, click **OK**.)

25 In QuickBooks Accountant, click **Company** from the menu bar and then click **Make General Journal Entries**.

26 Record the sale of the office desk based on the information provided in Figure 12.25 above. Your journal entry should look like Figure 12.26 below.

Figure 12.26

Journal Entry in QuickBooks Accountant to Record the Disposal of an Asset

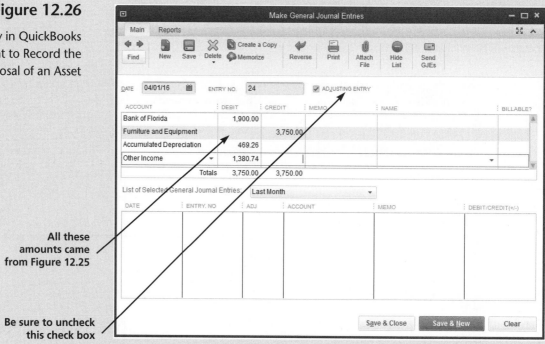

All these amounts came from Figure 12.25

Be sure to uncheck this check box

27   Click **Save & Close**.

28   Click **Manage Fixed Assets** from the Accountant menu.

29   Click **Display Report** from the Reports menu.

30   Select **Depreciation Schedule by G/L Account Number**.

31   Select the **Book** Use Basis option.

32   Type **4/30/16** as the Print depreciation through Date, and then click **OK**. Your report should look like Figure 12.27.

Figure 12.27

Depreciation Report for 4/30/16

Book Basis

Wild Water Sports, Inc.
Depreciation Schedule by G/L Account Number
For the 4 Months Ended 04/30/16

Asset No.	Asset Description	Date Acquired	Method	Life	Sold?	Cost	Accum Depr 01/01/16	Current Depreciation	Accum Depr 04/30/16
15000 Furniture and Equipment									
7	Office Desk	01/01/15	ST LINE	10/00	Y	3,750.00	375.00	94.26	469.26
8	Office Furniture	01/01/15	ST LINE	10/00	N	71,250.00	7,125.00	2,355.53	9,480.53
2	Computers, printers, and network	01/09/16	ST LINE	05/00	N	70,000.00	0.00	4,322.40	4,322.40
5	Marine Equipment	01/11/16	ST LINE	05/00	N	100,000.00	0.00	6,065.57	6,065.57
6	Truck	02/16/16	ST LINE	05/00	N	45,000.00	0.00	1,844.26	1,844.26
1	Computer	03/31/16	ST LINE	05/00	N	5,000.00	0.00	84.70	84.70
3	Computer/Printer	04/27/16	ST LINE	05/00	N	12,000.00	0.00	26.23	26.23
	Total for (Furniture and Equipment)					307,000.00	7,500.00	14,792.95	22,292.95
	Client Subtotal Before Sales					307,000.00	7,500.00	14,792.95	22,292.95
	Less Assets Sold					3,750.00			469.26
	Total					303,250.00	7,500.00	14,792.95	21,823.69

This report reflects the cost and accumulated depreciation of the asset sold

33   Print and then close the report.

34   Close the Fixed Asset Manager.

Karen summarizes the disposal effort as being a two-fold process. Step one: identify the asset being disposed and update the Fixed Asset Manager accordingly, and step two: record the general ledger effects of the disposal via a journal entry in QuickBooks Accountant.

End Note

You have now helped Karen use both QuickBooks Accountant and QuickBooks Fixed Asset Manager to account for the purchase, depreciation, and disposition of fixed assets.

Business Events Summary

Business Event	Process Steps	Page
Create new client	Use Manage Fixed Assets from Accountant menu	364
Fixed Asset Item List	Modify existing checks to reflect new fixed asset item or click Item and then click New from the Fixed Asset Item List	366
Synchronization	Use Manage Fixed Assets from Accountant menu after modifying the Fixed Asset List from within QuickBooks Accountant	371
Modify fixed asset	Double-click Asset Number from within Fixed Assets Manager	373
Depreciation report	Use Display Report from the Reports menu in Fixed Asset Manager	374
Depreciation entry	Use Post Journal Entry to QuickBooks from the QuickBooks Accountant menu in Fixed Asset Manager	375
Depreciation projections	Select an asset from the Fixed Assets Manager and then click the Projection tab	377
Asset disposal	Click Disposal tab from the Fixed Assets Manager and use the Make Journal Entries from QuickBooks Accountant	379

Chapter 12 Questions

1 What is the Fixed Asset Manager?

2 How do you create a new client for fixed asset management from within QuickBooks Accountant?

3 Describe the process for modifying a check, previously written to purchase a fixed asset, to establish a new fixed asset item in QuickBooks Accountant.

4 How is the fixed asset list automatically updated?

5 What circumstances require the fixed asset list to be manually updated?

6 When is the Fixed Asset Manager synchronized with the fixed asset list?

7 What information is provided by the Fixed Asset Manager's Depreciation Schedule by G/L Account Number report?

8 How does the Fixed Asset Manager calculate current period depreciation?

9 Can the Fixed Asset Manager provide you a schedule of future depreciation? If so, what information is part of this schedule?

10 Describe the financial accounting journal entry to record the sale/disposal of a fixed asset.

Chapter 12 Matching

Select the letter of the item below that best matches the definitions that follow. Use the text or QuickBooks Accountant Help to complete this assignment.

a. Fixed Asset Item List

b. Fixed Asset Manager

c. Fixed asset

d. Synchronization

e. Recovery period

f. Depreciation

g. Accumulated depreciation

h. Disposal date

_____ The transfer and update of any changed asset items from Fixed Asset Manager to the Fixed Asset Item List in QuickBooks Accountant.

_____ Estimated useful life of an asset.

_____ The process used to create two or more assets from one existing asset.

_____ Provides tight integration with QuickBooks Accountant data, a detailed, customizable asset entry screen, six depreciation bases (Book, State, Federal, Other, AMT, ACE), projected depreciation calculations, and disposition tracking.

_____ The process of allocating the cost expiration of tangible property against income.

_____ A long-term tangible piece of property that a firm owns and uses in the production of its income and is not expected to be consumed or converted into cash any sooner than at least one year's time.

_____ Shows the fixed asset items you've set up to track changes to the value of your fixed assets.

_____ Depreciation method that allows an equal amount of depreciation for each year in the asset's estimated life.

i. Split asset   _____ The amount of depreciation, including year-to-date depreciation, taken from an asset from the date the asset was placed in service.

j. Salvage value   _____ The date on which the asset was sold, lost, damaged, stolen, exchanged, used up, worn out, broken, retired, or given away.

k. Straight-line depreciation   _____ The value an asset is expected to have at the end of its useful life.

Chapter 12 Assignments

Chapter 12 Assignment 1

ADDING MORE INFORMATION: WILD WATER SPORTS

Restore the file Wild Water Sports Ch 12A (Backup) that you downloaded from the text web site, and then reflect the following additional events for April 2016:

*   4/1/16 – Purchased a portable building for $65,000 with a 12-year useful life, no salvage value, depreciated on a Sum of the Years Digits basis for financial accounting purposes by issuing check 1055 to AJ Marine Equipment. (**Hint**: Use the Item tab to record a new fixed asset item with a description "Portable Building.")

*   4/1/16 – Purchased a generator for $40,000 with a 6-year useful life, no salvage value, depreciated on a 200% Declining Balance basis for financial accounting purposes. This asset acquisition was accomplished with a 5-year loan payable to AJ Marine Equipment. (**Hint**: Record using a journal entry and then create a new fixed asset item with a description "Generator.")

Synchronize the newly modified Fixed Asset List with the Fixed Asset Manager, and then modify the two new assets in the Fixed Asset Manager to reflect the correct book depreciation methods, useful life, and general ledger accounts. (Note: once you start the Fixed Asset Manager you'll probably have to create a new client and set up accounts.) Post the depreciation journal entry to QuickBooks Accountant as of 4/30/16.

a. Print the Depreciation Schedule by G/L Account Number report from the Fixed Asset Manager using the book basis as of 4/30/16.

b. Print the journal entry in April 2016 that was posted by the Fixed Asset Manager. (**Hint**: Use the chart of accounts technique shown in the text to locate the journal.)

c. What is the expected book depreciation for the Portable Building in the third year ended 12/31/2018? (**Hint**: Use the Projection tab in the Fixed Asset Manager to reveal this information.)

Chapter 12 Assignment 2

ADDING MORE INFORMATION: CENTRAL COAST CELLULAR

Restore the file Central Coast Cellular Ch 12 (Backup) that you downloaded from the text web site, and then:

- Modify the 1/08/09 purchase of equipment using check 3002 to reflect the creation of a new fixed asset item using Equipment 1 as its purchase description and asset name.

- Modify the 1/22/09 purchase of equipment using check 3008 to reflect the creation of a new fixed asset item using Equipment 2 as its purchase description and asset name.

- Open the Fixed Asset Manager and create a new client.

- Synchronize the newly modified Fixed Asset List with the Fixed Asset Manager.

- Modify the two new assets in the Fixed Asset Manager to reflect straight-line book depreciation, a useful life of 10 years, and appropriate general ledger accounts for the asset, accumulated depreciation, and depreciation expense.

- Post the depreciation journal entry to QuickBooks Accountant as of 1/31/09 (*Note:* depreciation recorded in QuickBooks Accountant prior to using the Fixed Asset Manager was greater than that computed. Thus your journal entry will reflect a decrease in depreciation expense and accumulated depreciation.

a. Print the Depreciation Schedule by G/L Account Number report from the Fixed Asset Manager using the book basis as of 1/31/09.

b. Print the journal entry 1/31/09 that was posted by the Fixed Asset Manager. (**Hint**: Use the chart of accounts technique shown in the text to locate the journal.)

c. What is the expected book depreciation expense and ending accumulated depreciation for the Equipment 1 in the third year ended 12/31/2011? (**Hint**: Use the Projection tab in the Fixed Asset Manager to reveal this information.)

Chapter 12 Assignment 3

ADDING MORE INFORMATION: SANTA BARBARA SAILING

Restore the file Santa Barbara Sailing Ch 12 (Backup) that you downloaded from the text web site, and then do the following like you did in the chapter:

- Create a new client in the Fixed Asset Manager (current year 7/1/15–6/30/16, book depreciation method: straight-line).

- Modify fixed assets purchased with a check in QuickBooks Accountant. (Check 101 purchased a J-24 Boat [use J-24 as asset name and purchase description] with a life of 20 years being depreciated using the straight-line depreciation method.)

- Manually update the Fixed Asset Item List to account for the beginning balance in the Furniture and Equipment and Boat accounts in QuickBooks Accountant. The beginning balance in Furniture and Equipment represented $1,000 in office furniture that had been purchased on 3/1/15 and is depreciated using the straight-line depreciation method over four years and $1,450 in sailing equipment that had been purchased on 4/1/15 and is depreciated using the straight-line method over three years. The beginning balance in Boats represented several boats all purchased on 1/1/15 for $300,000 and depreciated using straight-line depreciation over 20 years.

- Synchronize the newly modified Fixed Asset Item List with the Fixed Asset Manager.

- Modify the new assets in the Fixed Asset Manager to reflect the correct useful life and general ledger accounts.

- Use the Split Asset process in the Fixed Asset Manager to allocate the $300,000 cost between the following assets: Catalina 28 (15%), Catalina 32 (25%), Catalina 42 (28%), and Catalina 50 (32%). Be sure to change the name of the newly created assets from (1) Boat to Catalina 28 etc. and to delete the original asset that was just split into four.

a. Create and print a Depreciation Schedule by G/L Account Number report on a book basis with depreciation through 7/31/2015.

b. Post the journal entry for the books basis as of 7/31/15 in the Fixed Asset Manager. You should notice that the resulting journal entry is out of balance. In this case, when the company first started using QuickBooks Accountant they failed to record accumulated depreciation when they first set the company up. The balancing adjustment at that time went to Capital Stock. Thus this journal entry (from the Fixed Asset Manager) must reduce the Capital Stock account to fix the error. To do so, once you request the journal entry in the Fixed Asset Manager, click the **Add Entry Line** button. Then add Capital Stock as an account and the type **7642.42** as the debit entry. Your entry should now be in balance. Now click **Post Entry to QuickBooks**. Now print the resulting journal entry recorded in QuickBooks Accountant. (***Hint***: Use the chart of accounts technique shown in the text to locate the journal.)

c. What is the expected book depreciation expense for the Catalina 32 in the second year ended 6/30/2016? (***Hint***: Use the Projection tab in the Fixed Asset Manager to reveal this information.)

d. What is the accumulated depreciation balance at 7/31/2015 for the company?

Chapter 12 Assignment 4

ADDING MORE INFORMATION: DRONE CITY

Restore the file Drone City Ch 12 (Backup) that you downloaded from the text web site and then do the following like you did in the chapter:

- Create a new client in the Fixed Asset Manager (current year 1/1/17–12/31/17, book depreciation method: straight-line).

- Modify fixed assets purchased with a check in QuickBooks Accountant. (Check 104 purchased three Max Transport drones [use Max Transport #1, Max Transport #2, and Max Transport #3 as asset names and purchase descriptions] with a life of 10 years being depreciated using the straight-line depreciation method. *Hint*: You are creating three different assets with an <u>effective start date</u> of **1/1/17** and cost of **$8,000** each.)

- Synchronize the newly modified Fixed Asset Item List with the Fixed Asset Manager.

- Modify the new assets in the Fixed Asset Manager to reflect a book useful life of 10 years and appropriate general ledger accounts (Furniture and Equipment and Accumulated Depreciation).

a. Create and print a Depreciation Schedule by G/L Account Number report on a book basis with depreciation through 1/31/2017.

b. Post the journal entry for the books basis as of 1/31/17 in the Fixed Asset Manager. Print the resulting journal entry recorded in QuickBooks Accountant. (*Hint*: Use the chart of accounts technique shown in the text to locate the journal.)

c. What is the expected book depreciation expense for the Max Transport #1 in the second year ended 12/31/18? (*Hint*: Use the Projection tab in the Fixed Asset Manager to reveal this information.)

d. Post the journal entry for the books basis as of 3/31/17 in the Fixed Asset Manager. Print the resulting journal entry recorded in QuickBooks Accountant.

e. Update the Fixed Asset Manager to reflect the sale of Max Transport #3 effective 3/31/17 for $6,000 cash. Create and print a Depreciation Schedule by G/L Account Number report on a book basis with depreciation through 3/31/2017.

f. Create and print a journal entry to reflect the disposal described above reflecting any gain or loss on the sale to a new other expense type of account called G/L on the Sale of Fixed Assets.

Payroll Taxes

Upon completion of this chapter, the student will be able to:

- Calculate federal income tax withholding
- Calculate Social Security and Medicare taxes
- Calculate federal unemployment taxes
- Learn about state income and unemployment taxes

Overview

Throughout this text, you have been provided information for employee payroll tax withholding and employer payroll tax expenses. QuickBooks Accountant has the ability to calculate each of these for you; however, they charge you an annual fee to do so. Some businesses will find this service very valuable and worth the cost, and some will not. Payroll tax computations are not straight-forward. They are, in fact, quite convoluted and depend on all sorts of exceptions and rules. For example, federal income tax withholding depends on an employee's income; how often he or she is paid (e.g., weekly, biweekly, semi-monthly, monthly); the number of exemptions claimed; filing status (married, single, or head of household); and so on.

This appendix is designed to provide you with a basic overview of the pay-roll tax conundrum and is focused on federal taxes only. Each state has its own rules for income tax withholding, unemployment, and so forth.

Federal Income Tax Withholding

As previously mentioned, federal income tax withholding depends on a number of factors. Guiding employers in this regard is Internal Revenue Service Circu-lar E (Employer's Tax Guide), which can be downloaded at **http://www.irs.gov/ pub/irs-pdf/p15.pdf**.

The IRS provides tables in this document for computing the specific amount to be withheld from each employee. It also provides a percentage method, which is much easier to produce for our purposes. Employees must supply employers with payroll tax information each year, such as their filing status (married, single, head of household) and the number of exemptions they are claiming.

To compute an employee's federal income tax withholding:

1 Determine the frequency of wage payments (weekly, biweekly, semi-monthly, monthly, etc.).

2 Determine the employee's filing status.

3 Based on the above, choose the appropriate table for Percentage Method of Withholding found in Figure A1.1. (*Note:* The IRS tables in this appendix are from 2014 and used as examples only. The concepts and formulas discussed here are applicable to the latest data, which can be downloaded from the IRS web site.)

Figure A1.1

Tables for Percentage
Method of Withholding

Percentage Method Tables for Income Tax Withholding

(For Wages Paid in 2014)

TABLE 1—WEEKLY Payroll Period

(a) SINGLE person (including head of household)—
If the amount of wages (after subtracting withholding allowances) is:
Not over $43 . . . . $0

Over—	But not over—	The amount of income tax to withhold is:	of excess over—
$43	—$218	$0.00 plus 10%	—$43
$218	—$753	$17.50 plus 15%	—$218
$753	—$1,762	$97.75 plus 25%	—$753
$1,762	—$3,627	$350.00 plus 28%	—$1,762
$3,627	—$7,834	$872.20 plus 33%	—$3,627
$7,834	—$7,865	$2,260.51 plus 35%	—$7,834
$7,865	. . . .	$2,271.36 plus 39.6%	—$7,865

(b) MARRIED person—
If the amount of wages (after subtracting withholding allowances) is:
Not over $163 . . . . $0

Over—	But not over—	The amount of income tax to withhold is:	of excess over—
$163	—$512	$0.00 plus 10%	—$163
$512	—$1,582	$34.90 plus 15%	—$512
$1,582	—$3,025	$195.40 plus 25%	—$1,582
$3,025	—$4,525	$556.15 plus 28%	—$3,025
$4,525	—$7,953	$976.15 plus 33%	—$4,525
$7,953	—$8,963	$2,107.39 plus 35%	—$7,953
$8,963	. . . .	$2,460.89 plus 39.6%	—$8,963

TABLE 2—BIWEEKLY Payroll Period

(a) SINGLE person (including head of household)—
If the amount of wages (after subtracting withholding allowances) is:
Not over $87 . . . . $0

Over—	But not over—	The amount of income tax to withhold is:	of excess over—
$87	—$436	$0.00 plus 10%	—$87
$436	—$1,506	$34.90 plus 15%	—$436
$1,506	—$3,523	$195.40 plus 25%	—$1,506
$3,523	—$7,254	$699.65 plus 28%	—$3,523
$7,254	—$15,667	$1,744.33 plus 33%	—$7,254
$15,667	—$15,731	$4,520.62 plus 35%	—$15,667
$15,731	. . . .	$4,543.02 plus 39.6%	—$15,731

(b) MARRIED person—
If the amount of wages (after subtracting withholding allowances) is:
Not over $325 . . . . $0

Over—	But not over—	The amount of income tax to withhold is:	of excess over—
$325	—$1,023	$0.00 plus 10%	—$325
$1,023	—$3,163	$69.80 plus 15%	—$1,023
$3,163	—$6,050	$390.80 plus 25%	—$3,163
$6,050	—$9,050	$1,112.55 plus 28%	—$6,050
$9,050	—$15,906	$1,952.55 plus 33%	—$9,050
$15,906	—$17,925	$4,215.03 plus 35%	—$15,906
$17,925	. . . .	$4,921.68 plus 39.6%	—$17,925

TABLE 3—SEMIMONTHLY Payroll Period

(a) SINGLE person (including head of household)—
If the amount of wages (after subtracting withholding allowances) is:
Not over $94 . . . . $0

Over—	But not over—	The amount of income tax to withhold is:	of excess over—
$94	—$472	$0.00 plus 10%	—$94
$472	—$1,631	$37.80 plus 15%	—$472
$1,631	—$3,817	$211.65 plus 25%	—$1,631
$3,817	—$7,858	$758.15 plus 28%	—$3,817
$7,858	—$16,973	$1,889.63 plus 33%	—$7,858
$16,973	—$17,042	$4,897.58 plus 35%	—$16,973
$17,042	. . . .	$4,921.73 plus 39.6%	—$17,042

(b) MARRIED person—
If the amount of wages (after subtracting withholding allowances) is:
Not over $352 . . . . $0

Over—	But not over—	The amount of income tax to withhold is:	of excess over—
$352	—$1,108	$0.00 plus 10%	—$352
$1,108	—$3,427	$75.60 plus 15%	—$1,108
$3,427	—$6,554	$423.45 plus 25%	—$3,427
$6,554	—$9,804	$1,205.20 plus 28%	—$6,554
$9,804	—$17,231	$2,115.20 plus 33%	—$9,804
$17,231	—$19,419	$4,566.11 plus 35%	—$17,231
$19,419	. . . .	$5,331.91 plus 39.6%	—$19,419

TABLE 4—MONTHLY Payroll Period

(a) SINGLE person (including head of household)—
If the amount of wages (after subtracting withholding allowances) is:
Not over $188 . . . . $0

Over—	But not over—	The amount of income tax to withhold is:	of excess over—
$188	—$944	$0.00 plus 10%	—$188
$944	—$3,263	$75.60 plus 15%	—$944
$3,263	—$7,633	$423.45 plus 25%	—$3,263
$7,633	—$15,717	$1,515.95 plus 28%	—$7,633
$15,717	—$33,946	$3,779.47 plus 33%	—$15,717
$33,946	—$34,083	$9,795.04 plus 35%	—$33,946
$34,083	. . . .	$9,842.99 plus 39.6%	—$34,083

(b) MARRIED person—
If the amount of wages (after subtracting withholding allowances) is:
Not over $704 . . . . $0

Over—	But not over—	The amount of income tax to withhold is:	of excess over—
$704	—$2,217	$0.00 plus 10%	—$704
$2,217	—$6,854	$151.30 plus 15%	—$2,217
$6,854	—$13,108	$846.85 plus 25%	—$6,854
$13,108	—$19,608	$2,410.35 plus 28%	—$13,108
$19,608	—$34,463	$4,230.35 plus 33%	—$19,608
$34,463	—$38,838	$9,132.50 plus 35%	—$34,463
$38,838	. . . .	$10,663.75 plus 39.6%	—$38,838

4 Determine the amount of wage payment.

5 Determine the number of employee withholding allowances.

6 Use Figure A1.2 to calculate the value of a single withholding allowance.

Table 5. Percentage Method—2014 Amount for One Withholding Allowance

Payroll Period	One Withholding Allowance
Weekly	$ 76.00
Biweekly	151.90
Semimonthly	164.60
Monthly	329.20
Quarterly	987.50
Semiannually	1,975.00
Annually	3,950.00
Daily or miscellaneous (each day of the payroll period)	15.20

Figure A1.2

One Withholding Allowance

7 Compute the employee's withholding amount by multiplying his or her withholding allowances by the value of a single withholding allowance just calculated.

8 Calculate net wages by subtracting the employee's withholding amount determined above from his or her wage payment.

9 Using net wages determined above, calculate the required federal income tax withholding using the table you selected from Figure A1.1.

Example 1: A single employee claiming two withholding allowances is paid $600 weekly.

To calculate the federal income tax withholding:

1 Frequency of wage payments: weekly.

2 Employee's filing status: single.

3 Appropriate table for Percentage Method of Withholding: Table 1.

4 Amount of wage payment: 600.

5 Number of employee withholding allowances: 2.

6 Value of a single withholding allowance: 76.00.

7 Employee's withholding amount: $2 \times 76.00 = 152.00$.

8 Net wages: $600.00 - 152.00 = 448.00$.

9 Required federal income tax withholding:
$17.50 + [15\% \times (448.00 - 218.00)] = 52.00$.

Example 2: A married employee claiming three withholding allowances is paid $1,500 semi-monthly.

To calculate the federal income tax withholding:

1   Frequency of wage payments: semi-monthly.

2   Employee's filing status: married.

3   Appropriate table for Percentage Method of Withholding: Table 3.

4   Amount of wage payment: 1,500.

5   Number of employee withholding allowances: 3.

6   Value of one withholding allowance: 164.60.

7   Employee's withholding amount: $3 \times 164.60 = 493.80$.

8   Net wages: $1,500.00 - 493.80 = 1,006.20$.

9   Required federal income tax withholding:
    $0.00 + [10\% \times (1,006.20 - 352.00)] = 65.42$.

Example 3: A married employee claiming five withholding allowances is paid $8,300 monthly.

To calculate the federal income tax withholding:

1   Frequency of wage payments: monthly.

2   Employee's filing status: married.

3   Appropriate table for Percentage Method of Withholding: Table 4.

4   Amount of wage payment: 8,300.

5   Number of employee withholding allowances: 5.

6   Value of one withholding allowance: 329.20.

7   Employee's withholding amount: $5 \times 329.20 = 1,646.00$.

8   Net wages: $8,300.00 - 1,646.00 = 6,654.00$.

9   Required federal income tax withholding:
    $151.30 + [15\% \times (6,654.00 - 2,217.00)] = 816.85$.

Social Security and Medicare Taxes

The Federal Insurance Contributions Act (FICA) provides for a federal system of old-age, survivors, disability, and hospital insurance. The old-age, survivors, and disability insurance part is financed by the Social Security tax. The hospital insurance part is financed by the Medicare tax. Each of these taxes is reported separately. Generally, you are required to withhold Social Security and Medicare taxes from your employees' wages, and you must also pay a matching amount of these taxes. Certain types of wages and compensation are not subject to Social Security taxes. Generally, employee wages are subject to Social Security and Medicare taxes regardless of the employee's age or whether he or she is receiving Social Security benefits.

Social Security and Medicare taxes have different rates, and only the Social Security tax has a wage base limit. The wage base limit is the maximum wage that is subject to the tax for the year. Determine the amount of withholding for Social Security and Medicare taxes by multiplying each payment by the employee tax rate. There are no withholding allowances for Social Security and Medicare taxes. In 2014 the employee tax rate for Social Security was 6.2% (amount withheld). The employer tax rate for Social Security is also 6.2% (12.4% total). The 2014 wage base limit was $117,000. The current employee tax rate for Medicare is 1.45% (amount withheld). The employer tax rate for Medicare tax is also 1.45% (2.9% total). There is no wage base limit for Medicare tax; all covered wages are subject to Medicare tax. Guiding employers in this regard is Internal Revenue Service Circular E (Employer's Tax Guide), which can be downloaded at **http://www.irs.gov/pub/irs-pdf/p15.pdf**.

To compute an employee's withholding and the employer's computation of Social Security and Medicare taxes:

1 Determine the employee's cumulative earnings (year to date) prior to this paycheck.

2 Determine the amount of wage payment for the current period.

3 Determine whether the employee's cumulative earnings exceed (or are close to) the Social Security wage base limit.

4 Calculate the Social Security tax by multiplying the appropriate wage payment by 6.2%.

5 Calculate the appropriate Medicare tax by multiplying the wage payment by 1.45%.

Example 1: In 2014, a single employee claiming two withholding allowances is paid $600 in the current week. Cumulative earnings to date are $3,000.

To calculate the Social Security and Medicare tax:

1 Cumulative year-to-date earnings: 3,000.

2 Wage payment: 600.

3 Cumulative earnings compared to the Social Security wage base limit: 3,000 is less than 117,000.

4 Social Security tax: $600 \times 6.2\% = 37.20$.

5 Medicare tax: $600 \times 1.45\% = 8.70$.

Example 2: In 2014, a married employee claiming three withholding allowances is paid $1,500 semi-monthly. Cumulative earnings to date are $6,000.

To calculate the Social Security and Medicare tax:

1 Cumulative year-to-date earnings: 6,000.

2 Wage payment: 1,500.

3 Cumulative earnings compared to the Social Security wage base limit: 6,000 is less than 117,000.

4 Social Security tax: $1,500 \times 6.2\% = 93.00$.

5 Medicare tax: $1,500 \times 1.45\% = 21.75$.

Example 3: In 2014, a married employee claiming five withholding allowances is paid $8,300 monthly. Cumulative earnings to date are $110,000.

To calculate the Social Security and Medicare tax:

1 Cumulative year-to-date earnings: 110,000.

2 Wage payment: 8,300.

3 Cumulative earnings compared to the Social Security wage base limit: 110,000 is less than 117,000 but close; difference is 7,000.

4 Social Security tax: $7,000 \times 6.2\% = 434.00$ (since this will bring the employee up to the wage limit).

5 Medicare tax: $8,300 \times 1.45\% = 120.35$.

Federal Unemployment Taxes

Use Form 940 (or Form 940-EZ) to report your annual Federal Unemployment Tax Act (FUTA) tax. This FUTA tax, together with state unemployment systems, provides for payments of unemployment compensation to workers who have lost their jobs. Most employers pay both federal and state unemployment taxes. Only the employer pays FUTA tax—do not collect or deduct it from your employees' wages. The FUTA tax rate for 2014 is 6.0% less state unemployment taxes paid up to 5.4%. Thus, the net tax (0.6%) applies to the first $7,000 you pay each employee in a year after subtracting any exempt payments. The $7,000 amount is the federal wage base. Your state wage base may be different. Instructions for Form 940 can be downloaded at **http://www.irs.gov/pub/ irs-pdf/i940.pdf**.

To compute a company's FUTA tax:

1 Determine the employee's cumulative year-to-date earnings prior to this paycheck.

2 Determine the amount of wage payment for the current period.

3 Determine whether the employee's cumulative earnings exceed (or are close to) the FUTA wage base limit.

4 Calculate the FUTA tax by multiplying the appropriate wage payment by 0.6%.

Example 1: In 2014, a single employee claiming two withholding allowances is paid $600 in the current week. Cumulative earnings to date are $3,000.

To calculate the FUTA tax:

1 Cumulative year-to-date earnings: 3,000.

2 Wage payment: 600.

3 Cumulative earnings compared to the FUTA wage base limit: 3,000 is less than 7,000.

4 FUTA tax: $600 \times 0.6\% = 3.60$.

Example 2: In 2014, a married employee claiming three withholding allowances is paid $1,500 semi-monthly. Cumulative earnings to date are $6,000.

To calculate the FUTA tax:

1 Cumulative year-to-date earnings: 6,000.

2 Wage payment: 1,500.

3 Cumulative earnings compared to the FUTA wage base limit: 6,000 is less than 7,000 but close; difference is 1,000.

4 FUTA tax: $1,000 \times 0.6\% = 6.00$.

Example 3: In 2014, a married employee claiming five withholding allowances is paid $8,300 monthly. Cumulative earnings to date are $110,000.

To calculate the FUTA tax:

1 Cumulative year-to-date earnings: 110,000.

2 Wage payment: 8,300.

3 Cumulative earnings compared to the FUTA wage base limit: 110,000 is more than 7,000.

4 FUTA tax: $0 \times 0.6\% = 0.00$.

State Income Tax Withholding and Unemployment Taxes

Each state has its own rules for withholding state income taxes and computing the employer's cost for unemployment. Some states, Florida and Nevada for instance, do not have a state income tax. Other states, such as California and Hawaii, have not only state income taxes but also training taxes.

Most of the state income tax computations are similar to the federal computations in that they have different tables for different filing status as well as tables for exemption allowances. This book cannot explain how to calculate taxes for each state in the union, so you should visit your local state tax agency to determine income tax and unemployment tax rates and requirements. Sample state payroll tax guidelines can be found at the following state web sites, which are current as of this writing:

California	**http://www.edd.ca.gov/Payroll_Taxes/**
Florida	**http://www.myflorida.com/dor/taxes/**
Hawaii	**http://hawaii.gov/tax/**

Appendix 1 Questions

1   What factors affect an employee's federal income tax withholding?

2   Where can employers obtain guidance on federal income tax withholding?

3   How do withholding allowances affect the computation of federal income tax withholding?

4   What does the Social Security tax finance?

5   What does the Medicare tax finance?

6   What is the Social Security tax rate?

7   Is there a wage base limit to the Social Security tax? If so, what was it for 2014?

8   What is the Medicare tax rate?

9   Is there a wage base limit to the Medicare tax? If so, what was it for 2014?

10   Who pays FUTA, and what is the current rate and computational structure?

Appendix 1 Assignments

1   In 2014, a married employee claiming one withholding allowance is paid $800 in the current week. Cumulative earnings to date are $4,000. Calculate the following:

   a.   Federal income tax withholding.

   b.   Employee Social Security taxes to be withheld.

   c.   Employee Medicare taxes to be withheld.

   d.   Employer Social Security tax.

   e.   Employer Medicare tax.

   f.   FUTA.

2   In 2014, a single employee claiming three withholding allowances is paid $2,000 semi-monthly. Cumulative earnings to date are $6,500. Calculate the following:

   a.   Federal income tax withholding.

   b.   Employee Social Security taxes to be withheld.

   c.   Employee Medicare taxes to be withheld.

   d.   Employer Social Security tax.

   e.   Employer Medicare tax.

   f.   FUTA.

3 In 2014, a single employee claiming no withholding allowances is paid $10,000 monthly. Cumulative earnings to date are $112,200. Calculate the following:

a. Federal income tax withholding.

b. Employee Social Security taxes to be withheld.

c. Employee Medicare taxes to be withheld.

d. Employer Social Security tax.

e. Employer Medicare tax.

f. FUTA.

Traditional Accounting: Debits and Credits

Student Learning Outcomes

Upon completion of this chapter, the student will be able to:

- Examine a trial balance and view underlying source documents
- Examine a general ledger and view underlying source documents
- Examine a journal and view underlying source documents

Case: **Wild Water Sports, Inc.**

You and Karen have been recording basic business transactions for Wild Water Sports without using journal entries or mentioning the terms "debit" and "credit" even once. This is another one of the benefits of using QuickBooks Accountant: It enables businesspeople who were not accounting majors to "do accounting." Moreover, accountants appreciate QuickBooks Accountant because they can use it with clients who want to have more control over their finances yet do not have formal training in accounting.

As a user of QuickBooks Accountant, you should know that, although you haven't actually used debits and credits in this book other than for adjusting journal entries, QuickBooks Accountant is based on a dual-entry (also known as double-entry) accounting system. Every transaction that you entered in Chapters 6 through 11 had an effect on two or more accounts in the chart of accounts. For example, every sales invoice increased Sales Revenue and Accounts Receivable. Every time you initiated a QuickBooks Accountant activity such as "receive payments," Cash was increased and Accounts Receivable was decreased.

QuickBooks Accountant actually provides three equivalent ways for you to record transactions using the double-entry system: You can record transactions by using business documents (what QuickBooks Accountant refers to as Forms), by using registers, or by making journal entries. So far in this textbook, you have used all three. Recall that using a document involves recording a transaction by completing a business document, such as a sales invoice or a check. When you correctly complete the document, the effect(s) of the transaction on the financial statements are automatically entered. For example, when Wild Water paid its yearly insurance premium of $22,000 on 1/31/16, the dual effects of this transaction on the Prepaid Insurance account (increased) and the Bank of Florida account (decreased) were processed by filling out a business document—specifically, a check. In contrast, using registers involves accessing a particular account's register and inputting the effects of the transaction. For example, you could choose either the Prepaid Insurance register or the Bank of Florida (cash) register and enter the changes (increase/decrease) as needed.

You ask if it is still possible to use debits and credits in QuickBooks Accountant, because your formal accounting training focused primarily on journal entries as the source of every transaction. Karen explains that, yes, it is indeed possible, and she offers to demonstrate QuickBooks Accountant's ability to prepare a trial balance, a general ledger, and a journal entry. You point out that, under normal circumstances, you would begin the accounting process with a journal entry. However, in this case, you will view the steps with her in reverse order, because the process has already been completed.

Trial Balance

The trial balance is a two-column listing of all asset, liability, owners' equity, revenue, and expense accounts. Accounts that have debit balances are listed in the debit column, and accounts that have credit balances are listed in the credit column. Although not foolproof, an equality between debits and credits generally indicates that the accounting process has been followed correctly.

With QuickBooks Accountant, you can quickly create a trial balance. All you need is the date as of which you want the trial balance. Then you can use QuickBooks Accountant's QuickZoom feature to view supporting accounts and supporting journals or business documents.

To create the trial balance and examine supporting detail:

1 Open the Wild Water Sports file you used in Chapter 11. Change the company name, using the Company menu, to include an A at the end. Your new Company name should be Wild Water Sports Ch 11A.

2 From the Reports Center, click **Accountant & Taxes** and then double-click **Trial Balance**.

3 Change the report dates to read from **1/1/16** to **3/31/16**; then click **Refresh** to view the trial balance you have prepared, as shown in Figure A2.1.

4 Double-click the **16,500.00** Prepaid Insurance amount to view the Prepaid Insurance account shown in Figure A2.2.

5 Double-click on the **5,500.00** amount to view the prepaid insurance adjusting journal entry in the Make General Journal Entries window, as shown in Figure A2.3. Recall that this adjusting journal entry increases an expense and decreases an asset.

6 Close all windows.

Wild Water Sports Ch 11A
Trial Balance
As of March 31, 2016

	Mar 31, 16	
	Debit	Credit
Bank of Florida	▶ 47,442.42 ◀	
Short-Term Investments	39,890.41	
Accounts Receivable	399,932.73	
Inventory Boats	243,600.00	
Inventory Parts	2,112.00	
Prepaid Advertising	20,000.00	
Prepaid Insurance	16,500.00	
Undeposited Funds	0.00	
Furniture and Equipment	295,000.00	
Accumulated Depreciation		17,833.00
Accounts Payable		216,200.00
MasterCard	0.00	
Unearned Revenue		10,000.00
Accrued Liabilities		1,760.97
Payroll Liabilities		2,934.66
Sales Tax Payable		28,457.66
Loan Payable		297,632.40
Capital Stock		400,000.00
Opening Balance Equity	0.00	
Retained Earnings	0.00	
Boat Sales		767,500.00
Part Sales		610.00
Service		6,685.00
Cost of Goods Sold	614,488.00	
Advertising and Promotion	6,700.00	
Bank Service Charges	75.00	
Depreciation Expense	10,333.00	
Insurance Expense	5,500.00	
Interest Expense	7,719.57	
Office Supplies	4,500.00	
Payroll Expenses	32,945.97	
Telephone Expense	5,020.00	
Utilities	2,870.00	
Interest Income		2,015.41
Other Income		3,000.00
TOTAL	1,754,629.10	1,754,629.10

Figure A2.1

Trial Balance

Figure A2.2

Prepaid Insurance

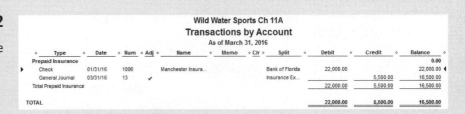

Type	Date	Num	Adj	Name	Memo	Clr	Split	Debit	Credit	Balance
Prepaid Insurance										0.00
Check	01/31/16	1006		Manchester Insura...			Bank of Florida	22,000.00		22,000.00
General Journal	03/31/16	13	✓				Insurance Ex...		5,500.00	16,500.00
Total Prepaid Insurance								22,000.00	5,500.00	16,500.00
TOTAL								**22,000.00**	**5,500.00**	**16,500.00**

Figure A2.3

Prepaid Insurance Adjusting Journal Entry

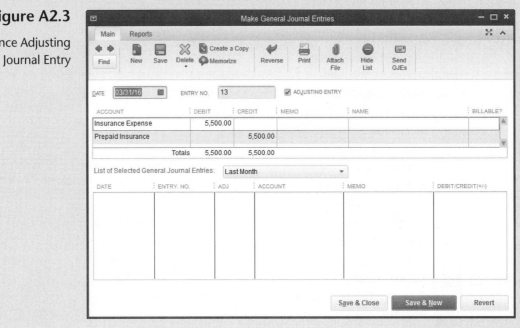

The Prepaid Insurance register actually reflects the entering of an adjustment via a journal entry. The adjustment itself was an adjusting entry prompted by the existence of a business source document, such as a check, an invoice, or a bill.

General Ledger

The general ledger is used in accounting information systems to store the effects of individual asset, liability, owners' equity, revenue, and expense accounts. In manual accounting systems, journals are used to record business transactions, the effects of which are then posted or transferred to a general ledger. This recording and posting is compressed into one step in QuickBooks Accountant as the transactions are recorded. Karen decides to use a sales invoice to demonstrate how the effects of a transaction are stored in the general ledger.

She explains that the invoice itself is used as a source business document. Information is entered into the invoice; then, when you click OK, the invoice is stored and the consequence of that invoice is immediately recorded. In accounting jargon: once you enter the invoice, a debit is posted to the Accounts

Receivable account in the general ledger and a credit is posted to the Sales Revenue account in the general ledger.

"In my accounting classes, we usually posted all the sales for a month with one journal entry," you comment. "In this case, it looks like each sale is recorded individually. Doesn't that take a lot of time?"

"Yes," Karen agrees. "But once you enter this invoice, several steps are completed simultaneously. Accounts Receivable is debited, and Sales Revenue is credited. If we're selling inventory, the same invoice updates the perpetual inventory record, credits the Inventory account, and debits the Cost of Goods Sold account. Plus, the customer's account is adjusted accordingly, so we know how much each customer owes and when amounts are due. Let's take a look at QuickBooks Accountant's general ledger and some underlying transactions."

To create the general ledger:

1 From the Reports Center, click **Accountant & Taxes** and then click **General Ledger**.

2 Change the report dates to read from **1/1/16** to **3/31/16** and then click **Refresh**.

3 Scroll down the general ledger until you can view the Accounts Receivable account, as shown in Figure A2.4.

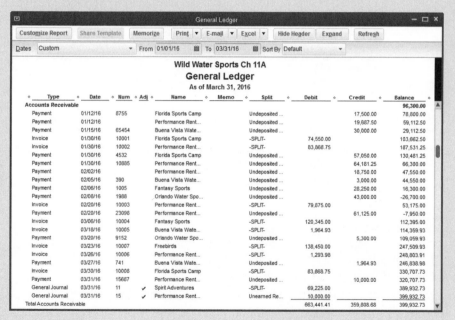

Figure A2.4

Accounts Receivable Portion of the General Ledger

4 Double-click Invoice No. **10001** dated 1/30/16 to Florida Sports Camp in order to view the underlying source document: the specific sales invoice that increased accounts receivable by $74,550, as shown in Figure A2.5.

Figure A2.5

Invoice

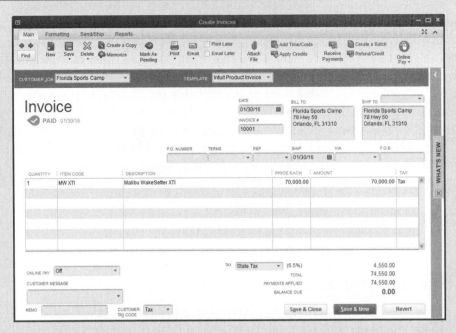

5   Close the Create Invoices window. Double-click the payment dated 1/30/16 from Florida Sports Camp via their Check No. **4532** to view the underlying source document: the specific payment that decreased accounts receivable by $57,050, as shown in Figure A2.6.

Figure A2.6

Receive Payment

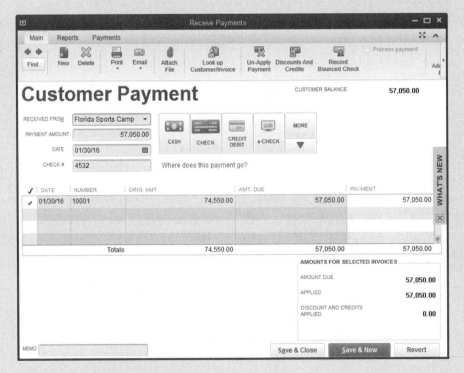

6 Print the first page of the General Ledger by clicking the **Print** button on the General Ledger window.

7 Click the **Pages** option button in the Page Range: section of the Print Reports window.

8 Type **1** in the To: text box and then click **Print**.

9 Close all windows.

After seeing how easy this is, you might wonder why QuickBooks Accountant—or some other similar program—isn't used all the time in business. The reason is that many companies often have their own accounting software that has been customized to their specifications. But many smaller businesses, which often can't afford the luxury of customized software, have found QuickBooks Accountant to be an inexpensive yet powerful and easy-to-use alternative.

General Journal

"I'm still not convinced that QuickBooks Accountant follows the debit and credit convention," you comment. "Most times you drill down from the general ledger or trial balance you get to a source document, not to a journal entry."

"That's true," Karen responds. "Remember, we entered most of these transactions from source documents, not from journal entries as you did in your accounting classes. However, I can still show you that, if needed, QuickBooks Accountant can provide you with the underlying debits and credits for all business transactions recorded."

To view journal entry support for business transactions:

1 From the Reports Center, click **Accountant & Taxes** and then double-click **Journal**.

2 Change the report dates to read from **2/1/16** to **2/29/16** and then click **Refresh**.

3 The first four transactions for the month of February are shown in Figure A2.7.

4 The first transaction shown debits the Inventory Parts account and credits the Bank of Florida account by $1,000. Double-click the transaction with **Delco** to reveal the check (source document) that was used to pay Delco for the parts purchased.

5 Close the check window. Scroll down the Journal window until you come to Sales Receipt 6005 recorded on 2/4/16, as shown in Figure A2.8.

Figure A2.7

Journal Showing the First Four Transactions for the Month of February

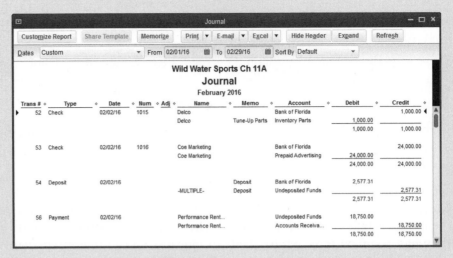

Figure A2.8

Journal Showing Receipt 6005

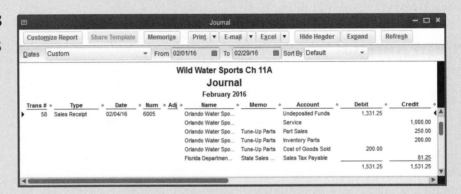

6   The sales receipt transaction shows debits to Undeposited Funds (an asset) and Cost of Goods Sold (an expense) as well as credits to Service (an income account), Parts (an income account), Inventory Parts (an asset), and Sales Tax Payable (a liability).

7   Double-click **Sales Receipt 6005** to view the underlying source document that created this journal entry.

8   Close the sales receipt window.

9   The transaction below Sales Receipt 6005 should be the deposit made on 2/5/16.

10 Double-click the **Deposit** journal entry to view the underlying source document that created this journal entry. This transaction shows a debit to the Bank of Florida account and two credits to the Undeposited Funds account. (Recall that the previous transaction recorded the collection of cash as an increase in Undeposited Funds because they were not immediately deposited into the company's bank account.)

11 Close the deposit window.

12 Print the first page of the Journal by clicking the **Print** button on the Journal window.

13 Click the **Pages** option button in the Page Range: section of the Print Reports window.

14 Type **1** in the To: text box, and then click **Print**.

15 Close all windows.

You can now see why accountants want to see the Journal information. It validates QuickBooks Accountant as a "real" accounting program with underlying debits and credits like those learned in their accounting courses.

End Note

Many accountants prefer to use journal entries (i.e., the debit–credit format) to record business transactions. But Intuit Inc. designed QuickBooks Accountant for businesspeople who did not want to use journal entries. Although Quick-Books Accountant allows you to enter all transactions using the journal entry format, doing so requires that you sacrifice QuickBooks Accountant's specialized invoicing, bill payment, payroll, and other useful features. The choice is yours!

Appendix 2 Questions

1 In what order does QuickBooks Accountant list accounts in the trial balance report?

2 What QuickBooks Accountant feature allows you to access supporting accounts or journals when viewing the trial balance?

3 What happens when you double-click an amount on the trial balance?

4 Explain how a transaction recorded through an account register also creates a general journal entry.

5 Why does QuickBooks Accountant have a general ledger?

6 What advantages does QuickBooks Accountant's document-initiated recording method have over the standard journal entry method?

7 What happens when you double-click on an amount in the general ledger?

8 How do you print one page of the General Ledger?

9 What information about business transactions is shown in the Journal?

10 Why would someone want to look at a QuickBooks Accountant Journal?

Appendix 2 Assignments

1 *Creating a Trial Balance, General Ledger, and Journal for Wild Water Sports*

Use the Wild Water Sports file you completed in Chapter 11 for the following tasks. (*Note:* Print without the date prepared, time prepared, and report basis fields as you did in this chapter.)

a. Create and print a Trial Balance for the period January 1 to April 30, 2016.

b. View the General Ledger for the period April 1 to April 30, 2016. Print Page 1 in landscape view.

c. View the Journal for the period April 1 to April 30, 2016. Print Page 1 in landscape view.

2 *Creating a Trial Balance, General Ledger, and Journal for Central Coast Cellular*

Use the Central Coast Cellular file you completed in Chapter 11 to perform the following tasks. (*Note:* Print without the date prepared, time prepared, and report basis fields as you did in this chapter.)

a. Create and print a Trial Balance for the period January 1 to January 31, 2009.

b. View the General Ledger for the period January 1 to January 31, 2009. Print Page 1 in landscape view.

c. View the Journal for the period January 1 to January 31, 2009. Print Page 1 in landscape view.

Appendix 2 Case Problems

1 *Creating a Trial Balance, General Ledger, and Journal for Aloha Properties*

Requirements:

Use the file you completed for the Aloha Properties case in Chapter 11 to perform the following tasks. (*Note:* Print without the date prepared, time prepared, and report basis fields as you did in this chapter.)

a. Create and print a Trial Balance for the period January 1 to February 29, 2008.

b. View the General Ledger for the period February 1 to February 29, 2008. Print Page 1 in landscape view.

c. View the Journal for the period February 1 to February 29, 2008. Print Page 1 in landscape view.

2 *Creating a Trial Balance, General Ledger, and Journal for Ocean View Flowers*

Requirements:

Use the file you completed for the Ocean View Flowers case in Chapter 11 to perform the following tasks. (*Note:* Print without the date prepared, time prepared, and report basis fields as you did in this chapter.)

a. Create and print a Trial Balance for the period January 1 to February 29, 2008.

b. View the General Ledger for the period February 1 to February 29, 2008. Print Page 1 in landscape view.

c. View the Journal for the period February 1 to February 29, 2008. Print Page 1 in landscape view.

Helpful References

Installing QuickBooks Accountant, Managing Files, Memorizing Reports, Uploading Files to Your Instructor and Getting QuickBooks Certified

Student Learning Outcomes

Upon completion of this Appendix, the student will be able to:

- Install and register a trial version of QuickBooks Accountant on their home computer
- Manage QuickBooks company and backup files using Window's file management system
- Memorize reports in groups
- Upload a QuickBooks company or backup file to an instructor
- Become QuickBooks certified

Overview

Many students using this text are completing chapter work and student assignments, cases, exercises, and comprehensive problems on a computer in their school's computer lab with a licensed version of QuickBooks Accountant installed. Included in this text is a trial version of QuickBooks Accountant, which can be installed on the student's personal computer if they choose to do some of their work somewhere other than in their school's computer lab. This appendix will provide a description of how that software is installed.

Throughout this text, you will need to manage your QuickBooks Company and backup files, memorize reports, and perhaps upload a file to an instructor. In prior editions, instructions to perform these tasks were included in the beginning chapters and student needed to refer to them in succeeding chapters. In this edition, they have been placed in an appendix so they are easily located.

Install and Register QuickBooks Accountant

Included with this text is a disk, attached to the back cover, that contains a student trial version of QuickBooks Accountant for Windows along with a license and product number. Be advised that if you purchase this book used there is a very good chance that even with the disk included you may not be able to use the student version of QuickBooks Accountant because the prior user might have already registered the software and the time for its use has expired. You now must install QuickBooks Accountant student version and then register the application. If you don't register, you will only have 30 days to use the software and then access will be denied.

To install the student version of QuickBooks Accountant on your personal computer:

1 Insert the QuickBooks Accountant (student version) disk into your computer's CD or DVD rom drive.

2 Open Windows Explorer and navigate to your computer's CD or DVD rom drive.

3 Double-click **Setup**. (Note: Your computer, once the CD has been inserted, may automatically run the setup process. If that occurs, you can skip this step and continue below.)

4 Click **Yes** if your computer asks you for permission to install this software. The setup application may take some time to load so be patient.

5 A Welcome to QuickBooks screen should appear. When the **Next** button appears, click it.

6 Click in the checkbox to indicate you accept the terms of the license agreement and then click **Next**.

7 Select the **Express** option button and then click **Next**. Your screen should look like Figure A3.1.

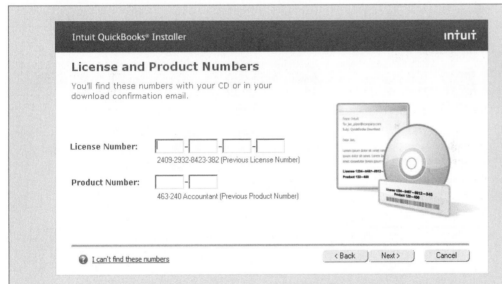

Figure A3.1

Entering the License and Product Numbers

8 Type the license number and product number shown on the yellow tag attached to the back cover of this text and then press **Next**.

9 Click **Next** to install QuickBooks Accountant. (This may take 10–15 minutes.)

10 Restart your computer to complete the installation.

It is important to register your copy of QuickBooks Accountant. There is no cost to register; however, if you don't register, you will only have 30 days of use and then nothing. After you register QuickBooks, you will have 160 days of use.

To register the student version of QuickBooks Accountant on your personal computer:

1   After you have installed the QuickBooks Accountant application, restart it.

2   Click the **Help** menu and then click **Register QuickBooks**.

3   Type your email address in the box provided.

4   Type a password and password confirmation and then click **Register**.

5   Enter additional information requested and then click **Next**.

6   Click the **Start Using QuickBooks Now** text.

File Management

This text includes a disk labeled Data Files that contains files needed for some chapters and some end of chapter assignments. These data files are also available from this text's student and instructor companion web sites at Cengage Publishing as illustrated in Figure A3.2.

Figure A3.2

Student Companion Web Site at Cengagebrain.com

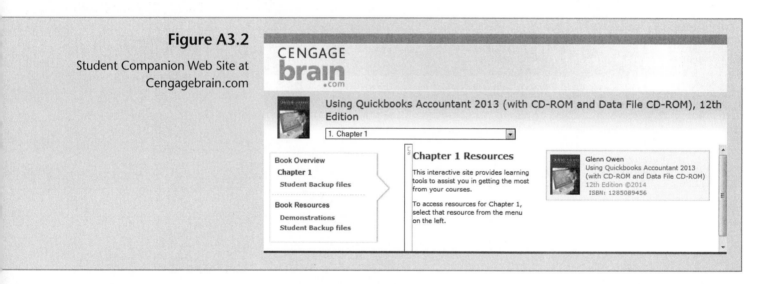

All of these files are backup files and must be restored from within Quick-Books Accountant before you can use them. Files that you modify from those provided and files that you create from scratch must be managed. This just means you need to know where they are on your computer or removable media.

It is recommended that you spend time managing your files, including both the backup files (with a file extension of .qbb) and full QuickBooks Accountant files (with an extension of .qbw). For example, in Figure A3.3, Windows Explorer shows a folder that was created to store all the student backup files from the text and a separate folder that was created to store all of QuickBooks working files. Once the backup was restored from within QuickBooks, the working file was stored here. Figure A3.4 illustrates the student backup files, whereas Figure A3.5 illustrates the actual working files created after the backup file for Larry's Landscaping was restored.

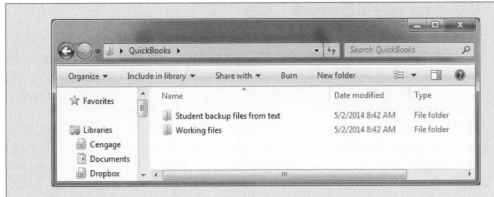

Figure A3.3

Using Folders and Windows Explorer to Manage QuickBooks Backups and Working Files

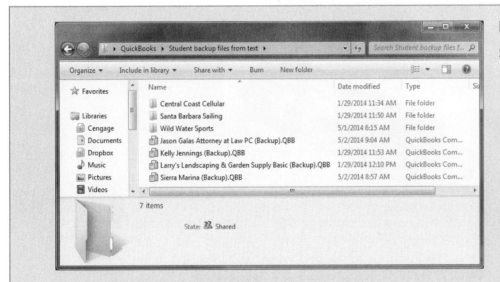

Figure A3.4

Student Backup Files

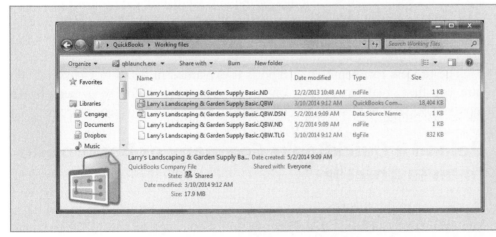

Figure A3.5

Student Working Files

Note that in restoring Larry's Landscaping & Garden Supply Basic (Backup).QBB (shown in Figure A3.4) QuickBooks Accountant created five files in the Working Files folder shown in Figure A3.5.

Use of a Flash Drive

A USB flash drive, shown in Figure A3.6, is a data storage device that includes flash memory with an integrated Universal Serial Bus (USB) interface. USB flash drives are typically removable and rewritable. Use of a USB flash drive to move your QuickBooks files between a lab, business, or home environment is highly recommended. However, it is recommended that you not open these files in QuickBooks from your USB flash drive. Doing so will result in very slow response times because QuickBooks saves each action. Instead, it is recommended that you move your file from the USB flash drive to your computer's hard drive and then open the file located on the hard drive from within QuickBooks. When you are done, close QuickBooks and then use Windows Explorer to move your updated file back to your USB flash drive for backup and transportation to another computer.

Figure A3.6

Flash Drive

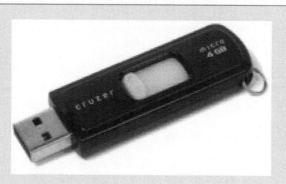

Memorize Reports in Groups

QuickBooks Accountant provide a means for you to memorize a report you create with specific dates, headings, groupings, statistics, etc., for use at a later time after additional business events have been recorded. This is also an easy way for instructors to see that you know how to create reports and for them to grade your work.

The process for memorizing reports is explained in detail in Chapter 2. Be sure you first create a report group with your name before you memorize a report. Also be sure to save your memorized report into your report group.

Upload a QuickBooks Company or Backup File to an Instructor

If your instructor directs you to upload your full QuickBooks file to a Course Management System (like Blackboard), you should upload the .QBW file only. See Figure A3.5 for an example. If instead your instructor directs you to upload a backup of your QuickBooks file, be sure you select the .QBB file you create from your working file. Do not send them the student backup file provided by the publisher.

Become QuickBooks Certified

According to Intuit, developer of QuickBooks, certification "validates newly acquired QuickBooks skills for an entry level position in professional accountancy and effectively demonstrates bookkeeping skills, including how to create purchase orders, track sales and expenses, produce and manage invoices, and monitor financial records."

The exams given use multiple choice questions through an online testing tool to help validate a test candidate's use of the QuickBooks software for accounting and bookkeeping principles and procedures.

Do I Need to Become QuickBooks Certified?

There are two schools of thought here. The first is that becoming certified provides employers/clients independent confirmation of an individual's skill and proficiency in using QuickBooks. Thus certification is a good resume builder. The second is that any employer/client that relies solely on certification to assure competency in using QuickBooks will eventually find themselves looking for a new QuickBooks professional.

Does it hurt? No. Does it help? Maybe. Is it necessary? No. What is important is the knowledge, skill, and proficiency in using QuickBooks as a tool to help businesses better understand the financial implications of their decisions.

In the opinion of the author, certification takes a back seat to accounting education and experience. Thus it is in the student's best interest to gain accounting knowledge (the more the better) through courses at accredited institutions in the topics of bookkeeping, financial accounting, managerial accounting, cost accounting, tax accounting, and the application of QuickBooks to different business situations. The next step is to gain experience through internships or part-time jobs working under a QuickBooks/Accounting professional. Add to that QuickBooks certification, after your education and experience, and you're ready for gainful employment.

How Do I Get Certified?

The steps that follow will help you get certified:

1   Get educated in bookkeeping and accounting concepts (see above).

2   Choose what kind of QuickBooks certification you wish to pursue: ProAdvisor, Enterprise Solutions, Point of Sale, or Advanced.

3   Choose a professional training service, computer training web site, or community college to take the classes that help you prepare for QuickBooks certification.

4   Acquire an exam prep guide and take as many practice exams as you can.

5   Schedule a seat for a QuickBooks exam.

6   Take your exam. You must pass with a score of 80% or higher on the exam to get certified.

What Do I Need to Know to Become Certified?

These are the topic areas you must know before attempting the exam. After each item, the author has provided a page reference to this text as to where instruction of that topic begins. If that particular topic is not covered in this text (as indicated by an *), a description and overview of that topic are listed at the end of this appendix.

QuickBooks Setup (6% of exam)

A student should know:

- What information is required before they set up a QuickBooks file (pg. 90)
- How to start a new company data file in QuickBooks (pg. 91)
- How to keep the lists and preferences from an old file while removing old transactions (*)
- How to customize the home page (pg. 95)
- How to set up lists (customers, vendors, items, etc.). This includes understanding which names and items should appear on which lists. (pg. 99)

QuickBooks Utilities and General Product Knowledge (10% of exam)

A student should know:

- How to navigate or move around QuickBooks: use home page, menus, icon bar, etc. (pg. 20)
- How to back up and restore a data file (pg. 124)
- How to determine the release number and how to update QuickBooks (pg. xix)
- How to use QuickBooks in single-user and multi-user mode (*)
- What editions of QuickBooks are available and how to find out which one he or she is using (pg. xix)
- How to password-protect QuickBooks (*)
- How and why to use preferences (pg. 95)

List Management (6% of exam)

A student should know:

- How to manage lists (customers, vendors, items, etc.) (pg. 106)
    - Adding new entries
    - Deleting entries
    - Editing entries
    - Merging entries

Items (8% of exam)

A student should know:

- How QuickBooks uses items to perform the necessary accounting behind the scenes (pg. 99)
- The different types of items and when to use each type (pg. 99)
- How to use items for different types of scenarios (pg. 99)

Sales (10% of exam)

A student should know:

- Who should be listed in the Customer Center (pg. 107)
- How to navigate and use the Customer Center (pg. 107)

- How to complete the workflow (from the sale to making the deposit) for:
  - Invoicing (pg. 164)
  - Sales receipts (pg. 158)
- How QuickBooks uses the Undeposited Funds, Accounts Receivable, and checking accounts in the invoicing cycle (pg. 161)
- How and why to record a customer credit (pg. 164)
- How and why to create statements (*)
- How to handle bounced (NSF) checks (*)

Purchases (10% of exam)

A student should know:

- Who should be listed in the Vendor Center (pg. 109)
- How to navigate and use the Vendor Center (pg. 109)
- The different workflows for making purchases:
  - Entering and paying bills (A/P) (pg. 235)
  - Writing checks (pg. 243)
  - Using a credit card (*)
  - Using a debit card (*)
- How to record the transactions in the purchase workflows (pg. 226)
- How and why to record a vendor credit (*)
- How to complete the inventory workflow (purchase order to payment) (pg. 226)
- How to set up, collect, and pay sales tax (pg. 242)
- Bank reconciliation (pg. 284)

Payroll (12% of exam)

A student should know:

- The differences between the payroll services available from QuickBooks (pg. 173)
- How to set up payroll (including employees, federal and state taxes, and basic payroll deductions) using the Payroll Setup Wizard (pg. 117)
- How to set up an employee's earnings and sick or vacation time (pg. 117)
- How to track sick or vacation time (accruing hours and using "banked" hours) (*)
- How and why to setup payroll schedules (*)
- How to run payroll (pg. 177)
- How and why to pay payroll liabilities (pg. 241)
- How to prepare payroll forms (Form 941, W-2) in QuickBooks (*)
- Track time and use it for payroll or for invoicing customers (pg. 174)

Reports (16% of exam)

A student should know:

- Why and how to use the Report Center (pg. 322)
- How to customize reports: collapsing subaccounts, etc. (pg. 334)
- The basic question that each report answers (all of Chapter 11)
- How and why to send reports to Excel (pg. 337)
- How and why to process multiple reports (*)
- How and why to memorize reports (pg. 35)

Basic Accounting (10% of exam)

A student should know:

- What the basic financial statements are and have a basic understanding of what they mean (pg. 7)
- The difference between cash and accrual reports (*)
- How and why to set a closing date (*)
- How to enter a Journal Entry if asked to do so by an accountant; i.e., they do not need to fully understand what accounts to debit or credit (pg. 391)

Customization/Saving Time and Shortcuts (12% of exam)

A student should know:

- How and why to memorize transactions (*)
- How to set up multiple users and what level of access can be granted or denied (*)
- How and why to create custom fields (customers, vendors, and employees) (*)
- How to customize an invoice (*)

Will This Text Prepare Me to Pass the QuickBooks Certification Exam?

The short answer is yes, this text does address most but not all of the certification exam questions. However, this book was not created as a guide on how to pass the certification exam. It is an accounting text, teaching students how to utilize their accounting knowledge in a computerized environment, specifically QuickBooks. Secondly, this is a case-based text designed to teach and evaluate a student's ability to analyze information, organize that information into a QuickBooks file, and use QuickBooks to answer business-related questions and generate reports that provide management insight into their business.

Texts that use multiple choice questions to assess a student's ability to use QuickBooks come up short on actually assessing a student's QuickBooks skills. This text focuses on educating and assessing students' ability to solve problems by asking them to create QuickBooks files, answer business questions, and generate business reports based on case data.

Thus, the long answer is no. This text was not designed as a certification preparation text. That is a side benefit, not the goal.

Certification Topics Not Specifically Covered in This Text

The following are certification topics not specifically covered in this text; thus, they are addressed in this appendix:

Topic Area	Topic	Explanation
QuickBooks Setup	How to keep the lists and preferences from an old file while removing old transactions	To create a new company file for a new year, perform the Archive & Condense Data procedure: 1. Select the File menu and select Utilities > Condense Data. 2. Click Yes to the message, "Budget data may be moved during cleanup. Do you want to continue anyway?" 3. Select ALL Transactions in the Condense Data window. 4. Click Yes to the confirmation message. 5. Click Begin Condense.

Topic Area	Topic	Explanation
QuickBooks Utilities and General Product Knowledge	How to use QuickBooks in single-user and multi-user mode	If QuickBooks is running in single-user mode, any number of users can work on the file, but only one at a time. If QuickBooks is running in multi-user mode, multiple users can access the same company file at the same time from different computers.
	How to password-protect QuickBooks	To password-protect your QuickBooks data file, click on Company in the menu bar and then click Set Up Users. From here, you can assign a password for the main (Administrator) account in QuickBooks. You can also set up user accounts, passwords, and different levels of access if you have multiple people using your QuickBooks file.
Sales	How and why to create statements	The primary reason for using statements in QuickBooks is to remind delinquent customers that they owe you money and to summarize the amount they owe.
		To create statements in QuickBooks for all customers that owe you money, select Create Statements from the Customers menu. Specify a statement date and statement period and then select customers for which you want statements created.
	How to handle bounced (NSF) checks	1. Record your bank's charges for a bounced check. 2. Record a credit memo to reverse the original sale. 3. Create a new customer invoice that should include all of the items from the original invoice, plus a line item for Bad Check Charge created above.
Purchases	Using a credit card	1. From the startup screen, click on Banking. 2. Then click on Credit Cards. 3. Use the drop-down box at the top of the screen to choose the card you are adding expenses for. (Note: Each credit card has its own register that lists all the charges and credits you've recorded and the payments you've made. You can enter new charges and payments directly in the register.) 4. In the Purchased From field, enter the name of the vendor you purchased the goods or services from. 5. In the Amount field, enter the amount of the charge. 6. Below, under the Expenses tab, enter the name of the account you use to track this type of expense (advertising, etc.).
	Using a debit card	Same as using a credit card above.
	How and why to record a vendor credit	Often a vendor will grant a business credit for returned items or allowances. To record this credit: 1. From the Vendors menu, click Enter Bills. 2. At the top of the Enter Bills window, click Credit. 3. Enter the vendor's name and the amount of the credit. 4. In the detail area, enter the expense accounts, customers, jobs, or classes to which you want to assign the credit. 5. Save the credit.
Payroll	How to track sick or vacation time	To set up the sick and vacation payroll items in QuickBooks: 1. Click the Lists drop-down menu on the top menu bar, and then select Payroll Item List. 2. Click the Payroll Item button in the bottom left corner, and then select New. 3. Select Custom Setup, and then click Next. 4. Select Wage, and then click Next. 5. Select either Annual Salary or Hourly Wages depending on whether you are setting up these payroll items for salaried or hourly employees, and then click Next. 6. Select Sick Pay or Vacation Pay, and then click Next. 7. Name the item (for example: Hourly Sick Pay), and then click Next. 8. Select the expense account that you want this item to report to. 9. Click Finish.

Topic Area	Topic	Explanation
	How and why to setup payroll schedules	Pay schedules make it easier to organize multiple pay frequencies. The Pay Employees window displays the next pay date and pay period for each pay schedule. Pay schedules make it easier to see who needs to be paid and when. 1. From the menu at the top, click Employees > Payroll Center. 2. In the Payroll Center, under the Pay Employees section, select Set up your payroll schedule. 3. In the New Payroll Schedule window, enter a name for your payroll schedule. 4. Enter how often you will pay your employees on this schedule. 5. Enter your pay period end date. 6. Enter the date that should appear on paychecks for this pay period. 7. Indicate if you pay your employees either monthly or semimonthly. 8. When finished, click OK. 9. Choose whether this schedule should be applied to all employees with the same pay frequency. Select Yes to globally assign this payroll schedule, or select No.
	How to prepare payroll forms (Form 941, W-2) in QuickBooks	1. From the Employees menu, select Payroll Tax Forms & W-2s. 2. Then select Process payroll forms if you have a payroll subscription. If not, select Tax form worksheets in Excel.
Reports	How and why to process multiple reports	To expedite the processing and printing of reports in QuickBooks: 1. Go to the Reports menu and click Process Multiple Reports. 2. Click the Select Memorized Reports From drop-down list and choose All Reports, Ungrouped Reports, or a specific memorized report group. 3. Click in the left column to select the reports that you want to display or print. Clear the checkmark for each report that you don't want to display or print.
Basic Accounting	The difference between cash and accrual reports	The accrual bookkeeping method is where you regard income or expenses as occurring at the time you ship a product, render a service, or receive a purchase. Under this method, the time when you enter a transaction and the time when you actually pay or receive cash may be two separate events. In QuickBooks, an accrual basis report shows income, regardless of whether all your customers have paid their invoices, and expenses, regardless of whether you have paid all your bills. The cash bookkeeping method is where you regard income or expenses as occurring at the time you actually receive a payment or pay a bill. A cash-basis report shows income only if you have received it and expenses only if you have paid them. For example, if you have not yet received a payment for an invoice, a cash-basis report on your sales will not include the amount of the invoice.
	How and why to set a closing date	You can choose whether or not to close your books at the end of the year. QuickBooks doesn't require you to do so. If you choose not to close your books in QuickBooks (the method chosen by the author of this text), you always have easy access to last year's data, including the details of every transaction. You can also create comparative reports between this year and last year. If you choose to close your books, QuickBooks performs certain year-end adjustments, based on your fiscal year start month. 1. QuickBooks adjusts your income and expense accounts at year end to zero them out. Therefore, you start your new fiscal year with a zero net income. 2. QuickBooks makes an adjusting entry to your net income. 3. On the first day of the new fiscal year, QuickBooks increases your Retained Earnings equity account by the previous year's net income. This way, you start each new fiscal year with a net income of zero.

Topic Area	Topic	Explanation
Customization/Saving Time and Shortcuts	How and why to memorize transactions	The QuickBooks memorized transaction feature can save valuable time. To memorize a transaction: 1. Enter a transaction or open a previous transaction that you wish to memorize. 2. Right-click on the transaction and then click Memorize. Later, QuickBooks will automatically launch a Memorize Transaction window. You can then select to have QuickBooks automatically enter the transaction (you set the specifics of how and when), and whether you want QuickBooks to remind you about the transaction.
	How to set up multiple users and what level of access can be granted or denied	For the most reliable multi-user setup, Intuit recommends that you install QuickBooks or the QuickBooks Server on the same computer as the company file and set up that computer to host multi-user access to company files. With multi-user QuickBooks, you can do all the same activities that you would normally do in QuickBooks. When more than one user needs to use the company file, you can open it and switch to multi-user mode. Once the file is in multi-user mode, the other users you set up can now open that same file from another computer. Some activities, such as backing up a file, can be done only when a single user is working on the company file. QuickBooks makes it easy to switch to single-user mode for those activities and then switch back to multi-user mode. To add users and give them access (Note: Only the QuickBooks Administrator can do this task.): 1. Go to the Company menu, click Set Up Users and Passwords, and then click Set Up Users. 2. Click Add User. 3. Assign a user name and password. 4. Choose whether this person will have access to selected areas of QuickBooks or all areas of QuickBooks. 5. If you granted access to all areas of QuickBooks, you have no more selections to make. Click Yes to confirm that you want this person to have full access. Click Finish to complete the setup process. 6. If you are selecting the areas the user has access to, make your selections in the window. Click Next to go to the next window. No access: Denies access of any kind to the area. Full access: Provides general access to the area, letting the user do everything except edit and delete transactions. You'll be asked near the end of the setup process if you also want the user to edit and delete transactions. Selective access: Provides a more limited access to the area than full access. Select this option if you want the user to have access, but not be able to do a particular activity. For example, you can allow someone to enter transactions but prevent them from printing them.
	How and why to create custom fields (customers, vendors, and employees)	You can add up to seven custom fields to each Customers list, Vendors list, or Employees list. Overlapping fields count as one field on each list. For example, if you add the same field to all three lists, you can still add six other fields to each list. You can add custom fields you've set up for customers to any sales form. Likewise, you can add custom fields you've set up for vendors to the purchase order form. If you want information you've entered in the custom fields to appear on a form, you must add the fields to the form. 1. Click the Customers icon, Vendors icon, or Employees icon. 2. Click the left tab in the left pane, either Customers, Vendors, or Employees. 3. Right-click any name on the list and then click Edit. 4. Click the Additional Info tab. 5. Click the Define Fields button. 6. For each field you want to add, enter the name you want to use in the Label column, and select which lists the custom field applies to.